Software Development, Design, and Coding

With Patterns, Debugging, Unit Testing, and Refactoring

Third Edition

John F. Dooley
Vera A. Kazakova

Apress®

Software Development, Design, and Coding: With Patterns, Debugging, Unit Testing, and Refactoring

John F. Dooley
Galesburg, IL, USA

Vera A. Kazakova
Columbia, MD, USA

ISBN-13 (pbk): 979-8-8688-0284-3
https://doi.org/10.1007/979-8-8688-0285-0

ISBN-13 (electronic): 979-8-8688-0285-0

Managing Director, Apress Media LLC: Welmoed Spahr
Acquisitions Editor: Melissa Duffy
Development Editor: Laura Berendson
Coordinating Editor: Gryffin Winkler

Cover designed by eStudioCalamar

Cover image by JJ Ying on Unsplash (www.unsplash.com)

Distributed to the book trade worldwide by Apress Media, LLC, 1 New York Plaza, New York, NY 10004, U.S.A. Phone 1-800-SPRINGER, fax (201) 348-4505, e-mail orders-ny@springer-sbm.com, or visit www.springeronline.com. Apress Media, LLC is a California LLC and the sole member (owner) is Springer Science + Business Media Finance Inc (SSBM Finance Inc). SSBM Finance Inc is a **Delaware** corporation.

For information on translations, please e-mail booktranslations@springernature.com; for reprint, paperback, or audio rights, please e-mail bookpermissions@springernature.com.

Apress titles may be purchased in bulk for academic, corporate, or promotional use. eBook versions and licenses are also available for most titles. For more information, reference our Print and eBook Bulk Sales web page at www.apress.com/bulk-sales.

Any source code or other supplementary material referenced by the author in this book is available to readers on GitHub (https://github.com/Apress). For more detailed information, please visit www.apress.com/gp/services/source-code.

If disposing of this product, please recycle the paper

John: For diane once again.

Vera: To all my students.

Table of Contents

About the Authors...xv

About the Technical Reviewer xvii

Acknowledgments..xix

Preface xxi

Chapter 1: Introduction to Software Development 1

What We're Doing..2

So, How to Develop Software?...2

Conclusion 7

References...7

Part I: Models and Team Practices 9

Chapter 2: Software Process Models..11

The 3(+3) Variables of Software Development 12

Software Development Approaches..15

Plan-Based Software Development..16

Agile Software Development 17

Agile Values, Principles, and Activities...19

Lean Software Development 21

Lean Principle 1: Eliminate Waste...22

Lean Principle 2: Build Quality In 23

Lean Principle 3: Create Knowledge 24

Lean Principle 4: Defer Commitment 24

Lean Principle 5: Deliver Fast..25

Lean Principle 6: Respect People..25

Lean Principle 7: Optimize the Whole...26

Implementations of Software Development Models 26

    The Waterfall Model: An Assembly-Line Approach 27

    The Code and Fix "Model": A Proto-Agile Approach 29

    Agile Development Implementations 30

Hybrid Software Development Approaches for Multi-Level Focus and Scope 44

References 46

Chapter 3: Project Management Essentials 49

Project Planning 50

    Project Planning: Organization 51

    Project Planning: Risk Analysis 51

    Project Planning: Resource Requirements 54

    Project Planning: Task Estimation and Schedule 54

    Project Planning: Defect Management 58

Soft-Aware Development 59

    Soft-Aware Development: The Dark Side of Teamwork 63

    Soft-Aware Development: Supporting the Individuals 65

    Soft-Aware Development: A Culture of Safety and Growth 68

    Soft-Aware Development: Teamwork Artifacts 79

Conclusion 84

References 84

Chapter 4: Ethics and Professional Practice 89

Introduction to Ethics 89

Ethical Theory 90

    Ethical Theory: Deontological Theories 91

    Ethical Theory: Consequentialism (Teleological Theories) 94

Ethical Drivers 99

    Legal Drivers 99

    Professional Drivers 99

Ethical Discussion and Decision Making 102

    Discussion 1: Identifying and Describing the Problem 102

    Discussion 2: Analyzing the Problem 103

Case Studies 104

   #1 Copying Software 104

   #2 Whose Computer Is It? 105

   #3 How Much Testing Is Enough? 105

   #4 How Much Should You Tell? 105

   #5 Abusive Workplace Behavior 106

The Last Word on Ethics 106

References 108

Chapter 5: Intellectual Property, Obligations, and Ownership 109

Who Owns What? 109

What Is Intellectual Property? 110

   Intellectual Property: Public Domain Works 111

   Intellectual Property: Copyright 112

   Intellectual Property: Patents 117

   Intellectual Property: Ownership and You 121

References 122

Chapter 6: Requirements 123

What Types of Requirements Are We Talking About? 124

   User Requirements 124

   Domain Requirements 125

   Non-Functional Requirements 125

   Non-Requirements 125

Gathering Requirements in a Plan-Driven Project 126

   Gathering Requirements: But I Don't Like Writing! 126

   Gathering Requirements: Outline of a Functional Specification 127

   Gathering Requirements: Design and New Feature Ideas 130

   Gathering Requirements: One More Thing 131

Gathering Requirements in an Agile Project 131

   Agile Requirements Gathering: The Three Cs 132

   Agile Requirements Gathering: INVEST in Stories 133

Agile Requirements Gathering: The Product Backlog 135

Agile Requirements Gathering: SMART Tasks.. 135

Agile Requirements Gathering: Sprint/Iteration Backlog 137

Requirements Digging 137

Why Requirements Digging Is Hard.. 138

Analyzing the Requirements 140

Conclusion 142

References... 142

Part II: Design Practices **143**

Chapter 7: Software Architecture **145**

Architectural Pattern: The Main Program - Subroutine 147

Architectural Pattern: Pipe-and-Filter 148

Architectural Pattern: Object-Oriented Model-View-Controller (MVC) 150

Object-Oriented Architecture:.. 152

An MVC Example—Let's Hunt! 152

Architectural Pattern: The Client-Server 155

Architectural Pattern: The Layered Approach.. 157

Conclusion 160

References... 160

Chapter 8: Design Principles **161**

Wicked Problems 162

Tame Problems 165

The Design Process 166

Desirable Design Characteristics (Things Your Design Should Favor) 167

Design Heuristics... 169

Designers and Creativity.. 171

Conclusion 173

References... 174

Chapter 9: Structured Design 177

Structured Programming 177

Stepwise Refinement.. 178

    Example of Stepwise Refinement: The Eight Queens Problem............... 180

Modular Decomposition 190

    Example: Keyword in Context.. 192

Conclusion 198

References... 198

Appendix 1: The Complete Non-Recursive Eight-Queens Program................ 199

Appendix 2: A Modular Version of the KWIC Solution 202

Chapter 10: Object-Oriented Overview 209

An Object-Oriented Analysis and Design Process.................................... 210

    Details of the OOA&D Process 213

Executing the Process.. 214

    Step 1: The Problem Statement... 214

    Step 2: The Feature List.. 215

    Step 3: Use Cases... 215

    Step 4: Decompose the Problem 216

    Step 5: Class Diagrams... 217

    Step 6: Code Anyone?.. 218

Conclusion 224

References... 224

Chapter 11: Object-Oriented Analysis and Design.......................... 225

Analysis.. 226

    Analysis: An Example... 228

Design.. 231

Change in the Right Direction 234

    Recognizing Change... 234

    Songbirds Forever 235

    A New Requirement.. 235

Separating Analysis and Design.. 237

Shaping the Design.. 238

Abstraction.. 240

Conclusion 244

References.. 244

Chapter 12: Object-Oriented Design Principles **245**

List of Fundamental Object-Oriented Design Principles 246

Encapsulate Things in Your Design That Are Likely to Change................................... 247

Code to an Interface Rather Than to an Implementation 248

The Open-Closed Principle (OCP).. 252

The Don't Repeat Yourself Principle (DRY) 254

The Single Responsibility Principle (SRP) 255

The Liskov Substitution Principle (LSP).. 258

Alternatives to Inheritance: Delegation, Composition, and Aggregation 262

The Dependency Inversion Principle (DIP) 267

The Interface Segregation Principle (ISP) 269

The Principle of Least Knowledge (PLK) 270

Class Design Guidelines.. 272

Conclusion 273

References.. 274

Chapter 13: Design Patterns.. **275**

Design Patterns and the Gang of Four.. 277

The Classic Design Patterns 278

Creational Patterns.. 279

Structural Patterns 279

Behavioral Patterns 279

Patterns We Can Use... 280

Creational Patterns.. 280

Structural Patterns 290

Behavioral Patterns 298

Conclusion 310

References 311

Chapter 14: Parallel Programming **313**

Concurrency vs. Parallelism.. 314

Parallel Architectures: Flynn's Taxonomy 317

Parallel Programming 319

Some Parallel Programming Definitions.. 319

Performance and Scalability 321

How to Write a Parallel Program 323

Parallel Programming Models 323

Designing Parallel Programs 325

Parallel Design Techniques.. 325

Programming Languages and APIs (with Examples).. 328

Parallel Language Features... 328

Parallel Language Features: Java Threads 330

Parallel Language Features: The OpenMP API 338

Conclusion 344

References 344

Chapter 15: Parallel Design Patterns **347**

Parallel Design Patterns Overview... 348

Overview: Parallel Design Spaces 348

A List of Parallel Patterns... 358

Pattern 1: Embarrassingly Parallel 358

Pattern 2: Manager/Worker 359

Pattern 3: Map and Reduce 360

Pattern 4: MapReduce 362

Pattern 5: Divide and Conquer 365

Pattern 6: Fork/Join.. 367

Conclusion 373

References... 373

Part III: Coding Practices 375

Chapter 16: Code Construction 377

A coding example.. 380

Size and Focus... 382

Formatting, Layout, and Style 383

General Layout Issues and Techniques 383

White Space... 387

Block and Statement Style Guidelines 387

Declaration Style Guidelines 389

Commenting Style Guidelines 391

Identifier Naming Conventions.. 394

Refactoring.. 397

    When to Refactor... 398

    Types of Refactoring.. 401

Defensive Programming... 404

    Defensive Programming: Assertions Are Helpful 406

    Defensive Programming: Exceptions.. 407

    Defensive Programming: Error Handling 407

    Defensive Programming: Exceptions in Java 410

Conclusion 413

References.. 414

Chapter 17: Debugging 415

What's an Error, Anyway?.. 417

What Not To Do... 418

An Approach to Debugging 419

    Debugging Step 1: Reproduce the Problem Reliably..................... 420

    Debugging Step 2: Find the Source of the Error 421

    Debugging Step 3: Fix the Error (Just That One)! 426

    Debugging Step 4: Test the Fix 427

    Debugging Step 5: Look for More Errors 427

Debugger Tools 428

    Gdb 428

    Eclipse 429

    XCode 430

Source Code Control 431

    Source Code Control: The Collision Problem.. 432

Source Code Control Systems... 435

    Subversion.. 435

    Git and GitHub.. 435

    Mercurial 437

One Last Thought on Coding and Debugging: Pair Programming 438

Conclusion 438

References.. 439

Chapter 18: Unit Testing **441**

The Problem with Testing... 443

Code Creator vs. Code Breaker Mindset 444

When to Test?... 445

Testing in an Agile Development Environment... 446

What to Test? 447

    Code Coverage: Test Every Statement... 447

    Data Coverage: Bad Data Is Your Friend? 449

Characteristics of Tests... 451

How to Write a Test 452

    Writing Tests: The Story 452

    Writing Tests: The Tasks 453

    Writing Tests: The Tests 453

JUnit: A Testing Framework 459

Testing Is Critical.. 464

Conclusion 465

References.. 465

Chapter 19: Code Reviews and Inspections 467

Walkthroughs, Reviews, and Inspections... 469

Walkthroughs.. 470

Code Reviews 470

Code Inspections.. 472

    Inspection Roles 473

    Inspection Defect Types... 475

    Inspection Phases and Procedures 476

Reviews in Agile Projects... 478

    Performing an Agile Peer Code Review 480

Summary of Review Methodologies 480

Defect Tracking Systems... 481

Defect Tracking in Agile Projects.. 483

Conclusion 484

References... 485

Chapter 20: Wrapping It All Up 487

What Have You Learned? 488

What to Do Next? 489

References... 492

Index.. 495

About the Authors

John F. Dooley is the William and Marilyn Ingersoll Professor Emeritus of Computer Science at Knox College in Galesburg, Illinois. Before returning to teaching in 2001, Professor Dooley spent more than 16 years in the software industry as a developer, designer, and manager working for companies such as Bell Telephone Laboratories, McDonnell Douglas, IBM, and Motorola, along with an obligatory stint as head of development at a software start-up. He has over two dozen professional journal and conference publications and seven books to his credit, along with numerous presentations. He has been a reviewer for the Association for Computing Machinery Special Interest Group on Computer Science Education (SIGCSE) Technical Symposium for the last 36 years and he reviews papers for the journal *Cryptologia* and other professional conferences. He has created short courses in software development and three separate software engineering courses at the advanced undergraduate level.

Dr. Vera A. Kazakova is a computer science educator and researcher, with expertise in artificial intelligence, experiential learning, and collaborative methodologies. With a PhD in AI focused on nature-inspired computation and emergent division of labor, her research spans CS education, evolutionary computation, narrative generation, decentralized multiagent systems, and cyber social science. Dr. Kazakova also has extensive experience as a CS educator, having taught programming, artificial intelligence, research, and software development courses. Dr. Kazakova coined the term "Soft-Aware development" to encapsulate a holistic approach for building software, building stakeholder relationships, and building up each developer along the way. An ardent proponent of experiential learning and agile methodologies, Dr. Kazakova champions a multi-sprint learning architecture that enables students to adapt and iterate, fostering a shared environment of continuous growth. Her passion for collaboration, from simplistic autonomous agents to human developers and members of large online communities, sets her apart as an advocate for a more interconnected, empathetic, and empowering approach to CS research, education, and software development.

About the Technical Reviewer

Dr. Takako Soma is an Associate Professor of Computer Science at Illinois College in Jacksonville, Illinois. She is also a co-author of *Guide to Java: A Concise Introduction to Programming* Second Edition (Springer 2023) and *Guide to Data Structures: A Concise Introduction Using Java* (Springer 2017).

Acknowledgments

We'd like to thank Melissa Duffy and Shonmirin P. A. of Apress for making this new edition possible. Our Technical Reviewer and all the staff at Apress have been very helpful and gracious. The book is much better for their reviews, comments, and edits.

Thanks also to all of the students in CS 292 over the years who have used successive versions of this material, first as course notes and then as the finished book, and to our Knox College Computer Science colleagues David Bunde and Jaime Spacco who've listened to us. Finally, thanks to Knox College for giving us the time and resources to finish all the editions of this book.

Preface

What's this book all about? Well, it's about how to develop software from a personal perspective. We'll look at what it means for you to take a problem and produce a program to solve it from beginning to end. That said, this book focuses a lot on design. How do you design software? What things do you take into account? What makes a good design? What methods and processes are there to help you design software? Is designing small programs different from designing large ones? How can you tell a good design from a bad one? What general patterns can you use to help make your design more readable and understandable?

It's also about code construction. How do you write programs and make them work? "What?" you say. "I've already written eight gazillion programs! Of course I know how to write code!" In this book, we'll explore what you already do and investigate ways to improve on it. We'll spend some time on coding standards, debugging, unit testing, modularity, and characteristics of good programs. We'll also talk about reading code, what makes a program readable, and how to review code that others have written with an eye to making it better. Can good, readable code replace documentation? How much documentation do you really need?

And it's about software engineering, which is usually defined as "the application of engineering principles to the development of software." What are engineering principles? Well, first, all engineering efforts follow a defined process, so we'll talk about what phases there are to this process, as well as how to best support development through becoming an effective facilitator. We'll talk a lot about agile methodologies, how they apply to small development teams, and how their project-management techniques work for small- to medium-sized projects. All engineering work has a basis in the application of science and mathematics to real-world problems. We will often ground our theoretical discussion by designing and implementing solutions to specific problems.

By the way, there's at least one other person (besides this book's authors) who thinks software development is not an engineering discipline. We're referring to Alistair Cockburn, and you can read his paper, "The End of Software Engineering and the Start of Economic-Cooperative Gaming," at http://alistair.cockburn.us/The+end+of+softw are+engineering+and+the+start+of+economic-cooperative+gaming.

Finally, this book is about professional practice, the ethics and the responsibilities of being a software developer, social issues, interpersonal skills, privacy, how to write secure and robust code, and the like. In short, those various non-technical things that you need in order to be a professional software developer.

This book covers many of the topics described for the ACM/IEEE Computer Society Curriculum Guidelines for Undergraduate Degree Programs in Computer Science (known as CS2023).[1] In particular, it covers topics in a number of the knowledge areas of the guidelines, including software development fundamentals, software engineering, systems fundamentals, parallel and distributed computing, programming languages, and social issues and professional practice. It's designed to be both a textbook for a junior-level undergraduate course in software design and development and a manual for the working professional. Although the chapter order generally follows the standard software development sequence, you can read the chapters independently and out of order. We're assuming that you already know how to program and that you're conversant with at least one of these languages: Java, C, or C++. We are also assuming you're familiar with basic data structures, including lists, queues, stacks, maps, and trees, along with the algorithms to manipulate them.

In this third edition, several chapters have been rewritten and all of the chapters have been updated, including new content and examples. The book discusses modern software development processes and techniques; notably the coverage of agile techniques has been updated and expanded. Much of the plan-driven process and project-management discussions from the second edition have been removed or shortened, and longer and new discussions of agile methodologies, including Scrum, lean software development, and Kanban have taken their place. There is a new chapter on intellectual property, ownership, and obligations. Finally, the chapter on project management essentials has been greatly expanded to include an introduction and discussion of Soft-Aware development, an approach to software development based on the idea that learning to make software is less crucial than *learning to work together while attempting to make software.*

---

[1] The Joint Task Force on Computing Education. 2023. "Computer Science Curricula 2023: Curriculum Guidelines for Undergraduate Degree Programs in Computer Science." New York, NY: ACM/IEEE Computer Society. https://csed.acm.org/wp-content/uploads/2023/03/Version-Beta-v2.pdf.

We have used this book in an upper-level course in software development and it has grown out of the notes we developed for that class. We developed our own notes because we couldn't find a book that covered all the topics we thought were necessary for a course in software development, as opposed to one in software engineering or just programming. Software engineering books tend to focus more on process and project management than on design and actual development. We wanted to focus on the design and writing of real code rather than on how to run a large project. This book is our perspective on what it takes to be a software developer on a small- to medium-sized team and help develop great software.

We believe that by the end of the book you'll have a much better idea of what the design of good programs is like, what makes an effective and productive developer, and how to develop larger pieces of software. You'll know a lot more about design issues. You'll have thought about working in a team to deliver a product to a written schedule. You'll begin to understand project management, know some metrics and how to review work products, and understand configuration management. We will not cover everything in software development—not by a long stretch—and we'll only be giving a cursory look at the management side of software engineering, but you'll be in a much better position to visualize, design, implement, and test software of many sizes, either by yourself or in a team.

CHAPTER 1

Introduction to Software Development

"Not only are there no silver bullets now in view, the very nature of software makes it unlikely that there will be any—no inventions that will do for software productivity, reliability, and simplicity what electronics, transistors, and large-scale integration did for computer hardware. We cannot expect ever to see twofold gains every two years."

—Frederick J. Brooks, Jr.[1]

So, you might be asking yourself, why is this book called *Software Development, Design, and Coding*? Why isn't it called *All About Programming* or *Software Engineering*? After all, isn't that what software development is? Well, no. Programming is a part of software development, but it's certainly not all of it. Likewise, software development is a part of software engineering, but it's not all of it.

Here's the definition of software development that we'll use in this book: software development is the process of taking a set of requirements from a user (a problem statement), analyzing them, designing a solution to the problem, and then implementing that solution on a computer.

But isn't that programming? Well, no. Programming is really just the implementation part, or possibly the design and implementation part, of software development. Programming is central to software development, but it's not the whole thing.

Well, then, isn't it software engineering? Again, no. Software engineering also involves a process and includes software development, but it also includes the entire management side of creating a computer program that people will use. Software

---

[1] Brooks, F. 1987. "No Silver Bullet." *IEEE Computer* 20 (4): 10–19. `www.inst.eecs.berkeley.edu/~maratb/readings/NoSilverBullet.html`.

© John F. Dooley and Vera A. Kazakova 2024
J. F. Dooley and V. A. Kazakova, *Software Development, Design, and Coding*,
https://doi.org/10.1007/979-8-8688-0285-0_1

engineering includes project management, configuration management, scheduling and estimation, baseline building and scheduling, managing people, and several other things. Software development is the fun part of software engineering.

So software development is a narrowing of the focus of software engineering to just that part concerned with the creation of the actual software. And it's a broadening of the focus of programming to include analysis, design, and release issues.

What We're Doing

It turns out that, after 80 or so years of using computers, we've discovered that developing software is hard. Learning how to develop software effectively, efficiently, and sustainably is also hard. You're not born knowing how to do it and many people, even those who take programming courses and work in the industry for years, don't do it particularly well. It's a skill you need to pick up and practice—a lot. You don't learn programming and development by reading books—not even this one. You learn it by developing software. That, of course, is the attraction: to work on interesting and difficult problems. The challenge is to work on something you've never done before, something you might not even know if you can solve. That's what has you coming back to create new programs again and again.

There are probably several ways to learn software development. But we think that all of them involve reading excellent designs, reading a lot of code, writing a lot of code, and thinking deeply about how to approach a problem and design a solution for it. Reading a lot of code, especially really beautiful and efficient code, gives you lots of good examples about how to think about problems and approach their solution in a particular style. Writing a lot of code lets you experiment with the styles and examples you've seen in your reading. Thinking deeply about problem solving lets you examine how you work and how you do design, and lets you extract from your labors those patterns that work for you; it makes your programming more intentional.

So, How to Develop Software?

Well, the first thing you should do is read this book. It certainly won't tell you everything, but it will give you a good introduction into what software development is all about and what you need to do to write great code. It has its own perspective, but it's a perspective based on our combined 40 years or so of writing code professionally and another 24 years trying to figure out how to teach others to do it.

Despite the fact that software development is only part of software engineering, software development is the heart of every software project. After all, *at the end of the day what you deliver to the user is working code.* A team of developers working in concert usually creates that code. So to start, maybe we should look at a software project from the outside and ask, what does that team need to do to make that project a success?

In order to succeed at software development, you need the following:

> *To realize that you don't know everything you need to know at the beginning of the project.* Software development projects just don't work this way. You'll always uncover new requirements; other requirements will be discovered to be not nearly as important as the customer thought; still others that were targeted for the next release are all of a sudden requirement number one. This is known as *churn.* Managing requirements churn during a project is one of the single most important skills a software developer can have. If you are using new development tools (say a new web development framework), you'll uncover limitations you weren't aware of and side effects that cause you to have to learn, for example, three other tools to understand them (e.g., that web development tool you want to use is Ruby-based, requires a specific relational database system to run, and needs a particular configuration of Apache to work correctly.)

> *A small, well integrated team.* Small teams have fewer lines of communication than larger ones. It's easier to get to know your teammates' strengths and weaknesses, understand their personalities and preferences, and establish who is the go-to person for particular problems or tools. Well-integrated teams have usually worked on several projects together. Keeping a team together across several projects is a major job of the team's manager and of the individual teammates themselves. Well-integrated teams are more productive, better at holding to a schedule, and more likely to produce code with fewer defects at release. The key to keeping a team together is to give them interesting work, give them the freedom to decide how to do the work, and facilitate the process by removing barriers and helping with conflict resolution.

Good communication among team members. Continuous direct communication among team members is critical to day-to-day progress and successful project completion. Teams that are co-located are generally better at communicating and communicate more than teams that are distributed geographically (even if they're just on different floors or wings of a building) or that are working virtually.[2] This is a major issue with larger companies that have software development sites scattered across the globe.

Good communication between the team and the customer. Communication with the customer is essential to controlling requirements and requirements churn during a project. On-site or close-by customers allow for constant interaction with the development team. Customers can give immediate feedback on new releases and can be involved in creating system and acceptance tests for the product. Agile development methodologies strongly encourage customers to be part of the development team and, even better, to be on site daily. See Chapter 2 for a quick introduction to some agile methodologies.

A process that everyone buys into. Every project, no matter how big or small, follows a process. Larger projects require more coordination and tighter controls on communication and configuration management. As a result, larger teams tend to be more plan-driven and follow processes with more rules and documentation required. Smaller projects and smaller teams will, these days, tend to follow more agile development processes, with more flexibility and less documentation required. This certainly doesn't mean there is *no* process in an agile project; it just means you do what makes sense for the current stage of your project, so that you can correctly uncover and satisfy all the requirements, meet the schedule, and produce a quality product. See Chapter 2 for more details on process and software life cycles.

---

[2] Note that teams that are distributed geographically can also be closer to clients and thus have better communication with them. Also, the advent of easy and fast conferencing software can mitigate the disadvantages of remote work.

The ability to be flexible about that process. No project ever proceeds as you think it will on the first day. Requirements change, people come and go, tools don't work out or get updated, and so on. This point is all about handling risk in your project. If you identify risks, plan to mitigate them, and then have a contingency plan to address the event where the risk actually occurs, you'll be in much better shape. Chapter 4 talks about requirements and risk.

A plan that everyone buys into. You wouldn't write a sorting program without an algorithm to start with, so you shouldn't launch a software development project without a plan. The project plan encapsulates what you're going to do to implement your project. It talks about process, risks, resources, tools, requirements management, estimates, schedules, configuration management, and delivery. It doesn't have to be long, it doesn't need to contain all the minute details of the everyday life of the project, and it doesn't even need to be written down, but everyone on the team needs to have input into it, they need to understand it, and they need to agree with it. Unless everyone buys into the plan, you're doomed. See Chapter 3 for more details on project planning.

To know where you are at all times. It's that communication thing again. Most projects have regular status meetings so that the developers can "sync up" on their current status, get a feel for the status of the entire project, and to create a sense of camaraderie within the team. This works very well for smaller teams (say, up to about 20 developers, many of which will have daily "stand-up" meetings to sync up at the beginning of each day. Different process models handle this "stand-up" meeting differently. For instance, plan-driven models don't require these meetings, depending on the team managers to communicate with each other. Agile processes often require all-hands daily meetings to facilitate constant team communication in a highly dynamic project environment.

To be brave enough to say, "hey, we're behind!" Nearly all software projects have schedules that are too optimistic at the start. It's what clients want to hear, what companies want to offer, and what managers and developers want to supply. "Sure, I can get that done in a week!" "I'll have it to you by the end of the day." "Tomorrow? Not a problem." No, no, no, no, no. Just face it. At some point you'll be behind. And the best thing to do about it is to tell your manager right away. Sure, they might be angry. But they'll be angrier when you end up a month behind and they didn't know it. Fred Brooks' famous answer to the question of how software projects get so far behind is "one day at a time." The good news, though, is that the earlier you figure out you're behind, the more options you have. These include lengthening the schedule (unlikely, but it does happen), moving some requirements to a future release, getting additional help, and so on. The important part is to keep your manager informed.

The right tools and the right practices for this project. One of the best things about software development is that every project is different. Even if you're doing version 8.0 of an existing product, things change. One implication of this is that, for every project, you need to examine and pick the right set of development tools. Picking tools that are inappropriate is like trying to hammer nails with a screwdriver; you might be able to do it eventually, but is sure isn't easy or pretty or fun, and you can drive a lot more nails in a shorter period of time with a hammer than with a screwdriver. Even if you have to first obtain a hammer and then learn how to use it for the very first time, you are leveling up your toolkit and your skills in the process, investing in your ability to work more efficiently going forward. The three most important factors in choosing tools are the application type you are writing, the target platform, and the development platform. You usually can't do anything about any of these three things, so once you know what they are, you can pick tools that improve your productivity. A fourth and nearly as important factor in tool choice is the composition and experience of the development team. If your team are all experienced developers with facility on multiple platforms, tool choice is much easier. If, on the other hand, you have a bunch of fresh-outs and your target platform is new to all of you, you'll need to be careful about tool choice and fold in time for training and practice with the new tools.

Conclusion

Software development is the heart of every software project, and it is the heart of software engineering. Its objective is to deliver excellent, defect-free code to users on time and within budget—all in the face of constantly changing requirements. This makes development a particularly hard job to do. But finding a solution to a difficult problem and getting your code to work correctly is just about the coolest feeling in the world.

> *"[Programming is] the only job I can think of where I get to be both an engineer and an artist. There's an incredible, rigorous, technical element to it, which I like because you have to do very precise thinking. On the other hand, it has a wildly creative side where the boundaries of imagination are the only real limitation. The marriage of those two elements is what makes programming unique. You get to be both an artist and a scientist. I like that. I love creating the magic trick at the center that is the real foundation for writing the program. Seeing that magic trick, that essence of your program, working correctly for the first time, is the most thrilling part of writing a program."*
>
> —Andy Hertzfeld (designer of the first Mac OS)[3]

References

Brooks, F. 1987. "No Silver Bullet." *IEEE Computer* 20 (4): 10–19. www.inst.eecs.berkeley.edu/~maratb/readings/NoSilverBullet.html.

Lammers, Susan. 1986. *Programmers At Work*. Redmond, WA: Microsoft Press.

---

[3] Lammers, Susan. 1986. *Programmers At Work*. Redmond, WA: Microsoft Press.

PART I

Models and Team Practices

CHAPTER 2

Software Process Models

If you don't know where you're going, any road will do.
If you don't know where you are, a map won't help.

—Watts Humphrey

The process of developing software is commonly described as the Software Development Lifecycle (SDLC). Every program, no matter how small, has a life cycle, broadly composed of the following steps:

1. Conception

2. Requirements gathering/exploration/modeling

3. Design

4. Coding and debugging

5. Testing

6. Release

7. Maintenance/software evolution

8. Retirement

Your development process may combine multiple steps or iterate over a subset of steps repeatedly between releases, but, in one form or another, all development should encompass all of the above life cycle steps in order to create high-quality software. The two most common variations are *plan-based models*[1] and the newer *agile development* models.[2]

---

[1] Paulk, Mark C. 1995. *The Capability Maturity Model: Guidelines for Improving the Software Process. The SEI Series in Software Engineering.* Reading, Mass.: Addison-Wesley Pub. Co.

[2] Martin, Robert C. 2003. *Agile Software Development, Principles, Patterns, and Practices.* Upper Saddle River, NJ: Prentice Hall.

With plan-based development, the project team will generally do a complete life cycle (at least steps 2 through 7) before going back in the SDLC to start working on the next version of the product. In plan-driven models, the methodology tends to be stricter in terms of process steps and when releases happen. Plan-driven models have more clearly defined phases and more requirements for sign-off on completion of a phase before moving on to the next phase. Plan-driven models require more documentation at each phase and verification of completion of each work product. They tend to work well for large contracts for new software with well-defined deliverables.

In agile development, which is more prevalent now, the project team will usually iterate over a partial life cycle (usually steps 3 through 5) several times before proceeding to the release step. The agile models are inherently incremental and operate under the assumption that small, frequent releases produce a more robust product than larger, less frequent ones. Phases in agile models tend to blur together more than in plan-driven models, and there tends to be less documentation of work products required, the basic idea being that code is what is being produced and so developer efforts should focus there. See the Agile Manifesto web page at `https://agilemanifesto.org` to get a good feel for the agile development model and goals.

There is no one best process for developing software. Each project must decide on the model that works best for its particular application and base that decision on the project domain, the scope of the project, the experience of the team, and the timeline of the project. In this chapter, we begin by reviewing the shared variables of software development projects, followed by a discussion of the different broadly defined approaches, and finally we take a look at several prominent specific software model implementations as well as how they can be hybridized together.

The 3(+3) Variables of Software Development

According to the Project Management Institute,[3] the three main *variables of software development* are cost, time, and scope.

- *Cost* (a.k.a. resources) is usually the most constrained; as a developer, you have very limited control over cost and you cannot spend your way to quality or to being on schedule. Cost can influence the size

---

[3] Project Management Institute. 2021. *A Guide to the Project Management Institute Body of Knowledge*. 7th ed. Project Management Institute, Inc. `www.pmi.org`.

of the team or the types of tools available during development. For
small companies and startups, cost also influences the environment
where the developers will work.

- *Time* is your delivery schedule and is typically imposed on you
  from the outside. For example, most consumer products (be they
  hardware or software) will have a delivery date somewhere between
  August and October in order to hit the holiday buying season. You
  can't move Christmas. If you are late, the only way to fix your problem
  is to drop features or lessen quality, neither of which is pretty. Time is
  also where Brooks' Law gets invoked (adding programmers to a late
  project just makes it later).

- *Scope* (a.k.a. features) is what the product actually does. This is what
  developers should always focus on. It's the most important of the
  variables from the customer's perspective and it is also the one you
  as a developer have the most control over. Controlling scope allows
  you to provide managers and customers control over quality, time,
  and cost. If the developers don't have control over the feature set for
  each release, then they are likely to blow the schedule. This is why
  developers should do the estimates for software work products.

Together, cost, time, and scope form the *Iron Triangle* of software development, in
which specifying two of the variables defines the third. In the real world, a customer will
often specify timeframe and budget for the task, which will then be your constraints to
estimate a realistic scope within the broader task.

Occasionally, a fourth variable is added (usually as the center of the triangle).

- *Quality* is the number/severity of defects, simplifications, or
  functionality reductions you are willing to release with. Thus, quality
  may be used to describe non-binary characteristics of features in
  your scope (e.g. the time to respond to a user query should be no
  more than n milliseconds, but the lower the better). This is not,
  strictly speaking, an input variable like cost, time, and scope, but
  rather a metric for the quality of your output. You can make short-
  term gains in delivery schedules by sacrificing quality, but the cost

is enormous. It will take more time to fix the next release and your credibility will be pretty well shot. More commonly, there is an expected minimum expected quality for the product, fixing this "variable".

In some definitions, the scope of the task/product is considered to be fixed or, otherwise, intertwined with quality, leading instead to an Iron Triangle consisting of cost, time, and quality.[4]

More recently, two more variables have been defined as part of the new six-variable set of constraints:[5]

- *Benefit* is the value delivered to the product provider and to the client. With new information about the market, client needs, or target audience, benefit may change, requiring changes to scope or to other variables.

- *Risk* is the likelihood of not meeting expected values for the other criteria (such as failing to implement features, increasing development time, or exceeding the expected budget). Managing one type of risk may increase another type of risk (e.g., increasing time makes scope less risky, but is likely to increase cost). To minimize risk, developers need to control as many of the variables as possible, always keeping in mind that the only constant of software development is change. If you pay attention and effectively cope with change as it occurs, you can keep the risk and cost of change manageable.

As shown in Figure 2-1, all constraints need to be balanced. Altering one will require adjusting others to compensate.

---

[4] https://ronjeffries.com/xprog/articles/practices/pracfourvariables/
[5] Siegelaub, J. M. 2007. "Six (Yes Six!) Constraints: An Enhanced Model for Project Control." In *Proceedings of the PMI Global Congress 2007*. Atlanta, GA: Project Management Institute, Inc. www.pmi.org/learning/library/six-constraints-enhanced-model-project-control-7294. See also https://prince2.wiki/.

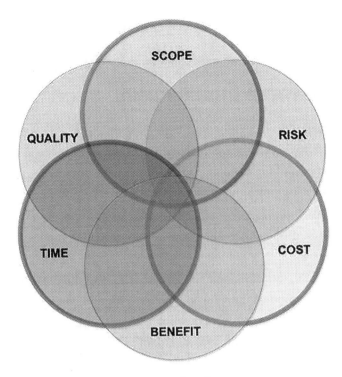

Figure 2-1. *The six variables of software development*

A number of other expansions to the variables that define a software development project have been suggested over the years. For example, The Square Route combines the Iron Triangle with additional considerations of project evaluation at the delivery stage and post-delivery stage.[6] Additional constrains external to the organization and the client may also play an important role in the creation of software products, including social, economic, legislative, environmental, and other factors.[7]

Software Development Approaches

When it comes to developing software, there are several general approaches, which can be employed separately or together within an organization or even within a single

---

[6] Atkinson, Roger. 1999. "Project Management: Cost, Time, and Quality, Two Best Guesses and a Phenomenon, It's Time to Accept Other Success Criteria." *International Journal of Project Management* 17 (6): 337–42.

[7] www.smartsheet.com/content/project-constraints

project. Below we discuss planning, reducing waste with lean methodologies, and adapting by remaining agile.

Plan-Based Software Development

The main characteristic of plan-based software development is to make a plan and then follow through with it. It seems simple enough...except that to make a reliable plan you need to have all of the information AND that information must not change. As we are neither omniscient nor clairvoyant, this poses a bit of a problem. We are at the mercy of imprecise language describing poorly understood requirements that are devised to solve problems for changing real-world scenarios by teams of predictably unpredictable humans.

Still, plans are comforting. It allows the illusion that we know what is going to happen. If we follow a plan and get a result, we hope that following the same plan in the future will yield the same result. Of course, controlling for all variables (both internal and external to the project) is impossible. Plans also allow for subplans and estimations for the entire hierarchy of plans. Granted, the further away the step, the less accurate our estimation. Plans also allow us to assess dependencies and schedule tasks accordingly. Of course, any change can tumble the carefully scheduled house of cards which we painstakingly designed, estimated, sorted, scheduled, and partially developed.

Let's say we do have a plan: we have devised steps and we will complete them one by one, in order. For a small project with a single developer, who is also the client, this may very well work out. In a more realistic scenario, the client is not us, the project is complex, and we have to coordinate with other stakeholders. Let's say our basic plan has a design phase, an implementation phase, a testing phase, and delivery. We take several months to come up with a beautiful design and show our client, but the client wants changes. We take a few weeks to make changes to the design; the client approves. We make a development plan and attempt to implement our design over the next several months. In that time, some of the libraries we were relying on have been deprecated, some developers leave, new ones join the team, the market changes, causing the client to request changes to the design, and ultimately our development plan and our design are both obsolete. Do-over time... To make matters worse, so far we have delivered no value to the client and they are starting to lose confidence that we ever will. To recap, making reliable short plans for small projects is doable; anything else is wishful thinking.

Agile Software Development

Starting in the mid-1990s, a group of process mavens began advocating a new model for software development. Targeting medium-sized software projects and smaller teams of developers, the new approach was intended to allow teams to quickly adjust to changing requirements and customer demands, while also releasing functional software much more quickly and frequently than under plan-driven models. The new model was, in a word, *agile*.[8]

In most *agile* process models, we start with the "known" requirements (a snapshot of the requirements at some time early in the process) and prioritize them, typically based on the customer's ranking of what features are most important to deliver first. Keep in mind that what we think we know or understand about these requirements is commonly only somewhat accurate: natural language is imprecise; the understood meanings differ based on communicator background, positionality, and other context; and clients often do not necessarily understand what they want or need to solve their problem. Thus, one of our most important challenges in software development is to *iteratively approach an accurate shared understanding of the problem and the prospective solution*. According to Tom DeMarco, iterative software development follows one basic rule:

> *Your project, the whole project, has a binary deliverable. On the scheduled completion day, the project has either delivered a system that is accepted by the user, or it hasn't. Everyone knows the result on that day.*

> *The object of building a project model is to divide the project into compo-nent pieces, each of which has this same characteristic: each activity must be defined by a deliverable with <u>objective completion criteria</u>. The deliver-ables are demonstrably done or not done.*[9]

Rather loosely, we can devise a series of iterations, where each iteration is a complete Minimum Viable Product (MVP), working and robust, albeit with fewer features than the final goal product. For each iteration, we will select a set of the next highest priority requirements (including some you or the customer may have discovered during the previous iteration), develop, test, and demo the MVP, and gather feedback. This feedback may drastically alter our initial plan, which is why our initial plan is only a loose sketch of future development iterations.

---

[8] Cockburn, A. 2002. *Agile Software Development*. Boston, MA: Addison-Wesley.

[9] DeMarco, Tom. 1983. *Controlling Software Projects: Management, Measurement and Estimation*. Yourdon Press.

So what happens if you estimate wrong? What if you decide to include too many new features in an iteration? What if there are unexpected delays? Well, if it looks as if you won't make your iteration deadline there are only two realistic alternatives: move the deadline or remove features. We'll come back to this problem later when we talk about estimation and scheduling. The key to iterative development is "live a balanced life— learn some and think some and draw and paint and sing and dance and play and work every day some,"[10] or in the software development world, *analyze* some and *design* some and *code* some and *test* some every day. We'll revisit this idea when we talk about the agile development models later in this chapter.

Overall, agile is composed of ongoing short-term experiments, iteratively reviewed to evaluate product and practices, and to find processes that work for the team and the client. In other words, some good old-fashioned trial and error. While some failure is inevitable, it is more informative and less costly to fail on small increments, to fail early, and to learn from it quickly. Thus, we reduce the pressure of needing our intermediates to be right, requiring only that these decision are useful in helping us learn more about what was actually needed.

Agile development works from the proposition that the goal of any software development project is working code. Consequently, the development team should spend most of their time writing code, not documentation. As opposed to the heavyweight plan-driven models mentioned above and espoused by groups like the Software Engineering Institute (SEI) at Carnegie Mellon University,[11] this new process model was *lightweight*, requiring less documentation and fewer process controls. Lightweight methodologies tend to emphasize writing tests before code, frequent product releases, significant customer involvement in development, common code ownership, and refactoring (rewriting code to make it simpler and easier to maintain). Lightweight methodologies do, unfortunately, suffer from several myths, the two most pernicious being that lightweight processes are only good for very small projects and that lightweight projects lack process discipline. Both of these are incorrect. The truth is that lightweight methodologies have been successfully used in many small and medium-sized projects (say up to about 500K lines of code), as well as in very large projects. Larger projects can nearly always be organized as a set of smaller projects, which together provide services to the single larger

---

[10] Fulghum, Robert. 1986. *All I Really Need to Know I Learned in Kindergarten.* New York, NY: Ivy Books.

[11] (Paulk 1995)

product. Lightweight methodologies also require process discipline, especially in the beginning of a project, when initial requirements and an iteration cycle are created, and in the test-driven-development used as the heart of the coding process.

In the remainder of the chapter, we will review the agile values, principles, and activities that have been defined over the years. Note, however, that *agility necessarily extends to how these concepts and practices are ultimately incorporated into development* (i.e., to iteratively determine what works and what does not for each particular product/organization/team/etc.).

Agile Values, Principles, and Activities

In early 2001, a group of experienced and innovative developers met in Snowbird, Utah, to talk about the state of the software development process. All of them were dissatisfied with traditional plan-driven models and had been experimenting with new lightweight development techniques. Out of this meeting came the Agile Manifesto.[12] The original description proposed by the group included two parts: values (the manifesto itself) and principles.

The four *Agile Values* showcase that while the authors recognize the value of the items on the right, they view the items on the left as the most crucial to successful software development:

- Individuals and interactions over processes and tools

- Working software over comprehensive documentation

- Customer collaboration over contract negotiation

- Responding to change over following a plan

The following 12 *Agile Principles* were defined by the authors to focus and guide development:

- Our highest priority is to satisfy the customer through early and continuous delivery of valuable software.

- Welcome changing requirements, even late in development. Agile processes harness change for the customer's competitive advantage.

- Deliver working software frequently, from a couple of weeks to a couple of months, with a preference to the shorter timescale.

---

[12] https://agilemanifesto.org/

- Business people and developers must work together daily throughout the project.

- Build projects around motivated individuals. Give them the environment and support they need, and trust them to get the job done.

- The most efficient and effective method of conveying information to and within a development team is face-to-face conversation.

- Working software is the primary way to measure progress.

- Agile processes promote sustainable development. The sponsors, developers, and users should be able to maintain a constant pace indefinitely.

- Continuous attention to technical excellence and good design enhances agility.

- Simplicity—the art of maximizing the amount of work not done—is essential.

- The best architectures, requirements, and designs emerge from self-organizing teams.

- At regular intervals, the team reflects on how to become more effective, then tunes and adjusts its behavior accordingly.

The following four main *Agile Activities* (although originally defined as part of the Agile variant called eXtreme Programming) are applicable for all Agile methodologies:

Design while you code. In real world domains, all the requirements aren't typically known or correctly understood in advance. Mistakes and oversights will be made in architectural design, detailed design, and coding. Additionally, during product development, requirements and constraints may change, as no project exists in a vacuum, away from real world events such as turnover in the development team, updates to customer needs due to market changes, the development of new technologies, and so on. Agile software development models build products a piece at a time, with each product increment allowing for several crucial events to happen earlier and more frequently: delivery of value to the customer, feedback gathering, and adaptation to changes. Designing while coding allows more developer freedom to choose how to deliver on the tasks, promoting developer agency while increasing their responsibility to self-manage.

Direct communication is best, although what "direct" means has shifted greatly in recent years. We see "direct communication" as happening in real time, with direct exposure to both verbal and non-verbal cues, which would encompass in-person discussions, video conferencing, and even advanced virtual environments. In any given software development project, there are two types of knowledge: 1) the customer has domain knowledge and what understanding of what the system is supposed to do and 2) the developers have technical knowledge about the target platform, programming language(s), and possible implementation issues. The customer doesn't know the technical side and the developers don't have the domain knowledge, so effective communication—on both sides—is a key activity in developing the product. Frequent communication means everyone is learning from everyone's process, creating a more well-rounded shared understanding faster.

Code is the main deliverable. The fundamental difference between plan-driven models and agile models is this emphasis on the code, as code is where system knowledge resides. In a plan-driven model, the emphasis is on producing a set of work products that together represent the entire work of the project with code being just one of the work products. In agile methodologies, the emphasis is placed squarely with code as the deliverable; in addition, by structuring the code properly and keeping comments up to date, the code itself becomes documentation for the project.

Test-driven development. Test cases for the required features are written before development takes place and should all initially fail. Once all tests for a feature pass, the feature implementation is completed. Test-driven development is instrumental for managing change, as continuous testing tells you when a new feature is completed and integrated into the system without breaking any of the pre-existing functionality.

Lean Software Development

Lean software development comes from the just-in-time manufacturing processes (also known as the Toyota Production System, among other names), which were introduced in Japan in the 1970s and then made their way around the world in the 1980s and 1990s, encouraged by the publication in 1990 of *The Machine That Changed The World*[13]

---

[13] Womack, James P., Daniel T. Jones, and Daniel Roos. 1990. *The Machine That Changed the World: The Story of Lean Production -- Toyota's Secret Weapon in the Global Car Wars That Is Now Revolutionizing World Industry.* New York, NY: Simon and Schuster.

(Womack et. al.). Just-in-time manufacturing evolved first into lean manufacturing and then into lean product management systems throughout the 1990s. The publication of Poppendieck & Poppendieck's *Lean Software Development: An Agile Toolkit*[14] in 2003 marked the movement of *lean* into the *agile* development community.

Lean software development is a set of principles designed to eliminate *waste* in order to improve productivity, quality, and customer satisfaction. *Waste* is anything that does not add value to the product. Thus, *lean* emphasizes that the team should only be focusing on activities that add immediate value to the product.

The Poppendiecks[14] transformed the *lean* principles that started at Toyota into seven key principles for software development:

- Eliminate waste
- Build quality in
- Create knowledge
- Defer commitment
- Deliver fast
- Respect people
- Optimize the whole

We will go through each of these principles briefly to illustrate how they apply to software development.

Lean Principle 1: Eliminate Waste

The main goal of *lean* software development is to eliminate *waste*, defined as anything that does not add value to the product or increases its cost or time. In software development, the main sources of *waste* are the following:

- *Partially done work*, as it adds no immediate value and may become obsolete before it is finished

---

[14] Poppendieck, Mary, and Tom Poppendieck. 2003. *Lean Software Development: An Agile Toolkit.* Upper Saddle River, NJ: Addison-Wesley Professional.

- *Extra processing,* such as excessive documentation/paperwork or unnecessary meetings

- *Extra features* that are rarely, if ever, used, while taking up resources and cluttering code

- *Task/context switching,* which reduces efficiency by introducing delays and increasing cognitive load for the developers

- *Waiting* for approvals and dependencies causes wasteful bottlenecks

- *Motion* of artifacts and of information can be wasteful without the necessary regulation to ensure artifact/data organization and labeling is usably clear and consistent

- *Defects,* which become increasingly expensive to fix as detection time moves further from the defect's inception

A general approach to reducing all forms of waste in a project is to continually reconsider how the team's development process is working and what can be improved (i.e., "What was wasteful and how can we change it to be less wasteful next time?"). Small iterative adjustments to the workflow will lead to an overall reduction of development *wastes.*

Lean Principle 2: Build Quality In

Quality issues lead to a variety of software development waste. Finding and logging defects, fixing defects, and re-testing all result in waste we'd like to eliminate. "Building quality in" refers to focusing on and incorporating quality directly into the software development processes.

There are many techniques to increase the quality of your development processes. Two popular techniques that improve code quality at the source are *pair programming* (two programmers coding together, following a set of predefined practices) and *Test-Driven Development* (TDD) (writing software with the goal of passing all previously defined test-cases). Both allow developers to write, test, and fix code quickly and before the code is integrated into the product code base where defects become harder to find and fix. Integrating new features as soon as they are done gives the testing team a new version of the product to test as quickly as possible and shortens the amount of time between code creation and testing. Another relatively painless, but somewhat controversial way to improve quality of your code: instead of logging discovered defects in a defect tracking system, fix it *NOW*. As soon as you find it. That builds quality in and eliminates waste simultaneously.[15] Another technique to improve software quality is *constant feedback*. One way to facilitate this feedback is to make the customer part of the development team, allowing for direct repeated evaluation of new iterations of the product and providing developers with crucial timely feedback on what is suitable and what needs to be changed.

Lean Principle 3: Create Knowledge

While working through requirements, creating the design, and implementing the code, the team is necessarily learning new things. You learn by working to understand requirements. You learn by beginning with an initial design and realizing how the design must change as the requirements become better understood. You learn more about the domain, the customer, the tools, the dependencies, and so on. Thus, you are jointly creating knowledge that is embodied in the code you produce and ship.

To ensure all this knowledge is truly "created" (meaning that it survives longer-term and allows the team to really "learn" by keeping this knowledge), some shorter-term practices are necessary. For example, if one teammate learns something crucial about the project's requirements or dependencies, they must ensure this information is made available to the rest of the team. This can be achieved through consistent code documentation, well organized wiki pages, dependency management tools, targeted trainings, etc. Overall, these practices can reduce the motion of artifacts and information, extra processing, and even defects. The focal point is to ensure that any new information doesn't just solve short-term problems for whoever encountered them, but truly turns into knowledge that helps the whole team level up their understanding, their skills, and their products.

Lean Principle 4: Defer Commitment

This lean principle really dates back to the early 1970s and the advent of top-down structured design. Deferring commitment means putting off decisions (particularly irreversible or highly consequential ones) for as long as possible and only making them when absolutely necessary.

---

[15] (Poppendieck & Poppendieck 2003, 25-26)

One way to defer commitment is to follow a flexible, hierarchical, and modular design. In top-down design, you can begin with a general formulation of the problem solution, increasing future flexibility, and pushing implementation decisions further down to whenever the design and the code need to become more detailed. Creating libraries and APIs can allow us to implement flexible functionality without committing to how it must be invoked, leaving those decisions to the individual developers of each feature. In this way, by the time you reach the level where these details are required, more information is typically available, allowing the code to be developed more naturally and with greater ease.

Lean Principle 5: Deliver Fast

The faster we can deliver value to the customers, the sooner we can obtain crucial customer feedback to guide future development. Additionally, minimizing the time between when requirements are generated and when product meeting those requirements is delivered, there is less time for the requirements—and the market— to change.

So how do you deliver fast? *Lean* into the principles (pun intended). Keep requirements clear and simple. Don't add too many features and don't spend time pre-planning future features. Don't over-engineer the solution. Find a reasonable approach, a reasonable set of data structures, and reasonable algorithms to implement your solution. Remember that the perfect is the enemy of the good—and the fast. Satisfice instead of optimizing: if it's a suitable solution for the immediate need, move on. Finally, a crucial path to deliver fast is to have an experienced, well-integrated, cooperative, self-organizing, respectful-of-each-other team with the right skill set for your product. The team quite literally makes or breaks the product.

Lean Principle 6: Respect People

Respecting people is the key to building cohesive, productive teams. The focal idea is that the people doing the work should make the decisions. Process and product creation decisions should not be imposed from above, but rather generated from the trenches. From the manager's perspective, respecting your team means empowering the team to make their own decisions, including about task time estimates and decomposition, processes, tools, and design. This empowerment means that the manager must learn to listen to their team and take their ideas and concerns into consideration. It also means that the manager must act as a facilitator and a shield for their team, allowing them to get the job done. Together, everyone must endeavor to create an environment where everyone is able to speak their mind and disagreements are resolved with respect for each other. This creates a team with open communication and decision-making transparency. More on this in the next chapter.

Lean Principle 7: Optimize the Whole

"A lean organization optimizes the whole value stream, from the time it receives an order to address a customer need until software is deployed and the need is addressed. If an organization focuses on optimizing something less than the entire value stream, we can just about guarantee that the overall value stream will suffer."[16]

The main idea behind optimizing the whole is to keep the entire product picture in sight as you develop. One way to prevent myopic views is to have diverse, multi-disciplinary, well-communicating teams, which contain all the skills and product creation functions needed to deliver a product that truly meets the customer's needs.

Implementations of Software Development Models

"When I read them, I want to shout, Draw me a map! Show me the way! But all the authors do is describe their footprints and talk about their shoes, which are always the best, the only true shoes."[17]

When it comes to implementing any software development model, there are endless accounts of general approaches, countless possible tweaks, and a cornucopia of books and other resources that aim to guide you through the process. Consequently, we do not aim to provide exhaustive nor prescriptive step-by-step implementation details. Instead, in this section, we review the most prominent implementations of the ideas presented earlier in this chapter. Our goal is to delineate the unique focal points of each approach,

---

[16] (Poppendieck & Poppendieck 2003, 39)

[17] Bancroft, Josiah. 2013. *Senlin Ascends (The Books of Babel)*. CreateSpace Independent Publishing Platform. www.amazon.com/Senlin-Ascends-Books-Babel-1/dp/1482590956.

which we hope will not only help you distinguish them, but also hybridize them in order to better suit your team, project, organization, and client needs.

The Waterfall Model: An Assembly-Line Approach

The first and most traditional of the plan-driven process models is the waterfall model. Shown in Figure 2-2, it was created in 1970 by Winston Royce[18] and addresses all the standard life cycle phases. It progresses nicely through requirements gathering and analysis, to architectural design, detailed design, coding, debugging, integration and system testing, release, and maintenance. It requires detailed documentation at each stage, along with reviews, archiving of the documents, sign-offs at each process phase, configuration management, and close management of the entire project.

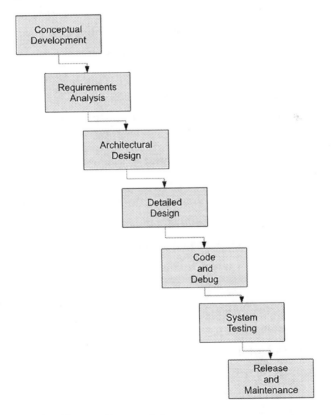

Figure 2-2. *The Waterfall process model*

---

[18] Royce, W. W. 1970. "Managing the Development of Large Software Systems." In *Proceedings of IEEE Wescon*, 1–9. Piscataway, NJ: IEEE Press.

It also doesn't work (at least not for anything beyond tiny projects). There are two fundamental and related problems with the *Waterfall* model that hamper its acceptance and make it very difficult to implement.

Problem 1: *Waterfall* requires that you finish phase N before you move on to phase N+1.

Problem 2: *Waterfall* has no provision for backing up to earlier stages for adjustments.

Waterfall is fundamentally modelled like an assembly-line for developing software. The initially comforting straightforward progression through the waterfall stages requires that all steps be completed in order and, since there is no way to go back and rework earlier development phases, each phase must be completed perfectly. In the simplest example, this means that you must precisely nail down *all* your requirements before you start your architectural design, finish your coding and debugging before you start unit testing, and so on. Additionally, each phase must be thoroughly documented along the way. In theory, this would be great. In practice, however, this never happens. No doubt having the complete set of perfectly understood requirements would be ideal before diving into designing the system. Alas, we have never seen a project where all requirements were known from the start, or where these requirements were correctly understood by all stakeholders, or where big things didn't change at some point during development of real-world projects with dynamic real-world needs and constraints.

Consequently, finishing one phase before the next begins is problematic, not to mention ensuring that nothing was missed or otherwise requires updating in any of the preceding phases. You never know everything you need to know at exactly the time you need to know it. This is why software is a *wicked problem*.

Nevertheless, the *Waterfall* is a terrific theoretical model. It isolates the different phases of the life cycle and forces you to think about what you really do need to know before you move on. It's also a way to start thinking about very large projects, breaking them down into smaller phases, and giving managers a warm fuzzy mirage of a plan. It's also a reasonable model for inexperienced teams working on a well-defined small project, because it leads them through the life cycle and clearly labels what's happening at each stage. Most organizations that implement the *waterfall* model modify it to have the ability to back up one or more phases so that missed requirements or unsuitable design decisions can be fixed. This helps and generally makes the waterfall model usable, but the requirement to update all the involved documentation when you do back up makes even this version problematic.

The Code and Fix "Model": A Proto-Agile Approach

Coding and fixing as you go is not a formal model, but it is what most of us do when we're working on small projects by ourselves or maybe with a single partner. This code and fix "model", depicted in Figure 2-3, is often used in lieu of actual project management. In this approach there are no formal requirements, no required documentation, no quality assurance or formal testing, and release is haphazard at best. Don't even think about effort estimates or schedules when using this model. And yet it is attractive enough and useful enough when we don't need to coordinate with others.

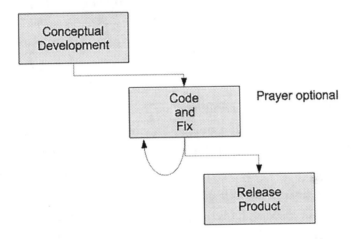

Figure 2-3. *The code and fix process model*

"*Code and fix*" requires a minimal amount of time to understand the problem (usually because we made up the problem/requirements ourselves) and jump straight into coding. Compile your code and try it out. If it doesn't work, fix the first problem you see and try it again. Continue this cycle of type-compile-run-fix until the program does what you want with no fatal errors and then ship it. We've all used it way more than once.

Software created using this model will be small, short on user interface niceties, and idiosyncratic. With no real mention of configuration management, little in the way of testing, no architectural planning, and probably little more than a desk check of the program for a code review, this approach can be very dangerous for most software development. It is, however, good for one thing: quick, disposable, maintenance-free projects developed by tiny 1-2 person teams. In other words, for quick and dirty proofs-of-concept, such as to validate architectural decisions, show a quick version of a user interface design, or to understand some larger problem you're working on.

If this reminds you of a mini version of agile, you are not wrong. This approach is wildly flexible and allows us to iteratively gain insights from our progress toward the goal. For this reason, we consider *code and fix* to be the proto-agile model.

Agile Development Implementations

The best practice is to iterate and deliver incrementally, treating each itera-tion as a closed-end "mini-project," including complete requirements, design, coding, integration, testing, and internal delivery. On the iteration deadline, deliver the (fully-tested, fully-integrated) system thus far to inter-nal stakeholders. Solicit their feedback on that work, and fold that feedback into the plan for the next iteration.

(From "How Agile Projects Succeed"[19]*)*

Agile development is all about adaptability, which can take on many different forms depending on the project scope and timeline, the development team, and so on. **Applying *agile* development prescriptively will break the very agility of *agile*.** Thus, although a number of specific *agile* approaches have been devised over the years, it is important to remain flexible in their understanding and implementation. Below, we discuss a number of these implementations, highlighting their core values and the accompanying nomenclature intended to help developers lean into these values.

Agile processes all aim to provide agility during software development, but how that agility is achieved can differ widely. As you read about each agile implementation, keep the following key differences in mind and consider the remaining specifications to be descriptive but non-prescriptive guidelines for how one might approach operationalizing each approach:

- eXtreme Programming delivers agility by prioritizing specific software engineering practices (in particular, pair programming and constant integration).

- Crystal delivers agility by prioritizing people and their interactions, allowing each team to self-organize as they see fit.

---

[19] www.adaptionsoft.com/on_time.html

- Scrum delivers agility through explicit short iterations ("sprints") that deliver product increments, although what is "short" depends on the scope of the project.

- Kanban delivers agility through a continuous flow of tasks from being needed to done, where the remaining tasks can be altered and reprioritized at any time.

Agile Methodology - eXtreme Programming (XP)

Kent Beck and Ward Cunningham created eXtreme Programming (XP) around 1995, describing it as a "lightweight, efficient, low-risk, flexible, predictable, scientific, and fun way to develop software."[20] XP focuses on productive technical development, particularly pair programming and constant integration.

XP relies on the following fundamental ideas:

- *Heavy customer involvement*: XP requires that a customer representative be on site at all times to define the content of each iteration of the product, as well as to create all the acceptance tests for each interim release.

- *Short iteration cycles and frequent releases*: XP typically uses release cycles in the range of a few weeks or months and each release is composed of several iterations of 3-5 weeks each.

- *Pair programming:* XP requires that all code be jointly written by pairs of developers, alternating as the driver and the navigator periodically (approximately every 30 minutes). The driver codes while the navigator watches, making suggestions, thinking about design and testing, and so on. While less code can be written in this way, the resulting code contains fewer defects, improving productivity.

- *Continuous unit testing* (also known as Test-Driven Development or TDD): XP calls for developers to first write the unit tests for any new features and then develop these features in a way that passes the predefined tests.

---

[20] This is a very short description of how XP works; for a much more eloquent and detailed explanation see the bible of XP: Beck, K. 2000. *Extreme Programming Explained: Embrace Change*. Boston, MA: Addison-Wesley.

While all Agile approaches favor direct communication, XP extends this notion to direct coding communication (both with a coding partner and with the rest of the code) and to direct client communication. Frequent releases require constant integration and building of the product. Whenever a programming pair finishes a feature or task and it passes all their unit tests, they immediately integrate and build the entire product. They then use all the unit tests as a regression test suite to make sure the new feature hasn't broken anything already checked in. If it does break something, they fix it immediately. So in an XP project, integrations and builds can happen several times a day. This process gives the team a good feel for where they are in the release cycle every day and gives the customer a completed build on which to run the acceptance tests. Having an on-site customer representative allows the XP team to get immediate feedback on new features and to uncover design and requirements issues early.

Implementing XP may vary depending on the team and the project, but should involve some form of the following practices:

- *The planning game*: Develop the scope of the next release by combining business priorities and technical estimates. The customer and the development team need to decide on the stories/features that will be included in the next release, the priority of each story, and timing of the release. The developers are responsible for breaking these stories into tasks and estimating the duration of each task. The sum of the durations will determine which tasks can get done by delivery date. If necessary, some stories are moved out of a release if the numbers don't add up.

- *Small releases*: Put a simple system into production quickly, and then release new versions on a very short cycle (1-2 months, with duration and size depending on what makes sense from a business perspective). The larger the release scope and duration, the harder it is to estimate.

- *Metaphor*: "A simple shared story of how the whole system works," which replaces your architecture. The metaphor must be a coherent explanation of the system, decomposable into smaller bits called *stories*. *Stories* should always be expressed in the vocabulary of the metaphor, and the language of the metaphor should be common to both the customer and the developers.

- *Simple design*: Keep the design as simple as you can each day. Redesign often to keep it simple. According to Beck, a simple design (1) runs all the unit tests, (2) has no duplicated code, (3) expresses what each story means in the code, and (4) has the fewest number of classes and methods that make sense to implement the stories so far.[21]

- *Testing*: Programmers constantly write unit tests. Tests must all pass before integration. Beck takes the hard line that "Any program feature without an automated test simply doesn't exist."[21] Although this works for most acceptance tests and should certainly work for all unit tests, this analogy breaks down in some instances, notably in testing the user interface in a GUI. Even this can be made to work automatically if your test framework can handle the events generated by a GUI interaction. Beyond this, having a good set of written instructions will normally fill the bill.

- *Pair programming*: Two programmers at one machine must write all production code in an XP project. Any code written alone is thrown away. This has the effect of reinforcing collective ownership by spreading the knowledge of the entire system around the entire team. It avoids the "beer truck problem," where the person who knows everything gets hit by a beer truck and thus sets the project schedule back months.

- *Collective ownership*: The team owns the entire project and all of its code, sharing the reasonability for designing, writing, altering, and testing all features. This supports "ego-less programming," promoting effective teamwork.

- *Continuous integration*: Integrate and build every time a task is finished, possibly several times a day (as long as the tests all pass). This helps to quickly detect and isolate bugs and defects by narrowing issues to the latest code and its interactions with the existing code base.

---

[21] (Beck 2000)

- *Refactoring*: Make small improvements of non-functional aspects of the code without changing its external behavior in order to make the code cleaner, less redundant, more readable, more efficient, and more maintainable. The principle of *simple design* imposes on you the responsibility to make refactoring changes when you see they are needed, while *collective ownership* allows you to refactor code written by others.

- *40-hour week*: Work a regular 40-hour week. Never work a second week in a row with overtime. The XP philosophy has a lot in common with many of Tom DeMarco's *Peopleware* arguments. People are less productive working overtime, having to handle personal affairs during the workday, being tired and making more mistakes, being stressed and irritable with their teammates, and so on. Having time to relax and recharge allows developers to focus on their work during the work day, making the team more productive.

- *On-site customer*: A customer is part of the team, is on-site, writes and executes functional tests, and helps clarify requirements. The customer's ability to give immediate feedback to changes in the system also increases team confidence that they are building the right system every day.

- *Coding standards*: Because of collective code ownership and ongoing refactoring, the team must follow sensible coding standards to improve communication in and out of the code base. These standards should make your code easier to read and maintain but should not constrict creativity.

Agile Framework - Crystal: Flexible Customization to Team/ Project Needs

Crystal is an agile method originally devised by Alistair Cockburn[22] while he was working at IBM in the early 1990s. He noticed that projects vary too much for any one set of project steps to suit them all. Instead, Crystal is thus organized around the people rather

---

[22] Cockburn, Alistair. *Crystal Clear*. Upper Saddle River: Addison-Wesley, 2004.

than around processes or tools. This means human interactions, as well as individual skills, talents, and needs, all of which are variable across teams, as well as within teams over time.

As we are not focusing on specific processes, Crystal has no formal structure. Instead, Crystal development believes the following:

- *All projects are unique.* Tools and processes need to be determined for each project, as well as adapted if/when changes occur.

- *Teams can self-optimize.* Tools and processes need to work for the project but also for the team, thus teams themselves should jointly determine the workflow that will work best for them, as well as adjust it as needed during development.

To support these characteristics, Crystal development is organized around the following 7 principles:

- *Frequent delivery*: Frequent (a relative term depending on project overall scope) testing and new releases.

- *Reflective improvement*: The team will periodically reflect on and make improvements to practices and tools.

- *Osmotic communication*: Osmotic for small teams, closed loop for larger teams.

- *Personal safety*: Create an environment where members feel safe to express their opinions, suggestions, and needs.

- *Focus*: Team members need a shared understanding of the big picture and of the individual tasks.

- *Easy access to expert users*: On-demand access to experts to resolve questions, concerns, or gaps in understanding.

- *Technical environment with automated tests, configuration management, and frequent integration*: When organizing around people, there is a lot of development flexibility, so frequently integrating everyone's work, automatically testing to ensure everything works individually and together smoothly, and using version control for backup and partial releases is paramount.

You can see that Crystal is very flexible and thus can be adapted to the needs of each team and project. For shorter projects, Crystal's reduced organizational scaffolding and required processes can be beneficial, as it allows focus on how the specific team can accomplish the required work. The main caveat here is that if the team is newer, larger, or remote, self-organization can get tricky.

Agile Framework - Scrum: Iterative Sprints Toward the Next Short-Term Goal

Scrum derives its name from rugby, where a *scrum* is a means of restarting play after a rule infraction: the 8 forwards on a rugby team (out of 15 players in the rugby union form of the game) attempt to (re)gain control of the ball and move it forward towards the opposing goal line. The idea in the agile Scrum methodology is that a small team is unified around a single goal and gets together for sprints of development that move them towards that goal.

The original process management idea for Scrum comes from Takeuchi and Nonaka's 1986 paper, "The New New Product Development Game"[23], while the first use of the term "Scrum" is attributed to DeGrace and Stahl's 1990 book *Wicked Problems, Righteous Solutions.*[24]

Like other *agile* methodologies, Scrum emphasizes the efficacy of small teams, direct communication, iterative development, learning from frequent feedback, and collective ownership. What distinguishes Scrum is its focus on team management and its structure of explicit time-boxed periods of development called *sprints*. Each *sprint* has a predetermined duration (commonly 1-4 weeks), with a fixed delivery date that does not move out. The scope of work to be delivered needs to be chosen so as to accommodate this delivery date, while still delivering the next Minimum Viable Product (MVP) to the client each sprint. The goal of each *sprint* is to provide a prototype that showcases your most current understanding of the client needs and your plan for delivering a solution. Showing this prototype (no matter how rudimentary) allows you to begin a conversation

---

[23] Takeuchi, Hirotaka, and Ikujiro Nonaka. "The New New Product Development Game." *Harvard Business Review* 64, no. 1 (1986): 137-146.

[24] DeGrace, Peter, and Leslie Hulet Stahl. 1990. *Wicked Problems, Righteous Solutions: A Catalogue of Modern Software Engineering Paradigms.* Yourdon Press Computing Series. Englewood Cliffs, N.J.: Yourdon Press.

about what was understood correctly and what needs adjustment. Ensuring this happens early limits the work that needs to be redone to make the necessary adjustments before developing further. Thus, *sprints* are "about creating conditions that enable better decision making, sooner."[25]

Scrum Roles

Scrum explicitly defines three roles in a development project:

The product owner is the person who generates and prioritizes the requirements for the product. These requirements commonly take the form of *user stories*, which are features that can be summarized into sentences like "As a <type of user>, we want to <do something>, so that <some value is created>." The product owner adds the user stories to the product backlog and prioritizes them. The product owner is also charged with making sure that the team understands the requirements behind the user stories.

The Scrum master is an expert in Scrum who facilitates development by coaching the team through Scrum values and practices (such as the daily Scrum meetings), helping the team self-organize (e.g., by increasing transparency), helping resolve internal and external blockers, and protecting the team from outside influences during the sprint. The scrum master is emphatically not team lead/manager because, as Scrum teams are teams of equals and arrive at decisions by consensus.

The development team is everyone else: designers, developers, writers, and so on. The team reviews the user stories generated and prioritized by the product owner, turning each highest priority story into one or more tasks that suggest how the necessary feature will be developed in order to deliver value. Selecting a subset of stories and tasks that can be accomplished within the given sprint duration, the team self-organizers by jointly deciding who will work tasks and what development processes they will employ. Regardless of task allocation, the team collectively owns all code and the project, sharing the goal of delivering the next functional MVP at the end of every sprint.

---

[25] www.linkedin.com/pulse/agile-consistently-lowering-standards-part-2-changing-andy-reid/

Scrum Artifacts

Scrum requirements are encapsulated in two backlogs:

- The *Product Backlog* is the prioritized list of all the requirements for the project. The product owner creates and prioritizes the product backlog composed of user stories, based on a desired *Product Goal.* The development team breaks the high-priority user stories into tasks and estimates them. This list of tasks becomes the *Sprint Backlog.*

- The *Sprint Backlog* is the prioritized list of user stories for the current sprint. Once the sprint starts, only the development team may add tasks to the sprint backlog; these are usually bugs found during testing. No outside entity may add items to the sprint backlog, only to the product backlog. The focus of the sprint backlog is the *Sprint Goal:* a guiding star for the team to follow; any changes during the sprint should protect this goal.

- The *Increment* is a contribution to the Product Goal that means the *definition of Done*, which is a formal quality measure decided upon by the organization (or by the team, if not otherwise defined). Multiple backlog items may reach Done state during a single Sprint.

Scrum Board

In most Scrum teams, the sprint backlog is *visual*, providing everyone with a clear shared view of the progress status of the sprint work. It is represented on a board using either Post-It notes or index cards, with one note or card per task; it may also be an online virtual board (e.g., Trello, Jira, Notion, or Pivotal Tracker). This *task board*, shown in Figure 2-4, always has at least three columns: *ToDo, Doing*, and *Done,* though more commonly it also includes a *Product Backlog*, a *Sprint Backlog*, and a column for testing such as *Quality Assurance/Review.* At the start of a sprint, the Development team selects some of the top priority items from the *Product Backlog* and moves them to the *Sprint Backlog.* These items are then broken down into tasks, which become the *ToDo* items for the sprint. These tasks will move across the board until reaching the *Done* column once fully developed, tested, and integrated into the code base.

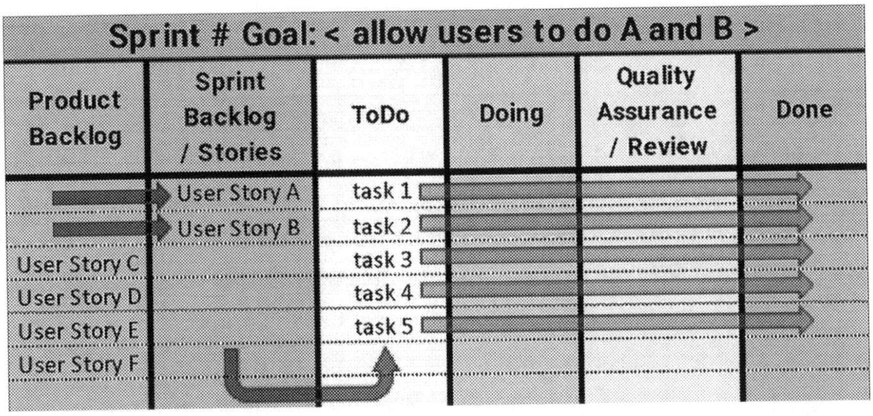

Product Backlog	Sprint Backlog / Stories	ToDo	Doing	Quality Assurance / Review	Done
		Sprint # Goal: < allow users to do A and B >			
	User Story A	task 1			
	User Story B	task 2			
User Story C		task 3			
User Story D		task 4			
User Story E		task 5			
User Story F					

Figure 2-4. *A generic single-sprint Scrum board. Dark arrows indicate the movement of items during sprint planning; light arrows indicate the movement of items during the sprint*

Scrum Values

In order to facilitate the teamwork necessary for an agile self-organizing team, SCRUM relies on individuals practicing the following:[26]

- Commitment to the shared goals and each other

- Focus on the Sprint Goal and Sprint Backlog

- Openness about the work and challenges (including interpersonal)

- Respect for each other as individuals and as capable contributors to the shared goals

- Courage to tackle difficult tasks, to bring up difficult conversations, and to generally "do the right thing"

Scrum Ceremonies

Scrum teams have several types of meetings that help the team self-organize.

Sprint planning: An initial planning phase that creates the product list of the initial requirements, decides on an architecture for implementing the requirements, divides

---

[26] https://scrumguides.org

the user stories into prioritized groups for the sprints, and breaks the first set of user stories into tasks to be estimated and assigned. They stop when their estimates occupy all the time allowed for the sprint. Tasks in a sprint should not be longer than one day of effort and ideally can be accomplished in one sitting (to avoid task switching). If a task is estimated to take more than one day of effort, it is successively divided into two or more tasks until each task's effort is the appropriate length. This rule comes from the observation that humans are terrible at doing exact estimations of large tasks and that estimating task efforts in weeks or months is basically just a guess. So breaking tasks down into smaller pieces gives the team a more reliable estimate for each.

The daily stand-up is a short meeting (15–30 minutes; the shorter the better) where the entire team discusses sprint progress. The daily scrum meeting allows the team to share information and track sprint progress. By having daily scrum meetings, any slip in the schedule or any problems in implementation are immediately obvious and can then be addressed by the team at once. "The Scrum Master ensures that everyone makes progress, records the decisions made at the meeting and tracks action items, and keeps the scrum meetings short and focused."[27] During the daily stand-up, each team member answers the following three questions in turn:

> *How have you furthered development since the last meeting?*
>
> *How will you further development between now and the next meeting?*
>
> *Is anything standing in your way?*

Note that the wording of these questions may be tweaked slightly, but the sentiment must remain. Discussions other than responses to these three questions are deferred to other meetings. Daily stand-ups are crucial to help everyone track progress towards the shared Spring Goal, facilitate collaboration, and improve accountability and engagement.

The sprint review happens at the end of each sprint, presenting the newly developed MVP to the product owner (commonly as a demo), who may perform acceptance testing on it. The meeting "reviews" everything that has been "Done" this sprint as part of fulfilling the Spring Goal, as well what was left out and why.

The sprint retrospective is held after the sprint review to "retrospect" on how the team worked together: their processes, communication, collaboration mechanics, meeting

---

[27] Rising, Linda, and Norman S. Janoff. 2000. "The Scrum Software Development Process for Small Teams." *IEEE Software* 17 (4): 26–32.

expectations, etc., searching for areas in which they can improve performance for the next sprint. Retrospectives are a crucial tool for improvement, as they are responsible for the agile iterative improvement of the teamwork itself. The retrospective marks the official end of the current sprint.

Backlog refinement or *story time* meetings are held periodically throughout the sprint (such as once a week) in order to refine backlog items, ensuring they are ready for future sprint planning. Product owner participates by adding and (re)prioritizing stories, and developers participate by breaking down high priority stories into tasks.

Although sprints usually end at the end of the predefined sprint period, a sprint can be terminated early if all work planned for the sprint has been completed. While new work could be added, it is generally most suitable to go through all the end-of-sprint and sprint-planning procedures in order to properly review what was done, retrospect on how it was done, and plan next development steps.

Scrum Velocity

With most teams, estimates of tasks become better as the project progresses, primarily because the team now has data on how they have done when estimating on previous sprints. The measure of the amount of work completed in a single sprint is called *velocity*. Over time, this allows the team decide how many tasks to include in each sprint. With meaningful retrospectives and the resulting iterative improvements to the team's processes and practices, velocity should increase over time as the team becomes better at breaking down and assigning tasks, creating accurate estimates of the work needed for each task, as well as at collaborating with each other.

Scrum End of Project

After the last scheduled development sprint, a final sprint may be done to bring closure to the project. This sprint implements no new functionality, but prepares the final deliverable for product release. It fixes any remaining bugs, finishes documentation, and generally productizes the code. Any requirements left in the product backlog are transferred to the next release. A Scrum retrospective is held before the next sprint begins to ponder the previous sprint and see if there are any process improvements that can be made.

Agile Framework - Kanban: Continuous Flow with Limited Current

The Kanban Method is a practice derived from Lean manufacturing (the Toyota Production System) and other change management systems; it draws most of its original ideas from the just-in-time manufacturing processes. Kanban is more methodology than process; it is an objective and a set of principles and practices to meet that objective.

The Kanban Board

To help organize development, Kanban employs the following notions:

- *Work in progress (WIP)* is the total number of tasks the team is currently working on, including all the states in which a task may find itself (in-progress, done, testing, review, etc.).

- *Flow* is the passage of tasks from one state to another on the way to completion.

- *Lead time*: The amount of time (in hours or days) it takes for the team to get a task from the initial ToDo state to the Done state. Over time, as the team finishes more and more tasks, the average lead time can be computed for the team, allowing for an estimation of how long it will take any one task to get Done, which serves as a measure of productivity.

What distinguishes Kanban is the continuous flow of the work. There are no timeboxed sprints and, consequently, no smaller sprint backlogs containing a subset of tasks for the team to focus on next. All remaining ToDos are in a single backlog and to help the team get organized, Kanban uses *swimlanes*: horizontal dividers to segment the tasks. Swimlanes can represent any useful separation, including task priority, task type, different projects/products, and even different teams.

With all remaining tasks sitting in the backlog, limited work-in-progress is how you allow the team to stay focused on the flow. Work-in-progress and flow can be asynchronously tracked by developers using the *Kanban board*, a variant on the Scrum *task board*. Figure 2-5 shows a generic task/Kanban board. These boards can be physical white boards that occupy one wall of a common space for the team or shared digital boards. On this board the team will add physical or digital post-it notes to identify tasks, which can then be moved from column to column (i.e., state-to-state) on the board.

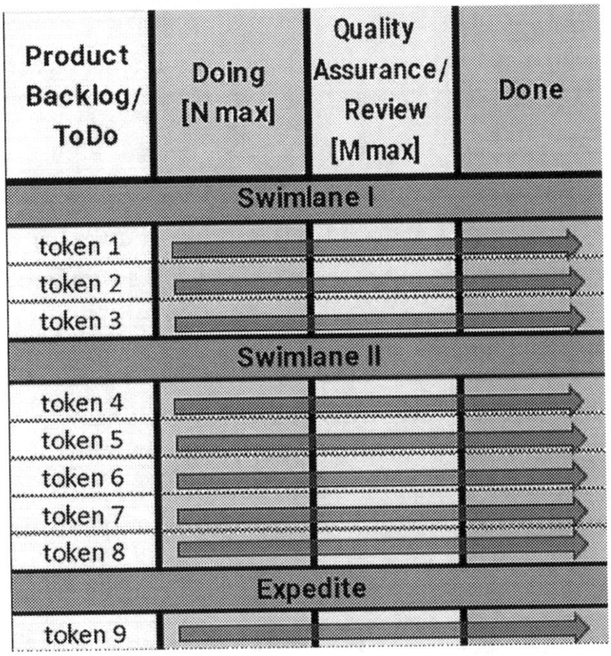

Product Backlog/ ToDo	Doing [N max]	Quality Assurance/ Review [M max]	Done
Swimlane I			
token 1			
token 2			
token 3			
Swimlane II			
token 4			
token 5			
token 6			
token 7			
token 8			
Expedite			
token 9			

Figure 2-5. *A generic task/Kanban board, with WIP maxima and swimlanes, with arrows depicting flow*

With this type of board, users have the option of changing the number and headings of the columns in order to make the board fit their process. Kanban works by using a *pull system*: instead of pushing items out to other stages, Kanban tells developers to pull items from a previous stage as they have the capacity to handle them. At the end of every task completion, the team will have working software with a new feature added.

The team can then specify the maximum number of tasks that are allowed to be worked on simultaneously (i.e., "Doing" and "Quality Assurance/Review") referred to as the work-in-progress or WIP, used to control the flow of work through the team. There is not hard rule for the WIP, but it should account for: 1) the number of people on the team and 2) how many tasks should each person be juggling concurrently. The general recommendation is somewhere between 1 to 2 tasks per person. For example, let's say that every state on the Kanban board is maxed-out (there are N tasks in development, M in review/testing) and a developer finishes developing a new task. This task cannot move to the Review state until one of the tasks currently under review is finished. We've just exposed a bottleneck in the flow of work. In Kanban, the developer would jump in to help review one of the tasks in that state. No new tasks can be pulled into the Develop state until there is room for the finished task downstream.

In Kanban, the objective is to maximize WIP within the constraint of the maximum number of tasks allowable at any time. There is no time-boxing as in Scrum; the goal is to move tasks through as quickly as possible (have the shortest *lead time*) while maximizing productivity by working up to the maximum number of tasks allowable.

You can note that when we say *maximizing WIP*, we don't mean giving the team more work. In fact, the goal in keeping the maximum number of tasks in each state low is to reduce the team's workload and allow them to focus on a smaller number of tasks (we want to avoid multitasking). The idea is that this will reduce stress and expensive task-witching, while increasing work quality *and* throughput. You'll notice that there are some things missing here, notably, how things get on the ToDo list, and what Done means. That's because Kanban isn't really a project management technique. In order to use Kanban, you need to have some process in place already and you need to manage it.

Hybrid Software Development Approaches for Multi-Level Focus and Scope

Multiple software development philosophies and even multiple implementations can coexist effectively within the same organization, team, or project. You may need to choose several approaches to help you get organized at different times and focus levels. Consider that the overall company needs to get organized, a project needs to get organized, and development needs to get organized.

> *"While all of the Agile processes have commonality, their sweet spots are attuned to specific organizational levels: different "views" for different audiences. Lean shines when applied to those with a strategic, organization and shareholder value focus: the Executive. Scrum shines when applied to those with a team organization, management, and project delivery focus: the Project Management. Extreme Programming shines when applied to those with a development delivery and tactical focus: the Development."*[28]

---

[28] Bourne, Geoffrey. 2010. "The Marriage of Lean, Scrum, and Extreme Programming (XP): How to Align Agile Across and Organization." *AgileConnection*. www.agileconnection.com/article/ marriage-lean-scrum-and-extreme-programming-xp.

Most notably, it is not *lean* versus *agile*, but rather crucially *lean* AND *agile*, where *lean* focuses on improving the process by reducing wastes, while *agile* focuses on improving the product by effectively adapting to new information throughout the project. Both are crucial to developing software. Additionally, *agile* does not mean no *planning*, as not thinking far enough ahead can lead to incorrect early decisions; a better perspective is to borrow l*ean's* deferring of commitment to ensure that early decisions to do not eliminate potentially useful future options. Here are a few ways that the implementations of these ideas can play off of each other:

- Lean can be naturally combined with Scrum, as agile allows early feedback, reducing how much needs to be reworked, and clear shared understanding among teammates can reduce motion, defects, non-utilizing talent, overproduction, and waiting.

- Since XP is mainly focused on programming, development can easily benefit from team management defined in Scrum.

- While coding individual features, developers naturally employ mini Waterfalls, creating a plan and following it to develop and test each new feature.

- While developing prior to an initial release to the public may be most fruitful with Scrum, providing continuous services and fast changing projects may be better represented through Kanban, allowing for a continuous approach.

- Scrum is well suited to projects where discrete increments are meaningful and for working toward an initial release, while Kanban lends itself naturally to ongoing operation such as providing a continuous service; Scrumban[29] is a fused approach that allows for the development of new features while also providing ongoing services.

As can be seen from the methodologies described in this chapter, iteration and collaboration are the key. The most effective way to build complex software is to incrementally gather insights, leaning what to make and how to make it better at each

---

[29] See www.agilealliance.org/scrumban/

following step. You must recognize that you never have all the knowledge at the start, and that designing, writing, testing, and delivering incrementally better code is the most reliable and effective path toward creating great software.

References

Anderson, David J. 2010. *Kanban: Successful Evolutionary Change for Your Technology Business.* Sequin, WA: Blue Hole Press.

Atkinson, Roger. 1999. "Project Management: Cost, Time, and Quality, Two Best Guesses and a Phenomenon, It's Time to Accept Other Success Criteria." *International Journal of Project Management* 17 (6): 337–42.

Bancroft, Josiah. 2013. *Senlin Ascends (The Books of Babel)*. CreateSpace Independent Publishing Platform. www.amazon.com/Senlin-Ascends-Books-Babel-1/dp/1482590956.

Beck, K. 2000. Extreme Programming Explained: Embrace Change. Boston, MA: Addison-Wesley.

Bourne, Geoffrey. 2010. "The Marriage of Lean, Scrum, and Extreme Programming (XP): How to Align Agile Across and Organization." Article. *AgileConnection.* www.agileconnection.com/article/marriage-lean-scrum-and-extreme-programming-xp.

Cockburn, A. 2002. *Agile Software Development.* Boston, MA: Addison-Wesley.

DeGrace, Peter, and Leslie Hulet Stahl. 1990. *Wicked Problems, Righteous Solutions: A Catalogue of Modern Software Engineering Paradigms.* Yourdon Press Computing Series. Englewood Cliffs, N.J.: Yourdon Press.

DeMarco, Tom. 1983. Controlling Software Projects: Management, Measurement and Estimation. Yourdon Press.

Fulghum, Robert. 1986. *All I Really Need to Know I Learned in Kindergarten.* New York, NY: Ivy Books.

Jeffries, Ron. 2015. *The Nature of Software Development: Keep It Simple, Make It Valuable, Build It Piece by Piece.* Programming. Dallas, TX: The Pragmatic Programmers, LLC. pragprog.com.

Martin, Robert C. 2003. *Agile Software Development, Principles, Patterns, and Practices.* Upper Saddle River, NJ: Prentice Hall.

McConnell, Steve. 1996. *Rapid Development: Taming Wild Software Schedules.* Redmond, WA: Microsoft Press.

Paulk, Mark C. 1995. *The Capability Maturity Model: Guidelines for Improving the Software Process*. The SEI Series in Software Engineering. Reading, Mass.: Addison-Wesley Pub. Co.

Poppendieck, Mary, and Tom Poppendieck. 2003. *Lean Software Development: An Agile Toolkit*. Upper Saddle River, NJ: Addison-Wesley Professional.

Project Management Institute. 2021. *A Guide to the Project Management Institute Body of Knowledge*. 7th ed. Project Management Institute, Inc.

Rising, Linda, and Norman S. Janoff. 2000. "The Scrum Software Development Process for Small Teams." *IEEE Software* 17 (4): 26–32.

Royce, W. W. 1970. "Managing the Development of Large Software Systems." In *Proceedings of IEEE Wescon*, 1–9. Piscataway, NJ: IEEE Press.

Siegelaub, J. M. 2007. "Six (Yes Six!) Constraints: An Enhanced Model for Project Control." In *Proceedings of the PMI Global Congress 2007*. Atlanta, GA: Project Management Institute, Inc. `www.pmi.org/learning/library/six-constraints-enhanced-model-project-control-7294`.

Takeuchi, H., and I. Nonaka. 1986. "The New New Product Development Game." *Harvard Business Review* 64 (1): 137–46.

Womack, James P., Daniel T. Jones, and Daniel Roos. 1990. *The Machine That Changed the World: The Story of Lean Production -- Toyota's Secret Weapon in the Global Car Wars That Is Now Revolutionizing World Industry*. New York, NY: Simon and Schuster.

CHAPTER 3

Project Management Essentials

"The first step of any project is to grossly underestimate its complexity and difficulty."

—Nicoll Hunt

Once your project begins, it needs to be managed. You need to manage the schedule, the people, the process, and above all, yourself (wherever you fit on the team). There is no one correct way to manage development, but there are some ways to do this well and even more ways to do it poorly. We have certainly uncovered some of both over the years, so let us try to make your journey less perilous. It's dangerous out there; take this chapter!

Working on anything other than personal development projects means working on a team; and working on a team means being managed, either from above or from within. Thus, learning about project management from both sides is an essential part of learning software development. Project management can be seen as managing the work and managing the people, so we divided this chapter into two major sections:

1. *Project planning*: Much of how daily tasks are managed depends on the chosen software development model, which you saw in the previous chapter. What's left are the parts of the project that need to be established before the project begins (i.e., project planning tasks):

   a. Organization

   b. Risk analysis

© John F. Dooley and Vera A. Kazakova 2024
J. F. Dooley and V. A. Kazakova, *Software Development, Design, and Coding*,
https://doi.org/10.1007/979-8-8688-0285-0_3

    c.   Resource requirements

    d.   Task estimation and schedule

    e.   Defect management

2. *Soft-Aware development*: The most important and complex aspect that must be managed in any project are the people. Developers and managers are not just a valuable resource, but rather the very biosphere of development. Maintaining and supporting this biosphere with all of its complex dynamics will not only impact the success of the current project but also all the projects to follow. In the second half of this chapter, we review how and why we must strive to be Soft-Aware ("soft-skill" aware) throughout development, by discussing

    a.   The dark side of teamwork

    b.   Supporting individuals

    c.   Supporting the culture

    d.   Conflict as opportunity

    e.   Teamwork artifacts

Project Planning

Project plans are a great tool for setting down what you think you're doing, an outline of how it will be done, and how you plan on executing the outline. The problem with a project plan is that, once it's written and signed off on, upper management thinks the project will run exactly as stated in the plan. But the reality of the project often thwarts the plan.

Project planning is forever; it continues throughout the entire duration of the project. "The Plan" is never really set in stone because typical software projects are usually in constant flux. In those projects that are using a plan-driven process model, a project plan is an actual document that is written by the project manager and that is approved and signed off on by the development team and by upper management.

It is, in effect, a *contract*, albeit a rolling one, of what the team is going to do and how they are going to do it. It says how the project will be managed, and in the most extreme plan-driven projects, even states how and when the document itself will be modified.

Project Planning: Organization

Before work can begin, you need to decide how you are going to organize development. If you're working with an experienced team, you can reuse your previous organizational documentation, but you should never skip this. The two main but often intertwined sides of project organization are the development and the people:

- How are you going to *organize the product*? (Waterfall or iterative development? Version control tools? Project scope and schedule?)

- How are you going to *organize the people* making this product? (What is the team organization/hierarchy? How and when will everyone communicate and coordinate?)

It is crucial to have explicit agreement and precise shared understanding of scheduling and expectations across all stakeholders. Choosing a development process model (see previous chapter) will provide many of the answers about how to organize your project. For instance, any agile project will be focused around features and require a schedule of iterations, each beginning with planning and culminating in a minimum viable product. Agile teams are hierarchically flat and self-organizing, with the team owning the agile project plan (not the project manager) and requiring frequent communication on a variety of open channels. Agile teams also co-own all code, thus requiring everyone to follow shared code-management practices, such as git-flow branching for source control. Narrowing down the process model from agile to a specific implementation (such as XP, Scrum, Crystal, feature-driven, etc.) will further specify details of organizing both the product and the people.

Project Planning: Risk Analysis

Next we need to think about risk analysis. What can possibly go wrong with a project and what will we do when it does? Let's look at some possible risks[1]:

- *Schedule slips*: That task that you estimated would take three days has just taken three weeks. In a plan-driven project, this can be an issue if you don't have regular status meetings. Waiting three weeks to tell your boss that you're late is always worse than telling her that

---

[1] McConnell, Steve. 1996. *Rapid Development - Taming Wild Software Schedules.* Microsoft Press.

you'll be late as soon as you know it. Don't put off delivering bad news. In an agile project, this is unlikely because most agile projects have a daily status meeting (or stand-up). This way schedule slips are noticed almost immediately, and corrective action can take place quickly.

- *Excessive defect rate*: Your testing is finding lots of bugs. What do you do: continue to add new features or stop to fix the bugs? Again, this can be a real issue in a project where integration builds happen according to a fixed schedule, say once a week. In a project where integrations happen every day, or every time a new feature is added, you can keep up with defects more easily. In either case, if you are experiencing a high defect rate, the best thing to do is to stop, take a look around, and find the root cause of the defects before adding more functionality. This can be very hard to do from a project management standpoint, but you'll thank yourself in the end.

- *Misunderstood requirements*: What you're doing isn't what the customer wanted. This classic problem is the result of the fact that customers and developers live in two different worlds. The customer lives in the application domain where they understand from a user's perspective what they want the product to do. The developer understands from a technical perspective how the product will work. Occasionally, these worlds intersect and that's good, but often they don't and that is where you get a misunderstanding of requirements. The best approach is to have the customer on site as often as possible and to produce deliverable products as often as possible.

- *Requirements churn*: New features, altered features, deleted features... Never-ending requirements churn is probably the largest single reason for missed delivery dates, high defect rates, and project failure. Churn happens when the customer (or your own marketing folks, or the development team itself) continues to change requirements while development is underway. It leads to massive amounts of rework in the code, retesting of baselines, and delay after delay. Managing requirements is the single most important job of the project manager. In a plan-driven process, a change control board

(CCB) examines each new requirement and decides whether to add it to the list of features to be implemented. There may be a member of the development team on the CCB, but that's not required, so the danger here is that the CCB adds new features without understanding all the scheduling and effort ramifications. In agile processes, the development team keeps control of the prioritized requirements list (called the product backlog in Scrum), and only adjusts the list at set points in the project—after iterations in XP and after each sprint in Scrum.

- *Turnover*: Your most experienced developer decides to join a start-up three weeks before product delivery. The best way to reduce turnover is to (1) give your developers interesting work, (2) have them work in a pleasant environment, and (3) give them control over their own schedules. Oddly enough, money is not one of the top motivators for software developers. This doesn't mean they don't want to get paid well, but it does mean that throwing more money at them in order to get them to work harder or to keep them from leaving doesn't generally work. Still, despite your best efforts, some developers will leave. The best way to mitigate the effect of turnover is to spread the knowledge of the project around all the members of the development team. Principles like *common code ownership* and techniques like *pair programming* work to invest all the team members in the project and spread the knowledge of the code across the entire team. We will talk more about how to support developers and maintain a healthy workplace culture in the "Soft-Aware Development" section of this chapter.

Once you've got a list of the risks to your project, you need to address each one and talk about two things: *avoidance* and *mitigation*. For each risk, think about how you can avoid it. Build slack into your schedule, do constant code reviews, freeze requirements early, do frequent releases, require pair programming so you spread around the knowledge of the code, and the like. Then you need to think about what you'll do if the worst-case scenario does happen; this is *mitigation*. Remove features from a release, stop work on new features and do a bug hunt, negotiate new features into a future release, and so on. If a risk becomes a reality, you'll have to do *something* about it; it's better to have planned what you'll do beforehand.

Once you address avoidance and mitigation, you'll have a plan on how to handle your identifiable risks. This doesn't completely let you off the hook because there are bound to be risks you miss, but the experience of addressing the risks you do come up with will enable you to better handle new ones that surprise you during the project. When using an iterative process model, it's a good idea to revisit your risks after each iteration and see which ones have changed, identify any new ones, and remove any that can no longer happen.

Project Planning: Resource Requirements

Your project needs resources. How many people do you need for the project? Do they all need to start at once, or can their starting dates on the project be staggered as phases are initiated? How many computers do you need? What software will you be using for development? What development environment do you need? Is everyone trained in that environment? What support software and hardware do you need? Yes, you do need a configuration management system and a stand-alone build machine (typically a virtual machine on a cloud server), no matter what process model you're using. Having a single machine where you build a new version of the product every day allows you to control all the variables in a compilation and build. This includes, but isn't limited to, the version of the operating system the build machine is using and the exact version of each library that your program is using. This consistent build environment makes sure that you get the correct version of the new product build every time.

The platform you're targeting and the application domain in which you are working answer many of these resource questions, so that's the easy part. Questions about team size, start dates, and phases of the project will likely not be able to be answered until you do a first cut at effort estimation and scheduling, so an iterative approach may be of use here. Additionally, some resources can present tradeoffs or force changes to the project's scope. Considering alternatives may require the participation of all immediate stakeholders.

Project Planning: Task Estimation and Schedule

The first step toward a project schedule is seeing what you'll be doing and how long each step will take. This is the classic chicken-and-egg problem: you can't really do estimation until you have a fairly detailed decomposition of the features or user-stories into tasks. But your manager always wants effort estimates and schedule data before you start doing the design. Resist this by prioritizing design once you've got some idea of the requirements. Select a small set of high priority requirements, design a solution for that feature set, and only then estimate the effort for that set. Don't worry that the requirements might change; they will, so there is very limited use in decomposing and estimating too far ahead. You need a detailed decomposition of features into implementable tasks before you can do effort estimation, so this will need to happen incrementally. Don't ever believe anyone who tells you "That feature will take six months to do." That is a wild guess and bears little to no relation to reality. You just cannot estimate something that big. The best you can do is to say, "I was once on a team that implemented a feature like that in six months." And even that only helps a little.

The estimation mantra is *estimate size first, then effort, finally schedule.* The overall work broken down into tasks that can be completed in at most a week, and ideally one or two days. Breaking down the work into small well-defined tasks forces you to think deeper about how you plan to get it done. Tasks small enough to be completed in one sitting already greatly reduce the cognitive and technical costs of task switching.

Size always needs to come first because you just can't figure out how long something will take until you have an idea of how big of a job it is. Once you have a sensible list of tasks, you can start doing size estimation. Size can be several things, depending on your work breakdown and your development model: functional modules, number of classes, number of methods, number of function points, number of object points, or story points.

Next is *effort* estimation. Tasks should be estimated as *person-hours.* There are several techniques for getting effort estimates: COCOMO II[2], function point analysis, and the Delphi method are just three. All, however, depend on being able to count things in your design. The Delphi method is a quick and relatively efficient estimation technique. Here's one simplified way it can work: find three of your most senior developers (folks who've got the most experience and who should therefore be able to give you a good guess) and give them the task breakdown (assuming they weren't already involved in doing the initial breakdown—the ideal situation). To estimate effort for each task, ask them to give you three numbers in person-hours: the shortest amount of time it should take, the longest amount of time it should take, and the typical amount of time it should take. Calculate the average shortest time, average longest time, and average typical time and use these averages to specify the expected range of hours (min-max) and the typical

---

[2] Boehm, Barry W., Chris Abts, A. Winsor Brown, Sunita Chulani, Bradford K. Clark, Ellis Horowitz, Ray Madachy, Donald J. Reifer, and Bert Steece. 2000. *Software Cost Estimation with COCOMO II.* Prentice Hall

expected effort for the task. Notice that you need developers to perform these estimates. Managers should never do development estimates. Even if a manager has been a developer in the past, unless one is deeply involved in the actual development work, they should not be involved in doing development estimates.

To increase task estimate accuracy over time, you need to track the *velocity* of each task, a term from agile methodologies,[3] defined as the estimated effort of a task divided by the actual effort. Velocity above 1.0 means the task took less time than estimated; velocity below 1.0 means the task took longer than estimated. Task velocities help you understand your pessimistic overestimation or your optimistic underestimation tendencies, ultimately helping you estimate better. Ideally, as a developer gains experience, their velocity will approach 1.0 on each task, settling closer to a 0.85-1.15 range, allowing the overall schedule to be more accurate. If a developer's velocity fluctuates wildly (one task is 0.6, another is 1.8, a third is 1.2), then a crash course in estimation techniques might be appropriate.

Once you have determined the size of the tasks and the person-hours effort estimates for each task in your first release or iteration, you can proceed with creating a *schedule*. Before you can look at that spiffy Gantt chart with the nice black diamond that marks the release date, there are several things to take into account:

- Get your developers to specify *dependencies* between tasks, as dependencies will push out your delivery date. While some tasks can start simultaneously, some tasks can't start before others finish or can start once others are half-finished.

- Figure out your *duty cycle* (the fraction of one period when the system is active). Out of each eight-hour day, how many hours do your developers actually *develop*? Remember that reading mail, attending meetings, doing code reviews, taking breaks, etc. all eat up time. Corporate culture as a whole has a big effect on the breakdown of work time utilization. You can't assume that an eight-hour task will be done in a single day. Realistically, out of each eight-hour day, 2-4 hours are eaten up with other stuff, so your development duty cycle can be as low as 50% (four hours, half of an eight-hour day.

---

[3] Beck, Kent. 2000. *Extreme Programming eXplained: Embrace Change*. Reading, MA: Addison-Wesley.

- Take weekends, vacations, sick days, training, and buffer time into account when you're making the schedule. If your senior developer has a task on the critical path of your project, you probably need to know that she's attending that week-long seminar in May.

- You should not schedule a developer to work on two tasks at the same time. Most project-scheduling software will not let you do this by default, but most of them will also let you override this. Don't. You will be tempted to do this to meet the deadlines your manager or marketing team wants, but do your best to resist the temptation. You'll only end up having to change the schedule when you miss the date anyway.

- Finally, you must have some way to track the project schedule, to specify tasks, deadlines, priorities, estimates, and developers working on the tasks. While full project management tools may seem like overkill at first, they are typically flexible enough to suit different project needs without too much overhead. Using real project management applications like Jira, Notion, or Trello provide lots of features that make keeping the schedule up to date much easier.

Consider the benefits that automation can bring to everyone's awareness of the project status: automatic reminders, calendar integration, assignment of tasks to developers, and notifications of updates. Project management tools can also automatically track a wide variety of metrics (such as task velocities), generate visualizations to better understand these metrics (such as showcasing the change of average velocity throughout the project), and organize project information into different handy layouts (such as grouping velocity data by type of task and by developer). With teams (even moderate teams of 10 or more developers), automated tracking of dependencies of your project can help manage who's working on what and when. This knowledge is even more critical for agile development with short time-boxed iterations. When planning each sprint, you need to know the priorities of each user story in the product backlog and how they relate to each other. You must track the progress of the tasks in the sprint backlog and knowing dependencies can be the difference between achieving your sprint goal versus not.

Project management tools can also help with effort estimation, as hourly estimates can be very hard on humans. Some project management tools have you create an estimate using magnitude instead. The simplest type lets you do *small, medium,* or *large* for estimates, while others let you give each task some number of points on a scale, say, 1, 2, 4, or 8 points for each task. This makes it easy to total the number of points the team is trying to implement in each time-boxed iteration and, over time, gives you the average numbers of points a team can implement per iteration.

Project Planning: Defect Management

Hope for the best; plan for the worst. Inevitably, you'll introduce defects into your program. The project plan should account for continuous testing needs, and the schedule should have room for handling any uncovered defects. As a developer, your aim is twofold:

- Introduce as few defects as possible into the code you write.

- Find as many of them as you can before releasing the code.

Despite your best efforts, though, you will release code with defects in it. It's just inevitable. For a program of any size, there are just too many possible paths through the program and too many different ways to introduce bad data for there not to be defects. Your objective is to release with as few defects as possible and to make those defects ones that don't really impact the product or its performance. To make this a reality, most development organizations have a set of defect levels to characterize defect severity, such as fatal (program crashes), severe (major functionality broken), serious (functionality broken but there is a workaround), trivial (small issue), and feature request (something that would be nice to have in the future). These defect levels are generally built into a defect tracking system.

Whenever you find a defect in a piece of code, file a defect report in the defect tracking system, allowing developers and managers to see how many and how severe the current defects are. When fixing defects, developers will start at the most severe and work their way down.

Soft-Aware Development

"When [project managers] kick off any project, they are given the herculean task of figuring out and managing the expectations of many different stake-holders. But when the [project managers] can recognize the roots of those expectations, step into the role of a couple's counselor, build meaningful, personal, trusting relationships, and ensure the broader team stays focused on the overall goal, they can successfully manage everyone's expectations as they steer that project across that coveted finish line."

—Amy Shoenthal[4]

"The manager's function is not to make people work, but to make it possible for people to work."

—Tom DeMarco, Timothy Lister[5]

What is the first thing that comes to mind when we say "team project"? Is it stress? Exasperation? Concern? Relief at an upcoming free ride? Consider how most of us learn about team-based work: we are asked to collaborate on school projects but usually not taught how. Ad-hoc short-term group projects self-managed by novices typically lead to deficient and long-term unsustainable coping strategies, such as carrying your team or freeloading. After all, we'll likely never have to work with these people again! Concerns also abound about credit and blame attribution. In the end, students end up perceiving teamwork as detrimental and unpleasant[6]. After repeatedly reinforcing these practices and beliefs through multiple stressful class projects, students graduate and are unleashed onto the world. The problem, of course, is that the real world runs on networking: making and maintaining relationships with your peers, bosses, underlings, clients, the public, etc. Those same short-term coping strategies simply won't do because the real world (like the North) remembers!

---

[4] Shoenthal, Amy. 2023. "The Art of Setting Expectations As a Project Manager." *Harvard Business Review.* https://hbr.org/2023/10/the-art-of-setting-expectations-as-a-project-manager.

[5] DeMarco, Tom, and Tim Lister. 2013. *Peopleware: Productive Projects and Teams.* Addison-Wesley.

[6] Wilson, Laura, Susie Ho, and Rowan H Brookes. 2018. "Student Perceptions of Teamwork Within Assessment Tasks in Undergraduate Science Degrees." *Assessment & Evaluation in Higher Education* 43 (5): 786–799.

In the remainder of this chapter, we introduce what it means to be Soft-Aware ("soft skill" aware) and how deficient teamwork negatively impacts developers and development. We then look at how supporting individuals and creating a safe shared culture promotes healthy and sustainable collaboration. Finally, we look at how to bring these theories into practice as an agile process of learning and improving together through a number of teamwork artifacts.[7]

Soft-Aware development is a new paradigm that centers individuals, interpersonal relationships, and workplace culture as the heart of healthy and sustainable joint creation of software. Being *Soft-Aware* encompasses building software, building stakeholder relationships, and building up each developer along the way. *Soft-Aware* development was first coined by Dr. Kazakova[8] while teaching team-based software development to undergraduate computer science students. The focus was on developing the developers' professional dispositions and interpersonal skills, because learning to make software is less crucial than *learning to work together* while attempting to make software. With high technology churn, increasingly higher-level programming practices, and the ever-evolving software development models, what remains unchanged is the power of social-emotional learning in allowing us to work with others toward making innovations much greater than anything we can achieve alone. Social-emotional learning is how people *"acquire and apply the knowledge, skills, and attitudes to develop healthy identities, manage emotions and achieve personal and collective goals, feel and show empathy for others, establish and maintain supportive relationships, and make responsible and caring decisions".*[9] While development often happens in sprints, teamwork is a marathon: it requires commitment, training, a sustainable pace, and working through discomforts. Openly valuing and practicing social-emotional learning is how we train for our teamwork marathon, support a shared *Soft-Aware* culture, and support each other.

---

[7] In software development, the term *artifact* refers to useful byproducts of the development process.

[8] Kazakova, Vera A, John F Dooley, and Monica M McGill. 2023. "Soft-Aware Development: Social Emotional Learning as an Agile Process." In *Proceedings of the 2023 ACM Conference on International Computing Education Research-Volume 2*, 39–40.

[9] Collaborative for Academic, Social, and Emotional Learning (CASEL). 2023. "FAQs." *CASEL.org.* https://casel.org/faq/.

Research shows that *"productivity depends on a work force that is socially and emotionally competent"*.[10] *Soft-Aware* development is all about the people; it places consistent focus on each individual teammate and on the emergent and dynamic teamwork that must be carefully nurtured and maintained. There is no single correct way to work together but rather only desirable teamwork outcomes. A team is always more capable and more complex than the sum of the teammates, as our emergent interactions can make or break our shared work. Working on a team is not only showing up for and adapting to a project, but also showing up for and adapting to each other.

It may seem that this section is written for the "power holders" but power comes in many forms, not just those with "management" in their job title. We all hold some type of power. Consider, for example, how being more outspoken may literally offer someone more say in meetings; consider also how using that outspokenness to bring everyone's ideas to the table may vastly improve the quality of the decisions being made. Consider how years of experience may inform many crucial ideas, but consider also that inexperienced points of view may allow us to innovate in directions that seemed impassable before. By *power* we mean the ability to effect change. Being mindful of yourself and of those around you will allow you to build a team who can effect that change with you. For truly cooperative work, rather than dividing ourselves into managers and those being managed, there should only be collaborators (some of whom have the task of facilitating the work of others). In this way, instead of a hierarchical power, we can each contribute our own individual super-powers to form the most well-rounded super dev[11] team. Find your power, find your voice to use that power, and help your teammates use their own powers along with you.

Why do we need everyone to get along anyway? While we could expect our employees or teammates to *just put their heads down and focus on the work* (an attitude we've unfortunately witnessed way too often in the real world), that would be very nearsighted. Working with a team we don't like takes a lot more emotional effort and makes us tired and unhappy, hindering software development. The sense of personal agency and happiness at work improve developer productivity,[12,13] while emotional

---

[10] Elias, M. J., J. E. Zins, and R. P. Weissberg. 2000. "Promoting Social and Emotional Learning: Guidelines for Educators." *Adolescence* 35 (137): 221.

[11] developer

[12] Graziotin, Daniel, Fabian Fagerholm, Xiaofeng Wang, and Pekka Abrahamsson. 2018. "What Happens When Software Developers Are (Un)Happy." *Journal of Systems and Software* 140:32–47.

[13] Meyer, Andr´e N, Earl T Barr, Christian Bird, and Thomas Zimmermann. 2019. "Today Was a Good Day: The Daily Life of Software Developers." *IEEE Transactions on Software Engineering* 47 (5): 863–880.

intelligence helps mitigate stress and build trust.[14] Workers feeling powerless in the face of uncontrollable stressful situations such as layoffs, task or project uncertainties, feeling unvalued, experiencing exclusion or discrimination, etc. can all lead to a variety of negative physical and psychological effects, including "learned helplessness," which is a sense of lacking personal agency, leading to reduced engagement in the workplace.[15] According to the *State of the Global Workplace 2023 Report* release by Gallup, Inc., 77% of the global workforce does not find their work meaningful or engaging, leading to 59% "quiet quitting" (doing the bare minimum or seat-warming) and 18% "loud quitting" (actively engaging in disruptive behavior), with 51% of employed workers considering or seeking new employment.[16] Gallup's report also indicates that 70% of team engagement is attributable to the manager. Healthier workplace culture is the antidote to employee disengagement and high turnover, and managers, supervisors, SCRUM masters, team leads, and anyone with authority and/or seniority must lead the charge. While most developers and managers have no explicit background in social-emotional learning, many companies are recognizing the need for a workplace culture shift and beginning to offer training seminars to develop their employees' interpersonal or *soft* skills.

Teamwork is not just what happens on the way to the deliverable; it is an ongoing crucial task in itself. Remember that most collaborations continue beyond the duration of a current project, so teammates are not to be treated as expendable development resources, but rather as the very biosphere in which development will thrive or perish. In fact, software development can be seen as "*a series of resource-limited, goal-directed games of invention and communication.*"[17] We have seen great developers fall apart together. We have also seen struggling developers rise together. Being the lone rockstar developer is not the goal. If you are doing great, you will be asked to help, guide, train, or supervise others. You will be asked to showcase your work to management and clients.

---

[14] Rezvani, Azadeh, and Pouria Khosravi. 2019. "Emotional Intelligence: The key to Mitigating Stress and Fostering Trust Among Software Developers Working on Information System Projects." *International Journal of Information Management* 48:139–150.

[15] Neogy, Rajkumari. 2023. "Neuroscience has the antidote for managers to address an overlooked behavior that blocks success." *fastcompany.com*. www.fastcompany.com/90973601/.

[16] GALLUP, Inc. 2023. "State of the Global Workplace 2023 Report. The Voice of the World's Employees." *Gallup.com*, www.gallup.com/workplace/349484/state-of-the-global-workplace.aspx.

[17] Cockburn, Alistair. 2004. "The End of Software Engineering and the Start of Economic-Cooperative Gaming." *Computer Science and Information Systems* 1 (1): 1–32.

You will be given larger projects where you will have to learn to delegate. You will have to work well with others. Teamwork is the key and it must be intentional. Any opportunities for joint brainstorming, direct collaboration, teamwide updates, and team-building activities are an anchoring part of all shared work and should be welcomed into even the tightest development schedules. Although we are all endlessly busy and time is expensive, not taking the time to be *Soft-Aware* is always going to cost us more that we can afford. Valuing and supporting teammates and teamwork is a smart investment (in their future, in the future of the team, and in the future of the product), never a waste.

Soft-Aware Development: The Dark Side of Teamwork

Not all joint work rises to the level of actual *teamwork*, meaningfully supporting and augmenting the team's joint output. Instead, development and developers often suffer from the darker side effects of poor teamwork. Let's consider some specific examples of common behaviors that lead to trouble:

- *Making work decisions based on social comfort zones*: Only reaching out to others of your own gender, age group, race, cultural background, etc. can alienate others, making them feel excluded from brainstorming or decision making. Not actively working with a teammate because you don't connect with them personally, instead of making an effort to understand the source of the friction, can only exacerbate the issue. Avoiding talking to developers who don't speak up themselves perpetuates unnecessary isolation. A small effort on our part may lead to substantial increase in the comfort, belonging, and agency others feel. The formation of implicit subteams can be okay based on current ongoing task division, but it is important to keep the whole team in mind whenever possible, such as during coffee breaks or daily standup meetings.

- *Keeping project information inaccessible to parts of the team* (e.g., discussing development issues in private threads or emails) can make it hard for everyone to stay on top of decisions, challenges, needs, etc. Make work discussions accessible on demand to the whole team, but without forcing everyone to be part of every discussion as it happens if they do not have the bandwidth or are otherwise engaged. For instance, you can respond to an issue brought up in a general thread by responding in a separate but visible thread. Consider also the benefits of messaging services such as Slack or Discord, which allow information to be grouped or pinned, reactions and threads can be added, and teammates to be tagged to bring relevant discussions to their attention.

- *Developers jumping right into making things.* Even within Agile methodologies, this is a mistake. Taking time to agree on the design, creating mood-boards to ensure that everyone shares the same overall vision, and clearly delineating tasks and subtasks (even if only for the next small iteration of the product instead of for the final deliverable) is crucial to avoid confusion and streamline decision-making during development. Poorly defined or poorly understood tasks commonly lead to overlap in work, merge conflicts, confusion, frustration, and strife on the team.

- *Shutting out the less experienced teammates.* Not allowing newer developers to take on meaningful and interesting parts of the project because you don't have confidence in their skills discourages learning and reduces creativity. Excluding less experienced team members from crucial discussions regarding development reduces agency and negatively impacts buy-in into the shared project vision.

- *Assuming that completing your tasks is sufficient for collaboration.* Being a productive island will not suffice if the rest of the development archipelago struggles. Collaboration revolves around a shared goal and checking on the team is checking on that goal. Not documenting found solutions and workarounds is detrimental to shared learning and to growing a shared knowledgebase. Not taking the time to understand the contributions of others can lead to a lot of strife, including members believing they are the only ones making meaningful contributions, or not noticing when someone's work was not correctly merged into the repository and thus excluded from a demo, which can be very discouraging for a developer.

- *Undervaluing interpersonal needs.* Not respecting each other's work, time, responsibilities, needs, and concerns is not respecting each other. Not informing the team of personal circumstances that will affect your work or your availability is likely to cause concern about whether some contribution will be available by the deadline, resulting in redundant work, stress, overtime, and breaching of trust. Not showing up on time to meetings showcases a lack of planning, a questionable reliability, and a lack of respect for others' time. Not checking with teammates when making decisions that may impact them is bound to create both code and interpersonal conflicts. Failing to update supervisors and clients on progress and difficulties can lead to disconnect in understanding, increased stress, and loss of business.

- *Not taking care of yourself.* Not taking the time and care to share your ideas of concerns clearly will have a direct negative impact on you and an indirect negative impact on the team. Not sharing difficulties and setbacks creates inaccurate expectations and reduces team support. Sticking to an unrealistic schedule or contributions is nearsighted, as it leads to resentment and burnout.

Soft-Aware Development: Supporting the Individuals

Everyone knows that user-stories matter, but we must remember that developer-stories do too, because both sides are stakeholders of the development process. If we expect developers to work for us and with us, we must invest in them as individuals by supporting meaningful work, paying attention to developers and their needs, supporting their agency, valuing their personal and professional growth, and understanding creative time.

Micromanagement is not sustainable for either side: managers cannot be everywhere nor have all the information at all times, while developers cannot have their hands tied at all times or else no development can take place. Consider how it is harder to think when someone is looking over your shoulder, or to get groceries from someone else's list without knowing which substitutions are acceptable, or to solve a problem in some specific way that you don't understand. Ron Jeffries describes *Dark Scrum*, which stems from incorrect implementation of agile practices: *"But the power holder already knows his job. His job is to stay on top of what everyone is doing, make sure they're doing the right things, and redirect them if they're not. How convenient that there's a mandatory meeting where he can do that, every single day![18] The result: instead of the team rallying around their joint mission and sorting out a good approach for the day, someone else drags information out of them, processes it in their head, and then tells everyone what to do. Since nothing ever goes quite as we expected yesterday morning, this improper activity often comes with a lot of blame-casting and tension. Dark Scrum oppresses the team every day. Self-organization cannot emerge."[19]* Developers need to be trusted to do the work and managers need to facilitate this work by addressing needs, removing barriers, and enabling bottom-up self-organization.

Let's think of development *like driving a vehicle* through an unknown terrain to some destination. Clients, managers, or product owners choose the destination but not the path. Developers are the drivers who choose how to best reach the goal. The scrum master or project manager should not back-seat drive, but they can keep track of progress and keep everyone focused on the general direction to the finish line. Product owner can call the cabin, but they are not in the car, and calling the driver distracts them from the road and should be done judiciously. The drivers need to have the freedom to decide which path they should take, based on their comfort level with the car they are driving, the speed they are going, their skills in navigating each type of terrain, the weather, unexpected car breakdowns, and anything else they deem relevant from their insider vantage point. The drivers should not be pushed to take paths or speeds they are not comfortable with; you can give them more information on their progress to help them better assess the needs, and you can choose to not hire them for the next trip, but you need to let them drive. Even crucial information needs to be provided non-disruptively. Consider that a driver is about to miss a turn but it may be too late to adjust course; sometimes it is safer to make the mistake and correct it after, not to mention that learning from mistakes can be more instructional in the long run. Giving developers some space and some planned-in time to make mistakes is important for their personal development, programming and debugging skills, confidence in their problem solving and trial and error, etc., which in turn makes it important for software development.

---

[18] Meaning the daily stand-up meeting.

[19] Jeffries, Ron. 2016. "Dark Scrum." *ronjeffries.com*. https://ronjeffries.com/articles/016-09ff/defense/.

Leaders must pay attention. Leaders/supervisors/managers can only be truly effective by being *close to the team* and to its problems. Leadership has to be personable, accessible, and adaptable. Create relationships and adapt structures around the people and their needs. Values in the workplace culture should be shared and supported across all individuals, but structures should be flexible to support the different ways in which people learn, communicate, and work. Pay attention to context (team context, personal context, and project context) and use it to make better decisions. Context also dictates whether an incident is actually an issue to be addressed and how to best address it. Note, however, that the same objective context may translate to different subjective contexts for different teams and for individual developers, so it is crucial for leaders to ask for feedback and make that feedback feel welcome, valued, and accounted for moving forward.

A key aspect of a productive and creative development environment is *meaningful work*. All teammates (especially those in managerial roles) need to help all stakeholders find meaning in the work, as it will drive the most dedication and creativity. While employment or academics typically provides extrinsic motivation (e.g., paycheck or grades), this can generally only engage compliance. To tap into true motivation, we should also engage intrinsic motivation by helping connect the project/company goals with all stakeholder goals,[20,21,22] such as desire for agency, personal growth, and fulfilment. A crucial starting off point for meaningful work is communicating the work's *impact* and helping others buy into that impact, sometimes by flexibly altering the work to fit all stakeholders. A shared vision helps everyone understand the goal and focus on it like a guiding North Star or a sprint goal Prioritizing together, understanding which elements are crucial and why, negotiating the schedule, and addressing concerns openly and as a team will all help ensure that everyone buys into the work plan and

---

[20] Cerasoli, Christopher P, Jessica M Nicklin, and Michael T Ford. 2014. "Intrinsic Motivation and Extrinsic Incentives Jointly Predict Performance: A 40-year Meta-Analysis." *Psychological Bulletin* 140 (4): 980.

[21] Mikkonen, Tommi. 2016. "Flow, Intrinsic Motivation, and Developer Experience in Software Engineering." *Agile Processes in Software Engineering and Extreme Programming* 104.

[22] Fairlie, Paul. 2011. "Meaningful Work, Employee Engagement, and Other Key Employee Outcomes: Implications for Human Resource Development." *Advances in Developing Human Resources* 13 (4): 508–525.

allow individuals to make the right development decisions within their tasks along the way. Understanding, agreeing with, and contributing to the plan increases everyone's personal agency, crucial for developers.[23]

Mutual dedication promotes trust and support. If you want your developers to go the extra mile, you must do the same by investing in their growth and well-being.[24] If you need developers to work overtime to handle unpredictable circumstances, then you need to invest in their personal time and needs too (extra vacation days, shorter week to compensate for extended days, etc.). If we want individuals to respect company time, then the company must respect individual time. Facilitate a *reasonable workload* and celebrate a work-life balance as opposed to working overtime. If we need everyone to be willing to put in the occasional longer hours to fulfill temporary emergent needs, there must be accountability on the side of management, not only for the extra hours, but also for the workers' willingness to accommodate for them outside of standard work time. Consider that two extra hours today cannot be meaningfully compensated by two fewer hours tomorrow. Any changes in work schedule, especially on short notice, create a non-negligible amount of overhead for individuals (ranging from working while tired, missing sleep, cancelling plans, skipping going to the gym, rearranging family and pet care, etc.). If this overhead is not meaningfully accounted for, workers will miss out on crucial recharge time, eventually leading to burnout, quiet quitting, reduced quality of work, and increased turnover.

Soft-Aware Development: A Culture of Safety and Growth

Teamwork does not happen in a vacuum. No matter how well we take care of each developer individually, our emergent collaborative environment is the biosphere of software development, which will ultimately determine whether we can thrive together. If only output is valued, then learning can become unsafe. If all conflict is perceived negatively, then diversity can become unsafe. A sustainable workplace culture requires a focus on learning and growth, a commitment to accountability, and a strong emphasis of interpersonal skills to support healthy relationships.

---

[23] Neogy, Rajkumari. 2023. "Neuroscience has the antidote for managers to address an overlooked behavior that blocks success." *fastcompany.com*. www.fastcompany.com/90973601/.

[24] Graziotin, Daniel, Fabian Fagerholm, Xiaofeng Wang, and Pekka Abrahamsson. 2018. "What Happens When Software Developers Are (Un)Happy." *Journal of Systems and Software* 140:32–47.

Safety in Learning

Soft-Aware development requires a safe environment for learning. All our work must be informed by the *context* in which that work takes place, and each new context should be approached with curiosity and a focus on growth. There are no one-size-fits-all solutions in teamwork: working with a new team, new project, or new client will require care, accountability, and readaptation. It will also require room to safely make mistakes and time when development may not happen, while knowledge is created and new skills are acquired.

Learning teamwork differs for each team composition, so trial and error is required. Teammates must welcome the process of learning and adaptation, which also means welcoming mistakes in both technical and non-technical aspects of the work, and even celebrating them as opportunities for growth. *Growth* requires learning new things, which starts from not knowing and often not succeeding on the first try. A *growth focus* normalizes learning from failure, allowing developers to feel safe to express difficulties, ask for help, or admit a mistake. Developers can use an agile approach here: try, get feedback, adjust, try again. Creating a safe environment for growth requires minimizing guilt and blame, focusing instead on supporting each other through the growing pains that typically accompany learning experiences.

When developers have the necessary freedom to do their work, accountability is spread across the team. As a result, the teammates must constructively hold each other *accountable but blameless.*[25] Blame focuses on the past, while accountability focuses on formulating a better plan for the future. An environment where taking accountability feels safe will lead to open and honest discussions about how to course-correct moving forward. A growth mindset naturally helps manage fear, minimize blame, and foster accountability when things do not work out. Consider that when a mistake happens and is not caught by anyone on the way to the client, everyone on the team is responsible. Anyone could have caught the mistake, but no one did. Finding someone to blame for the initial mistake will not solve the problem. The problem is not the mistake. Mistakes will happen. The real problem is that deficient protocols were likely in place, failing to setup protective redundancies to ensure mistakes are caught earlier in the shared process. How did each individual on the team passively or actively contribute to the problem? What can each teammate do to prevent it moving forward? Given any less-than-ideal outcome,

---

[25] Iqbal, Mary. 2023. "Why 'Accountable but Blameless' Is my New Favorite Phrase." *Scrum.org*. www.scrum.org/resources/blog/why-accountable-blameless-my-new-favorite-phrase.

the team should consider how all available information, technologies, practices, personnel, and circumstances contributed to the undesirable outcome, and how they can jointly safeguard against such outcomes in the future. Even in the simplest case of someone forgetting a task, the team can revise their practices to improve task-tracking with shared task boards, automatic deadlines and reminders, calendar integration, pair programming, etc.

Joint ownership of the project supports collective accountability and promotes mutual support across all tasks. While some light competition can be good, the team and company should all win or lose together to truly develop a sense of camaraderie and shared purpose. Shared ownership breeds support instead of competition. Shared ownership also ensures that work and understanding are distributed across the team more evenly, while a culture of learning values the acquisition of new skills along the way. The result is a team that is more balanced in workload and more prepared for handling unpredictable situations and future needs (helping test each other's code, cover for a sick teammate, etc.). To help foster a more collaborative environment, supervisors should notice, value, and model collaboration, sharing of resources, and maintaining a supportive and encouraging attitude.

On the technical side, a safe environment supports experimentation. Boldness, creativity, and innovation require exploratory trial and error. They also require considerable time when development may not happen while knowledge is being created. Some attempts will not immediately improve the product, but will instead create new skills, improve understanding, and explore new ideas. Incorrect productivity metrics and short-sighted incentives can lead to deficient development and teamwork practices. If nothing beyond the output is valued, teams will inevitably fall into unsustainable and self-preserving behaviors, such as:

- Developers only taking smaller tasks they can complete quickly so it sounds more productive

- Mistrust and zero-sum behaviors (e.g., competing and seeking personal safety through blame)

- Risk aversion, causing developers to avoid any tasks they are unsure of how to complete, shunning the more creative and challenging opportunities, and optimizing toward less learning along the way

- Skipping creative brainstorming to jump straight into coding up the next deliverable

Do not undervalue the process, the failures, the learning, and the discussions, in favor of looking solely at the results. Create space for experimentation and learning together, because no one will have all the answers (not those supervising, not the clients, and not the most experienced developers) and the suitable answer will change over time and across teams and team members. Additionally, while it is natural to focus on problematic behaviors as the main items to address, remember to also highlight the behaviors we value in our teammates.

Safety in Clarity

Regardless of what values are listed in the company bio, the culture we ultimately create is the one we promote throughout our daily operations. Our shared culture will reflect what is consistently noticed, valued, and modeled by everyone, but especially by those in charge.

As Adena Friedman said, "*Ideas are only as good as your ability to communicate them.*" For Soft-Awareness to truly permeate an organization's culture, it must be modeled by all levels of the organizational hierarchy. Meetings are a great opportunity for leaders to demonstrate and facilitate the expected constructive behaviors and responses: encourage and model open and rational dialogue, show and reward curiosity, offer support, and ask questions instead of making assumptions. Expressing needs or dissenting opinions should be rewarded to showcase that speaking up is not fruitless but instead very much worth the effort, courage, and vulnerability it takes. For example, if a teammate expresses a need or a preference, reasonable effort should be made to accommodate that need.

Consistency and clarity is safe. Requirements and constraints may change, but preparing for them can stay consistent. Work and teamwork context may change, but expectations can stay explicit and consistent. Giving clear feedback may feel unsafe in the short term but is ultimately crucial for workplace sustainability. According to Brené Brown, "*Of the ten behaviors and cultural issues that leaders identified as barriers to courage, there was one issue that leaders ranked as the greatest concern: Avoiding tough conversations, including giving honest, productive feedback.*"[26] Avoidant behaviors diminished trust and engagement, increased problematic behaviors, reduced a sense of shared purpose, and negatively impacted productivity. Brown summarized this as "*Clear is kind. Unclear is unkind.*"

---

[26] Brown, Brené. 2018. "Clear Is Kind. Unclear Is Unkind." *brenebrown.com*. https://brenebrown.com/articles/2018/10/15/clear-is-kind-unclear-is-unkind/.

Let's consider some other examples of being kind by being clear:

- Be explicit in all assumptions and plans across the team (frequently compare understanding, use visuals, discuss steps); make sure everyone understands the vision and their individual roles in helping bring that vision to life.

- Be specific about the distinction between minimum required targets vs. nice-to-have reach goals. Working based on guesswork is dangerous, costly, and breeds anxiety within the team.

- Clearly state constraints such as urgent needs or being understaffed. Transparency will help validate concerns and create a culture of open communication, trust, and shared problem solving.

- Don't leave others wondering whether they did enough or not, as this only leads to anxiety. Avoiding telling developers how to improve or what to change is not sustainable in the long run. Be specific and explicit about expectations so everyone can meaningfully retrospect, learn, and adapt by considering what was asked for, what was done, and why.

- Conversations are interpreted and digested differently by individuals. To ensure a shared understanding, explicitly recap takeaways and next steps for everyone.

- Be open, honest, courageous, and vulnerable with yourself and your team. Include a vibe-check in daily stand-up meetings to help improve shared clarity regarding the teammates' daily context.

- Direct all critique toward support and growth, not shame or tear down. Instead of pointing out undesirable or unproductive practices, guide each other to find better alternatives, always accompanied with reasoning regarding why one practice is preferable to another and how to implement it.

Safety in Diversity

While getting along may come easiest through similarities, heterogeneous teams showcase improved critical thinking and innovation.[27] Building and maintaining a culture that welcomes our differences requires everyone's commitment to a number of personal and interpersonal practices. *"But to build anything 'inclusively,' we must first saliently understand where we are excluding."*[28].

As you saw in the last chapter, Scrum explicitly defines a set of values for developers to practice commitment, focus, openness, respect, and courage. When in doubt, lead with empathy. Empathy allows us to better understand our client requirements, developer needs, and the challenges of our emergent collaboration. Empathy is about valuing others as individuals, not just as resources for joint work. This includes paying attention to their needs and difficulties, communication and work styles, and personal circumstances. Empathy requires vulnerability, authenticity, and a willingness to be wrong. Consider that you may not see the full complexity and scope of someone's work, that everyone has a different cultural and technical background, that our brains all process information very differently, and that all this diversity is our shared strength.

Making everyone feel safe, respected, and valued on your team requires a commitment to *diversity, equity, and inclusion.* Inclusion strategist Vernā Myers famously said, *"Diversity is being invited to the party; inclusion is being asked to dance."*[29] Equity then, at a minimum, requires ensuring that invitees can get to the party, the facilities are suitable for the invitees, and all invitees had a voice in planning the activities, music, and refreshments. Yes, that is much more involved, but without these steps, we cannot possibly claim that everyone is truly welcome at the party. It requires paying attention to personal needs and preferences, to historical and cultural contexts, and to personal goals, not just to software development tasks.

---

[27] Garousi, Vahid, Gorkem Giray, Eray Tuzun, Cagatay Catal, and Michael Felderer. 2019. "Closing the Gap Between Software Engineering Education and Industrial Needs." *IEEE Software* 37 (2): 68–77.

[28] Neogy, Rajkumari. 2020. "Exclusion and trauma are impacting the workforce. Here's how to fix it and heal." *fastcompany.com* (July). www.fastcompany.com/90526659/exclusion-and-trauma-are-impacting-the-workforce-heres-how-to-fix-it-and-heal.

[29] Myers, Vernā. 2015. "Diversity Is Being Invited to the Party; Inclusion Is Being Asked to Dance." In *American Bar Association*, vol. 1. 11.

An often overlooked dimension of diversity is the *type of work* expected from the teammates. Paul Graham's "Maker's Schedule vs. Manager's Schedule"[30] discusses the fundamental differences between creative work and management work. By default, a manager's schedule is broken down into small (e.g., hourly) intervals intended to schedule lots of meetings. Makers (e.g., developers) cannot create in small time slots, needing larger intervals such as half a day, because creative tasks require some windup time and extended chunks of time for deep focus and inventiveness. Meetings break up the available chunks of time and, if not scheduled carefully, can destroy a maker's entire day: "*A single meeting can blow a whole afternoon, by breaking it into two pieces each too small to do anything hard in. Plus, you have to remember to go to the meeting. That's no problem for someone on the manager's schedule. There's always something coming on the next hour; the only question is what. But when someone on the maker's schedule has a meeting, they have to think about it. For someone on the maker's schedule, having a meeting is like throwing an exception.*"[31, 32] To minimize damage to the productivity of developers and any other makers on your team, you can schedule meetings with maker-attendees at the beginning or end of a workday.

Another important dimension of diversity is neurodivergence, which is common on software development teams and accompanied by many unique strengths and challenges.[33] Research shows that many neurodivergent individuals are diagnosed later in life and do not disclose their diagnosis nor ask for accommodations, even while having specific ideas for meaningful accommodations, such as alternative performance evaluations and quieter working environments.[34] One inclusive approach may be to offer alternatives to be freely chosen by the individuals on the team based on their needs: alternative work spaces, alternative means of communication, alternative schedule, etc.

---

[30] Graham, Paul. 2009. "Maker's Schedule vs. Manager's Schedule." `www.paulgraham.com`. `www.paulgraham.com/makersschedule.html`.

[31] An *exception* indicates something went wrong and the program must be interrupted until it is handled.

[32] Graham, 2009.

[33] Gama, Kiev, and Aline Lacerda. 2023. "Understanding and Supporting Neurodiverse Software Developers in Agile Teams." *In Proceedings of the XXXVII Brazilian Symposium on Software Engineering*, 497–502. SBES '23. Campo Grande, Brazil: Association for Computing Machinery.

[34] Morris, Meredith Ringel, Andrew Begel, and Ben Wiedermann. 2015. "Understanding the Challenges Faced by Neurodiverse Software Engineering Employees: Towards a More Inclusive and Productive Technical Workforce." *In Proceedings of the 17th International ACM SIGACCESS Conference on Computers & Accessibility*, 173–184.

Keep in mind that some approaches and behaviors do not have to be objectively wrong in order to be contextually detrimental. All social interactions are contextually dense, with much of the context remaining implicit and invisible to all sides. Consider, for instance, the theoretically thoughtful idea of getting everyone breakfast for the 9 a.m. meeting. Were everyone's dietary restrictions accounted for or did some teammates end up feeling less valued than before the gesture? As another example, consider that people have different thresholds for feeling safe enough to speak up during a discussion. Simply asking whether anyone has questions or comments may not sufficiently open up the floor to invite everyone's opinions. Note also that the more dissenting the opinion, the more daunting it can be to voice it in a group setting. Consider also how not making eye contact is considered rude in some cultures and polite in others, and how rigidly adhering to one's social norms and customs can come across as exclusionary. Finally, consider how off-handedly saying "just" (e.g., "why don't you just...") in giving advice actually presumes extensive background similarities (such as specific technological skills), ultimately demoralizing and alienating instead of providing the intended support.[35] Humility, curiosity, and empathy are fundamental to working together in a sustainable, healthy, and productive way. Missteps will happen on all sides, but a shared commitment to growth will create a safer environment where everyone can try, observe, discuss, learn, and do better next time, while allowing others to learn and do better also.

Safety in Conflict

The biggest threat to safety is conflict, but conflict cannot and should not be avoided. Conflicts are a way to assess different ideas, approaches, and interpersonal needs. When handled constructively, conflicts are an invaluable opportunity to make the product and the team stronger.

Conflicts happen in any team, but can be especially prevalent in engaged self-organizing teams with open communication, developer agency, joint code ownership, and room for experimentation. Differences of opinion are a sign of a diverse and creative team. When faced with disagreement, conflicting opinions should not be disregarded. The opinion of any one person represents some percentage of the opinions of users who might consider using your product, of clients who may want to contract your development services, and of competitors who might decide to develop an alternative solution. Disregarding conflicting opinions will create tension, jeopardize the shared

---

[35] Frost, Brad. 2015. "Just." *bradforst.com* (September). https://bradfrost.com/blog/post/just/

vision, and disrupt the work. Accounting for different views early is an opportunity to improve overall quality and robustness of both the team and the product, and thus should be welcomed and handled with care. The team is your earliest focus group; do not leave their crucial insights on the table.

All conflict has the potential for positive or negative outcomes. *Constructive controversy "exists when one person's ideas, information, conclusions, theories, and opinions are incompatible with those of another, and the two seek to reach an agreement."*[36] Note how this differs from *consensus seeking*, which *"occurs when members of a group emphasize agreement, inhibit discussion to avoid any disagreement or arguments, and avoid realistic appraisal of alternative ideas and courses of action."*[37] Our goal is not to merely reach agreement but rather to jointly construct new understanding based on active cooperative learning. The following are some conditions that have been identified as necessary for constructive controversy:[38]

1. Cooperative goal structure, as competition hinders effective communication

2. Skilled disagreement to effectively navigate differences of opinion

3. Rational argument to generate, present, and update opinions in the face of evidence and logic

4. Active discussion by all participants, in place of avoidance, dominance, or submission

According to the Thomas-Kilmann Conflict Mode Instrument (TKI), people favor a particular conflict resolution style depending on their level of cooperativeness and assertiveness, alternatively defined as concern for others vs. concern for oneself.[39] Recognizing the conflict management style is important for teamwork management:

---

[36] Johnson, David W, and Roger T Johnson. 2011. "Constructive Controversy: Energizing Learning." *Small Group Learning in Higher Education: Research and Practice, Cooper, JL & Robinson, P.(editors), New Forums Press, Stillwater, Oklahoma*, 114–121.

[37] Johnson, Johnson. 2011

[38] Johnson, David W, and Roger T Johnson. 2009. "Energizing Learning: The Instructional Power of Conflict." *Educational Researcher* 38 (1): 37–51.

[39] Thomas, K. W. and Kilmann, R. H. 1974. Thomas-Kilmann Conflict Mode Instrument (TKI). *APA PsycTests.*

- *Avoiding* style: delays or failures to reach resolution can breed further discontent, resentment, and frustration; only works temporarily while gathering information, waiting for an opening in the schedule, or after some other ongoing situation is addressed.

- *Competing* style: detrimental to teamwork, as it values some contributors' needs over others; resolution is likely to breed resentment, disparity, and beget future conflict and hurt the work environment.

- *Accommodating* style: does the opposite of the competing style, but often with a similar overall effect, as it can lead to burnout due to not having one's needs met.

- *Compromising* style (lose-lose): everyone ends up making sacrifices toward some middle ground that is acceptable but ultimately not what anyone wanted.

- *Collaborating* style: the true ideal win-win; it's the most time consuming as it requires meaningful discussions to truly find ways to accommodate everyone's needs.

Brené Brown suggests that we all get ready to rumble: "*A rumble is a discussion, conversation, or meeting defined by a commitment to lean into vulnerability, to stay curious and generous, to stick with the messy middle of problem identification and solving, to take a break and circle back when necessary, to be fearless in owning our parts, and, as psychologist Harriet Lerner teaches, to listen with the same passion with which we want to be heard.*"[40]

Development teams will inevitably encounter both task conflicts and personal conflicts. *Task conflicts* are differences in understanding, conflicting opinions on which approach to take, assessments of risks and costs, etc. Resolving task conflicts improves the product by helping brainstorm alternatives, address weak points, or clarify requirements. *Personal conflicts* are differences in communication styles, cultural background, neurodivergence, personality, boundaries, triggers, etc. Personal conflicts can be a huge drain on the developers. Resolving interpersonal conflicts improves the teamwork, job satisfaction, and productivity.

---

[40] Brown, Brené. 2018. "Clear Is Kind. Unclear Is Unkind." brenebrown.com. https://brenebrown.com/articles/2018/10/15/clear-is-kind-unclear-is-unkind/.

Conflicts are invaluable to growth but they must not be allowed to fester. Timely proactive resolution is key, which requires a culture that welcomes difficult conversations, praises the courage they take, and helps everyone learn the skills necessary to both communicate, listen, and collaborate on finding a new common ground. Interpersonal tensions need to be brought to the surface and resolved in a timely manner in order to prevent deterioration of the relationship. Teams may need external contribution of resources, information, or impartial arbitration to resolve conflicts and prevent resentments from snowballing. So how can we constructively resolve a conflict? A series of *skilled disagreement* techniques have been proposed[41]:

- Criticize ideas, not people.

- Separate self-worth from criticism of your ideas.

- Focus on winning as a team, not individually.

- Encourage everyone to get informed and participate in the discussion.

- Listen to all ideas, regardless of your personal views.

- Restate ideas to ensure shared understanding.

- Clearly state all arguments, clarify differences, and then integrate through points of agreement.

- Try to understand opposing perspectives.

- Update your own perspective in the face of evidence.

- Emphasize rationality and data.

- Follow the *golden rule of conflict*: treat others as you want to be treated.

Workplace hierarchy will inevitably also affect conflicts. The following tips have been proposed to help higher positioned individuals through effective conflict management[42]:

---

[41] Johnson, David W, and Roger T Johnson. 2009. "Energizing Learning: The Instructional Power of Conflict." *Educational Researcher* 38 (1): 37–51.

[42] Tannenbaum, Scott, and Eduardo Salas. 2020. *Teams That Work: The Seven Drivers of Team Effectiveness.* Oxford University Press.

- Make time to resolve interpersonal conflicts. Recognize that conflicts do not just go away and waiting them out is detrimental.

- Determine whether a conflict needs to be addressed with individuals, subgroups, the whole team, or some combination of the above.

- To avoid blind agreement and to encourage discussion instead, refrain from imposing a personal point of view early in the conversation.

- Encourage the team to surface small concerns and irritants before they turn into conflicts.

- Look for opportunities to set the tone and model the behaviors you want to see from the team (e.g., thank others for speaking up, disagree constructively, acknowledge mistakes, etc.)

- Help frame and focus disagreements constructively by discussing why some approaches may not work contextually without being objectively wrong.

- Take the time to explain your decisions and, wherever possible, involve the team in decision-making.

Soft-Aware Development: Teamwork Artifacts

Being Soft-Aware improves teamwork and the team's output. But how do we make time for all these practices? How do we keep an eye on the teamwork and the culture? How do we make sure conflicts are resolved before they can corrode our team from the inside? In order to stay close enough to pay attention, but far enough to give development some creative room, some artifacts can be added to the development process.

Let's look at some artifacts and practices we found helpful for developer teams in the past:[43]

- Begin with an individual and confidential *assessments* to determine everyone's needs, practices, and personal traits to help put together effective balanced teams, establish helpful team protocols, and implement appropriate training sessions.

---

[43] You can download artifact templates we used for an undergraduate software development course and adapt them to your own projects: https://drive.google.com/drive/folders/1FaWT2YOV1CXPIXeOoLDOuNlxId5Bt6bk.

- Have teammates fill out regular (e.g., once per development iteration) *self and peer evaluations* (individual, confidential, and to be used solely for helping with teamwork): a streamlined form for subjective reflection on each developer's own performance, attitude, and contributions, as well as perceptions of the teammates' performances, attitudes, and contributions. Making explicit room to reflect is crucial to begin gathering the full picture of the teamwork and allow for timely interventions.

- *Play* is the essence of creative thinking. Having shared channels for memes or non-project news can help create a more personable and vibrant space that is not all work and no play. Create large and small team-building opportunities. Even spaces for coffee and some recharging conversation can turn a hard and stressful day into a worthwhile and fulfilling shared experience that can bring a team closer. Larger events can bring greater excitement and create shared memories.

- Normalize mistakes and learning, both in technical and non-technical aspects of the work. Don't ambush and don't single out. Schedule *routine check-ins* as part of the workflow to create opportunities for sharing and to help everyone prepare to be receptive. If a situation is sensitive, warn teammates that you will all need to work through the discomfort with empathy and courage.

- Have *open multi-directional communication channels*, such as short scheduled updates, in-person team working sessions, shared knowledge repositories, and convenient channels for on demand synchronous and asynchronous communication.

- Fill out *team contracts* with minimum requirements, which can be expanded by the teammates to best suit their collective comfort levels. The contract should cover team meeting frequency (e.g., time and location of daily stand-ups), frequency of checking and updating asynchronous communication channels (e.g., checking the Slack channel once a day and updating the Agile board after each work session), timeliness of unavailability notices (e.g., informing your team when you are running late), required technologies (e.g., git), protocols (e.g., adhering to git flow), and deliverables (e.g., standup reports and Minimum Viable Product demos every two weeks). The contract allows for a clear setting of expectations and responsibilities for the team and gives supervisors a view into the team's practices.

It is helpful to approach teamwork as an agile development process of its own: teamwork starts right away, is checked on frequently, and is course-corrected as needed. In fact, if you are already using agile methodologies, agile artifacts can directly allow to watch over the teamwork:

- Status *reviews/demos/presentations* are how you review the status of the product. When reporting the status, clearly state where the project is and where it's heading before the next status report:

  o What has been achieved since the last review/demo/iteration?

  o What has not been achieved from the work originally planned for this iteration?

  o What are the next steps?

Notice how reviews and stand-up meetings (see previous chapter) both examine the project status by discussing accomplishments, setbacks, and next steps. Reviews cover a larger timespan (typically a single development iteration) and engage an audience outside of the immediate developers working on the product (such as supervisors, product owners, and clients) to provide updates and request feedback. You should not embellish, make excuses, nor obscure issues. Be honest about problems and where you are in the schedule. While no one likes to report problems, and no one likes to have problems reported to them, this conflict must be embraced and handled in a timely manner. The best way to mitigate the problem is to get others involved in helping to find a solution, maintaining a culture of trust and safety. Make sure you know your audience so you can tailor the content to their level of expertise and their involvement in your work (managers, clients, and end users will want to be shown different things about the project and its status). A representative review of the completed work will allow you to gather the most relevant and helpful feedback from stakeholders.

- *Retrospectives* are how the team can review, assess, and modify the processes involved in their work. Retrospectives are typically held either after the product release or after each major iteration of the product (e.g., after every iteration or sprint), so you can use them as built-in opportunities to see how the team is reflects on their own innerworkings, as well as provide support, clarity, or an external perspective. The goal of a retrospective is to determine whether current processes and practices are serving the needs of the team as a whole, as well as the needs of the individual teammates:

  o What went right in our teamwork? (Did we meet our schedule? Did we communicate and collaborate effectively? Did everyone feel supported and respected?)

  o What went wrong in our teamwork? (Did teammates deviate from expected practices? Did we merge too close to the deadline? Did we work on the same features due to not clearly defining everyone's tasks? Did we have to work overtime?)

  o How should we update our processes, attitudes, or environment moving forward?

This is the most crucial meeting for Soft-Aware development and must be afforded time, care, and respect from both developers and supervisors. Consider how we are often taught to put aside personal issues to keep our head in the game. It is frequently discouraged and even regarded as unprofessional to discuss anything but the tasks at hand. But how do we discuss having last-minute merge conflicts in our repository without creating tension and blame if we are not to discuss personal needs, circumstances, and emotions? To modify our shared processes effectively, we must understand the big picture of our emergent shared context, and humans are at the very center of this context. Say we merged late the night before a demo. The demo went poorly, features were missing due to hastily resolved merge conflicts, everyone was tired and upset, and fingers are pointing at one developer. It may seem reasonable and expeditious to tell that developer off, threatening with dire consequences should this happen again. This is not the way. Was the developer struggling and afraid of asking for help? Of seeming unprepared or unqualified? Or had they been feeling isolated in general? Or perhaps they've tried to express needing help and no one stepped up? Had the team skipped stand-up meetings and missed this? Or perhaps the developer's feature just broke unrecoverably during final tweaks? Did our development process fail to properly encourage small incremental commits and merging with enough time to handle the unexpected? Meaningful resolutions require time and care for fruitful discussion on areas of improvement, both in our products and in the product creators.

- *Postmortems* (team-wide and individual) are a bigger *retrospective* that allows developers to reflect on the project as a whole, challenges, lessons, and perceptions. Some questions to consider are:

  o   What were the project goals and were they achieved?

  o   What went well in the project? What didn't?

  o   What went well in the team? What didn't?

  o   What were the main lessons learned by the team over the course of the project?

  o   What would the team do differently if given the chance to redo this project?

  Afterward, the teammates should complete individual postmortems where they each get a chance to further reflect on their own challenges and lessons:

  o   What were my own goals for this project and were they achieved?

  o   What went well for me with regards to the project? What didn't?

  o   What went well for me with regards to the team? What didn't?

  o   What were the main lessons I learned over the course of the project?

  o   What would I do differently if given the chance to redo this collaboration?

Postmortems are often treated as perfunctory by developers, who are eager to jump into the next creative adventure instead of filling out "paperwork." Slow down; this is no busy-work. Taking an opportunity to reflect between projects is one of the most crucial practices in growing as a developer. Research shows that reflection is key for turning our experiences into meaningful learning.[44] So think back: gather up what happened (technically and interpersonally), look at it from your future vantage point, and develop new insights about what empowered you, what held you back, and how you plan to use this new knowledge going forward. Congratulations, now you've leveled up!

Conclusion

In this chapter, we discuss how to manage the project by looking at the needs of both the product and the people creating the product. To anticipate and support the needs of the product, we consider options for organization, analyze risks, consider resource requirements, estimate schedules, and plan for the unavoidable management of defects. To anticipate and support the needs of the people jointly creating the product, we first consider some practices that may hinder teamwork. Then, we discuss how to become Soft-Aware through supporting individual developers, creating a safe culture in which we can thrive together, and welcoming conflict as opportunity for growth. Finally, we present a series of practices and artifacts that can help us watch over the complex emerging dynamics of our teams. For further discussion and examples of what leads to good teamwork, consider reading *Teams That Work* by Scott Tannenbaum and Eduardo Salas.[45]

References

Beck, Kent. 2000. *Extreme Programming eXplained: Embrace Change.* Reading, MA: Addison-Wesley.

Boehm, Barry W., Chris Abts, A. Winsor Brown, Sunita Chulani, Bradford K. Clark, Ellis Horowitz, Ray Madachy, Donald J. Reifer, and Bert Steece. 2000. *Software Cost Estimation with COCOMO II.* Prentice Hall.

---

[44] Boud, David, Rosemary Keogh, and David Walker. 2013. *Reflection: Turning Experience into Learning.* Routledge.

[45] Tannenbaum, Scott, and Eduardo Salas. 2020. *Teams That Work: The Seven Drivers of Team Effectiveness.* Oxford University Press.

Boud, David, Rosemary Keogh, and David Walker. 2013. *Reflection: Turning Experience into Learning*. Routledge.

Brown, Brené. 2018. "Clear Is Kind. Unclear Is Unkind." *brenebrown.com* (October). https://brenebrown.com/articles/2018/10/15/clear-is-kind-unclear-is-unkind/.

Cerasoli, Christopher P, Jessica M Nicklin, and Michael T Ford. 2014. "Intrinsic Motivation And Extrinsic Incentives Jointly Predict Performance: A 40-Year Meta-Analysis." *Psychological bulletin* 140 (4): 980.

Cockburn, Alistair. 2004. "The End of Software Engineering and the Start of Economic-Cooperative Gaming." *Computer Science and Information Systems* 1 (1): 1–32.

Collaborative for Academic, Social, and Emotional Learning (CASEL). 2023. "FAQs." *CASEL.org* (October). https://casel.org/faq/

DeMarco, Tom, and Tim Lister. 2013. *Peopleware: Productive Projects And Teams*. Addison-Wesley.

Elias, M. J., J. E. Zins, and R. P. Weissberg. 2000. "Promoting Social And Emotional Learning: Guidelines For Educators." *Adolescence* 35 (137): 221.

Fairlie, Paul. 2011. "Meaningful Work, Employee Engagement, and Other Key Employee Outcomes: Implications for Human Resource Development." *Advances in Developing Human Resources* 13 (4): 508–525.

Frost, Brad. 2015. ""just."" *bradforst.com* (September). https://bradfrost.com/blog/post/just/.

Gallup, Inc. 2023. "State of the Global Workplace 2023 Report. The Voice of the World's Employees." Gallup.com, www.gallup.com/workplace/349484/state-of-the-global-workplace.aspx.

Gama, Kiev, and Aline Lacerda. 2023. "Understanding and Supporting Neurodiverse Software Developers in Agile Teams." *In Proceedings of the XXXVII Brazilian Symposium on Software Engineering*, 497–502. SBES '23. Campo Grande, Brazil: Association for Computing Machinery.

Garousi, Vahid, Gorkem Giray, Eray Tuzun, Cagatay Catal, and Michael Felderer. 2019. "Closing the Gap Between Software Engineering Education and Industrial Needs." *IEEE software* 37 (2): 68–77.

Graham, Paul. 2009. "Maker's Schedule vs Manager's Schedule." *www.paulgraham.com* (July). www.paulgraham.com/makersschedule.html.

Graziotin, Daniel, Fabian Fagerholm, Xiaofeng Wang, and Pekka Abrahamsson. 2018. "What Happens When Software Developers Are (Un)Happy." *Journal of Systems and Software* 140:32–47.

Iqbal, Mary. 2023. "Why 'Accountable but Blameless' Is my New Favorite Phrase." *Scrum.org* (May). www.scrum.org/resources/blog/why-accountable-blameless-my-new-favorite-phrase.

Jeffries, Ron. 2016. "Dark Scrum." *ronjeffries.com* (September). https://ronjeffries.com/articles/016-09ff/defense/.

Johnson, David W, and Roger T Johnson. 2009. "Energizing Learning: The Instructional Power of Conflict." *Educational Researcher* 38 (1): 37–51.

Johnson, David W, and Roger T Johnson. 2011. "Constructive Controversy: Energizing Learning." *Small Group Learning in Higher Education: Research and Practice, Cooper, JL & Robinson, P.(editors), New Forums Press, Stillwater, Oklahoma*, 114–121.

Kazakova, Vera A, John F Dooley, and Monica M Mcgill. 2023. "Soft-Aware Development: Social Emotional Learning as an Agile Process." In *Proceedings of the 2023 ACM Conference on International Computing Education Research-Volume 2*, 39–40.

McConnell, Steve. 1996. *Rapid development - Taming Wild Software Schedules.* Microsoft Press.

Meyer, André N., Earl T. Barr, Christian Bird, and Thomas Zimmermann. 2019. "Today Was a Good Day: The Daily Life of Software Developers." *IEEE Transactions on Software Engineering* 47 (5): 863–880.

Mikkonen, Tommi. 2016. "Flow, Intrinsic Motivation, and Developer Experience in Software Engineering." *Agile Processes in Software Engineering and Extreme Programming* 104.

Morris, Meredith Ringel, Andrew Begel, and Ben Wiedermann. 2015. "Understanding the Challenges Faced by Neurodiverse Software Engineering Employees: Towards a More Inclusive and Productive TechnicalWorkforce." *In Proceedings of the 17th International ACM SIGACCESS Conference on computers & accessibility*, 173–184.

Myers, Vernā. 2015. "Diversity Is Being Invited to the Party; Inclusion Is Being Asked to Dance." In *American Bar Association,* vol. 1. 11.

Neogy, Rajkumari. 2020. "Exclusion and trauma are impacting the workforce. Here's how to fix it and heal." *fastcompany.com* (July). www.fastcompany.com/90526659.

Neogy, Rajkumari. 2023. "Neuroscience has the antidote for managers to address an overlooked behavior that blocks success." fastcompany.com (October). www.fastcompany.com/90973601.

Rezvani, Azadeh, and Pouria Khosravi. 2019. "Emotional Intelligence: The Key to Mitigating Stress and Fostering Trust Among Software Developers Working on Information System Projects." *International Journal of Information Management* 48:139–150.

Shoenthal, Amy. 2023. "The Art of Setting Expectations as a Project Manager." *Harvard Business Review* (October). https://hbr.org/2023/10/the-art-of-setting-expectations-as-a-project-manager.

Tannenbaum, Scott, and Eduardo Salas. 2020. *Teams That Work: The Seven Drivers of Team Effectiveness.* Oxford University Press.

Thomas, K. W. and Kilmann, R. H. 1974. Thomas-Kilmann Conflict Mode Instrument (TKI). *APA PsycTests.*

Wilson, Laura, Susie Ho, and Rowan H Brookes. 2018. "Student Perceptions of Teamwork Within Assessment Tasks in Undergraduate Science Degrees." *Assessment & Evaluation in Higher Education* 43 (5): 786–799.

CHAPTER 4

Ethics and Professional Practice

Ethics is knowing the difference between what you have a right to do and what is right to do.

—Potter Stewart

We will continue our exploration of software development by spending some time talking about ethics and professional practice. That is, how you should act as a computing professional in situations that pose an ethical dilemma. We'll talk about what ethics is and how it applies to the software industry, what ethical theories exist that will give us some tools, what an ethical argument or discussion is, and how to evaluate ethical situations. Finally, we will go through some case studies to give you an idea of how these evaluation techniques will work.

Introduction to Ethics

Simply put, *ethics* is the study of how to decide if something is *right or wrong*. For now, we are going to assume that everyone knows what *right* and *wrong* means, but as we'll see in some of the examples, even this can be dicey at times. As for *computer ethics*, we'll say it is those ethical issues that a computer professional (in our case, software developers) will face over the course of their profession, whether they are on the job or working on their own projects. Computer ethics includes figuring out how make critical decisions that can affect you and others (your company, clients, users, and even society as a whole), both personally and professionally.

© John F. Dooley and Vera A. Kazakova 2024
J. F. Dooley and V. A. Kazakova, *Software Development, Design, and Coding*,
https://doi.org/10.1007/979-8-8688-0285-0_4

Many decisions made in your professional life will have an ethical component. What if you are asked to ship software that you think has a serious bug? What if your company is making or using illegal copies of software? What if your company is making it easy for others to infringe on the intellectual property of others (such as by releasing software that allows users to convert files that use digital rights management (DRM) protection into unprotected files)? What do you do if you believe you have a conflict of interest regarding a project you are working on? What do you do if you are offered a job developing software that you find morally objectionable? What if you discover that your company is keeping track of everyone's web searches or keystrokes? How much data is fair to collection from web site visitors and should visitors be made aware of this data collection? Is it ethical to ask employees to stay late or work weekends to meet company deadlines?

The ethical situations you will encounter in your professional life aren't categorically or substantially different from those that you will encounter outside of your profession (though their impact on your life and the lives of others may be amplified). You will still need to examine these situations using general ethical principles and theories, so that is where we will start.

Ethical Theory

Ethics is the study of what it means to *do the right thing* and how to do the right thing in different situations. Ethics is a huge branch of philosophy and we will not be able to cover more than a small part of it here. We will focus on just a couple of different theories and the tools those theories will give us to figure out how to do the right thing.

Firstly, "ethical theory is based on the assumption that people are rational and make free choices."[1] This isn't always true, obviously, but we'll assume it is and that for the most part people are responsible for their own decisions and actions.

Ethical rules are rules that we follow when we deal with other people and in actions or decisions that affect other people. Most ethical theories have the same goal, "to enhance human dignity, peace, happiness, and well-being."[2] We'll also assume that the ethical rules from an ethical theory apply to everyone and in all situations. These rules should help to clarify our decision making and help lead us to an ethical decision in

---

[1] Baase, Sara. 2003. *A Gift of Fire, 2nd Ed*. Upper Saddle River, NJ: Prentice-Hall, 403.
[2] (Baase 2003, 404)

a particular situation. While behaving ethically is not always easy, it does commonly directly conform to standard social and legal expectations. According to Baase,

> Behaving ethically, in a personal or professional sphere, is usually not a burden. Most of the time we are honest, we keep our promises, we do not steal, we do our jobs. This should not be surprising. If ethical rules are good ones, they work for people, that is, they make our lives better. Behaving ethically is often practical. Honesty makes interactions among people work more smoothly and reliably, for example. We might lose friends if we often lie or break promises. Also, social institutions encourage us to do right: We might be arrested if caught stealing. We might lose our jobs if we do them carelessly. In a professional context, doing good ethically often corresponds closely with doing a good job in the sense of professional quality and competence. Doing good ethically often corresponds closely with good business in the sense that ethically developed products are more likely to please customers. Sometimes, however, it is difficult to do the right thing....Courage in a professional setting could mean admitting to a customer that your program is faulty, declining a job for which you are not qualified, or speaking out when you see someone else doing something wrong.[3]

We'll now explore some different ethical theories from two different schools, the deontological school and the consequentialist school.

Ethical Theory: Deontological Theories

The word *deontology* is derived from the Greek word *deon* and means duty or obligation. Deontologists believe that people's actions ought to be guided by moral laws and that these laws are universal (and in some cases, absolute). Deontological arguments focus on the *intent* of an act, and how that act is or is not defensible as an application of a moral law. They usually do not concern themselves with the consequences of an act, instead emphasizing duty and absolutist rules for how to act.

Deontological school of ethical theory comes out of the work of Immanuel Kant (1724–1804), who believed that all moral laws were based on rational thought and behavior. Kant stresses fidelity to principles and duty. His arguments focus on duty divorced from any concerns about happiness or pleasure. Kant's philosophy is not

---

[3] (Baase 2003, 404)

grounded in knowledge of human nature, but in a common idea of duty that applies to all rational beings: one should do the right thing in the right spirit.[4]

Among Kant's many contributions to deontological theory, the three of the most fundamental ideas are:

1. *There are ethical constants and rules that must apply universally.* This is known as the *Categorical Imperative* or the *Principle of Universality.* In the simplest terms, the categorical imperative is a test of whether an action is right or wrong. If you propose a moral law or rule, can your conception of that law when acted upon apply universally? "Can the action in question pass the test of universalization? If not, the action is immoral and one has a duty to avoid it. The categorical imperative is a moral compass that gives us a convenient and tenable way of knowing when we are acting morally."[5]

2. *You should always act so as to treat yourself and others as ends in themselves and not means to an end.* That is, it is wrong to use a person, meaning every interaction with another person should respect them as a rational human being. "The principle of humanity as an end in itself serves as a limiting condition of every person's freedom of action. We cannot exploit other human beings and treat them exclusively as a means to our ends or purposes."[6]

3. *Logic or reason determine the rules of ethical behavior.* Actions are intrinsically good if they follow from logic or reason. Rationality is the standard for what is good.

Deontologists believe that it is the act that is important in evaluating a moral decision and that the consequences of the act do not enter into determining if the act is morally good or not. Kant takes an extreme position on the absolutism of moral rules. For example, take the moral rule: *It is always wrong to lie.* If a murderer is looking for

---

[4] Spinello, Richard A. 1997. *Case Studies in Information and Computer Ethics.* Upper Saddle River, NJ: Prentice-Hall.

[5] (Spinello 1997, 33)

[6] (Spinello 1997, 34)

his intended victim (whom you just hid in your basement) and asks where they are, according to the *It is always wrong to lie* moral rule, it is ethically wrong for you to lie to protect the intended victim. In the real world, most people would agree that this is a circumstance where the ethical rule should be broken because of the consequences if you do not.[7] We'll come back to this problem with Kant a little later.

As another example of a deontological argument and its problems, let's reflect on the experience of being torn between what we want to do and what we ought to do. Kant says that what we want to do is of no importance. We should always focus on what we ought to do; in other words, we must do our duty. The moral value of an action depends on the underlying moral law.[8] People who act in a dutiful way feel compelled to act that way out of belief and respect for some moral law.

In order to determine if a moral rule is correct or good, we try to apply the principle of universality. Let's work through the example of keeping promises. Say we are in a difficult situation. In order to get out of that situation, we must make a promise that we later intend to break. The moral rule here would be: I am allowed to make promises with the intention of breaking them later. Following the categorical imperative we attempt to universalize this rule, so the universal version of the rule is: it is morally correct for everyone in a difficult situation to make a promise they later break. If this is true, then promises become worthless because everyone would know that there was the possibility they'd be broken later. So there'd be no such thing as a promise anymore. Hence, the moral rule that applies to me becomes useless when we try to universalize it. So this is how, when you are analyzing an ethical dilemma, you apply the principle of universality. In this case, we discover that the rule we started with cannot be extended universally, and so it cannot be a moral rule.

So where are we with respect to deontological ethics? Well, we have a set of assumptions (or axioms) and a means of testing whether new, potential moral laws are correct or not (or right or wrong)—the principle of universality. How well does this work? Let's try to formulate some pros and cons.

What's good about the deontological approach to ethics?

---

[7] (Baase 2003, 405)

[8] Quinn, Michael J. 2005. *Ethics for the Information Age*. Boston: Addison-Wesley. 63.

(1) *It is rational.* It's based on the idea that rational humans can use logic to explain the why behind their actions.

(2) *The principle of universality produces universal moral guidelines.* These guidelines allow us to make clear moral judgments.

(3) *All people are treated as moral equals.* So this gives us an ethical framework to combat discrimination.

What's not so good about the deontological approach to ethics?

(1) *Sometimes no single rule can fully characterize an action.* Example: Stealing food to feed starving children. While there is an ethical rule against stealing, there is also an ethical rule that you should protect children. In this case, these two rules are in conflict.

(2) *Deontological arguments don't provide a way to resolve conflicts between two or more moral rules.* Kant's absolutist position on rules results in the idea that the deontological approach doesn't tell us which rules are more important than others.

(3) *Deontological theories (particularly Kant's) don't allow any exceptions to the moral rules.* This makes them difficult to apply in the real world, where we often need to bend the rules to avoid bad consequences. (But remember, deontological theory doesn't care about consequences; it cares about the act and the rule that the act embodies.)[9]

Ethical Theory: Consequentialism (Teleological Theories)

There is another way to reason about ethical situations, known as a *teleological theory*, which derives its name from the Greek word *telos*, meaning end or goal. Teleological theories focus only on the consequences of an act to determine if the act is good or bad,[10] for which they are also known as *consequentialism*.

---

[9] (Quinn 2005, 66-67)
[10] (Spinello 1997, 27-28)

The classic form of consequentialism is called *utilitarianism*, developed by British philosophers Jeremy Bentham (1748-1832) and John Stuart Mill (1806-1873). Utilitarianism is based on the *Principle of Utility*, which says that an action is morally good or right to the extent that it increases the total happiness (or utility) of the affected parties. The action is morally wrong if it decreases the total happiness. Thus, utility is the tendency of an action to produce happiness (or prevent unhappiness) for an individual or a group of individuals or a community.[11] An action might increase utility for some people and decrease it for others. This is the source of Mill's aphorism "the greatest good for the greatest number."

Consequently, according to utilitarianism we must have a way to calculate the increase or decrease of happiness. This means we also need some common metric for how to measure happiness and we need to be able to calculate the total happiness or unhappiness of an action. This leads us to two variations on utilitarianism.

Act utilitarianism is the theory that an act is good if its net effect (over all the affected people) is to produce more happiness than unhappiness. So act utilitarians apply the principle of utility to individual acts and all the morally significant people that they affect.

For example, say the local county is considering replacing a stretch of very curvy highway with a straight stretch. We need to consider whether this is a good idea or not. In order to do this, we must figure out who is affected by this new construction (who are the stakeholders) and what effect will the construction have on them (what is the cost). Say that in order to construct the highway, the county must take possession of 100 homes that the highway will cut through. Thus, these property holders are stakeholders who will be compensated for their property. Also, say about 5,000 cars drive on the highway every day; these drivers are also stakeholders because the new road may make their commutes shorter, reducing their monetary and time expenditures. More broadly, there will be some kind of an environmental impact because of the new road, which must be calculated as well. If we use money as the measure of utility, then we can attempt to calculate the utility of building the road. Say that the homeowners are compensated with $20 million. On the other hand, say that the car drivers incur a savings of about $2 each or $10,000 per workday for using the road, there are 250 workdays a year and the road will last for 20 years. It costs the county $12 million to build the road and the environmental cost to animal species of lost habitat is calculated to be about $1 million. So the total costs for the highway are about $33 million and the benefit to the drivers is

---

[11] (Quinn 2005, 67-68)

about $50 million. Following act utilitarianism, the action is good and the road should be built. Nevertheless, there are several problems with our calculations. We've not taken into account the unhappiness of the homeowners because some or all of them might not want to sell their homes. The impact on neighborhoods that may be divided by the new road is another cost. The cost of maintenance over 20 years to the county is another, but the value of having fewer accidents on a straight road is a benefit.[12] So, it seems for act utilitarianism we need to take into account more consequences than just the costs involved in the proximate action. It is not practical and often not even feasible to perform this type of calculation on every ethical decision we have to make. Act utilitarianism also doesn't take into account people's innate sense of duty or obligation and how these are accounted for during ethical decisions. It also forces us to reduce all ethical decisions to a positive or negative outcome, many of which are not easily quantifiable. Finally, act utilitarianism leads us to the *problem of moral luck*, where, when faced with an ethical decision, you do not have complete control over all the factors that determine the ethical goodness or badness of an action. The example Quinn uses for moral luck is of a dutiful nephew who sends his bedridden aunt a bouquet of flowers, only to discover that she is allergic to one of the flower species in the bouquet and ends up even sicker. Since the consequences for the aunt were very negative, the action is morally bad, but the nephew's intentions were good.[13] So what's the answer? Maybe we need to make some changes.

A variation of act utilitarianism is *rule utilitarianism*, which applies the principle of utility to general ethical rules instead of to individual actions. So we make the utilitarian calculation for a general ethical rule rather than for individual actions: "rule utilitarianism is the ethical theory that holds we ought to adopt those moral rules which, if followed by everyone, will lead to the greatest increase in happiness."[14] There is that "greatest good for the greatest number" thing again. Let's look at an example.

A computer worm is a self-contained computer program that exploits a security vulnerability, usually in operating system software, to release a payload that will normally do harm to an infected system and also to reproduce itself so it can propagate to other systems. On August 11, 2003, a worm called Blaster was released into the Internet. Blaster exploited a buffer overflow vulnerability in the remote procedure call (RPC) subsystem in the Windows XP and Windows 2000 operating systems in order

---

[12] (Quinn 2005, 69)

[13] (Quinn 2005, 72)

[14] (Quinn 2005, 72)

to access the system, release its payload and propagate. Microsoft had patched this vulnerability back in July 2003, but not all Windows users applied the patch. In roughly four days Blaster infected over 423,000 computers.[15]

On August 18, 2003 a new worm called Welchia was released and it exploited the same RPC vulnerability as the Blaster worm. However, when Welchia installed itself on a target system instead of doing anything harmful it first looked for and deleted the Blaster worm if it was on the target system. It then downloaded the Microsoft patch for the RPC vulnerability, installed it, and rebooted the target system. All copies of Welchia deleted themselves on January 1, 2004. The Welchia worm did all its work without the permission of the target system owner. In the computer security community, a worm like Welchia is known as an anti-worm or a helper worm. The ethical question we have is: was the action of the person who released the Welchia worm ethically good or bad? And, if bad, what might they have done instead? Let's analyze this ethical problem from a rule utilitarian perspective.

To analyze this ethical problem, we must create an appropriate ethical rule and then decide if its universal adoption would increase the utility of all the stakeholders. We first need a rule. "If a harmful computer worm is infecting the Internet, and I can write a helpful worm that automatically removes the harmful worm from infected computers and shields them from future attacks, then I should write and release the helpful worm."[16] What would be the benefits? Well, clearly, every Windows user who had not already updated their computer with the Microsoft patch would benefit because Welchia deletes Blaster, installs the patch, and shields their computer from any further attacks by Blaster. A clear win.

What about harm? Firstly, if everyone followed this rule, then every time there was a new malicious worm released, there would be a flood of helper worms released. This would slow down or clog network traffic. Secondly, what if some of the helper worms contained accidental bugs? Not all helpful programs are perfect, so there is a high probability that some of the helper worms would damage the target systems. This would decrease the safety of the individual computer systems, ultimately harming their owners. Finally, network or system administrators would have a hard time differentiating between malicious worms and helper worms. All they would see is a worm attempting to attack systems, causing false alarms, requiring overtime, and potentially causing missing real threats in the meantime.

---

[15] https://en.wikipedia.org/wiki/Blaster_(computer_worm)

[16] (Quinn 2005, 73)

The harm caused by the ethical rule that allows the release of the helper worms seems to decrease the happiness or utility on the Internet. Consequently, this ethical rule should not be created and the actions of the person who released the Welchia worm are ethically wrong.

It appears that rule utilitarianism keeps the useful parts of act utilitarianism but makes the overall calculation of ethical costs and benefits more straightforward by amplifying the consequences due to the hypothesized universal rule adoption. Additionally, since we use this theory on ethical rules, we also don't have to recalculate the costs and benefits for every act. We're also free to choose which rule we will enforce, which can get us out of ethical dilemmas. Finally, it can eliminate the problem of moral luck. So rule utilitarianism seems like it could be the way to go. Except for one problem.

In both forms of utilitarianism there is the problem that there can be an *unequal distribution of good consequences* across all of the stakeholders. This problem arises because utilitarianism only cares about the total amount of increase in happiness, not how it is distributed across all the stakeholders. For example, suppose acting one way results in everyone getting 100 units of happiness, but acting a different way results in half of stakeholders getting 201 units of happiness each. According to the utilitarian calculation, we should choose the second option because that will result in more total happiness, regardless of the fact that in the second option half the stakeholders are treated unfairly by getting nothing.[17]

John Rawls (1921-2002) tried to fix this problem by proposing two *Principles of Justice*. These principles say that when making ethical decisions that social and economic inequalities are acceptable if they meet the following two conditions: (1) every person in society should have an equal chance to rise to a higher level of social or economic standing and (2) that "social and economic inequalities must be justified. The only way to justify a social or economic inequality is to show that its overall effect is to provide the most benefit to the least advantaged."[18] This second condition is known as the *difference principle*, which provides justification for social policies such as graduated income tax, where those with more income pay higher taxes, while those with less income are entitled to more benefits from society. The two principles of justice are meant to increase equity, providing an overall more level playing field when making ethical decisions.

---

[17] (Quinn 2005, 75)
[18] (Quinn 2005, 79)

Ethical Drivers

In all ethical systems there are a set of constraints and rules that help guide any ethical discussion. Discussing ethical issues in computing and software development is no different. We will look briefly at two of these ethical drivers and how they relate to ethical problems in software development.

Legal Drivers

In all ethical discussions we must remember to consider the law because laws constrain our actions and also guide us down ethical paths that society has decided are acceptable behavior. These kind of legal drivers include laws (federal, state, and local) and government regulations (which are really interpretations of how the laws should be enforced), governing areas like intellectual property, health and safety issues, privacy issues, and data protection.

Professional Drivers

Every profession has a set of ethical drivers that describe how members of the profession are expected to behave. In the case of software development, two professional societies of computing, the *Association for Computing Machinery* (ACM) and the *IEEE Computer Society* (IEEE-CS), have each developed and published codes of conduct for their members. Every software developer should adhere to these codes of conduct. Links to the *ACM Code of Ethics and Professional Conduct*,[19] and the *ACM/IEEE-CS Software Engineering Code of Ethics*[20] are in the footnotes. We will let the ACM/IEEE-CS code's preamble finish off this section. We have highlighted particularly relevant sections.

Professional Drivers: Preamble to the ACM/IEEE-CS Software Engineering Code of Ethics

Computers have a central and growing role in commerce, industry, government, medicine, education, entertainment, and society at large. Software engineers are those

---

[19] Association for Computing Machinery. 2018. *ACM Code of Ethics and Professional Conduct.* New York, NY: ACM. www.acm.org/code-of-ethics.

[20] Gotterbarn, Don, Keith Miller, and Simon Rogerson. 1997. "ACM/IEEE Joint Software Engineering Code of Ethics and Professional Practice." *Communications of the ACM* 40 (11): 110-118. https://ethics.acm.org/code-of-ethics/software-engineering-code/

who contribute by direct participation or by teaching to the analysis, specification, design, development, certification, maintenance and testing of software systems. *Because of their roles in developing software systems, software engineers have significant opportunities to do good or cause harm, to enable others to do good or cause harm, or to influence others to do good or cause harm. To ensure, as much as possible, that their efforts will be used for good, software engineers must commit themselves to making software engineering a beneficial and respected profession.* In accordance with that commitment, software engineers shall adhere to the following Code of Ethics and Professional Practice.

The Code contains eight Principles related to the behavior of and decisions made by professional software engineers, including practitioners, educators, managers, supervisors and policy makers, as well as trainees and students of the profession. *The Principles identify the ethically responsible relationships in which individuals, groups, and organizations participate and the primary obligations within these relationships.* The Clauses of each Principle are illustrations of some of the obligations included in these relationships. *These obligations are founded in the software engineer's humanity, in special care owed to people affected by the work of software engineers, and in the unique elements of the practice of software engineering. The Code prescribes these as obligations of anyone claiming to be or aspiring to be a software engineer.*

It is not intended that the individual parts of the Code be used in isolation to justify errors of omission or commission. The list of Principles and Clauses is not exhaustive. The Clauses should not be read as separating the acceptable from the unacceptable in professional conduct in all practical situations. *The Code is not a simple ethical algorithm that generates ethical decisions.* In some situations, standards may be in tension with each other or with standards from other sources. These situations require the software engineer to use ethical judgment to act in a manner that is most consistent with the spirit of the Code of Ethics and Professional Practice, given the circumstances.

Ethical tensions can best be addressed by thoughtful consideration of fundamental principles, rather than blind reliance on detailed regulations. These Principles should influence software engineers to consider broadly who is affected by their work; to examine if they and their colleagues are treating other human beings with due respect; to consider how the public, if reasonably well informed, would view their decisions; to analyze how the least empowered will be affected by their decisions; and to consider whether their acts would be judged worthy of the ideal professional working as a software engineer. In all these judgments concern for the health, safety and welfare of the public is primary; that is, the "Public Interest" is central to this Code.

The dynamic and demanding context of software engineering requires a code that is adaptable and relevant to new situations as they occur. However, even in this generality, the Code provides support for software engineers and managers of software engineers who need to take positive action in a specific case by documenting the ethical stance of the profession. *The Code provides an ethical foundation to which individuals within teams and the team as a whole can appeal. The Code helps to define those actions that are ethically improper to request of a software engineer or teams of software engineers.*

The Code is not simply for adjudicating the nature of questionable acts; it also has an important educational function. As this Code expresses the consensus of the profession on ethical issues, it is a means to educate both the public and aspiring professionals about the ethical obligations of all software engineers.

The eight principles mentioned above are:

1. PUBLIC – Software engineers shall act consistently with the public interest.

2. CLIENT AND EMPLOYER – Software engineers shall act in a manner that is in the best interests of their client and employer consistent with the public interest.

3. PRODUCT – Software engineers shall ensure that their products and related modifications meet the highest professional standards possible.

4. JUDGMENT – Software engineers shall maintain integrity and independence in their professional judgment.

5. MANAGEMENT – Software engineering managers and leaders shall subscribe to and promote an ethical approach to the management of software development and maintenance.

6. PROFESSION – Software engineers shall advance the integrity and reputation of the profession consistent with the public interest.

7. COLLEAGUES – Software engineers shall be fair to and supportive of their colleagues.

8. SELF – Software engineers shall participate in lifelong learning regarding the practice of their profession and shall promote an ethical approach to the practice of the profession.[21]

---

[21] https://ethics.acm.org/code-of-ethics/software-engineering-code/

Similarly, the ACM Code of Ethics contains a set of general ethical principles that all computer scientists should follow. They include (using the ACM's numbering):

> 1.1 Contribute to society and to human well-being, acknowledging that all people are stakeholders in computing.
>
> 1.2 Avoid harm. That is, any negative consequences.
>
> 1.3 Be honest and trustworthy.
>
> 1.4 Be fair and take action not to discriminate.
>
> 1.5 Respect the work required to produce new ideas, inventions, creative works, and computing artifacts.
>
> 1.6 Respect privacy.
>
> 1.7 Honor confidentiality.[22]

Ethical Discussion and Decision Making

Given the above theories, a decision to an ethical problem can be reached by first identifying and describing the problem, and then by analyzing the problem and coming to a decision. A sample plan for how to carry out these two tasks is presented below.

Discussion 1: Identifying and Describing the Problem

1. Write down the statement of the ethical problem. This will help to clarify what exactly you're talking about.

2. List the risks, problems, and possible consequences.

3. List all the stakeholders. This will include you and anyone else involved in the ethical situation, as well as anyone affected by the consequences of the decision, both directly and indirectly.

4. Identify all the possible ethical issues in each case. Try to establish the rights and wrongs of the situation and figure out what ethical rules might be involved.

---

[22] www.acm.org/binaries/content/assets/about/acm-code-of-ethics-booklet.pdf

5. Identify all the possible legal issues. This includes intellectual property issues and health and safety issues.

6. List possible actions if the problem is more complex than a simple yes/no.

Discussion 2: Analyzing the Problem

1. What are your first impressions or reactions to these issues? What does your *moral intuition* say?

2. Identify the responsibilities of the decision maker. This involves things like reporting ethical problems if you're an employee and what your responsibilities might be as a manager.

3. Identify the rights of all stakeholders.

4. Consider the consequences of the action options on the stakeholders. Analyze the consequences, risks, benefits, harms, and costs for each action considered.

5. Find the sections of the SE Code and the ACM code that pertain to the problem and the actions. This will help you with the ethical rules and in laying out the situation so you can consider alternatives.

6. Consider the deontological and utilitarian approaches to the problem. You'll need to have the ethical rules you've considered in front of you, as well as the sections of the SE and ACM codes of ethics. Then run through our examples here of other ethical situations and follow those examples for your own situation.

7. Do the ethical theories point to one course of action? If more than one, which one should take precedence? List the different courses of action and then, if necessary, try to prioritize them. This will help you think about different courses of action.

8. Which of the potential actions do you think is the right one?
    Pick it. If you're using a utilitarian approach, you might consider
    picking a metric and seeing if you can measure the effects of the
    decision.

9. If there are several ethically acceptable options, pick one. Reflect
    on your decision.

Case Studies

In this section, we'll present several short case studies that illustrate the types of ethical
problems you might encounter as a software developer. These case studies will cover
ethical situations involving intellectual property, privacy issues, system safety issues,
and conflicts of interest. Your job is to analyze each case study, identify the ethical issues,
and propose a course of action. Be aware that there may not be one "right" answer to the
particular ethical problem.

#1 Copying Software

Jane Hudson teaches mathematics at an inner city high school in Chicago. Like many
rural and inner city high schools, Jane's school has very little money to spend on
computers and software. While her students do very well and have even placed in
a statewide math competition, many of her students come to high school woefully
underprepared for high school mathematics, so Jane and her colleagues spend a lot of
time on remedial work. Recently, a local company has offered to donate 24 iMacs to
Jane's high school. It has been decided that a dozen of these computers will be used to
create a mathematics computer lab specifically to help students with remedial work in
pre-algebra, algebra, geometry, and trigonometry. Jane wants to use a software program
called MathTutor for the computer lab, but a site-wide license for the titles she wants is
$5,000, money that her school just does not have. The high school already has one copy
of MathTutor and there is no copy protection on the program. Jane's department chair
has suggested that they just make copies of the program for the new computers. Jane
does not think that this is a good idea, but she is desperate to use the new computers
to help her students. What should Jane do? What are the ethical issues here? (See ACM
Code 1.5 and 2.3; SE Code 2.02.)

#2 Whose Computer Is It?

At Massive Corporation, you are a software development manager. A developer on one of your software projects is out sick. Another developer asks that you copy all the files from the sick developer's computer to his, so that he can do some important work. What should you do? What are the ethical issues here? (See ACM Code 1.7, 2.8, and 3.3.)

#3 How Much Testing Is Enough?

You are the project manager for a development team that is in the final stages of a project to create software that uses radiation therapy to destroy cancerous tumors. Once set up by an operator, the software controls the intensity, duration, and direction of the radiation. Since this is a new piece of software in a new product, there have been a series of problems and delays. The program is in the middle stages of system testing and the routine testing that has been done so far has all gone well, with very few software defects found. Your project manager wants to cut the rest of the testing short in order to meet the (updated) software delivery deadline. This will mean just doing the routine testing and skipping the scheduled stress testing. You are trying to decide whether to ship the software on time and then continue the testing afterwards, shipping patches for any defects found. What are the ethical issues here? (You should look up the Therac-25 problem as a similar instance of a case like this at `https://en.wikipedia.org/wiki/Therac-25`.) (See ACM Code 1.1, 1.2, 2.1, and 3.4; SE Code 1.03, 1.04, 3.06, and 3.10.)

#4 How Much Should You Tell?

You are a principal in the J2MD computer software consulting company. One of your clients, the City of Charleston, SC, wants your company to evaluate a set of proposals for a new administrative computing system and provide a recommendation to the city on which proposal to accept. The contract for the new system would be worth several million dollars to the winning company. Your spouse works for LowCountry Computing (one of the bidding companies) and she is the project manager in charge of writing their proposal to the city. You have seen early copies of her proposal and judge it to be excellent. Should you tell the project manager in the City of Charleston about your spouse's employment at LowCountry Computing? If so, when, and how much else should you reveal? (See ACM Code 1.3 and 2.5; SE Code Principle 4, 4.05, and 4.06.)

#5 Abusive Workplace Behavior[23]

Jane is a new hire in a high-tech company's generative AI research team. Jane did well in graduate school and her advisor worked closely with her and made sure she received appropriate credit for all her contributions. She generally does excellent work and was hired for her potential as a top-notch researcher. The technical lead of her new department, Gary, has a reputation as an excellent researcher. However, he usually insists on claiming primary authorship on every publication the team produces. He also has a very short temper, doesn't tolerate even minor errors, and retaliates against those who he thinks are questioning him or making mistakes—all of them women—by removing their names from submitted research articles. Jane soon comes under Gary's gaze when she checks in some code containing a minor timing error into the shared repository. Gary refuses to let Jane participate in a live demo of the software. Jane goes to her supervisor to complain. What ethical principles is Gary violating and what should Jane's supervisor do?

Gary's behavior certainly seems unprofessional and abusive. It clearly violates ACM guidelines 1.1, 1.2, 1.4, and 1.5. Jane's supervisor needs to confront Gary about his behavior. This comes under ACM guideline 3.3 which talks about leaders "providing for the psychological well-being and human dignity of the team," and guideline 3.4 which "has leaders articulate, apply, and support policies that reflect the principles of the Code."[24]

The Last Word on Ethics

Every software development professional will encounter ethical problems during the course of their career. How you handle those ethical situations will say a lot about your professional behavior and moral character. To wrap up this discussion of professional practice, let's look at one more list of fundamental ethical principles that you should carry with you throughout your career. The original list comes largely from Quinn, though it has been modified over the years.[25]

---

[23] This case study is modeled on one from the ACM Code of Ethics booklet.

[24] (ACM Code of Ethics booklet 2018, 19)

[25] (Quinn 2005, 383-384)

1. *Be impartial.* You will have some amount of loyalty to your company, but you also must have loyalty to society as a whole and to yourself. Make sure you remember that.

2. *Disclose information that others ought to have.* Don't hide information from people who need to know it. Don't be deceptive or deliberately misleading. Make sure you disclose any conflicts of interest.

3. *Respect the rights of others.* This includes intellectual property rights, civil rights, and other property rights. Don't steal, misuse, or misrepresent the property and contributions of others.

4. *Treat others fairly.* Don't discriminate against others. Make sure that others receive fair wages and benefits and credit for work done.

5. *Take responsibility for your own actions and inactions.* Take responsibility for everything you do—or don't do—whether good or bad.

6. *Take responsibility for the actions of those you supervise.* The old saying "The buck stops here" applies to you as a manager as well. This also includes making sure you communicate effectively with your employees.

7. *Maintain your integrity.* Deliver on your commitments. Be loyal to your employer (as long as they also operate in an ethical manner). Do not ask someone to do anything you would not do yourself.

8. *Continually improve your abilities.* Software development and the computer industry as a whole are in a constant state of flux. Tools and languages you used in college will be obsolete five years later. Make sure you are a lifelong learner.

9. *Share your knowledge, expertise, and values.* The more experience you acquire in your profession, the more you are obligated to share your knowledge and expertise with your coworkers and subordinates. You should also set an example for others by living these values.

References

Association for Computing Machinery. 2018. *ACM Code of Ethics and Professional Conduct*. New York, NY: ACM. `www.acm.org/code-of-ethics`.

Gotterbarn, Don, Keith Miller, and Simon Rogerson. 1997. "ACM/IEEE Joint Software Engineering Code of Ethics and Professional Practice." *Communications of the ACM* 40 (11): 110–18. `https://ethics.acm.org/code-of-ethics/software-engineering-code/`.

Baase, Sara. 2003. *A Gift of Fire, 2nd Ed.* Upper Saddle River, NJ: Prentice-Hall.

Quinn, Michael J. 2005. *Ethics for the Information Age*. Boston: Addison-Wesley.

Spinello, Richard A. 1997. *Case Studies in Information and Computer Ethics*. Upper Saddle River, NJ: Prentice-Hall.

Spinello, Richard A., and Herman T. Tavani. 2004. *Readings in CyberEthics, 2nd Ed.* Sudbury, MA: Jones and Bartlett Publishers.

CHAPTER 5

Intellectual Property, Obligations, and Ownership

He who receives an idea from me, receives instruction himself without less-ening mine; as he who lights his taper at mine, receives light without dark-ening me. That ideas should freely spread from one to another over the globe, for the moral and mutual instruction of man, and improvement of his condition, seems to have been peculiarly and benevolently designed by nature, when she made them, like fire, expansible over all space, without lessening their density in any point, and like the air in which we breathe, move, and have our physical being, incapable of confinement or exclusive appropriation.

—Thomas Jefferson

In this chapter, we will talk about a number of issues concerning teams and companies that, while not necessarily affecting software development, are central to the ultimate end of your work, the software itself.[1]

Who Owns What?

When you are working for an established company, or working on a team on a project, or in a start-up, the question of *who owns the software* you are producing comes up regularly. If you work for an established company, say Microsoft, Google, Amazon,

---

[1] Caveat: We are not lawyers. This chapter is based on our own research and experiences working on teams and for companies developing software. If you have any questions or issues with intellectual property rights, consult with a lawyer.

© John F. Dooley and Vera A. Kazakova 2024
J. F. Dooley and V. A. Kazakova, *Software Development, Design, and Coding*,
https://doi.org/10.1007/979-8-8688-0285-0_5

or even General Motors, ownership is usually pretty straightforward. On your first day of work you'll fill out a number of forms, mostly for taxes. But there will be one form in which you are required, as a condition of employment, to give away the rights to all the intellectual property you create while you are working for the company and/or using the company's resources.[2] From that day on everything you create or modify for the company is known as a "work for hire" and belongs to the company.[3]

Start-ups are somewhat different, particularly if you are one of the original creators of the start-up company. In that case, all of you will create and sign a contract that describes what you'll be producing as a company and allocates a certain percentage of the company or a percentage of the product proceeds to each of the creators. You will essentially all own the intellectual property and all "joint work" together and will agree how things are divided up. Team projects as part of a class or college project work similarly to start-ups. There may be many unique team-specific and project-specific quirks in this process and lots of discussion about actual percentages for each person on the team. These discussions need to happen early, they need to happen constructively, and they need to happen with accurate understanding of everyone's rights and responsibilities with respect to the "joint work." Neglecting to reach an explicit agreement by properly and preemptively addressing everyone's concerns can destroy your teamwork, project, or even company before it gets off the ground, so it is important to understand what intellectual property is, who owns it, and how it can be divided.

What Is Intellectual Property?

Intellectual property (IP) is a category of property that includes intangible creations of the human intellect. The products of human intellect are characterized in the law as *non-rivalrous public goods*.[4] This means that the same product may be used simultaneously by more than one person without diminishing the availability of that product for use by others. So while only one person can drive your car at a time, many people can use Microsoft Excel at once.

---

[2] This does not include any software you write on your own time, using your own computer and software. All that work is yours.

[3] www.nolo.com/legal-encyclopedia/copyright-ownership-rights-29953.html

[4] https://en.wikipedia.org/wiki/Rivalry_(economics)

The law of intellectual property is designed to provide an incentive to authors and inventors to produce works for the benefit of the public. The public's use of such works is regulated to ensure that authors and inventors are compensated for their efforts. So intellectual property law protects the work of authors and inventors and also allows limited use of those works by others, allowing the authors and inventors to profit from their work.

In the United States, intellectual property protections are enshrined in the U.S. Constitution, Article I, Section 8, Clause 8, which says "The Congress shall have power ... To promote the progress of science and useful arts, by securing for limited times to authors and inventors the exclusive right to their respective writings and discoveries."[5] All other countries also have intellectual property laws, but they may differ in certain particulars from those of the United States.

We'll look at three different types of intellectual property protection that will likely come into play when one is writing computer software. They are *public domain*, *copyright*, and *patents*.

Intellectual Property: Public Domain Works

Copyright, patents, and trademarks all provide a degree of protection to the original creator or inventor of a work from others using their work without fair compensation, for a fixed period of time. The length of time that a creative work or invention is protected varies from country to country and by the type of the original work. Any creative work that is not so protected is considered to be in the *public domain*. Note that eventually, all creative works and inventions end up in the public domain, and public domain is forever. Public domain means that anyone can reproduce the work, change it, perform it, create physical products from it, and so on, and they do not have to provide compensation to the original creator or inventor, nor do they have to get permission to make their changes. For example, you can perform your modern version of Hamlet and not have to send William Shakespeare a check because all of his works are in the public domain.

---

[5] https://constitution.congress.gov/browse/essay/artI-S8-C8-1/ALDE_00013060/

Intellectual Property: Copyright

According to the U.S. Copyright Office, "Copyright is a type of intellectual property that protects **original works of authorship** as soon as an author **fixes** the work in a **tangible form of expression**. In copyright law, there are a lot of different types of works, including paintings, photographs, illustrations, musical compositions, sound recordings, computer programs, books, poems, blog posts, movies, architectural works, [and] plays."[6]

As mentioned, copyright is enshrined in the U.S. Constitution, which was ratified in 1788. The first copyright law was passed by Congress in 1790. This law provided for a term of 14 years for the initial copyright, with an allowance for a renewal of the copyright for 14 more years.[7] You were required to register the copyright with the U.S. Copyright Office and to register it again in order to renew the copyright. You were also required to label your work as copyrighted.

In 1830, the terms for initial copyright and renewal were extended to 28 years each.

The Copyright Act of 1976 eliminated the requirement for mandatory formal registration and the requirement for renewal. So since 1976 any creative work is automatically copyrighted as soon as it is created and put it into a "tangible" or "fixed" form, including paper, film, computer memory, and so on. The act also extended the term of copyright to either 75 years or the life of the author plus 50 years, as well as removed the requirement to label your work as copyrighted. Notwithstanding, it is usually good practice to label your work with a copyright notice, even though it is no longer required. Note that this book has a copyright notice on the back side of the title page.

An update to the Copyright Act in 1998 further extended the term of copyright to either 120 years or the life of the author plus 70 years.[8] This update is colloquially known as the "Mickey Mouse Protection Act" because it was widely thought that the very long extension of copyright protection was designed to protect the Walt Disney Company's copyright of the Mickey Mouse character well into the 2020s.

---

[6] www.copyright.gov/what-is-copyright/
[7] After the renewal period, the work passed into the public domain.
[8] www.copyright.gov/title17/

What Rights Do You Have Under Copyright?

In the United States, once your work is copyrighted, you are entitled to six exclusive rights with regard to the work:[9]

- The right to reproduce the work
- The right to create derivative works (for example, adapting a book into a play)
- The right to distribute copies, or transfer ownership of the work
- The right to perform the work publicly
- The right to display the work publicly
- The right to perform the work publicly via digital audio or video transmission

Nobody else has these rights unless you formally assign them to someone else.

What Can You Copyright?

Only creative intellectual property in a fixed form is eligible for copyright. In the United States, you can copyright the following types of works:[10]

- Literary works
- Musical works
- Dramatic works
- Pantomimes and choreographic works
- Pictorial, graphic, and sculptural works
- Audio-visual works
- Sound recordings
- Derivative works
- Compilations

---

[9] www.copyright.gov/what-is-copyright/
[10] www.copyright.gov/circs/circ01.pdf

- Architectural works

- Computer software

What You Cannot Copyright

You are not allowed to copyright the following:[11]

- Unfixed works that have not been recorded in a tangible, fixed form (for example, that song that you made up and sang in the shower today)

- Work that is already in the public domain

- Titles, names, short phrases, and slogans

- Familiar symbols or designs

- Numbers and facts about math, including formulas

- Ideas and facts

- Processes and systems (for example, the Dewey Decimal System can't be copyrighted)

- Grammatical tropes (for example, "I before E except after C" can't be copyrighted)

- Recipes (but just the list of ingredients. The instructions on how to combine the ingredients can be copyrighted. You can also use the recipe to make a dish for your family without getting permission.)

- Anything produced as a result of working for the U.S. Federal Government cannot be copyrighted; all such work is automatically in the public domain.

- User interfaces (but you can get a design patent for user interfaces. More on this below.)

---

[11] www.copyright.gov/circs/circ01.pdf

Copyright Conflicts: Apple vs. Microsoft and User Interface Design

In the mid-1980s, after the release of the first Apple Macintosh computer and its advanced graphical user interface (GUI), Apple licensed parts of the graphical interface to Microsoft, who wanted to use the parts in its Windows 1.0 product. In 1987, when Microsoft revealed details of the next Windows iteration, Windows 2.0, Apple sued Microsoft for copyright infringement, claiming that many of the user interface elements of the new Windows were stolen from the Macintosh. In their case, Apple emphasized that the court should consider the "look and feel" of the entire user interface, rather than just individual elements. They claimed that the "look and feel" of the Macintosh GUI was covered by copyright.[12]

In the midst of this case, Xerox Corporation sued Apple for copyright infringement claiming that the Macintosh user interface itself was copied from the Xerox Alto computer, which had been introduced in the late 1970s. In 1981 and 1982, Apple Macintosh engineers, including Apple CEO Steve Jobs, had visited Xerox's Palo Alto Research Center (PARC) and had been shown the Alto and its unique (at the time) graphical user interface. Xerox contended in their suit that the Mac's GUI was directly derived from the Alto's, and its implementation went beyond a similar technology sharing agreement between Apple and Xerox PARC.

At the end of the day, the Microsoft and Apple settled prior to a jury trial of the case. The judge wrote that you could copyright the expression of an idea, but not the idea itself, and that Apple's "look and feel" was an idea. So it was the individual pieces of the user interface that were copyrightable, and not the entire thing. For example, you cannot copyright the idea of a clickable button, but you can copyright the artistic design of a specific button. Hence Apple's Trashcan icon is protected by copyright, but the idea of throwing files away in a particular location is not. Similarly, you cannot copyright the use of a pop-up dialog box (the idea), but you can copyright your specific written explanation in a pop-up that you create.

The more artistic and original your design is, the more protection copyright offers. But protection by copyright is limited and, while copyright may protect some individual design elements, copyright is not a good way to protect an entire user interface. For that, one should use a *design patent* (see the "Patents" section below).

---

[12] See https://en.wikipedia.org/wiki/Apple_Computer,_Inc._v._Microsoft_Corp.

Fair Use: The Copyright "Get out of Jail Free" Card

Occasionally, you can use parts of a copyrighted work without having to get permission. This is known as "fair use."[13] A use of a copyrighted work must meet four criteria in order to be considered as fair use:

1. *Purpose and character of the use*: How the party claiming fair use is using the copyrighted work. Not-for-profit and educational uses are considered acceptable, while commercial uses are not.[14] For example, the use of some or all of a copyrighted work in a classroom as part of a course is usually okay.

2. *Nature of the copyrighted work*: More creative works get more protection. For example, written fiction and poetry are presumed to have higher copyright protection.

3. *Amount of the work used*: The amount used in relation to the size of the whole copyrighted work. Smaller is better. For novels, a few hundred words is likely okay, for songs and video productions, less than 10% of the work is also typically allowed.

4. *Effect of the use on the potential market for or value of the copyrighted work.* If your use of part of a copyrighted work does not diminish the market or value of the work, it's probably okay.

The bottom line with respect to use of copyrighted works is that things like criticism, comment, news reporting, teaching, scholarship, parody/satire, and research are all examples of activities that generally qualify as fair use. Copying a song from a CD or the Internet and sharing or selling it would definitely not qualify as fair use. For an example, see the Napster case.[15]

---

[13] www.copyright.gov/fair-use/more-info.html

[14] This applies to both for-profit and not-for-profit educational institutions. See https://tmupublic.blob.core.windows.net/public-archive/Media/578456/Comparison.pdf.

[15] https://en.wikipedia.org/wiki/Napster

Intellectual Property: Patents

Under United States law, a patent is a right granted to the inventor of a process, machine, article of manufacture, or composition of matter that

1. is new and useful,

2. is non-obvious,

3. has industrial applicability, also known as *functional utility* (that is, it has to do something),

4. and it cannot be *"prior art,"* meaning it can't have been patented before.[16]

The inventor gets a patent—protection from the government for a fixed amount of time—in exchange for the public disclosure of their invention.

What Is a Patent?

A patent is the *right to exclude others* for a limited time (usually 20 years in the U.S.) from profiting off a new invention or technology without the consent of the patent holder. The patent holder can license the patent to someone else in order to manufacture, sell, import or export the device. However, unless you have a license, you cannot use the patent. Patent licenses can be free, or they can involve a royalty payment to the patent holder. Patents are also only usually recognized in the country where the patent is issued, so if you want to market your new device in the United States, the European Union, the United Kingdom, and China, you must obtain patents in all those jurisdictions. There are treaties that allow some patents to be recognized in several jurisdictions.

You cannot renew a patent. Once its term has expired it is considered to be in the *public domain*. Once the patent is in the public domain, anyone can create products from the patent without needing to obtain a license or paying any licensing fees to the original patent holder. This non-renewal is one reason of many why pharmaceutical companies charge so much for new drugs. They only have 20 years to make back all the money invested in creating it and to make a profit for their shareholders. Once a drug has entered the public domain, any other drug company can make that drug, which become the *generic* versions. The only way around the non-renewal is for the original patent holder to get a new patent for an *improvement* or *modification* of the original patent.

---

[16] www.uspto.gov/patents/basics/essentials

What You Can't Patent

You are not allowed to patent

- an abstract idea,

- physical phenomena,

- mathematical equations,

- laws of nature,

- living things,

- the elements,

- mental processes,

- printed matter,

- most business methods, and

- computer software (sort of. We'll talk about patenting software in some detail next.)

Software Patents

Any computer source code that you write is automatically protected by copyright, but this only covers the actual source code text. Copyright doesn't protect any of the new or novel algorithms in your code, nor your new process for implementing an existing algorithm, and so on. For that you would need a patent. For mechanical or electrical inventions that end up as physical products or novel processes to create a product, describing, submitting an application for, and acquiring a patent is pretty straightforward. Securing software patents is, unfortunately, a bit more complex.

Firstly, software is not a physical product. For another, it changes form in order to be useful. You can write a novel program, but your source code is not an executable format. You first have to change the form of your software from source code into machine code, for a particular target machine, via a compiler, in order to get it to execute. Secondly, even as an executable, your software cannot work on its own. It must execute under a particular operating system, which in turn must operate on a particular type of computer (a piece of hardware) to produce the output it is designed to create. (Your Mac app won't run on Windows unless you rewrite and recompile it to do so.) Also, remember that list of things that cannot be patented; we cannot patent abstract ideas, mathematical equations, mental processes, and most business methods. This issue alone would make acquiring a meaningfully protective patent on a piece of software difficult. And just to make matters even more interesting, software is not mentioned anywhere in U.S. patent law, nor is the phrase "software patent" defined.[17]

The U.S. government has been wrestling with the idea of software patents since at least 1972 when the Patent Office issued a patent for an algorithm to convert binary-coded decimal (BCD) numbers into purely binary representations.[18] However, 42 years later, in 2014, the U.S. Supreme Court upended that case and invalidated most other software patents in a case called *Alice Corp vs. CLS Bank International*[19] by deciding that most software was not patentable because it represented *abstract ideas* and should therefore be considered *prior art*. In an effort to provide some clarity for software patent applications, the Supreme Court defined a test which is now known as the *Alice-Mayo* framework. Under the two-part Alice-Mayo framework, the Patent Office requires that (1) the newly discovered mathematical formula or algorithm be assumed as known (i.e. it is *prior art*), and (2) the patent application must contain an additional "inventive concept" that limits the application of (1) to a specific and non-trivial use.[20]

In the years subsequent to the Alice Corp decision and the creation of the Alice-Mayo framework, the courts and the U.S. Patent Office have continued to wrestle with how to categorize software innovations that may be patentable. They have focused on patent claims that were "directed to a specific improvement to the way computers operate, embodied in the self-referential table."[21] This implies that even though algorithms are typically considered prior art, software patent claims that emphasize "a specific improvement to the way computers operate" can be patentable. The story continues...[22]

---

[17] https://en.wikipedia.org/wiki/Software_patents_under_United_States_patent_law
[18] https://en.wikipedia.org/wiki/Gottschalk_v._Benson
[19] https://arstechnica.com/tech-policy/2014/06/
supreme-court-smashes-do-it-on-a-computer-patents-in-9-0-opinion/
[20] https://en.wikipedia.org/wiki/Patentable_subject_matter_in_the_United_States
[21] https://arstechnica.com/tech-policy/2016/12/
these-three-2016-cases-gave-new-life-to-software-patents/
[22] www.uspto.gov/web/offices/pac/mpep/s2106.html#ch2100_d2e7df_24a6e_1bd

Types of Patents

There are three general types of patents:

1. *Design patents* are patents issued for original, new, and ornamental designs for manufactured products. Design patents protect the design or look of something. They require the design of the invention to be original and useful. Design patents last for 15 years for applications filed after May 13, 2015. While you can't copyright a "look and feel," you can patent it as a design patent. Design patents can protect the "look and feel" of a graphical user interface (GUI). A design patent is infringed if another GUI would be confused for yours by an ordinary observer. Note that design patents do not protect the functional aspects of a UI. For that you need a utility patent.

2. *Utility patents*, or patents for invention, give legal protection to people who invent a new and useful process, an article of manufacture, or a composition of matter. Utility patents are normally used to protect new physical devices, say a particular type of electric bicycle or a new type of ceiling fan. Utility patents last for 20 years and require periodic maintenance fees. If you don't pay the maintenance fee, the patent lapses. Utility patents are what most people think of when you use the word "patent."

3. *Plant patents*[23] (yes, the growing/living kind) go to anyone who produces, discovers, and invents a new kind of plant capable of reproduction. So, for example, a new variety of rose that you create is patentable. These patents are granted for 20 years from the date of filing and no maintenance fees apply. Note that plant patents do not apply to things like DNA, RNA, drugs, genomes, and such, which require utility patents.

---

[23] www.uspto.gov/patents/basics/apply/plant-patent

Intellectual Property: Ownership and You

At the beginning of this chapter we discussed how working on team projects, principally in classes, research labs, and start-ups, is different with respect to ownership of intellectual property, particularly computer software. This is especially true for copyright, as the Copyright Act distinguishes between *individual work, derivative work,* and *joint work.*

An *individual work* is obviously a work created—and owned—by a single person.

A *derivative work* is a product based on an existing, copyrighted work.[24] Copyright holders have the right to create derivative works from their own work. If someone else creates a derivative work, say a video of a novel, without getting permission from the copyright holder, that is *copyright infringement* and the copyright holder can sue for damages.

This brings us to *joint work.*[25] A *joint work*[26] is a product made by more than one creator. Section 101 of the U.S. Copyright act defines joint work as "a work prepared by two or more authors with the intention that their contributions be merged into inseparable or interdependent parts of a unitary whole." This includes the kind of work that a class team project entails or the shared output of a start-up. All members of the creative team (not just the developers) own the copyright to the final product jointly and equally. This has a number of ramifications. For instance, since all the participants on the team own the copyright, any one of them can make changes to the source code, creating a derivative work. Second, without consulting their co-owners, they can also license the source code to someone else who intends to use the product or make changes to it, creating their own derivative work. Needless to say, most organizations require the participants to sign a contract explicitly laying out what each person can and cannot do with the joint work and who would own the copyright to any derivative works.[27]

There is one more wrinkle in the *joint work* complexity. If a single person has an idea for a product and puts that idea into a fixed form, say in a notebook, or as a prototype of a software implementation, then they own the copyright to that work product (that specific expression or implementation of the idea). If they then join a team or create a start-up

---

[24] www.legalzoom.com/articles/what-are-derivative-works-under-copyright-law

[25] www.law.cornell.edu/wex/joint_work

[26] www.law.cornell.edu/wex/joint_work

[27] https://copyright.universityofcalifornia.edu/ownership/joint-works.html

whose purpose is to implement and expand the original idea, then the idea of *joint work* gets a bit murky. First of all, the original person owns the copyright to the original work product. But, once the team engages in the endeavor of creating a joint work, essentially creating a derivative work of the original, then the members of the team own the copyright of the subsequent joint work equally. Any member of the team can license the work or make changes to it themselves, so it is important to agree on the ownership of the derivative work before creating it. There is, however, also the issue that the original work is copyrighted by the original author, and so the team member who creates a new, independent, derivative work will need to get the original author's permission, or obtain a license, to use any parts that were in the original copyrighted work. If not handled properly, preemptively, and equitably, any of these complexities could result in major problems for the team, both legally and interpersonally, hindering collaboration, and ultimately the product itself.

In short, for team projects not bound by preimposed ownership agreements (such as those of an employer), make sure you have an explicit and detailed signed agreement before you begin creating the work.

References

ACM. 1992. *ACM Code of Ethics and Professional Conduct.* New York, NY: ACM. Retrieved August 18, 2017. www.acm.org.

Nolo. 2023. *Who Owns the Rights to a Copyright?* Los Angeles, CA. www.nolo.com/legal-encyclopedia/copyright-ownership-rights-29953.html.

United States Copyright Office. 2020. *Copyright in Derivative Works and Compilations.* Washington, DC. www.copyright.gov/circs/circ14.pdf.

United States Copyright Office. 2020. *Copyright Law of the United States (Title 17).* Washington, DC. www.copyright.gov/title17/.

United States Patent and Trademark Office. 2021. *Laws, regulations, policies, procedures, guidance and training.* Washington, DC. www.uspto.gov/patents/laws.

CHAPTER 6

Requirements

The hardest single part of building a software system is deciding <u>what to build</u>. No other part of the conceptual work is as difficult in establishing the detailed technical requirements, including the interfaces to people, to machines, and to other software systems. No other part of the work so cripples the results if done wrong. No other part is more difficult to rectify later. Therefore, the most important function that the software builder performs for the client is the iterative extraction and refinement of the product requirements.

—Fred Brooks[1]

Before you start coding—yes, *before* you start coding—you need to know what it is you're going to build. That's what requirements are: a list of stuff you have to implement in order to create your terrific program. Most developers hate requirements. Really. All we'd like to do is sit down and start coding. All of us have that super-programmer mentality; just give us the problem and we can sit down and design and code it on the fly. Not! If you want to be a productive developer and make fewer errors and come up with a good, clean design, you need requirements. The more detailed they are, the better. A good set of requirements tells you just what the program is supposed to do. It gives you the scaffolding around which you'll hang your design. You'll do requirements anyway— it's one of those steps in a standard development lifecycle that you can't avoid—but if you don't make room for it in your project, you won't create a great program. Being intentional about requirements forces you to think about the details of the program, and it also lets you listen to the users so you have a better idea of what they really want. So let's talk about requirements.

---

[1] Brooks, Frederick P. 1995. *The Mythical Man-Month : Essays on Software Engineering, Silver Anniversary Edition*. Paperback. Vol. Anniversary. Boston, MA: Addison-Wesley.

© John F. Dooley and Vera A. Kazakova 2024
J. F. Dooley and V. A. Kazakova, *Software Development, Design, and Coding,*
https://doi.org/10.1007/979-8-8688-0285-0_6

What Types of Requirements Are We Talking About?

We're really talking about *functional requirements*. That is, the list of features the user will see and be able to use when they fire up your program. These are the "black box" requirements that show the external behavior of your program. As far as the user is concerned, these are the only requirements that matter. In a plan-driven process, the output of this activity of identifying requirements is a *functional specification* of what the software system is supposed to do. For an agile process, the output is a set of *user stories* that define the *product backlog*.

During the course of uncovering requirements for your project, you will usually see four different types: user requirements, domain requirements, non-functional requirements, and non-requirements.

User Requirements

User requirements are nearly always expressed in natural language. They are the details of what the user expects to see as they use the program. They also include descriptions of screen layouts, dialog boxes, and menus. Any interaction element in the program should be described in the user requirements. For example:

Logging into the system: When Gloria clicks on the Login button on the main page, a login dialog box appears in the middle of the screen. The login dialog must contain two text boxes, labeled "Username" and "Password." There must also be two buttons in the dialog box, labeled "Submit" and "Cancel." If at any time Gloria presses the Cancel button, the dialog box shall disappear and she will be taken back to the previous screen. In normal usage, she will click in the Username text box and type in her username, and then click in (or tab to) the Password text box and type in her password. The text typed in the Password text box must be hidden. Once Gloria is finished typing in her username and password she must press the Submit button. If she has entered a correct username/password combination, she will then be taken to the main menu page. If Gloria's username/password combination is incorrect, an "Invalid username or password, please try again" message will appear in the dialog box, the text boxes will be cleared, and she will be given the opportunity to login again.

You can express user requirements as scenarios and/or as detailed screen-by-screen descriptions. Remember to use pictures as much as you can when defining user requirements. If your program is web-based, you can create lots of quick and dirty digital or even hand-drawn mockups to show the user before development takes place. This will help clarify expectations and greatly aid in the discussion of both functional elements and stylistic choices.

Domain Requirements

These are the requirements imposed on you by the application domain of the program. If you're writing a new version of an income tax program, you will be constrained by the latest IRS regulations. A general ledger program will have to abide by the latest edition of the Generally Accepted Accounting Principles (GAAP), and a smartphone will need to implement the latest Global System for Mobile communication (GSM) protocols. You don't need to write down all these requirements, just refer to them. A set of detailed domain requirements gives the developers information they will need during the design of the program. Domain requirements are usually considered "middle layer" software because they are the heart of the application, below the user interface and above the operating system, networking, or database software. A lot of domain requirements will get implemented as separate classes and libraries with their own APIs. Users are concerned with domain requirements only insofar as they affect the user requirements above.

Non-Functional Requirements

Non-functional requirements are constraints on the services and functions of the program and also expectations about its performance. They can include target platform specifications, timing constraints, performance requirements, memory usage requirements, file access privileges, security requirements, response times, minimum number of transactions per second, and so on. These are usually requirements that may not be visible to the user but which do affect the user experience. An example of a non-functional requirement is the need for your web page to load and display within 3 seconds.

Non-Requirements

Non-requirements are things the product is not going to do. You will need to communicate these to the customer, because after laying out what the program will do, the most important thing to do in the requirements phase is *manage expectations*.

One of the worst phrases a customer can utter at that final demo before you release is, "But I thought it was going to do...." You need to tell all the stakeholders in a project what the program is going to do and also what it's not going to do. In particular, you need to let them know all requirement-related aspects that won't be implemented—at least not in the current release, such as "only one countdown timer may run at a time" or "there will not be a defrost cycle that allows defrost modes to be selected by food type." Be careful, however, because the actual list of things that your program will not do is nearly infinite. Nevertheless, crucial non-requirements should be discussed explicitly with the client and stated clearly in your design documentation.

Gathering Requirements in a Plan-Driven Project

A *functional specification* describes what the program will do entirely from the user's perspective. It doesn't care how the software is implemented. It talks about the features of the program and specifies screens, menus, dialogs, and the like. Think of it as a badly written user manual. A second kind of spec can be called a *technical specification*. The technical specification describes the internal implementation details of the program. That is, it talks about data structures, algorithms used, database models, choice of programming language, and so on. We're not going to talk about technical specs, just functional specs.

"Wait," you say. "What about all those agile methodologies we talked about in Chapter 2? *They* don't write functional specs. So there! I'm off the hook." Well, in fact, agile methodologies *do* write functional specifications. They're just in a different format from the 300-page single-spaced requirements document that some plan-driven methodologies require. Agile methodologies require that, together with the customer representative or product owner, you write *user stories* that lay out what the program will do. That's a spec. We will discuss how agile methodologies do requirements later in this chapter. The important part and the idea behind this entire chapter is to *write down what your program is supposed to do before you start coding*.

Gathering Requirements: But I Don't Like Writing!

A standard argument made by software developers is that they can't write. Nonsense! Everyone can learn to write functional specs. But writing is work. You have to get in there and practice writing before you'll be any good at it. If you're still in school (be it undergrad or graduate school), take a course in writing, one where you've got to write analytical essays or fictional stories or poetry or scientific reports every single week. You should also have to read other works critically; reading other people's writing, whether good or bad, is a great way to learn how to write better.

Functional requirements should always be written in a natural language. Why? Well, it's the Sapir-Whorf linguistic relativity hypothesis, don't you know?[2] In a nutshell, language not only determines what you *do* say, it determines what you *can* say (and think). That is, the language you use determines what kinds of thoughts you are able to have; it tends to constrain your thinking processes, and thus what you can think about and how you express your thoughts. If the language doesn't have room for certain kinds of thoughts, you are much less likely to think them. Natural languages are much more expressive and varied than programming languages, so you want to write requirements and do your designs in natural languages and save the programming languages for implementation later. Whether you believe the Sapir-Whorf hypothesis or not, it's nearly always a good idea to develop your functional requirements in a natural language so you don't get bogged down in the syntactic and semantic details of a programming language before you need to. This doesn't mean that you can't think about implementation while you're doing the functional requirements (you inevitably will, trust us), but just shunt those thoughts over into a "technical note" sidebar of your specification or a completely separate document.[3] You might also look at Kenneth Iverson's Turing Award lecture, "Notation as a Tool of Thought," for a similar discussion.[4]

Gathering Requirements: Outline of a Functional Specification

In general, functional specification should have the elements we will discuss below. Lots of the ideas here are from Spolsky.[5] Keep in mind that every functional specification is different, just as every software development project is different. So take this outline with a grain of salt and just use the parts that apply to your project.

---

[2] http://en.wikipedia.org/wiki/Linguistic_relativityretrieved, September 15, 2009.

[3] Spolsky, Joel. 2004. *Joel on Software*. Berkeley, CA: Apress.

[4] Iverson, Kenneth E. 1980. "Notation as a Tool of Thought." *Communications of the ACM* 23 (8): 444–65.

[5] (Spolsky 2004)

Overview

This is your executive summary. It's a paragraph or two of what the program is supposed to do. For example:

"This program runs your microwave oven. It interfaces to a keypad and an LCD display that provides user input and output functionality. Its functions are limited to those that a standard microwave would have, with the addition of single buttons for pizza and coffee reheating. It also will run a time of day clock and a standalone countdown timer. It doesn't control the light. It has a safety interlock that will prevent the microwave from starting if the door is open."

Disclaimer

You should always put in a statement right at the start stating that "This specification isn't done yet. If you think something is missing or wrong, send me an email." That helps keep all the marketing guys off your back and lets you file new feature requests in your mail trash bin. Lots of people will put a big, black DRAFT in the header or footer of the document. That can work as well, but folks tend to ignore it. Some people will use a big DRAFT watermark on their specs, so that every page has the word embedded behind the text. This doesn't stop people from yelling at you either. At some point, your disclaimer should change to something like "This specification is as complete as it will be for this release. If you think something is missing or wrong, send an email to the author and we'll consider it for the next release."

Author's Name

Somebody needs to be responsible for the functional specification. Not a committee, not the development team, *one person*. This is usually either the development manager or the project manager, depending on how your company sets up development projects. There are pros and cons to all the different organizational arrangements.

If the development manager (the person to whom the developers report) is in charge of the functional spec, then that person is usually up to speed on all the technical aspects of the project. That's good. On the other hand, if your boss writes the functional spec, it might be harder to tell her that there's something wrong with the specification or that you don't agree with the design. Also, development managers were probably developers at one time and so they may not have the people skills (read: charm and schmoozing skills) necessary to talk to marketing, the customer, documentation, testing, and so on.

If your company puts project managers in charge of specifications, design, and schedule, but don't have developers directly reporting to them, then you run the risk of getting someone that isn't as technically savvy as a former developer. On the other hand, these folks can usually charm the socks off the other teams so negotiations are a lot smoother. Project managers do need to have some technical skills and to be very good at getting all the stakeholders to reach consensus on the contents of the functional specification.

Scenarios of Typical Usage

These are the actual requirements. A great way to get customers to respond to your requirements list is to present several scenarios of typical usage of the program as part of the specification. These are known as *user stories* and they have a couple of advantages:

- First, if you write the requirements as if they're user stories, the customer is more likely to read them.

- Second, customers are more likely to understand what you're doing and come up with ideas for things you've missed or gotten wrong. This is always a good thing, because the more customer input you get early in the process, the more likely you'll actually create something they want.

In many agile methodologies, including Scrum, requirements are often written as user stories. As the customer is usually part of the agile project team, you can get constant feedback on user stories and daily program builds. In Scrum, the customer isn't required to be part of the project team, but they are strongly encouraged to keep in close contact with the team. Also, in Scrum, shorter sprint lengths allow the customer to see working versions of the product more often. In the Unified Modeling Language (UML, see `www.uml.org`), there is an entire notation used to create use cases (another word for scenarios or user stories). But, as discussed, nothing beats natural language for describing requirements. We'll come back to use cases in Chapter 10.

Once you've written a couple of scenarios, you will have a much better idea of how your program will flow, as well as what screens, dialog boxes, menus, and so on you'll need. This lets you go through each one of those screens and flesh out the details of how they're laid out, what buttons, text boxes, icons, graphics, and so on they'll have, and what other screens they connect to. Use pictures! Natural language is great, but it is also inherently ambiguous, so a picture of a screen or a dialog box is worth way more than a thousand words. It gives the reader a clearer picture (pun intended) of what you are planning and gets them thinking about program flow and their user interface needs and wants.

Open Issues

When you first write the functional specification, there will be one or two or twenty things you don't know. That's okay. Just put them in the "Open Issues" section. Then every time you meet with the customer, point to this section and try to get answers. Some of these questions will move to requirements sections and some will end up in the "Non-requirements" section, after you get those answers. By the end of the project, though, this section should be empty. If it's not, well, you've got issues that will haunt you.

Gathering Requirements: Design and New Feature Ideas

If you're like most developers, you'll be trying to design and code the program in your head all the time you're doing your requirements gathering and analysis. That's just what developers do. The two types of notes developers and project managers typically create are technical notes containing design or coding ideas for developers and marketing notes containing feature ideas for the marketing folks and the customer. So to keep from forgetting the design and implementation ideas you have during the requirements phase, write a separate notebook. This notebook is just a separate document that contains notes for later. Ideally it is a document that is shared with the entire team.

Finally, as your project proceeds through development, new requirements and features will surface. This always happens. But if you want to keep to a schedule and deliver a working product, you simply *cannot* implement everything that will come up. If you want your requirements to be up to date, you need a place to put all the tasks you will do later. That's what a *backlog* is for, all the requirements you are going to consider for the next release of the product. This does a couple of good things for you. It tells the customer you haven't forgotten these features, and that by moving them to the next release you are committed to delivering the current release as close to the published schedule as possible. And it tells the developers that you're not out of control and that the project has a good shot at being done with high quality and on time. For more information on backlogs, take a look any of the Scrum agile methodology descriptions in Chapter 2.[6]

---

[6] Schwaber, Ken, and Mike Beedle. 2002. *Agile Software Development with Scrum.* Series in Agile Software Development. Upper Saddle River, N.J.: Prentice Hall.

Gathering Requirements: One More Thing

One more thing about the functional specification: don't obsess. Chances are that you'll do a good job of picking out requirements and writing them down in the functional spec, but that it won't be as detailed as you like and it won't be complete. Don't worry. The only time a functional specification is complete is when you ship the release. Don't spend time trying to get every single detail correct; don't spend time trying to tease every requirement out of your customer. It just won't happen. Set a time limit, do your best, and let it go. You don't want to have a bunch of developers sitting around twiddling their thumbs with nothing to do, waiting for the spec, do you? Also, keep in mind that software development is a wicked problem, so our requirements need only to be satisfactory and sufficient. We are satisficing, as optimizing software development is not realistic.

Gathering Requirements in an Agile Project

First things first: in an agile development project, there is no formal functional specification. That is because agile developers recognize from the beginning that the requirements will change, so they should embrace change and defer making decisions about requirements and design as long as possible. Also, because in an agile project the customer is an integral part of the team, the agile developers also know that they can get immediate feedback on feature implementations and they can get timely updates on requirements from the customer. This doesn't necessarily make the process of gathering requirements any easier, but it gives everyone more confidence that the current set of requirements is the right set.

For most agile methodologies, the key idea in requirements gathering is the *user story*. The user story is just that: a description of some feature or scenario that the customer wants to execute in order to get some type of work done. The classic way to describe the contents of a user story is to say

"*As a <role>, I want to do <action>, so that <reason/benefit>.*"

By expressing a user story this way, you get to the *who*, *what*, and *why* of the requirement.

Agile Requirements Gathering: The Three Cs

A user story has three fundamental components, expressed by Ron Jeffries in 2001[7]: the card, the conversation, and the confirmation.

Card

All user stories are written on *cards*. A card can be a Post-It note, an index card, a piece of paper, or even a digital card. Basically, it can be any physical or digital 2D rectangle that can be moved across some physical or digital board. While the card contains the text of the story "As a <role> I want to <action> so that <benefit/result>," it is really an invitation to a collaborative conversation about what the story really means and what the user really wants. Note that the card is not generally very detailed; it typically only contains an outline of the story. It's a placeholder for the real requirement that will be subsequently hashed out. Stakeholders can, however, write on the card, adding estimates, questions, etc.

Conversation

The *conversation* about a user story takes place between all the important stakeholders in the project, the product owner or user, the development team, the testers, marketing folks, and maybe others. This is a substantive discussion about what the product owner really wants from the story. The conversation is ideally held in person (or the closest available technological approximation) and the discussion includes more details about the story, possibly estimates of size, and an estimate of the relative priority of the story. The conversation may also include breaking the original story into two or more smaller stories, if the initial estimates indicate the effort to implement the story may be too large (stories that can be finished in one working session are ideal, but no story should exceed the planned length of an individual development Sprint, although its future iterations might).

Confirmation

The last component of a user story is *confirmation*. The user or product owner provides this information in the form of *acceptance criteria* for the story, usually written on the

---

[7]http://ronjeffries.com/xprog/articles/expcardconversationconfirmation/

back of the card as a short bullet list. These criteria become the *acceptance tests* that the product owner will use to confirm that the implementation of the story is acceptable to the user. The best way to create acceptance tests is for the product owner to generate examples of the story in use and then for the development team to automate the examples. This way, the product owner can execute the acceptance tests on the delivered feature and confirm whether the implementation works or not.

Agile Requirements Gathering: INVEST in Stories

If we are to structure our development around user stories, how do we make sure that our user stories are good? A lot of the details of a user story come out during the conversation and the confirmation, but those details do not directly help us judge the *quality* of the story nor its overall usefulness. Bill Wake laid out the characteristics of a good user story using the acronym INVEST[8]:

Independent

The idea here is that your user stories should be *independent of each other*, (i.e. each able to be scheduled and implemented separately from any other user story, even if it ended up taking several agile iterations to fully implement). Wake gives the example of a multi-layered cake: if you take a slice out of the cake, you can eat (implement) just that one slice, independently of any other. This may not always be possible; think of things like the radio software in a mobile phone. In order to fully test the user interface embodied in a user story, you may have to have all of the radio software working first. You'll see this same idea later on as loose coupling in object-oriented design.

Negotiable

A good story leaves room for all stakeholders to *negotiate the details* of its implementation. The story provides the essence of the requirement but is not so specific that it reads like a contract. Rather, it provides the developer with a goal, while allowing the owner and the developer to jointly create a workable interpretation that will allow for a feasible and satisfactory implementation.

---

[8] http://xp123.com/articles/invest-in-good-stories-and-smart-tasks/

Valuable

A good user story must be *valuable to the customer*. It must describe a feature or a service that the customer wants. Since user stories will be scheduled and implemented in a development iteration, they must add value to the product after each iteration. In addition, if the team decides a user story is too large (see "Small" below) and must be split into multiple stories, each of them must provide value to the customer. This idea gives the development team guidance on how to split stories—based on value to the customer, not on technology.

Estimable

User stories must be able to be *estimated*, allowing the product owner to assign a relative priority to each story. Estimation is part of the negotiation in the conversation and is also the first step in decomposing the story into implementable tasks. If the development team struggles to estimate a story or if the estimated effort required for its implementation is too large, then the story is likely too large and should be broken down.

Small

Good user stories should be *small*, allowing for story independence, facilitating negotiability, clarifying value determination, simplifying effort estimation, and streamlining testing. Ideally, a user story should be implementable in a single sprint or iteration, immediately adding value to the customer. Small stories also allow the development team to decompose them into a number of small tasks—ideally of 8 person-hours or less of effort. To reduce overhead of re-estimation as requirements change, you can focus on estimating only the high priority stories, ensuring they are ready for implementation. As a story moves up in the product backlog, its importance will increase until a detailed estimate of its effort and task breakdown is warranted. If at that time the story is larger than a single iteration, you should attempt splitting it into smaller stories.

Testable

Good stories must be *testable*. In agile, this practice is usually implemented using Test-Driven Development: 1) the developers will implement unit tests to determine whether a yet-to-be-implemented feature functions as expected (it doesn't, yet) and 2) the feature is then developed and tested repeatedly until it passes all unit tests. The *testable* characteristic also allows the development team to test any non-functional requirements (performance, response time, usability, etc.).

This harkens back to the plan-driven idea of *traceability*. Once implemented, you should be able to trace a feature back through the implementation and design and into the original requirements. Based on the initial requirements discussed in the conversation about the user story, the product owner writes the acceptance criteria, which translate into acceptance tests used to confirm that the user story is implemented satisfactorily. This is typically the definition of "done" in an agile environment. If the product owner is unsure or unclear about how to write the acceptance criteria for a given user story, this may mean that the story details are unclear and the story conversation should be restarted to clear up any confusion.

Agile Requirements Gathering: The Product Backlog

At this point, the total number of user stories generated by the product owner and agreed upon by the development team is added to a list of the total number of things that need to be done to create the product. This is known as the *product backlog*. Where a plan-driven process team will have a long, detailed document—the functional specification—an agile product team will have a stack of cards that ends up defining the product. This stack of cards is only preliminary, though. As the development process moves along, an agile product team will be adding, removing, and dividing user story cards constantly. The product owner will be the primary person doing this job and it's the product owner's job to decide when the product is done and should be released. There may still be cards left in the stack when a product is released. Those cards are destined for the next product effort.

Agile Requirements Gathering: SMART Tasks

Once the team agrees on a set of user stories and adds them to the product backlog, the developers can begin planning for the next iteration or sprint. This planning includes taking each user story and breaking it down into a set of implementable tasks that are easy to estimate and whose effort requires a relatively short amount of developer time. In short, tasks are the work to be done in order to implement user stories.

Decomposing stories into tasks is the work of the development team, not the product owner, and it takes place during planning out the next iteration or sprint. The estimates for the tasks are added up until the amount of effort reaches the amount of time available to the team in the next iteration. In Scrum, tasks can be assigned point values based on their perceived required effort: the more effort, the higher the point value. The team will add up the effort points for the high priority tasks until the point value reaches the team's average velocity. These tasks are then presented to the product owner, who either approves the list of work to be done or suggests changes by changing the priorities of stories in the product backlog. Eventually everyone agrees on the stories and tasks for the iteration and work can begin.

In order to perform this story decomposition and task effort estimation, the team must be able to identify tasks within stories and write them out on cards so they can be put on a task or Kanban board. Each task must meet certain goals, characterized by the acronym SMART: specific, measurable, achievable, relevant, and time-boxed.

Specific

While user stories are defined in a way that leaves room for interpretation and negotiation, the tasks generated from each story must be maximally specific to facilitate implementation, including any relevant details about the necessary data structures or user interfaces. Generating specific tasks is also likely to uncover hidden requirements or unforeseen complexities in the stories. This can lead to a reconsideration of the requirements and a renewed conversation about the current story, as well as to the creation of a new user story that will then get put in the product backlog.

Measurable

The team needs to know when each task can be considered *done*. Each team will have a different definition of *done*, but it should include things like "the feature works as listed on the task," "all the unit tests pass," and "the code has been reviewed and integrated."

Achievable

The task must be something that a developer can do within the timeframe of the iteration or sprint. The developer must also have the skill set necessary to complete the task, which may include asking for help or learning new skills in the process. This goal can also integrate with *pair programming*, which will spread the required skill set across two developers.

Relevant

This goal ties in with the Valuable story component above. With respect to tasks, this means that the task must do something that makes progress towards the creation of the user story implementation. It should add value to the iteration for the customer.

Time-Boxed

This goal means that the task, as estimated, can be finished within the iteration or sprint. If the task turns out to be harder than expected, the team is expected to divide it into two or more tasks and estimate them separately. The other goal implied here is that the total number of points assigned to the tasks included in the iteration is doable within the team's average velocity.

Agile Requirements Gathering: Sprint/Iteration Backlog

As highest priority user stories are selected and broken down into tasks, these tasks are estimated and added to the sprint/iteration backlog, becoming the things to get "done" in the next sprint/iteration. Depending on the agile methodology being used, once the sprint/iteration begins, the number of tasks in the backlog may or may not be changed. In Scrum, no more tasks may be added, except by the developers themselves, for the duration of the sprint. Any newly discovered work must be added to the product backlog instead.

Requirements Digging

Most software engineering texts use the phrase "requirements elicitation" to talk about the process of getting your users to tell you what they want. Hunt and Thomas, in their book *The Pragmatic Programmer* use the much more descriptive phrase "requirements digging" to emphasize the point that what you're really doing is digging for all those requirements that your customer doesn't know they want yet.[9] Hunt and Thomas also state that "It's important to discover the underlying reason *why* users do a particular thing, rather than just *the way* they currently do it. At the end of the day, your

---

[9] Hunt, Andrew, and David Thomas. 2000. *The Pragmatic Programmer: From Journeyman to Master.* Boston, MA: Addison-Wesley.

development has to solve their *business problem*, not just meet their stated requirements. Documenting the reasons behind requirements will give your team invaluable information when making daily implementation decisions."

Hunt and Thomas also make the terrific distinction between requirements, policies, and implementations as a way to illustrate the requirements digging process. To understand how these differ, let's consider some deficient examples of potential requirements:

"The system must let the user choose a loan term" is a nice succinct requirement. It says that there's something you must do. It isn't specific enough for implementation yet, but it tells the developer something concrete that must be built.

"Loan terms must be between 6 months and 30 years" is not a requirement, although it kind of looks like one. This statement is an example of a *business policy*. When statements like this are presented to developers as requirements, they have a tendency to hard-code the statement in the program. Wrong, wrong, wrong. Policies like this can change, so you need to be very careful about putting business policies in your requirements. It is almost always the case that you need to implement a more general version of the business policy than is stated. The real requirement is probably something like, "Loan terms are of finite length, but the length of the loan will vary by type of loan." This tells you that you probably need to build a table-driven subsystem to handle this feature. That way, the loan term for a particular type of loan can be changed by making a single change in a data table and the code doesn't need to change at all.

"The user must be able to select a loan term using a drop-down list" isn't a requirement either, although, again, it may look like one. This is only a requirement if the customer absolutely must have a drop-down menu box to choose their loan term. Otherwise, this is an example of the *implementation* that the customer would like to see, and it may not be a requirement.

Why Requirements Digging Is Hard

There are several reasons why dragging requirements out of your customer is a really hard exercise. Let's look at a few.

Difficulties with Scope

The actual boundaries of what your program is supposed to do are often fuzzy, for a variety of reasons. The program may be part of a larger system and the integration of the parts is ill-defined. The customer may not have thought through exactly what they want the program to do, so they start throwing out all sorts of ideas, many of which may not even apply to the problem at hand. Finally, the customer may have dropped into implementation-land, providing unnecessary levels of detail.

As ideas develop, customers often want more and more complex features. Overcoming such problems of scope creep can take a lot of focus, discipline, and patience, accompanied by many instances of saying "no" and of repeatedly asking "why does this need to be part of the program?" Scope is directly related to requirements creep, so beware.

Difficulties with Understanding

Let's face it: the customer and you as the developer speak different languages. Your customer is the domain expert and they speak the domain language (accounts receivable, accounts payable, reconciliation, general ledger, and so on). You speak the design and implementation language (class, object, method, use case, recursion, activation record, and the like).

There are usually two ways to overcome problems of understanding. The first is to have someone in the middle who has lived in both worlds and who can translate between the two. Some companies have *system engineers* or *technical marketers* who fulfill this role. These folks have done development and have also worked on the customer side so they can speak both languages. Good system engineers are worth their weight in user stories. The second way to promote understanding is to have the customer as part of the development team. This is the approach taken by most agile methodologies. When the customer is part of the development team, you get to talk to them every day, ask them questions, and even teach them some technical elements to clarify constraints and capabilities. And because the on-site customer sees intermediate product builds as soon as they available, you can get crucial immediate feedback. Everybody wins.

Difficulties with Volatility

Things change. This is by far the hardest part of requirements gathering and analysis and the biggest reason why schedules slip. You can't do anything about it. Get used to it. As Kent Beck says, "Embrace change." What you can do is *manage* change. Create a backlog of new features that get added as they arrive. In the Scrum methodology, new requirements are always added to the product backlog, but not to the current sprint backlog; this allows the current sprint to proceed as planned and the requirements are all reviewed when planning for the next sprint. Another way to manage change is to push the decision onto the user. Give the user a choice. "If we implement this new feature, it will add 6 weeks to the schedule. Do you still want it?" Alternatively, "If you want to keep to the original schedule we can only implement and test one of A, B, or C. You pick the one you want most." This is one of the things that the agile folks mean by *courage*.[10] Sometimes you have to take a stand to protect the viability of the project as a whole.

Non-Technical Difficulties

From a developer's perspective, non-technical difficulties with requirements are the worst ones you will encounter. Ideally, managers should shield developers from ever dealing with non-technical difficulties. Examples of non-technical difficulties are often somewhat political. For instance, one group of customers in an organization has a different view of the program requirements than another group. Or worse, one manager has a different view than another manager. The program being developed will reduce the influence of one department by automating a function where they used to be the sole source of expertise. The program will distribute data processing across several departments where it was once centralized in a single department. The list goes on and on. The best advice for non-technical difficulties with requirements digging is to run away—quickly. Let your vice-president deal with it; that's why they are paid the big bucks.

Analyzing the Requirements

Once you've written down a set of requirements, you need to make sure that these are the right requirements for the program; you need to *analyze* them. Analysis has three basic parts.

First, you *categorize* the requirements and organize them into related areas. This will help the designers a lot.

Second, you or, better yet, the customer *prioritizes* them. This is critical because you won't be able to implement all the requirements in the first product release (trust us, you won't), so this prioritized list will be what you'll use to set the targets for each interim release.

---

[10] Beck, K. 2000. *Extreme Programming Explained: Embrace Change.* Boston, MA: Addison-Wesley.

Lastly, you need to *examine* each requirement in relation to all the others, to make sure they fit into a coherent whole. Ask yourself a series of questions:

1. Is each requirement *consistent* with the overall project objective? If your program is supposed to sell your users books, it doesn't also have to allow book binding services.

2. Is this requirement *really necessary*? Have you added something that can be removed without impairing the essential functionality of the program? If your first release is supposed to allow users to buy books, then you probably don't need to also allow lawn mowers.

3. Is this requirement *testable*? This is probably a key question when you're doing requirements analysis. If you cannot figure out how to test a requirement, then you cannot know that you've implemented it correctly or that you are finished. All requirements *must* be testable or else they are not requirements. In most agile methodologies, the rule is to write the test first and then write the code (i.e., test-driven development).

4. Is this requirement *doable* in the technical environment you've got to work in? This question normally applies to those non-functional requirements mentioned previously. Are your requirements feasible given the particular target platform or set of hardware constraints you must work under for this project? For example, if your target platform is a Macintosh running OS X, a requirement that the DirectX graphics library be used is not doable because DirectX is a Windows-only library.

5. Is this requirement *unambiguous*? Your requirements need to be as precise as possible (refer to the previous testable questions) because as sure as you're sitting here reading this, someone will misinterpret an ambiguous requirement and you'll discover the error the day after you ship. Your requirements should never contain the words "or" or "may."

Conclusion

Once you're done with your functional specification or set of user stories and the analysis of your requirements, you're done with the requirements phase, right? Well, of course not. As we've said before, requirements change, so relax; don't obsess about the requirements; do the best you can to get an initial list of clear, testable requirements; and then move on to design. You'll always come back here later.

References

Beck, K. 2000. *Extreme Programming Explained: Embrace Change.* Boston, MA: Addison-Wesley.

Brooks, Frederick P. 1995. *The Mythical Man-Month : Essays on Software Engineering, Silver Anniversary Edition.* Paperback. Vol. Anniversary. Boston, MA: Addison-Wesley.

Hunt, Andrew, and David Thomas. 2000. *The Pragmatic Programmer: From Journeyman to Master.* Boston, MA: Addison-Wesley.

Iverson, Kenneth E. 1980. "Notation as a Tool of Thought." *Communications of the ACM* 23 (8): 444–65.

Jeffries, Ron. 2001. "Essential XP: Cards, Conversation, and Confirmation." Ron Jeffries (blog). August 30, 2001. https://ronjeffries.com/xprog/articles/expcardconversationconfirmation/.

Schwaber, Ken, and Mike Beedle. 2002. *Agile Software Development with Scrum. Series in Agile Software Development.* Upper Saddle River, N.J.: Prentice Hall.

Spolsky, Joel. 2004. *Joel on Software.* Berkeley, CA: Apress.

Wake, William. 2003. "INVEST in Good Stories and SMART Tasks." Agile Advice (blog). August 17, 2003. http://xp123.com/articles/invest-in-good-stories-and-smart-tasks/.

Wikipedia, *Sapir-Whorf Linguistic Relativity Hypothesis.* 2009. https://en.wikipedia.org/wiki/Linguistic_relativity retrieved, September 15, 2009.

PART II

Design Practices

CHAPTER 7

Software Architecture

What do we mean by a software architecture? To me the term architecture conveys a notion of the core elements of the system, the pieces that are difficult to change. A foundation on which the rest must be built.

—Martin Fowler[1]

Once you have an idea of *what* you're going to build, then you can start thinking about *how* you're going to build it. Of course, you've likely already been thinking about this from the very first requirement, but now you are finally ready to meaningfully delve into design.

There are really two levels of software design. The level we typically operate on when writing programs is called *detailed design*. What operations do we need? What data structures? What algorithms are we using? How is the database going to be organized? What does the user interface look like? What are the calling sequences? These are all very detailed questions that need to be answered before you can really get on with the detailed work of coding (well, sort of—we'll get to that later).

The second level is *architectural design*. What major components does your software need? How will these components interact? How will the system interact with its environment? Here you are designing the structure of the entire system, black-boxing (temporarily) the internal details of each component. As Fowler describes in this chapter's opening quote, you need the foundation before you can build the rest of the structure. *Software architecture* is a set of ideas that tells you which foundation is right for your program.

---

[1] Fowler, Martin. 2004. "Is Design Dead?" Retrieved from `http://martinfowler.com/articles/designDead.html` on July 3, 2017.

The idea of software architecture began as a response to the increasing size and complexity of programs. As Garlan and Shaw put it in their seminal document on software architecture, "As the size and complexity of software systems increases, the design problem goes beyond the algorithms and data structures of the computation: designing and specifying the overall system structure emerges as a new kind of problem.... This is the software architecture level of design."[2] However, is it really the case that *all* programs of any size and complexity have an architecture? Yes, though for larger programs you need to be more intentional about your thinking about the architecture. You must ensure you have the right set of architectural patterns incorporated into your design in order to form a solid foundation for your system. Mistakes here are costly because architectural features are so fundamental to the structure of the program that it becomes much harder to change things at the architectural level once the program has been written.

Whenever a software architect starts thinking about an architecture for a program, they usually start by drawing pictures. Diagrams of the architecture allow people to see the structure and framework of the program much more unambiguously than via text. Software architectures are normally represented as black box *graphs,* where graph nodes are *computational structures* and the graph edges are *communication conduits* between the structures. The conduits can represent data flow, object message passing, or procedure calls. Notations of this type vary and there are several standard notations, the most popular being the Unified Modeling Language (UML).

A particular architectural style is a pattern that can represent a set of similar structures. There are many different styles of software architecture, and in any given project you'll probably use more than one. As you'll see, different types of programs in different domains will lead us to different architectural styles or *architectural patterns.* Let's look at several different common architectural patterns (which share many characteristics with *design patterns* you'll see in the next chapter).

---

[2] Garlan, D., and M. Shaw. 1994. "An Introduction to Software Architecture." CMU/SEI-94-TR-21. Translated by School of Computer Science. Pittsburgh, PA: Carnegie Mellon University.

Architectural Pattern: The Main Program - Subroutine

The most traditional and oldest architectural pattern is the *main program – subroutine pattern*. While it descends from Niklaus Wirth's 1971 paper "Program Development by Stepwise Refinement,"[3] Wirth was just the first to formally define the top-down problem decomposition methodology that naturally leads to the *main program – subroutine pattern*.

The idea is to start with some big problem and then try to decompose this problem into several smaller semi-independent problems or pieces of the original problem. For example, nearly every problem that is amenable to a solution by top-down decomposition can be divided into three parts immediately: input processing, computation of the solution, and output processing. Once you have a problem divided into several pieces, you pick a single piece and continue dividing, setting aside all the other pieces as you go, akin to a depth-first search. Eventually, you'll have a very small problem where the solution is obvious; that is the time to write code. Thus, we are breaking down the problem from the top down, and writing solution code from the bottom up, although many variations exist.

Figure 7-1 gives an example of how the *main program - subroutine pattern* works. We'll discuss top-down decomposition of problems much more in Chapter 9.

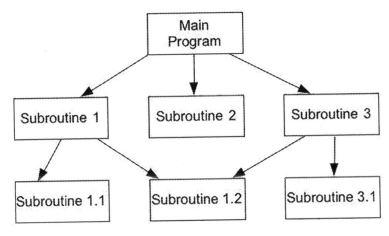

Figure 7-1. *An example of the main program – subroutine pattern*

---

[3] Wirth, N. 1971. "Program Development by Stepwise Refinement." *CACM* 14 (4): 221–27.

Wirth's paper makes the following four conclusions about programming by stepwise refinement:

1. *Program construction consists of a sequence of refinement steps. In each step a given task is broken up into a number of subtasks. Each refinement in the description of a task may be accompanied by a refinement of the description of the data, which constitute the means of communication between the subtasks...*

2. *The degree of modularity obtained in this way will determine the ease or difficulty with which a program can be adapted to changes or extensions of the purpose...*

3. *During the process of stepwise refinement, a notation which is natural to the problem in hand should be used as long as possible... Each refinement implies a number of design decisions based upon a set of design criteria...*

4. *The detailed elaborations on the development of even a short program form a long story, indicating that careful programming is not a trivial subject.*

Architectural Pattern: Pipe-and-Filter

In a pipe-and-filter style architecture, the computational components are called *filters* and they act as transducers that take input, transform it according to one or more algorithms, and then output the result to a communications conduit. The input and output conduits are called *pipes*.

A typical pipe-and-filter architecture is linear, as the example in Figure 7-2.

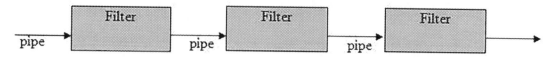

Figure 7-2. *An example of the pipe-and-filter architecture pattern*

The filters must be independent components. That is one of the beauties of a pipe-and-filter architecture: joining independent filters in different orders leads to different results. The classic example of a pipe-and-filter architectural style is the Unix shell, where there are a large number of small programs, which typically do a single thing and can be chained together using the Unix pipe mechanism. An example from Jon Bentley's book *Programming Pearls*[4] showcases how a pipe-and-filter works:

The Problem: Given a dictionary of words in English, find all the anagrams in the dictionary. That is, find all the words that are permutations of each other. For example, "pots," "stop," and "spot" are anagrams of each other.

So, what do we know? All the anagrams have the same letters and the same number of letters in each word. That gives us a clue to the method we'll use to find the anagrams: if we sort the letters of each word, we'll end up with a string of characters that has all the word's letters in alphabetical order. We call this creating a *sign* for the word. Let's break down the solution:

1. Create a sign for each word in the list by sorting the letters in each word; keep the sign and the word together as a pair.

2. Sort the resulting list of sign-word pairs by their signs; all the anagrams should now be together as their signs are identical.

3. Output all anagram groups of words (removing the signs) on separate lines, by starting a new group each time the sign changes.

This example has all the features of a standard pipe-and-filter architecture: independent computational components that perform a transformation on their input data and communication conduits that transmit the data from the output of one component to the input of the next. The pipe-and-filter pattern of this solution may be more clearly shown in Unix-speak:

sign `<dictionary.txt` | **sort** | **squash** `>anagrams.txt`

where `sign` is the filter we use to do step 1, with input file `dictionary.txt`. Then `sign` outputs a list of signs and their associated words which is piped to the Unix `sort` utility (we didn't need to write that one), which sorts the list by the first field on each line (its default behavior), which happens to be the sign of each word. It then outputs the sorted list to the next pipe. Then `squash` takes the sorted list from the incoming pipe and compresses it by putting all the words with the same sign on the same line, eliminating the signs as it does so. This final list is sent via one last pipe (this time a Unix I/O redirection) to the output file called `anagrams.txt`.

---

[4] Bentley, Jon. 2000. *Programming Pearls, Second Edition*. Paperback. Boston, MA: Addison-Wesley.

Note that not all applications should use the pipe-and-filter architecture. For example, it won't work so well for interactive applications or applications that respond to events or interrupts. So let's look at more architectural styles.

Architectural Pattern: Object-Oriented Model-View-Controller (MVC)

The advent of object-oriented analysis, design, and programming in the early 1980s (well, it really started in the '60s, but no one was paying attention) brought with it a number of architectural and design patterns. We'll focus on one object-oriented architectural pattern here and save discussion of the rest to the chapter on design patterns.

The *Model-View-Controller* (MVC) architectural pattern is a way of splitting an application, or even just a piece of an application's interface, into three parts: the model, the view, and the controller. MVC was originally developed to map the traditional input, processing, and output roles of many programs into the GUI realm:

Input ➤ Processing ➤ Output
Controller ➤ Model ➤ View

The user input, the modeling of the external world, and the visual feedback to the user are separated and handled by model, view, and controller *objects,* as shown in Figure 7-3.

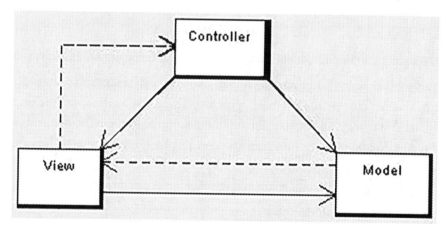

Figure 7-3. *The Model-View-Controller architecture*

- The *controller* interprets mouse and keyboard inputs from the user and maps these user actions into commands that are sent to the model and/ or view to effect the appropriate change. The controller handles input.

- The *model* manages one or more data elements, responds to queries about its state, and responds to instructions to change state. The model knows what the application is supposed to do and is the main computational structure of the architecture; it *models* the problem you're trying to solve. The model knows the rules.

- The *view* or *viewport* manages a rectangular area of the display and is responsible for presenting data to the user through a combination of graphics and text. The view doesn't know anything about what the program is actually doing; all it does is take instructions from the controller and data from the model and displays them. It communicates back to the model and controller to report status. The view handles the output.

The flow of an MVC program typically looks like this:

- The *user* interacts with the user interface (e.g., the user presses a button) and the controller handles the input event from the user interface, often via a registered handler or callback. The user interface is displayed by the view but controlled by the controller. Oddly enough, the controller has no direct knowledge of the view as an object; it just sends messages when it needs something on the screen updated.

- The *controller* accesses the model, possibly updating it in a way appropriate to the user's action (e.g., the controller causes the user's shopping cart to be updated by the model). This usually causes a change in the model's state as well as in its data.

- A *view* uses the model to generate an appropriate user interface (e.g., the view produces a screen listing the shopping cart contents). The view gets its own data from the model. The model has no direct knowledge of the view. It just responds to requests for data from whomever and to requests for transforming data from the controller.

- The controller, as the user interface manager, waits for further user interactions, which begins the cycle anew.

The main idea here is separation of concerns—and code. The objective is to separate how your program works from what it is displaying and how it gets its input data. This is classic object-oriented programming; you create objects that hide their data and hide how they manipulate that data, and then just present a simple interface to the world to interact with other objects. You'll see this again in Chapter 11.

Object-Oriented Architecture:
An MVC Example—Let's Hunt!

A classic example of a program that uses the MVC architectural pattern is the Nifty Assignment presented by Dr. David Matuszek at the 2004 Association for Computing Machinery SIGCSE Technical Symposium.[5]

The Problem

The program is a rudimentary simulation of a fox trying to find the rabbit in a grid environment, while the rabbit is trying to get away. There are bushes that the rabbit can hide behind and there are some restrictions on movement.

Figure 7-4 is a typical picture of the game in action.

---

[5] Matuszek, David. 2004. "Rabbit Hunt." In *Proceedings of the SIGCSE 2004 Technical Symposium.* ACM Press. http://nifty.stanford.edu/2004/RabbitHunt.

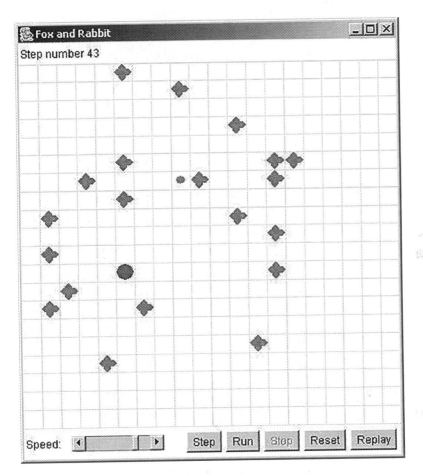

Figure 7-4. *A typical fox and rabbit hunt instance*

The fox is the large red dot, the rabbit is the small brown dot, and the bushes are the thick green crosses.

The objective of the programming assignment is to make the rabbit smarter so it can escape from the fox. Our focus, however, is solely on how the program is organized. Figure 7-5 shows the organization of the program using an object diagram taken from the BlueJ IDE. The key parts of the program are the three classes of objects (Bush, Fox, Rabbit), as well as the model, view, and controller components.

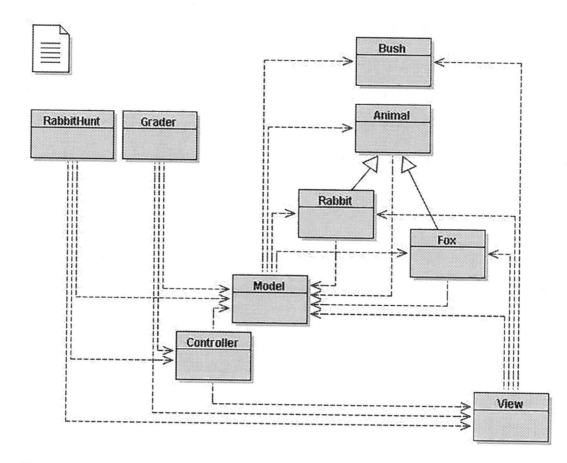

Figure 7-5. *The fox and rabbit hunt class structure*

The MVC Model

The model represents the rules of the game. It does all the computation, all the work of deciding whose turn it is, what happens during each turn, and whether anyone has won. The model is strictly internal and has practically nothing to do with the other parts of the program.

The model portion of this program is actually composed of five classes: Model (the "main" model class), Animal, Rabbit, Fox, and Bush. (Rabbit and Fox are subclasses of Animal, as you can see from the solid arrows in the Figure 7-5 diagram). This is the part of the program that you really need to understand.

The RabbitHunt class just creates model, view, and controller objects, and turns control over to the controller object. The controller object starts the model object and then waits for the user to press a button. When a button is pressed, a message is sent to the model object, which decides what to do.

The model object:

- places the fox, rabbit, and bushes in the field;

- gives the rabbit and the fox each a chance to move (one moves, then the other; they don't both move at the same time);

- tells the view to display the result of these two moves; and

- determines which animal won.

The MVC View

The view displays what is going on. It puts an image on the screen so the user can see what is happening. The view is completely passive; it does not affect the hunt in any way, it's just a news reporter that gives you a (partial) picture of what is happening inside the model.

The MVC Controller

The controller is the part of the program that displays the controls (the five buttons and the speed controls at the bottom of the window). It tells the model when to go and when to stop, without knowing anything about how the model works on the inside.

There are many advantages of splitting the program up into these separate parts. We can safely rewrite the GUI in the controller object or the display in the view object without changing the model. We can make the fox and/or the rabbit smarter (or dumber!) without changing the GUI or the display. We can reuse the GUI for a different application with very little effort. The list just goes on.

In short, MVC is your friend; use it wisely and often.

Architectural Pattern: The Client-Server

Moving back to a more traditional architecture, we once again go back in time. Back in the day, all programs ran on big iron and your entire program ran on a single machine. If you were lucky enough to be using a time-shared operating system, several people could be using the same program—albeit usually different copies—simultaneously. Then came personal computers and networks and someone had the bright idea of dividing up the work between that big iron and your tiny desktop machine. Thus was born the *client-server architecture.*

In a client-server architecture, your program is split up into two different pieces that typically run on two separate computers. A *server* does most of the heavy lifting and computation; it provides services to its *clients* across a high-bandwidth network. Clients, on the other hand, mostly just handle user input, display output, and provide communication to the server. In short, the client program sends requests for services to the server program. The server program then evaluates the request, does whatever computation is necessary (including accessing a database, if needed), and responds to the client's request with an answer.

The most common example of a client-server architecture today is the World Wide Web. In the web model, your browser is the client. It presents a user interface to you, communicates with a web server, and renders the resulting web pages to your screen. The web server does a number of things. It serves web pages in HTML, but it also can serve as a database server, a file server, and a computational server (consider everything Amazon.com does when you access it to make a purchase).

Clients and servers don't have to be on different computers, though. Two examples of programs written using a client-server architecture where both sides can reside on the same computer are *print spoolers* and the *X Windows graphical system.*

In a print spooler application, the program you are running (e.g., a word processor, a spreadsheet program, or your web browser) runs as a client that makes request to a printing service that is implemented as a part of the computer's operating system. This service is typically known as a print spooler because it keeps a spool of print jobs and controls which jobs get printed as well as the printing order. So, from your word processor, you select *Print* from a menu, set certain attributes, pick a printer, and then click *OK* on some dialog box. This sends a print request to the print spooler on your system. The print spooler adds your file to a queue of print jobs that it manages, then contacts the printer driver, and makes requests for printing to occur. The difference here is that once you've clicked the OK button, your client program (the word processor) typically does not have any more contact with the print spooler, and the print *service* runs unattended.

The X Window System (see `www.x.org/wiki/`) is a graphical windowing system available on all Unix- and Linux-based systems and also for Apple Macintosh and Microsoft Windows systems as an add-on windowing system. The X system uses a client-server architecture where the client programs and the server typically both reside on the same computer. The X system server receives requests from client programs, processes them for the hardware that is attached to the current system, and provides an output service that displays the resulting data in bitmapped displays. Client program examples include *xterm* (a windowed terminal program that provides a command line interface to Unix), *xclock* (you guessed it – a clock), and *xdm* (the X Window display manager). The X system allows hierarchical and overlapping windows, and provides the ability to configure menus, scroll bars, open and close buttons, background and foreground colors, and graphics. X can also manage a mouse and keyboards. These days, the main use of the X system is as a springboard to build more sophisticated window managers, graphical environments, graphical widgets, and desktop management windowing systems like GNOME and KDE.

Architectural Pattern: The Layered Approach

The layered architectural approach suggests that programs can be structured as a series of layers, much like geologic strata, with a sequence of well-defined interfaces between the layers. This has the effect of isolating each layer from the ones above and below it so that we can change the internals of any layer without having to change any of the other layers in the program. That is, of course, as long as your changes don't involve any changes to the interface. In a layered approach, interfaces should not be altered unless absolutely necessary. Two classic examples of a layered approach to programming are operating systems (OSs) and communications protocols.

An operating system's architecture has several objectives, among them to centralize control of the limited hardware resources and to protect users from each other. A layered approach to the operating system architecture does both of these things. Take a look at a standard picture of an OS architecture in Figure 7-6.

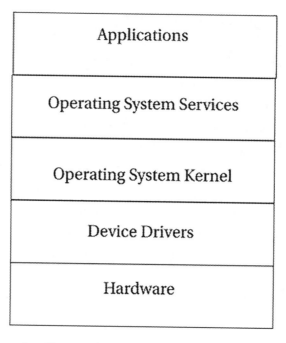

Figure 7-6. *An example of layered architecture for an operating system*

In this layered model, user applications request operating system services via a system call interface. This is normally the only way for applications to access the computer's hardware. Most operating system services must make requests through the kernel and all hardware requests must go through device drivers that talk directly to the hardware devices. Each of these layers has a well-defined interface, so that, for example, a developer may add a new device driver for a new disk drive without changing any other part of the OS. This is an example of information hiding.

The same type of interface happens in a communications protocol. The most famous of these layered protocols is the International Standards Organization (ISO) Open Systems Interconnection (OSI) seven-layer model, depicted in Figure 7-7.

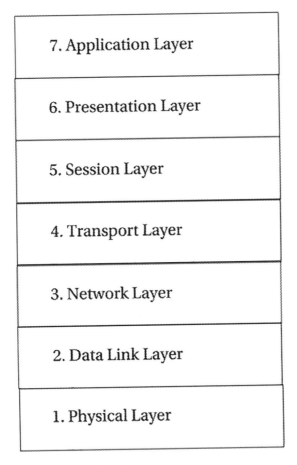

Figure 7-7. *The ISO-OSI layered architecture*

In this model, each layer contains functions or services that are logically similar and are grouped together. An interface is defined between each layer and communication between layers is only allowed via the interfaces. A particular implementation need not contain all seven layers, and sometimes two or more layers are combined to make a smaller protocol stack. The OSI model defines both the seven-layer approach and all the interface protocols. The model can be downloaded as a PDF file from www.itu.int/rec/T-REC-X.200/en. (The ITU or International Telecommunications Union is the new name for the ISO.)

Examples of protocols that are implemented at each layer are shown in Table 7-1.

Table 7-1. *Example Layered Protocols Using the ISO-OSI Architecture*

Layer	Protocol
7. Application	http, ftp, telnet
6. Presentation	MIME, SSL
5. Session	Sockets
4. Transport	TCP, UDP
3. Network	IP, IPsec
2. Data Link	PPP, Ethernet, SLIP, 802.11
1. Physical	

Conclusion

The software architecture is the core of your application. It is the foundation on which you build the rest of the program and which drives the rest of your design. There are many different styles of software architecture and in any given project you'll probably use more than one. The architectural style used for a program depends on what it is you're doing. That's the beauty of these styles; it may not always be true that form follows function but for software, design follows architecture. These foundational architectural patterns lead you down the path of design, shaping how your program will be constructed and lived in.

References

Bentley, Jon. 2000. *Programming Pearls, Second Edition.* Paperback. Boston, MA: Addison-Wesley.

Fowler, Martin. 2004. "Is Design Dead?" *MartinFowler.Com* (blog). May 2004. www.martinfowler.com/articles/designDead.html.

Garlan, D., and M. Shaw. 1994. "An Introduction to Software Architecture." Translated by School of Computer Science. Pittsburgh, PA: Carnegie Mellon University.

Matuszek, David. 2004. "Rabbit Hunt." In *Proceedings of the SIGCSE 2004 Technical Symposium.* ACM Press. http://nifty.stanford.edu/2004/RabbitHunt.

Wirth, N. 1971. "Program Development by Stepwise Refinement." *CACM* 14 (4): 221–27.

CHAPTER 8

Design Principles

There are two ways of constructing a software design. One way is to make it so simple that there are obviously no deficiencies. And the other way is to make it so complicated that there are no obvious deficiencies.

—C. A. R. Hoare

One way to look at software problems is with a model that divides the problems into two different layers:

- "Wicked" problems fall in the upper layer. These are problems that typically come from domains outside of computer science (e.g. biology, business, meteorology, sociology, political science, etc.). These types of problems tend to be open-ended, ill-defined, and large in the sense that they require much work. For example, pretty much any kind of a web commerce application is a wicked problem. Horst W. J. Rittel and Melvin M. Webber, in a 1973 paper on social policy,[1] gave a definition for and a set of characteristics used to recognize a wicked problem that we'll look at later in this chapter.

- "Tame" problems fall in the lower layer. These problems tend to cut across other problem domains; they tend to be better defined and small. Sorting and searching are great examples of tame problems. Small and well-defined don't mean "easy," however. Tame problems can be very complicated and difficult to solve. It's just that they

---

[1] Rittel, H. W. J., and M. M. Webber. 1973. "Dilemmas in a General Theory of Planning." *Policy Sciences* 4 (2): 155–69. https://doi.org/10.1007/BF01405730.

161

© John F. Dooley and Vera A. Kazakova 2024
J. F. Dooley and V. A. Kazakova, *Software Development, Design, and Coding*,
https://doi.org/10.1007/979-8-8688-0285-0_8

are clearly defined and you know when you have a solution. These are the kinds of problems that provide computer scientists with foundations in terms of data structures and algorithms for the wicked problems we solve from other problem domains.

What does this have to do with design principles, you ask? Well, realizing that most of the larger software problems you'll encounter have a certain amount of "wickedness" built into them influences how you think about design issues, how you approach the design of a solution to a large, ill-formed problem, and gives you some insight into the design process. In this chapter, we will talk more about wicked and tame problems, why you can abandon the waterfall model with a clear conscience, what are the characteristics of good designs, and which unifying heuristics you can apply to help you solve complex design problems.

Wicked Problems

According to Rittel and Webber, a *wicked problem* is one for which the requirements are completely known only after the problem is solved, or for which the requirements and solution evolve over time. It turns out this describes most of the "interesting" problems in software development. Jeff Conklin has revised Rittel and Webber's description of a wicked problem[2] and provided a more succinct list of the characteristics of wicked problems.[3] To paraphrase:

1. *A wicked problem is not understood until after the creation of a solution.* Another way of saying this is that the problem is defined and solved at the same time.[4]

---

[2] Conklin, E. Jeffrey, and William Weil. 1997. *Wicked Problems: Naming the Pain in Organizations.* Vol. 2005. Group Support Systems, Inc. www.3m.com/meetingnetwork/readingroom/gdss_wicked.html.

[3] Conklin, Jeff. 2005. "Wicked Problems & Social Complexity." In *Dialogue Mapping: Building Shared Understanding of Wicked Problems*, Paperback, 256. New York, NY: John Wiley & Sons. Retrieved from http://cognexus.org/wpf/wickedproblems.pdf on 8 September 2009. Paper last updated October 2008.

[4] DeGrace, Peter, and Leslie Hulet Stahl. 1990. *Wicked Problems, Righteous Solutions: A Catalogue of Modern Software Engineering Paradigms.* Yourdon Press Computing Series. Englewood Cliffs, N.J.: Yourdon Press.

2. *Wicked problems have no stopping rule*; that is, you can create incremental solutions to the problem, but there's nothing that tells you that you've found the correct and final solution.

3. *Solutions to wicked problems are not right or wrong*; they are better or worse, or good enough or not good enough.

4. *Every wicked problem is essentially novel and unique.* Because of the "wickedness" of the problem, even if you have a similar problem next week, you basically have to start over again because the requirements will be different enough and the solution will still be elusive.

5. *Every solution to a wicked problem is a "one shot operation."* See the bullet point above.

6. *Wicked problems have no given alternative solutions.* That is, there is no small finite set of solutions from which to choose.

Wicked problems crop up all over the place. For example, creating a word processing program is a wicked problem. You may think that you know what a word processor needs to do: insert text, cut and paste, handle paragraphs, print. But this list of features is only one person's list. As soon as you "finish" your word processor and release it, you'll be inundated with new feature requests: spell checking, footnotes, multiple columns, support for different fonts, colors, styles, and the list goes on. The word processing program is essentially never done—at least not until you release the last version and end-of-life the product.

Wicked problems include instances where you don't really know if you can solve the problem at the start. Expert systems require a user interface, an inference engine, a set of rules, and a database of domain information. For a particular domain, it's not at all certain at the beginning that you can create the rules that the inference engine will use to reach conclusions and recommendations. So you have to iterate through different rule sets, send out the next version, and see how well it performs. Then you do it again, adding and modifying rules. You don't really know if the solution is satisfactory (even just for the time being) until you're done. Now that's a wicked problem.

Conklin and Rittel and Webber say that when faced with a large, complicated problem (a wicked one), traditional cognitive studies indicate most people will follow a linear problem-solving approach, working top-down from the problem to the solution. This is equivalent to the traditional waterfall model described in Chapter 2.[5] Figure 8-1 shows this linear approach.

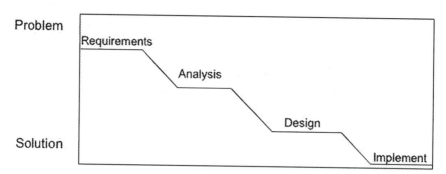

Figure 8-1. *Linear problem-solving approach*

Instead of this linear, waterfall approach, real wicked problem solvers tend to use an approach that swings from requirements analysis to solution modeling and back until the problem solution is good enough. Conklin calls this an *opportunity-driven* or *opportunistic* approach because the designers are looking for any opportunity to make progress toward the solution.[6] The opportunity-driven approach looks something like Figure 8-2.

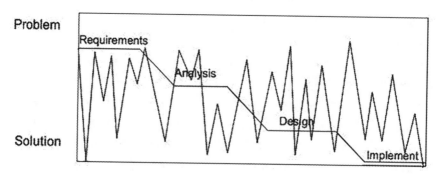

Figure 8-2. *The opportunity-driven development approach*

---

[5] (Conklin 2005)

[6] (Conklin 2005)

164

In this figure, the jagged line indicates the designer's work moving from the problem to a solution prototype and back again, slowly evolving both the requirements understanding and the solution iteration and converging on an implementation that is good enough to release. As an example, let's take a quick look at a web application.

Say that a not-for-profit organization keeps a list of activities for youth in your home county. The list is updated regularly and is distributed to libraries around the county. Currently, the list is kept on a spreadsheet and is distributed in hard copy in a three-ring binder. The not-for-profit wants to put all its data online and make it accessible over the web. It also wants to be able to update the data via the same web site. Simple, you say. It's just a web application with an HTML front end and a database and middleware code to update and query the database as the back end. Not a problem.

Ah, but this is really a wicked problem in disguise. Firstly, the customer has no idea how they want the web page(s) to look or behave, so whatever you give them the first time will not be precisely what they want; the problem won't be understood completely until you are done. Secondly, as you develop prototypes, they will want more features— so the problem has no stopping rule. And finally, as time goes on, the not-for-profit will want changes, so there is no "right" answer, there are only a variety of "good enough" answers. Very wicked.

Tame Problems

Conklin also provides a list of characteristics of "tame" problems, ones for which you can easily and reliably find a solution. "A tame problem

1. has a well-defined and stable problem statement;

2. has a definite stopping point (i.e., when the solution is reached);

3. has a solution that can be objectively evaluated as right or wrong;

4. belongs to a class of similar problems that are all solved in the same similar way;

5. has solutions that can be easily tried and abandoned; and

6. comes with a limited set of alternative solutions."[7]

---

[7] (Conklin 2005)

A terrific example of a tame problem is sorting a list of data values:

- The problem is easily and clearly stated: sort this list into ascending order using this function to compare data elements.

- Sorting has a definite stopping point: the list is sorted.

- The result of a sort can be objectively evaluated (the list is either sorted correctly or it isn't.)

- Sorting belongs to a class of similar problems that are all solved in the same way. Sorting integers is similar to sorting strings is similar to sorting database records using a key and so on.

- Sorting has solutions that can easily be tried and abandoned.

- Finally, sorting has a limited set of alternative solutions; sorting by comparison has a set of known algorithms and a theoretical lower bound.

The Design Process

Design is messy. Even if you completely understand the problem requirements (given a tame problem), you typically have many alternatives to consider when you're designing a software solution. You'll also usually make lots of mistakes before you come up with a solution that works. As you saw in Figure 8-2, your design will change as you understand the problem better over time. This gives the *appearance* of messiness and disorganization, but really, you're making progress.

Design is about tradeoffs and priorities. Most software projects are time-limited, so you usually won't be able to implement all the features that the customer wants. You have to figure out the subset that will give the customer the largest number of high priority features in the time you have available. So you have to prioritize the requirements and trade off one subset for another.

Design is heuristic. Design is largely about decomposing a larger problem into smaller, more manageable pieces.[8] For the overwhelming majority of projects there is no set of cut and dried rules that says, "First we design component X using technique Y.

---

[8] Parnas, D. 1972. "On the Criteria to Be Used in Decomposing Systems into Modules." Communications of the ACM 15 (12): 1053–58

Then we design component Z using technique W." Software just doesn't work that way. Software design is done using a set of ever-changing heuristics (cognitive shortcuts) that each designer acquires over the course of a career. Over time good designers learn more heuristics and patterns (see Chapter 13), which allow them to quickly get through the easy bits of a design and to reach the heart of the wickedness of the problem. The best thing you can do is to shadow an experienced designer and learn the heuristics.

Designs evolve. Good designers recognize that for any problem, tame or wicked, the requirements will change over time. This will then cascade into changes in your design, causing it to evolve over time. This is particularly true across product releases and new feature additions. The trick here is to create a software architecture (Chapter 7) that is amenable to change with limited effect on the downstream design and code.

Desirable Design Characteristics (Things Your Design Should Favor)

Regardless of the size of your project or what process you use to do your design, there are a number of desirable characteristics that every software design should have. These are the principles you should adhere to as you develop your design. Your design doesn't necessarily need to exhibit all of these characteristics, but having a majority of them will certainly make your software easier to write, understand, and use.

- *Fitness of purpose*: Your design must work and work correctly in the sense that it must satisfy the requirements you've been given, within the constraints of the platform on which your software will be running. Don't add new requirements as you go; the customer will do that for you.

- *Separation of concerns*: Related closely to modularity, this principle says you should separate out functional pieces of your design cleanly in order to facilitate ease of maintenance and simplicity. Modularity is good.

- *Simplicity*: Keep your design as simple as possible. This will let others understand what you're up to. If you find a place that can be simplified, do it! If simplifying your design means adding more modules or classes to your design, that's okay. Simplicity also applies to interfaces between modules or classes. Simple interfaces allow others to see the data and control flow in your design. In agile methodologies, this idea of simplicity is kept in front of you all the time. Most agile techniques have a rule that says if you're working on part of a program and you have an opportunity to simplify it (called *refactoring* in agile-speak), do it right then and there. Keep your design and your code as simple as possible at all times.

- *Ease of maintenance*: A simple, understandable design is amenable to changes needed for code maintenance. The most inevitable kind of necessary change you'll encounter is fixing errors. Errors occur at all phases of the development process, requirements, analysis, design, coding, and testing. The more coherent and simple your design is, the easier it will be to isolate and fix errors.

- *Loose coupling*: When you are separating your design into modules (or in object-oriented design, into classes), the degree to which the modules depend on each other is called *coupling*. *Tightly coupled* modules may share data or procedures, so a change in one module is much more likely to require a change in the other module. This increases the maintenance burden and makes the modules more likely to contain errors. *Loosely coupled* modules, on the other hand, hide the details of how they perform operations from other modules. Any data they share must be passed between procedures or methods via an *interface*. An example of loose coupling is the qsort() function in the Standard C library; it takes a provided list and sorts it in place. You don't need to know which particular sorting algorithm is used because you just give the function the original list and you get back the sorted one. Loose coupling lightens the maintenance burden because a change to one class or function will not likely affect how another class or function operates, as long as the interface is invariant. In this way changes are isolated and errors are much less likely to propagate.

- *High cohesion*: The complement of loose coupling is high cohesion. *Cohesion* within a module is the degree to which the module is self-contained with regards both to the data it holds and the operations that act on the data. A module with high cohesion has all the data it needs and all the operations allowed on the data are defined within the module itself. In the cases of object-oriented classes, any object instantiated from highly cohesive class template is very independent and only communicates with other objects via its published interface.

- *Extensibility*: An added benefit of simplicity and loose coupling is the ability to easily add new features to the design. This is extensibility. One of the features of software solutions to wicked problems is that they're never really finished. So after every product release, the customer typically asks for new features. The easier it is to add new features or make any other changes, the cleaner your design will remain over time.

- *Portability*: While not high on the list, keeping in mind that your software may need to be ported to another platform (or two or three) is a desirable characteristic. There are many issues involved with porting software, including operating system issues, hardware architecture, and user interface issues. This is particularly true for web applications.

Design Heuristics

Speaking of heuristics, here's a short list of good, time-tested heuristics. The list is clearly not exhaustive and it's somewhat idiosyncratic, but it's a reliable starting point for all your software designs. Think about these heuristics and try some of them during your next design exercise. We will come back to all of these heuristics in much more detail in later chapters.

Find real world objects to model. Alan Davis[9] and Richard Fairley[10] call this "intellectual distance." It's how far your design is from a real-world object. The heuristic here is to try to find real world objects that are close to things you want to model in your program. Keeping the real-world object in mind as you are designing your program helps keep your design closer to the problem. Fairley's advice is to minimize the intellectual distance between the real-world object and your model of it.

Abstraction is key. Whether you're doing object-oriented design (creating interfaces and abstract classes) or doing a more traditional layered design, you want to use abstraction. Abstraction lets us think clearly, by allowing us to remain on one level of specificity as we plan out our design. You can remain focused by putting off or

[9] Davis, Alan M. 1995. *201 Principles of Software Development*. New York, NY: McGraw-Hill, Inc.
[10] Fairley, R. E. 1985. *Software Engineering Concepts*. McGraw-Hill Series in Software Engineering and Technology. New York: McGraw-Hill.

black-boxing some of the decisions, pushing them higher in the design hierarchy (more abstraction) until you are ready to decide on the details. Abstraction is key for managing the complexity of a large problem. By abstracting away the details you can see the kernel of the real problem.

Information hiding is your friend. Information hiding is the concept that you isolate information—both data and behavior—in your program so that you can isolate errors and isolate changes; you also only allow access to the information via a well-defined interface. You hide the details of a class away and only allow communication and modification of data via a public interface. This means that your implementation can change, but as long as the interface is consistent and constant, nothing else in your program need change. If you're not doing object-oriented design, think about using libraries for hiding behavior and using separate data structures (structs in C and C++) for hiding state.

Keep your design modular. Breaking your design up into semi-independent pieces has many advantages. It keeps the design manageable in your head; you can just think about one part at a time and leave the others as black boxes. A fundamental part of object-oriented design is encapsulation, which is the practice of grouping data and its operations together, facilitating a modular design. It isolates changes, helping with extensibility and maintainability. Modularity is always the most robust approach.

Identify the parts of your design that are likely to change. If you make the assumption that there will be changes in your requirements, then there will likely be changes in your design as well. If you identify the areas of your design that are likely to change, you can modularize them, thus mitigating the impact of any changes you need to make. What things are likely to change? Well, it depends on your application and its domain. Business rules can change (think tax rules or accounting practices), user interfaces can change, hardware can change, and so on. The point here is to anticipate the elements most likely to change and to divide up your design so that the necessary changes are contained and simplified.

Use loose coupling, interfaces, and abstract classes. Along with modularity, information hiding, and change, using loose coupling will make your design easier to understand and to change as time goes along. Loose coupling minimizes dependencies of one class (or module) on another, so that a change in one module won't cause changes in other modules. If the implementation of a module is hidden and only the interface exposed, you can swap out implementations as long as you keep the interface constant. So you implement loose coupling by using well-defined interfaces between modules (in object-oriented design, by using abstract classes and interfaces to connect these classes).

Use your knapsack full of common design patterns. Robert Glass[11] describes great software designers as having "...a large set of standard patterns" that they carry around with them and apply to their designs. This is what design experience is all about: doing design over and over again and learning from the experience. In Susan Lammer's book *Programmers at Work,*[12] Butler Lampson says, "Most of the time, a new program is a refinement, extension, generalization, or improvement of an existing program. It's really unusual to do something that's completely new...." That's what design patterns are: they're descriptions of things you've already done that you can apply to a new problem.

Adhere to the Principle of One Right Place. In his book *Programming on Purpose,* P.J. Plauger says, "My major concern here is the Principle of One Right Place—there should be One Right Place to look for any nontrivial piece of code, and One Right Place to make a likely maintenance change."[13] When your design adheres to the Principle of One Right Place, debugging and maintenance are much easier.

Use diagrams as a design language. The two of us are visual learners. For us, a picture really is worth more than a thousand or so words. As we design and code, we are constantly drawing diagrams so we can visualize how our programs will flow, which classes or modules will be talking to each other, what data is dependent on what function, where do the return values go, what is the sequence of events, and so on. This type of visualization can settle the design in your head, help the same understanding to be shared with clients and other developers, and it can point out errors or possible complications in the design. Whiteboards, paper, digital tools...just get drawing! Even as computer scientists (or maybe especially so), drawing is the best problem-solving tool we know.

Designers and Creativity

Don't think that design is cut and dried, or that formal processes rules can be imposed to crank out software designs. It's not like that at all. While there are formal restrictions and constraints on your design that are imposed by the problem, the problem domain, and the target platform, the process of reaching the design itself need not be formal.

---

[11] Glass, R. L. 2006. *Software Creativity 2.0.* Paperback. Atlanta, GA: developer* Books.

[12] Lammers, Susan. 1986. *Programmers At Work.* Paperback. Redmond, WA: Microsoft Press.

[13] Plauger, P. J. 1993. *Programming on Purpose : Essays on Software Design.* Englewood Cliffs, N.J.: PTR Prentice Hall.

It is at bottom a creative activity. Bill Curtis, in a 1987 empirical study of software designers came up with a process that seems to be what most of the designers followed:[14]

1. Understand the problem.

2. Decompose the problem into goals and objects.

3. Select and compose plans to solve the problem.

4. Implement the plans.

5. Reflect on the design product and process.

Frankly, this is a pretty general list and doesn't really tell us everything we'd really need for software design. Curtis, however, then went deeper in #3 on his list, "select and compose plans," and found that his designers used the following steps:

1. Build a mental model of a proposed solution.

2. Mentally execute the model to see if it solves the problem. Make up input and simulate the model in your head.

3. If what you get is not correct, change the model to remove the errors and go back to step 2 to simulate again.

4. When your sample input produces the correct output, select some more input values and go back and do steps 2 and 3 again.

5. When you've done this enough times (you'll know because you're experienced) then you've got a good model and you can stop.[15]

This deeper technique makes the cognitive and the iterative aspects of design clear and evident. You see that design is fundamentally a function of the mind, is idiosyncratic, and depends on things about the designer that are outside the process itself.

---

[14] Curtis, Bill, R. Guindon, H. Krasner, D Walz, J. Elam, and N. Iscoe. 1987. "Empirical Studies of the Design Process: Papers for the Second Workshop on Empirical Studies of Programmers." Austin, TX: MCC.

[15] (Glass 2006)

John Nestor, in a report to the Software Engineering Institute, came up with a list of what are some common characteristics of great designers. Great designers

- have a large set of standard patterns;

- have experienced failing projects;

- have mastery of development tools;

- have an impulse towards simplicity;

- can anticipate change;

- can view things from the user's perspective; and

- can deal with complexity.[16]

Conclusion

So what have you learned about software design?

Design is ad hoc, heuristic, and messy. Designing software is a trial-and-error heuristic process, which is both necessary and sufficient for good designs.

Design depends on understanding of prior design problems and solutions. While designers need some knowledge of the problem domain (which can be supplied by a client), more crucially, they need knowledge of design and patterns of good designs. They need to have a knapsack of these design patterns that they can use to approach new problems. The solutions are tried and true. The problems are new but they contain elements of problems that have already been solved. The patterns are *malleable templates* that can be applied to those elements of the new problem that match the pattern's requirements.

Design is iterative. Requirements change and so must your design. Even if you have a stable set of requirements, your *understanding* of the requirements changes as you progress through the design activity and so you'll go back and change the design to reflect this deeper, better understanding. The iterative process clarifies and simplifies your design at each step.

Design is a cognitive activity. You're not writing code at this point, so you don't need a machine. Your head and a drawing tool are all you need to do design. As Dijkstra says,

---

[16] (Glass 2006)

"We must not forget that it is not our business to make programs; it is our business to design classes of computations that will display a desired behavior."[17]

Design is opportunistic. Glass sums up his discussion of design with "The unperturbed design process is opportunistic—that is, rather than proceed in an orderly process, good designers follow an erratic pattern dictated by their minds, pursuing opportunities rather than an orderly progression."[18]

All the characteristics above argue against a rigid, plan-driven design process and for a creative, flexible way of doing design. This brings us back to the first topic in this chapter: *design is just wicked.*

And finally

A designer can mull over complicated designs for months. Then suddenly the simple, elegant, beautiful solution occurs to him. When it happens to you, it feels as if God is talking! And maybe He is.

—Leo Frankowski (in *The Cross-Time Engineer*)

References

Conklin, E. Jeffrey, and William Weil. 1997. *Wicked Problems: Naming the Pain in Organizations.* Vol. 2005. Group Support Systems, Inc. www.3m.com/meetingnetwork/readingroom/gdss_wicked.html.

Conklin, J. 2005. *Dialogue Mapping: Building Shared Understanding of Wicked Problems.* Paperback. New York: John Wiley & Sons. www.wiley.com/en-us/Dialogue+Mapping%3A+Building+Shared+Understanding+of+Wicked+Problems-p-9780470017685.

Curtis, Bill, R. Guindon, H. Krasner, D Walz, J. Elam, and N. Iscoe. 1987. "Empirical Studies of the Design Process: Papers for the Second Workshop on Empirical Studies of Programmers." Austin, TX: MCC.

Davis, Alan M. 1995. *201 Principles of Software Development.* New York, NY: McGraw-Hill, Inc.

---

[17] Dijkstra, Edsger W. 1972. "The Humble Programmer." *Communications of the ACM* 15 (10): 859–66.

[18] (Glass 2006)

DeGrace, Peter, and Leslie Hulet Stahl. 1990. *Wicked Problems, Righteous Solutions: A Catalogue of Modern Software Engineering Paradigms.* Yourdon Press Computing Series. Englewood Cliffs, N.J.: Yourdon Press.

Dijkstra, Edsger W. 1972. "The Humble Programmer." *Communications of the ACM* 15 (10): 859–66.

Fairley, R. E. 1985. *Software Engineering Concepts.* McGraw-Hill Series in Software Engineering and Technology. New York: McGraw-Hill.

Glass, R. L. 2006. *Software Creativity 2.0.* Paperback. Atlanta, GA: Developer.* Books.

Lammers, Susan. 1986. *Programmers At Work.* Paperback. Redmond, WA: Microsoft Press.

McConnell, Steve. 2004. *Code Complete 2: A Practical Handbook of Software Construction.* Redmond, WA: Microsoft Press.

Parnas, D. 1972. "On the Criteria to Be Used in Decomposing Systems into Modules." *Communications of the ACM* 15 (12): 1053–58.

Plauger, P. J. 1993. *Programming on Purpose: Essays on Software Design.* Englewood Cliffs, N.J.: PTR Prentice Hall.

Rittel, H. W. J., and M. M. Webber. 1973. "Dilemmas in a General Theory of Planning." *Policy Sciences* 4 (2): 155–69. https://doi.org/10.1007/BF01405730.

CHAPTER 9

Structured Design

Invest in the abstraction, not the implementation. Abstractions can survive the barrage of changes from different implementations and new technologies.

—Andy Hunt and Dave Thomas[1]

Structured Programming

Structured design has its genesis in Edsger Dijkstra's famous 1968 letter to the *Communications of the ACM*, "Go To Statement Considered Harmful." Dijkstra's paper concludes with

> The **go to** statement as it stands is just too primitive; it is too much an invitation to make a mess of one's program. One can regard and appreciate the clauses considered (ed. if-then-else, switch, while-do, and do-while) as bridling its use. I do not claim that the clauses mentioned are exhaustive in the sense that they will satisfy all needs, but whatever clauses are suggested (e.g. abortion clauses) they should satisfy the requirement that a programmer independent coordinate system can be maintained to describe the process in a helpful and manageable way.[2]

Programming languages created from this point onward, while not eliminating the goto statement (except for Java, which has none), certainly downplayed its use, and courses that taught programming encouraged students to avoid it. Instead, problem solving was taught in a top-down structured manner, where one begins with the problem statement and attempts to break the problem down into a set of solvable subproblems.

---

[1] Hunt, Andrew, and David Thomas. 2000. *The Pragmatic Programmer: From Journeyman to Master*. Boston: Addison-Wesley.

[2] Dijkstra, E. 1968. "GoTo Statement Considered Harmful." *CACM* 11 (3): 147–48.

© John F. Dooley and Vera A. Kazakova 2024
J. F. Dooley and V. A. Kazakova, *Software Development, Design, and Coding*,
https://doi.org/10.1007/979-8-8688-0285-0_9

The process continues until each subproblem is small enough to be either trivial or very easy to solve. This technique is called *structured programming*. Before the advent and acceptance of object-oriented programming in the mid-1980s, this was the standard approach to problem solving and programming. It is still one of the best ways to approach a large class of problems.

Stepwise Refinement

Niklaus Wirth formalized the structured design technique in his 1971 paper, "Program Development by Stepwise Refinement."[3] *Stepwise refinement* contends that designing programs consists of a set of refinement steps. In each step, a given task is broken up into a number of subtasks. Each refinement of a task must be accompanied by a refinement of the data description and the interface. The degree of modularity obtained will determine the ease or difficulty with which a program can be adapted to changes in requirements or environment.

During refinement, you use a notation that is natural to the problem space. You avoid using a programming language for description as long as possible. Each refinement implies a number of design decisions based on a set of design criteria. These criteria include efficiency of time and space, clarity, and regularity of structure (simplicity).

Refinement can proceed in two ways, top-down or bottom-up. *Top-down* refinement is characterized by moving from a general description of the problem to detailed statements of what individual modules or routines do. The guiding principle behind stepwise refinement is that humans can concentrate on only a few things at a time—Miller's famous 7 +/- 2 chunks of data rule.[4] One works by

- Analyzing the problem and trying to identify the outlines of a solution and the pros and cons of each possibility

- Then designing the top levels first

- Steering clear of language-specific details

- Pushing down the details until you get to the lower levels

---

[3] Wirth, N. 1971. "Program Development by Stepwise Refinement." *CACM* 14 (4): 221–27.
[4] Miller, G. A. 1956. "The Magical Number Seven, plus or Minus Two: Some Limits on Our Capacity for Processing Information." *Psychological Review* 63: 81–97.

- Formalizing each level

- Verifying each level

- Then moving to the next lower level to make the next set of refinements. (That is, repeat.)

One continues to refine the solution until it seems as if it would be easier to code than to decompose; you'll see an example of this process later in this chapter.

The point is that you work until you become impatient at how obvious and easy the design becomes. The downside here is that you really have no good metric on "when to stop." It just takes practice.

If you can't get started at the top, then start at the bottom using *bottom-up* refinement:

- Ask yourself, "What do I know that the system needs to do?" This usually involves lower level I/O operations, other low-level operations on data structures, and so on.

- Identify as many low-level functions and components as you can from that question.

- Identify common aspects of the low-level components and group them together.

- Continue with the next level up or go back to the top and try again to work down.

Bottom-up refinement usually results in early identification of utility routines, which can lead to a more compact design. It also helps promote reuse because you are reusing the lower level routines. On the downside, bottom-up assessment is hard to use exclusively—you nearly always end up switching to a top-down approach at some point because sometimes you find you just can't put a larger piece together from the bottom-up. This isn't really stepwise refinement but it can help get you started. Most real stepwise refinements involve alternating between top-down and bottom-up design elements. Fortunately, top-down and bottom-up design methodologies can be very complementary.

Example of Stepwise Refinement: The Eight Queens Problem

The eight queens problem requires finding a placement of eight queens on a standard 8 x 8 chessboard in such a way that no queen can be attacked by any other. Remember that queens can move any number of spaces horizontally, vertically, or diagonally. One possible solution to the eight-queens problem is depicted in Figure 9-1.

Figure 9-1. *One solution to the eight queens problem*

It turns out that no one has yet found an analytical solution to this problem, and it's likely one does not exist. So how would you approach this problem? Take a moment to think about it on your own before continuing.

Done? Okay. Let's look at one possible way to decompose this problem.

Eight Queens: Proposed Solution 1

The first thing you need to do is to look at the problem and tease out the requirements and the outline of a solution. This will start you down the road of answering the question of what the top-level decomposition should be.

You might initially consider solving the problem using brute force: just try all the possible arrangements of queens and pick the ones that work. With 8 queens and 64 possible squares there are

$$\frac{n!}{k!(n-k)!} = \frac{64!}{56!8!} \approx 2^{32}$$

possible board configurations, where n is the number of squares on the board and k is the number of queens (or square positions to be chosen from the available), which is only 4,294,967,296 (a bit over 4 billion configurations). These days, that's not very many, so brute force could be a viable option.

If you generate a set A of all the possible board combinations, you can create a test called $q(x)$ that returns *true* if the board configuration x is a solution or *false* if x is not a solution. Then you can create a program that looks like the following:

```
Generate the set A of all board configurations;
while there are still untested configurations in A do
      x = the next configuration from A
      if (q(x) == true) then print the solution x and stop
      go back to the top and do it again.
```

Notice that all the work is getting done in two steps: generating the set A and performing the test $q(x)$. The generation of the set A only happens once but performing the test $q(x)$ happens once for every configuration in your set A, until you find a solution. While this approach will surely work, it's not at all efficient. So let's try to reduce the number of combinations to consider to speed things up.

Eight Queens: Proposed Solution 2

In the process of considering your initial brute-force approach, you've done some analysis so you have a clearer idea of what has to happen. In order to reduce the number of total possible configurations and then come up with a more efficient algorithm, you need to think about the problem more creatively. The first thing to notice is that you can never have more than one queen in a column (yes, also per row, but let's keep things simpler for now). Having exactly one queen per column reduces the number of possible combinations to 2^{24} or just 16 million (consider that to place a queen into each column will now have only 8 possible choices: the rows; so 8^8 or 2^{24} choices total). Although this is good, it doesn't really change the algorithm very much. Your proposed solution now looks like the following:

```
Generate the set B of restricted board configurations;
while there are still untested configurations in B do
    x = the next configuration from B
    if (q(x) == true) then print the solution x and stop
    go back to the top and do it again.
```

This version requires generating the set B of board positions with one queen in each column and still requires visiting up to 16 million possible board positions. Generating B is now slightly more complicated than generating A because you now have to test to see if a proposed board position meets the one queen per column restriction. However, because you'll have fewer configurations to test, Solution 2 still better than Solution 1 above. You can do better.

Eight Queens: Proposed Solution 3

Let's be even more clever about generating and testing board. Instead of generating a complete board configuration and then testing it, you can test partial solutions as they are being generated. As soon as a board configuration has any queens in conflict, you can reject the board without waiting to place the rest of the queens. Also, if you can back up from a bad board configuration to the last good partial configuration, you can explore the possible configurations more quickly.

Now you're at the point where you can do that top-level design, formalize it, and move down to the next refinement level.

Solution 3: Refinement 1

To start generating your board, you will place one queen at a time, trying alternatives if you create a conflict and backing up if you run out of alternatives. Let's now formalize the steps:

Starting from row 0 and column 0:

1. Put down a new queen on the next row in the next available column.

2. Test to see if new queen is safe from every other queen already on the board. (That's a variation on the *q(x)* test above.)

a. If new queen is not safe:

i. Try placing her on the next row in the current column and repeat step 2.

ii. If there are no rows left to try, remove the new queen from the board; go back to the previous column and move the previous queen to the next row; repeat step 2.

b. If new queen is safe:

i. Leave her here and go to the next column.

ii. Starting from the first row, begin placing the next queen.

With this method, you're ensuring that the partial solution up to your current column j is correct. You then attempt to expand to the next partial solution by adding a queen in column j+1. As new queens are only added when all previous queens are safe, the solution must only test the safety of the one new queen, which reduces the amount of work in the testing routine. If your safety check fails, you back up to your previous valid partial solution at column j and reconsider remaining alternative positions for the last successfully placed queen. Wirth calls this technique of creating and testing partial solutions a *stepwise construction of trial solutions*. And the backing up technique is, of course, called *backtracking*.

Here's more formal pseudo-code to find a single solution:

```
do {
    while ((row < 8) && (col < 8))  {
        if (the current queen is safe)
            advance: keep the queen on the board and advance to the next
            column and next queen
        else
            the queen is not safe; try moving her to the next row.
    }
    if (we've exhausted all the rows in this column) then
        backtrack: retreat a column, move that column's queen to the next
        row, and start again.
} while ((col < 8) && (col >= 0));

if (we've reached column 8) then
    we have a solution, print it.
```

This algorithm is the first formal view of the solution. Notice that above we're using pseudo-code rather than a real programming language, pushing language details even further down the refinement levels. Also, while we've got a general outline of the method, there are a lot of details still to be considered. These details have been pushed down in the hierarchy of control we're creating, and we'll get to them in the next refinement iteration. This is also a function of the stepwise refinement.

Now that you have a description of the algorithm, you can also work to verify it. The final verification will be watching the program produce a correct solution, but you're not at that point yet. Nevertheless, you can surely take a chessboard (or a piece of paper) and walk through this algorithm by hand to verify that you can generate a placement of queens on the board that is a solution to the problem.

At this point you've got a more formal top-level description, you've seen how verification can be done, and you're ready to expand those fuzzy steps shown above.

Solution 3: Refinement 2

Now that you've got a first cut at the program, you need to examine each of the steps in the program and see what they are made of. Let's focus on that innocent-sounding "Test to see if new queen is safe from every other queen already on the board." It's secretly been doing all the heavy lifting in your planned solution and it's time to figure out how.

While stepwise refinement is mostly about describing the control flow of the program, at some point you need to decide on exactly what the data will look like. For each problem you try to solve, this will happen at a different point in your refinement process. For this problem, you are finally at a place where your next refinement should be writing more detailed pseudo-code. That is pretty much forcing you to think about data structures. You need to ask yourself how you are going to represent the board with all the queens as well as all the empty positions. You need a data structure that will allow you to represent queens and check whether they can be attacked. A first cut at this might be an 8 x 8 two-dimensional array where you place our queens at some (row, column) positions. As you are only storing the presence or absence of a queen, you can save space by making it a boolean array. This data structure also allows you to easily check a new queen's safety. Let's break that down.

When placing a new queen at some position (row, col), you need to check the following:

- Is this row still free?

- Is this column still free?

- Is this main diagonal still free?

- Is this anti-diagonal still free?

If you choose to systematically place one queen per column, you can skip the first check, as each following column will still necessarily be free (note that you could do the same with rows). This leaves you with the other three checks: row, main diagonal, and anti-diagonal. The row check is easy: you can just check all the other squares in the same row as the newly placed queen. To check the diagonals, you need to find a way to calculate what positions are along either of the diagonals from any given (row, col).

Looking at the sets of diagonal positions closely in Figure 9-2, you can see on the left image, depicting the main diagonals, that the *difference* between the row and column values of all the squares along any single main diagonal is a constant value (e.g. zero along the center main diagonal, -1 for the diagonal above it, and 1 for the diagonal below it). Similarly, looking at the right side of Figure 9-2, you can see that the *sum* of the row and column values of all the squares on any of the anti-diagonals is also a constant (e.g. 7 along the center anti-diagonal, 6 for the diagonal above it, and 8 for the one below it). Thus, given any cell, you can determine if it falls on either of the diagonals for queen at a given position.

	0	1	2	3	4	5	6	7
0	(0,0)	(0,1)	(0,2)	(0,3)	(0,4)	(0,5)	(0,6)	(0,7)
1	(1,0)	(1,1)	(1,2)	(1,3)	(1,4)	(1,5)	(1,6)	(1,7)
2	(2,0)	(2,1)	(2,2)	(2,3)	(2,4)	(2,5)	(2,6)	(2,7)
3	(3,0)	(3,1)	(3,2)	(3,3)	(3,4)	(3,5)	(3,6)	(3,7)
4	(4,0)	(4,1)	(4,2)	(4,3)	(4,4)	(4,5)	(4,6)	(4,7)
5	(5,0)	(5,1)	(5,2)	(5,3)	(5,4)	(5,5)	(5,6)	(5,7)
6	(6,0)	(6,1)	(6,2)	(6,3)	(6,4)	(6,5)	(6,6)	(6,7)
7	(7,0)	(7,1)	(7,2)	(7,3)	(7,4)	(7,5)	(7,6)	(7,7)

	0	1	2	3	4	5	6	7
0	(0,0)	(0,1)	(0,2)	(0,3)	(0,4)	(0,5)	(0,6)	(0,7)
1	(1,0)	(1,1)	(1,2)	(1,3)	(1,4)	(1,5)	(1,6)	(1,7)
2	(2,0)	(2,1)	(2,2)	(2,3)	(2,4)	(2,5)	(2,6)	(2,7)
3	(3,0)	(3,1)	(3,2)	(3,3)	(3,4)	(3,5)	(3,6)	(3,7)
4	(4,0)	(4,1)	(4,2)	(4,3)	(4,4)	(4,5)	(4,6)	(4,7)
5	(5,0)	(5,1)	(5,2)	(5,3)	(5,4)	(5,5)	(5,6)	(5,7)
6	(6,0)	(6,1)	(6,2)	(6,3)	(6,4)	(6,5)	(6,6)	(6,7)
7	(7,0)	(7,1)	(7,2)	(7,3)	(7,4)	(7,5)	(7,6)	(7,7)

Figure 9-2. *Main diagonals (left) and Anti-diagonals (right)*

Note, however, that you still need to check all the cells and perform the addition and subtraction of its coordinates to check if it happens to fall along either diagonal of interest for each new queen. That is functional but slow. You can do even better!

Solution 3: Refinement 3

Using your previously devised two-dimensional array, you can store the exact position of every queen as well as all the empty positions. However, all you really need to track is whether a given row, column, or diagonal is already protected by an existing queen. Meaning you do not need to know exactly where the queens are—only the columns and diagonals that they are protecting.

Thus, instead of storing boolean information (queen or no queen) about your 8*8=64 positions, you can store boolean information (protected or not protected) about your 8 rows, 15 main diagonals, and 15 anti-diagonals (38 booleans total). For larger boards, the reduction in space complexity would be much more substantial (e.g. consider placing 1000 queens on a 1000x1000 chess board). Additionally, you will now only need to look at three booleans (the row and both diagonals) to determine if a new queen is safe, which makes your safety check constant time. Overall, this solution will run in O(n) for n queens.

To check whether a given row is still free, you only need a one-dimensional boolean array:

```
boolean rows[8]; //indices 0-7 are the chessboard row numbers
```

where `rows[r]` = true means that the rth row is still unprotected.

To store information about your diagonals in similar one-dimensional arrays, you can use the property about the constant difference or sum of up and down diagonals to create two other arrays. For your 15 main diagonals, as the difference values range from -7 to 7, inclusively, you will calculate the correct diagonal index as (row-col+7), shifting the range into standard valid indices 0-14.

```
boolean mainDiagonals[15]; // indices 0-14 are obtained as row-col+7
boolean antiDiagonals[15]; //indices 0-14 are obtained as row+col
```

where `mainDiagonals [d]` = true means that the dth diagonal is still unprotected.

With this arrangement,[5] the test for the safety of a queen at position (row, col):

```
( rows[row] AND mainDiagonals[row-col+7] AND antiDiagonals[row+col] )
```

This is a pretty great solution, but is it good enough? Well, that depends. In general, constant-time safety checks can't be beat, and if you need to place n queens, then O(n) can't really be beat either. Still, you may have other constraints and priorities. Currently, you are storing one boolean per row and one per diagonal; for a board of size n*n, you are storing n+(n+n-1)*2=5n-2 booleans. If you had a very large board and your storage space was very limited, you could reduce your space complexity at the expense of your time complexity.

Solution 3: Refinement 4

There's yet another way to think about how to store the data. This time let's try to store even less than one boolean per row and one per diagonal. Turns out, you can get by with just one one-dimensional array of the length equal to our columns:

```
int board[8]; // for an 8x8 board, indices 0-7 represent rows, values 0-7
              represent columns
```

where each *index* into the array represents a column (0 through 7 in the eight-queens case) and each *value* stored at that index represents the row on which a queen was placed (also 0 through 7 in the eight-queens case). This encoding provides you with the exact coordinates of each queen. As each new queen is placed, you can check all previously placed queens, one at a time, and assess whether their rows, their main diagonals, or their anti-diagonals match with those of the newly placed queen. If any matches are found, then the queens are in conflict and the new queen must be moved. In this way, you can eliminate the separate arrays for had previously used to store the safety of each diagonal. Note that this test for safety is no longer constant time, and the overall solution is slower since now you have to check for safety from 0 previous queens, then 1, then 2, then 3... (0+1+2+3+...+n-1), which is $O(n^2)$.

This might be the time for some more code. At this point, it seems appropriate to move from pseudo-code to a real language. You'll have to make this move at some point in the refinement process. Just like deciding when to define your data structures, exactly

[5] Dahl, O. J., E. Dijkstra, and C. A. R. Hoare. 1972. *Structured Programming*. London: Academic Press.

when to insert language-specific features depends on the problem and how detailed the refinement is at this point. A Java method to test for safety might look like

```
// int[] board indices represent columns, values represent queen's row
// row, col are the coordinates of the newly placed queen whose safety is
being assessed
```

```java
public boolean isSafe () {
    boolean safe = true;
    for (int c = 0; c < col; c++) { // c is each previous column
        if ((board[c] == row) ||  // occupied row == this row?
            ((board[c] - c) == (row - col) ) || // main diagonals match?
            ((board[c] + c) == (row + col) ) )  // antidiagonals match?
        safe = false; //any matches mean conflict!
    }
    return safe;
}
```

Remember that, because you're creating partial solutions by adding one queen to a column at a time, you only need to test all the columns *before* current col where the new queen is being placed.

Solution 3: Refinement 5

Now that you have the safety procedure out of the way and you've decided on a simple data structure to represent the current board configuration, you can proceed to the remaining procedures in the decomposition. The remaining tasks are

1. Keep a safe queen on the board and move on to the next column.

2. Try moving an unsafe queen down to the next row.

3. If there are no rows left to try, remove the new queen from the board; go back to the previous column and move the previous queen to the next row.

These are all simple enough to solve in code without further decomposition. This is a key point of structured programming: keep doing the decompositions until a procedure becomes obvious and then you can try coding it up directly. The three tasks above might look like the following when written in code:

```java
/** "keep a safe queen on the board and move on to the next column"
 *  the queen at (row, col) is safe, so we have a partial solution;
 *  advance to the next column
 */
public void advance () {
    board[col] = row;          // put the queen at (row, col) on the board
    col++;                     // move to the next column
    row = 0;                   // and start at the beginning of the column
}
```

For *try moving an unsafe queen down to the next row* you don't even need a method. The test in the main program for safety moves the queen up a row if the isSafe() method determines that the current (row, col) position is unsafe. The code for this is

```java
if (isSafe())
    advance();
else
    row++;
```

Finally, you have the following:

```java
/**
 * "if there are no rows left to try, remove the new queen from the board;
 * go back to the previous column and move the previous queen to the next row"
 * could not find a safe row in current col given current placements of other
 * queens so back up one col and move the previous queen to next row down
 */
public void retreat () {
    col--;
    row = board[col] + 1;
}
```

The complete Java program is in the Appendix.

Modular Decomposition

In 1972, David Parnas published a paper titled "On the Criteria to Be Used in Decomposing Systems into Modules" where he proposed that one could design programs using a technique called modularity.[6] Parnas' paper was also one of the first papers to describe a decomposition based on *information hiding*, one of the key techniques in object-oriented programming and which we will discuss later in this section. In his paper, Parnas highlighted the differences between a top-down decomposition of a problem based on the flow of control of a problem solution versus a decomposition of the problem that used encapsulation and information hiding to isolate data definitions and their operations from each other. His paper is a clear precursor to object-oriented analysis and design (OOA&D), which you'll see in the next chapter.

While Parnas' paper predates the idea, he was really talking about a concept called *separation of concerns*. "In computer science, separation of concerns is a design principle for separating a computer program into distinct sections. Each section addresses a separate concern: a set of information that affects the code of a computer program. A program that embodies separation of concerns well is called a modular program. Modularity, and hence separation of concerns, is achieved by encapsulating information inside a section of code that has a well-defined interface. Encapsulation is a means of information hiding."[7] Traditionally, separation of concerns was all about separating functionality of the program. Parnas added the idea of separating the data as well, so that individual modules would control data as well as the operations that acted on the data, and the data would be visible only through well-defined interfaces. This concept was later expanded upon by Edsger Dijkstra.[8]

There are three characteristics of modularity that are key to creating modular programs:

- Encapsulation

- Loose coupling

- Information hiding

---

[6] Parnas, D. 1972. "On the Criteria to Be Used in Decomposing Systems into Modules." *Communications of the ACM* 15 (12): 1053–58.

[7] Wikipedia. *Separation of Concerns.* 2023. https://en.wikipedia.org/wiki/Separation_of_concerns. Retrieved on September 7, 2023.

[8] Dijkstra, Edsger W. 1982. "On the Role of Scientific Thought." In *Selected Writings on Computing: A Personal Perspective*, Hardcover, 60–66. New York, NY: Springer-Verlag. https://link.springer.com/book/10.1007/978-1-4612-5695-3.

Encapsulation means to bundle a group of services defined by their data and behaviors together as a module and keep them together. This group of services should be coherent and clearly belong together. (Like a function, a module should do just one thing.) The module then presents an *interface* to the user and that interface is ideally the only way to access the services and data in the module. An objective of encapsulating services and data is *high cohesion*: your module should do one thing and all the functions inside the module should work towards making that one thing happen.

The complement of encapsulation is *loose coupling*, which describes how strongly two modules are connected to each other. We want to minimize the dependence any one module has on another, so we separate modules to minimize interactions and make modules interact through the module interface. The goal is to create modules with internal integrity (strong cohesion) and small, few, direct, visible, and flexible connections to other modules (loose coupling). Good coupling between modules is loose enough that methods in one module can easily be called by methods in another module, while the data in each module is independent and can only be changed by methods within the module where it is defined. This way, two modules can communicate and request changes to data without the fear of erroneously changing the data.

Loose coupling falls into four broad categories, ranging from good to awful:

- *Simple data coupling:* Where unstructured data is passed via parameter lists. This is the best kind of coupling because it lets the sending module structure the data as it sees fit and it allows the receiving module to decide what to do with the data.

- *Structured data coupling*: Where structured data is passed via parameter lists. This is also a good kind of coupling because the sending module keeps control of the data formats and the receiving module gets to do what it wants to with the data.

- *Control coupling*: Where data from the sending module is passed to a receiving module and the content of the data tells the receiving module what to do. This is not a good type of coupling: the sender and receiver are too closely coupled because the sender is controlling how functions in the receiving module will execute.

- *Global-data coupling*: Where the two modules make use of the same global data. This is just awful as it violates a basic tenet of encapsulation by having the modules share data. This invites unwanted side effects and ensures that at any given moment during the execution of the program neither of the coupled modules will know precisely what is in the globally shared data. In general, global variables are considered bad programming practice.

Information hiding is often confused with encapsulation, but they are not the same. Encapsulation describes a process of wrapping both data and behaviors into a single entity—in our case, a module. Data can be publicly visible from within a module and thus not hidden. Information hiding, on the other hand, says that the data and behaviors in a module should be controlled and visible only to the operations that act on the data within the module, so it's invisible to other, external, modules. This is an important feature of modules (and later of objects as well) because it leaves control of the data to the module that understands best how to safely manipulate this data, while safeguarding against the side effects that can arise from other modules reaching in and tweaking said data.

Parnas was not just talking about hiding data in modules. His definition of information hiding was even more concerned with hiding design decisions in the module definition. "We propose ... that one begins with a list of difficult design decisions or design decisions which are likely to change. Each module is then designed to hide such a decision from the others."[9] Hiding information in this manner allows clients of a module to use the module successfully without needing to know any of the design decisions that went into constructing the module. It also allows developers to change the implementation of the module without affecting how the client uses the module.

Example: Keyword in Context

Back in the day, when Unix was young and the world was new, the Unix documentation was divided into eight different sections and the entire manual started with a *permuted index*. The problem with Unix is not the command line interface nor the inverted tree file system structure. No, the problem with Unix is in practically every nearly unreadable Unix command name, including- `ls`, `cat`, `cp`, `mv`, `mkdir`, `ps`, `cc`, `as`, `ld`, `m4` ... we could go

---

[9] (Parnas 1972)

on. Unix probably has the most cryptic command line set of any operating system on the planet. The cardinal rule for creating Unix command line tools was apparently, "why use three characters when two will do?"

So, finding anything in any of the eight sections of Unix documentation could have been a real trial. Enter the *permuted index*. Every Unix man page starts with a header line that contains the name of the command and a short description of what the command does. For example, the cat(1) man page begins as follows:

```
cat - concatenate and print files
```

But what if you don't know the name of a command but you do know what it does? The permuted index solves this problem by incorporating most of the words of the command description (the articles were ignored) into the index itself. So that *cat* could be found under "cat" and also "concatenate," "print," and "files." This is known as a *Keyword in Context* (KWIC) index. It works just dandy.

So your problem is to create a KWIC index given two input files: the first file containing words to ignore (sometimes called "stop words") and the second file containing lines of text we want to index. For example, say your first file contains *for, the, and*, as the words to ignore and the second file looks like

```
The Sun also Rises
For Whom the Bell Tolls
The Old Man and the Sea
```

Your resulting KWIC index, with the sorted words in all caps, would be

```
            The Sun ALSO Rises
       For Whom the BELL Tolls
           The Old MAN and the Sea
               The OLD Man and the Sea
        The Sun also RISES
The Old Man and the SEA
               The SUN also Rises
     For Whom the Bell TOLLS
               For WHOM the Bell Tolls
```

Shifting each line left until the next valid keyword (skipping articles), you obtain n copies of each line with n keywords. After each shift, the index keyword (shown in all caps) ends up at the front of each copy of the line. All lines are then sorted in alphabetical order by their index keyword. In the case of a tie (two lines of text have the same index word), the lines should appear in the same order as in the input file.

The questions you need to answer are 1) how do you create the KWIC index? and 2) how do you store the index data?

KWIC: Top-Down Decomposition

You'll start by designing the problem solution using a top-down decomposition. Top-down decompositions, as you saw with the eight queens problem earlier in this chapter, are all about control flow: you want to figure out how to sequentially solve the problem, making progress with each step you take. It is assumed that the data are stored separately from the routines and that each subroutine in the control flow can access the data it needs. The alternative is to pass the data along to each subroutine as you call it; this can be cumbersome and time consuming because the data usually has to be copied each time you pass it to a routine.

A first decomposition of this problem might look like the following:

1. Input the words to ignore and the text.

2. Shift each line of text and store a copy of the line for each word that ends up at the front of the line (skipping any articles).

3. Sort all of the resulting shifted lines of text by their first word (i.e. by each line's index word).

4. Format and output the text.

Note that these steps can easily become separate subroutines that are all called in sequence from a main program. The data structure used for the input text could be an array of characters for each line, a String for each line, or an array of Strings for the entire input file. You could also use a map data structure that uses each index word as the key and a String containing the input text line as the value of the map element. There are certainly other possible data structures to be used. Sorting can be done by any of the stable sorting algorithms and which algorithm to use would depend on the data structure chosen and on the expected size of the input text. Your sort must be stable because of the requirement that identical index words sort their respective lines in the same order that they appear in the input text file. Depending on the programming language you use and the data structure you choose, sorting might be done automatically for you. The data structure you choose will affect how the circular shifts are done and how the output routine does the work of formatting each output line.

Now that you've got a feel for how a top-down decomposition might proceed, let's move on and consider a modular decomposition.

KWIC: Modular Decomposition

A modular decomposition of the KWIC problem can be based on information hiding in the sense that you will hide both data structures and design decisions. The modules you create will not necessarily represent elements of the sequential list you have above but will instead cooperate by calling each other as needed. One possible list of modules for generating a KWIC index is the following:

- Line module (for lines of input text)
- Keyword-Line pair module
- KWICIndex module to create the indexed list itself
- Shift module
- Module to format and print the output
- Master control module – the main program

The Line module will use the Keyword-Line module to create a map data structure (i.e., key-value pairs) where each key is a keyword and its value is the list of lines that begin with that keyword. The KWICIndex module will use the Line module to create the indexed list. The Shift module will use the KWICIndex module (and, consequently, the Line and Keyword-Line modules) and create the shifted set of lines. Sorting will be handled internally in the KWICIndex module; the index will be created as a sorted list and any additions to the list will maintain the sorted order. The format and print module will format the keyword lines so that the keywords are printed in all caps. For an alternative view, the lines could also be unshifted and keywords would be lined up under each other on consecutive output lines. Finally, the master control module will read the input, create the KWICIndex, and cause it to print correctly.

The key of these modules is that you can describe the modules and their interactions without needing the details of how each module is implemented and how the data is stored. That is hidden in the module description itself. Other designs are also possible. For example, it might be better to subsume the circular shift operations inside the Line module, allowing it to store the input lines and their shifts. Regardless, the next step in the design is to create the interface for each module and to coordinate the interfaces so that each module can communicate with every other module regardless of the internal implementation.

For this implementation, let's create four Java classes:

- Line, which creates the data structure for the lines that are input from a text file.

- KwicIndex, which takes the words to ignore and the input lines and creates a sorted permuted index. Lines are shifted and added to the index based on the keyword.

- Print, which takes the KwicIndex object and prints the permuted index in the right order and shifted as preferred (e.g., in original sentence order but with keywords lined up under each other).

- Main, checks that the command line arguments are correct, creates the initial KwicIndex object, and calls the methods to add new lines and to do the printing.

Give this program a file called input.txt with the following input:

```
Descent of Man
The Ascent of Man
The Old Man and The Sea
A Portrait of the Artist As a Young Man
A Man is a Man but Bubblesort is a dog
this is dumb
```

and ignoring the words "the," "of," and "and" (provided in the stop words input file) produces the following KWIC output:

```
                                        A Portrait of the Artist As a Young Man
                          A Man is A Man but Bubblesort is a dog
      A Man is a Man but Bubblesort is A dog
          A Portrait of the Artist As A Young Man
                                        A Man is a Man but Bubblesort is a dog
```

```
                A Portrait of the ARTIST As a Young Man
           A Portrait of the Artist AS a Young Man
                          The ASCENT of Man
             A Man is a Man but BUBBLESORT is a dog
                          DESCENT of Man
      something i do not know how to DO
                    something i DO not know how to do
A Man is a Man but Bubblesort is a DOG
                          this is DUMB
          something i do not know HOW to do
                    something I do not know how to do
               A Man IS a Man but Bubblesort is a dog
      A Man is a Man but Bubblesort IS a dog
                          this IS dumb
          something i do not KNOW how to do
                    A MAN is a Man but Bubblesort is a dog
                  Descent of MAN
            A Man is a MAN but Bubblesort is a dog
              The Old MAN and The Sea
            The Ascent of MAN
A Portrait of the Artist As a Young MAN
               something i do NOT know how to do
               The OLD Man and The Sea
                    A PORTRAIT of the Artist As a Young Man
          The Old Man and The SEA
                    SOMETHING i do not know how to do
                    THIS is dumb
     A Portrait of the Artist As a YOUNG Man
```

In Appendix 2 we show an implementation of the KWIC index program written in Java that somewhat closely follows the discussion above. We'll continue this discussion on modular decomposition in much more detail in the next chapter on object-oriented design.

Conclusion

Structured design describes a set of classic design methodologies. These design ideas work for a large class of problems. The original structured design idea, stepwise refinement, has you decompose the problem from the top down, focusing on the control flow of the solution. It also relates closely to some of the architectures mentioned in Chapter 7, particularly the main program subroutine and pipe-and-filter architectures. Modular decomposition is the immediate precursor to the modern object-oriented methodologies and introduced the ideas of encapsulation and information hiding. These ideas are the fundamentals of your design toolbox.

References

Dahl, O. J., E. Dijkstra, and C. A. R. Hoare. 1972. *Structured Programming.* London: Academic Press.

Dijkstra, E. 1968. "GoTo Statement Considered Harmful." *CACM* 11 (3): 147–48.

Dijkstra, Edsger W. 1982. "On the Role of Scientific Thought." In *Selected Writings on Computing: A Personal Perspective*, Hardcover, 60–66. New York, NY: Springer-Verlag. https://link.springer.com/book/10.1007/978-1-4612-5695-3.

Hunt, Andrew, and D. Thomas. 2000. *The Pragmatic Programmer: From Journeyman to Master.* Boston: Addison-Wesley.

Miller, G. A. 1956. "The Magical Number Seven, plus or Minus Two: Some Limits on Our Capacity for Processing Information." *Psychological Review* 63: 81–97.

Parnas, D. 1972. "On the Criteria to Be Used in Decomposing Systems into Modules." *Communications of the ACM* 15 (12): 1053–58.

Wikipedia. Separation of Concerns. 2023. http://en.wikipedia.org/wiki/Separation_of_concerns. Retrieved on September 7, 2023.

Wirth, N. 1971. "Program Development by Stepwise Refinement." *CACM* 14 (4): 221–27.

Appendix 1: The Complete Non-Recursive Eight-Queens Program

```java
/*
 *   NQueens.java
 *   8-Queens Program
 *   A non-recursive version for a single solution
 */

import java.util.*;

public class NQueens {

    static int totalcount = 0;
    static int row = 0;
    static int col = 0;
    static int[] board;

    /*
     *   the queen at (row, col) is safe,
     *   so we have a partial solution.
     *   advance to the next column
     */
    public void advance () {
        board[col] = row;
        col++;
        row = 0;
    }

    /*
     *   could not find a safe row in current col
     *   so back up one col and move that queen up a row
     */
    public void retreat () {
        col--;
        row = board[col] + 1;
    }
```

```java
/*
 *    check to see if queen at (row, col)  can be attacked
 */
public boolean isSafe () {
    boolean safe = true;
    totalcount++;
    /*
     * check diagonals and row for attacks
     * since we're just checking partial solutions
     * only need to go up to current col
     */
    for (int c = 0; c <col; c++){ //c is each previous column
        if ( (board[c] == row) || // occupied row == this row?
        ((board[c] - c) == (row - col) ) || // main diagonals match?
        ((board[c] + c) == (row + col)) ) // antidiagonals match?
            safe = false; //any matches mean conflict!
        }
    }
    return safe;
}

public static void main(String args[]) {
    int N = 8;       // default board size

    System.out.print("Enter the size of the board: ");
    Scanner stdin = new Scanner(System.in);
    N = stdin.nextInt();
    System.out.println();

    NQueens queen = new NQueens();
    /*
     *    index into board is a column number
     *    value stored in board is a row number
     *    so board[2] = 3; says put a queen on col 2, row 3
     */
    board = new int [N];         /*
     * simple algorithm to build partial solutions
```

```
 *    for N-queens problem. Place a queen in the
 *    next available column, test to see if it
 *    can be attacked. If not, then move to the next
 *    column. If it can be attacked, move the queen
 *    up a row and try again.
 *    If we exhaust all the rows in a column, back up
 *    reset the previous column and try again.
 */
do {
    while ((row < N) && (col < N))  {
        if (queen.isSafe())
            queen.advance();
        else
            row++;
    }
    if (row == N)
        queen.retreat();
} while ((col < N) && (col >= 0));

/* If we've placed all N queens, we've got a solution */
if (col == N) {
    for (int i = 0; i < N; i++) {
        System.out.print(board[i] + " ");
    }
} else
    System.out.println("No solution. ");

System.out.println();

System.out.println("after trying " + totalcount +
    " board positions.");

    }
}
```

Appendix 2: A Modular Version of the KWIC Solution

```java
/**
 * CLASS Line
 * Handle the storage of 3 key pieces of information.
 * the current line, the keyword, and the index of the
 * keyword in the line.
 *
 * Basically just like a struct in C.
 *
 */

public class Line implements Comparable<Line> {
    public String line;
    public String keyword;
    public int indexOf;

    public Line(String line, String keyword, int indexOf) {
        this.keyword = keyword;
        this.indexOf = indexOf;

        // capitalize the keyword in the line
        // grab the first part of the line
        String first = line.substring(0, indexOf);
        // capitalize the entire keyword
        String middle = keyword.toUpperCase();
        // grab the rest of the line after the keyword
        String last = line.substring(indexOf + keyword.length());
        // put it all back together
        this.line = first + middle + last;
    }

    /**
     * We want to sort lines based on keyword alone.
     * This will do a lexicographical comparison of the keywords
     * Remember that keyword is a String
     */
    @Override
```

```java
    public int compareTo(Line other) {
        return this.keyword.compareToIgnoreCase(other.keyword);
    }
}

import java.util.Scanner;
import java.util.*;

/**
 * CLASS KwicIndex
 * A KwicIndex object contains a collection of Lines
 * and the words we are ignoring as keywords.
 *
 * We use a HashSet for the words to ignore because
 * we only ever want one of each of these words.
 *
 * We use a PriorityQueue for the lines because we
 * want to store them sorted by keywords and the PQ
 * does that for us automatically.
 *
 */

public class KwicIndex {
    public HashSet<String> wordsToIgnore;
    public PriorityQueue<Line> lines;

    /**
     * Constructor that initializes the lists and
     * reads all the words to ignore
     */
    public KwicIndex(Scanner ignore) {
        this.wordsToIgnore = new HashSet<String>();
        this.lines = new PriorityQueue<Line>();

        while (ignore.hasNext()) {
            this.wordsToIgnore.add(ignore.next());
        }
    }
```

```
/**
 * Create an entry in the index for the given line.
 * @param str; a string to examine
 * @return
 */
public void add(String str) {
    Scanner scan = new Scanner(str);

    int offset = 0;
    int words = -1;
    while (scan.hasNext()) {
        // grab the next word
        String temp = scan.next();
        words++;
        /** if this word is not to be ignored create a new line
          *  with the line shifted with the new word removed
          *  then add it to the list of lines
          */
        if (!wordsToIgnore.contains(temp.toLowerCase())) {
            Line version = new Line(str, temp, offset + words);
            this.lines.add(version);
        }
        offset += temp.length();
    }
}

/**
 * return the index so we can print it
 */
public PriorityQueue<Line> getLines() {
    return lines;
}
}
```

```java
import java.util.*;

/**
 * CLASS Print
 * Print the resulting KWIC index
 *
 */

public class Print {
    public PriorityQueue<Line> lines;

    public Print(PriorityQueue<Line> lines) {
        this.lines = lines;
    }

    /**
     * Print to System.out the contents of the index
     * lines formatting adjusted so
     * keywords are in the same column
     */
    public void printIndex() {
        // make a new PriorityQueue
        PriorityQueue<Line> newLines = new PriorityQueue<Line>();

        // lets figure out the length of the longest line
        int longest = 0;
        for (Line l : lines) {
            if (l.indexOf > longest) {
                longest = l.indexOf;
            }
        }

        /**
         * do the printing
         */
        while (!lines.isEmpty()) {
            /** grab the line with smallest keyword */
```

```java
            Line l = lines.poll();

            /** save the line */
            newLines.add(l);

            /**
             * figure out the whitespace
             * Here we figure out how far over to print
             * the keyword based on putting the longest line
             * right in the middle
             */
            String retval = "";
            for (int i = 0; i < (longest - l.indexOf); i++) {
                retval += " ";
            }

            /**
             * construct the line
             */
            retval += l.line;

            // output
            System.out.println(retval);
        }
        /** Save the lines from all that polling */
        this.lines = newLines;
    }
}

import java.io.File;
import java.io.FileNotFoundException;
import java.util.Scanner;

/**
 * CLASS Main
 * Manage the KWIC indexing system.
 *
 * @author jfdooley
```

```
 *
 */

public class Main {

    public static void main(String[] args) {
        /**
         * declare the Scanners to read the files
         */
        Scanner scan = null;
        Scanner ignore = null;
        /**
         * usage and file opening
         *
         * if we have the correct number of input args
         * we try to open the input files
         */
        if (args.length == 2) {
            try {
                ignore = new Scanner(new File(args[0]));
                scan = new Scanner(new File(args[1]));
            } catch (FileNotFoundException ex) {
                System.out.println(ex.getMessage());
                System.exit(1);
            }
            /**
             * wrong number of input args. Give user a usage
             * message and leave
             */
        } else {
            System.out.println("Usage: java Main <inputFile> <wordsToIgnore>");
            System.exit(1);
        }
        /**
         * first we create an KwicIndex object & add
```

```
      * the words to ignore to it
      */
      KwicIndex index = new KwicIndex(ignore);

    /**
      * Now we add all the lines to the index
      *  the add() method does the work of the circular shift
      *  and adding the shifted lines to the priority queue
      */
      while (scan.hasNextLine()) {
          index.add(scan.nextLine());
      }

    /**
      * Finally we print the index we just created
      */
      Print prt = new Print(index.getLines());
      prt.printIndex();
  }
}
```

CHAPTER 10

Object-Oriented Overview

The object has three properties, which makes it a simple, yet powerful model building block. It has state, so it can model memory. It has behavior, so that it can model dynamic processes. And it is encapsulated, so that it can hide complexity.

—Trygve Reenskaug, *Working With Objects*

Well, yes, we've all learned about the object-oriented programming paradigm before, but it never hurts to go over some basic definitions so that we're all on the same page for our discussion about object-oriented analysis and design.

First of all, objects are *things*. They have an *identity* (i.e., a name), a *state* (i.e., a set of attributes that describes the current data stored inside the object), and a defined set of *behaviors* that operate on that state. A stack is an object, as is an automobile, a bank account, a window, a button in a graphical user interface, a book, and even a stack of books. In an object-oriented program, a set of cooperating objects pass messages among themselves. The messages make requests of the destination objects to invoke methods that either perform operations on their data (thus changing the state of the object), or to report on the current state of the object. Eventually work gets done. Objects use *encapsulation* and *information hiding* (remember, they're different) to isolate data and operations from other objects in the program. Shared data areas are (usually) eliminated. Objects are members of *classes* that define attribute types and operations.

Classes are *templates* or blueprints for objects. Classes can also be thought of as factories that generate objects. So an `Automobile` class will define and create instances of autos, a `Stack` class will create a new stack object, and a `Queue` class will create a new queue. Classes may *inherit* attributes and behaviors from other classes. Classes may be arranged in a class hierarchy where one class (a *super class*, also called a *parent* or *base class*) is a generalization of one or more *subclasses* (also called *child classes*). A subclass

209

© John F. Dooley and Vera A. Kazakova 2024
J. F. Dooley and V. A. Kazakova, *Software Development, Design, and Coding*,
https://doi.org/10.1007/979-8-8688-0285-0_10

inherits the attributes and operations from its super class and may add new methods or attributes of its own. In this sense a subclass is more specific and detailed than its super class; hence, we say that a subclass *extends* a superclass. For example, a BankAccount object may include the customer's name, address, balance, and a unique BankAccount id number; it will also allow deposits and withdrawals and the current balance can be queried. A CheckingAccount is a more specific version of a BankAccount; it has all the attributes and operations of a BankAccount, but also adds data and behaviors that are specific to CheckingAccounts, like check numbers and a per check charge. In Java this feature is called *inheritance*.

There are a number of advantages to inheritance. It is an *abstraction mechanism* that may be used to classify entities. It is a *reuse mechanism* at both the design and the programming level. An *inheritance graph* is a source of organizational knowledge about domains and systems.

And, of course, there are problems with inheritance, as well. It makes object classes that are not self-contained: subclasses cannot be understood without reference to their superclasses. Inheritance introduces complexity, which is undesirable, especially in critical systems. Inheritance also usually allows *overloading* [1] of operators (methods in Java), which can be good (polymorphism) or bad (screening useful methods in the superclass).

Object-oriented programming (OOP) has a number of advantages, among them easier maintenance, because objects can be understood and manipulated as stand-alone entities. Objects are also appropriate as reusable components. But, for some problems there may be no clear or useful mapping from real-world objects to system objects, meaning that OOP may not be appropriate for all problems.

An Object-Oriented Analysis and Design Process

Object-oriented analysis (OOA), design (OOD), and programming (OOP) are related but distinct.

OOA is concerned with developing an *object model of the application domain*. So, for example, you take the problem statement, generate a set of features and (possibly) use cases,[2] tease out the objects and some of the methods within those objects that you'll

---

[1] Overloading means that an operator is redefined to perform a different operation while retaining the same name.

[2] Cockburn, Alistair. 2000. *Writing Effective Use Cases.* Boston, MA: Addison-Wesley.

need to satisfy the use case, and you put together an architecture of how the solution will hang together. That's object-oriented analysis.

OOD is concerned with developing an *object-oriented system model* to satisfy requirements. You take the objects generated from your OOA, figure out whether to use inheritance, aggregation, composition, abstract classes, interfaces, and so on, in order to create a coherent and efficient model. You draw the class diagrams, flesh out the details of what each attribute is and what each method does, and describe the interfaces. That's the design.

Some people like object-oriented analysis, design, and programming[3] and some people don't.[4]

So, object-oriented analysis allows you to take a problem model and recast it in terms of objects and classes, and object-oriented design allows you to take your analyzed requirements and connect the dots between the objects you've proposed and to fill in the details with respect to object attributes and methods. But how do you really do all this?

Here is a proposed process that starts to fill in some of the details.[5] We'll figure out the rest as we go along.

1. Write (or receive) the *problem statement*. Use this to generate an initial set of features.

2. Create the *feature list*. The feature list is the set of program features that you derive from the problem statement; it contains your initial set of requirements. The feature list may be a set of *user stories*. To help generate the feature list, you can put together a set of *scenarios*, where a scenario is a narrative description of how the user will walk through using the program to accomplish a task. User stories are very brief and high level, while scenarios are longer and provide more detail. A user story might generate several scenarios. The scenario should be technology agnostic and should be explicit from the user's perspective. It's not how the

---

[3] Beck, K., and B. Boehm. 2003. "Agility through Discipline: A Debate." *IEEE Computer* 36 (6): 44–46.

[4] Graham, Paul. 2000. "Why Arc Isn't Especially Object Oriented." Blog. *PaulGraham.Com*. www.paulgraham.com/noop.html. Retrieved on 12 October 2009.

[5] McLaughlin, Brett D., Gary Pollice, and Dave West. 2007. *Head First Object-Oriented Analysis and Design*. Head First Books. Sebastopol, CA: O'Reilly Media, Inc.

program works; it's about what the user wants to accomplish and how the user gets the task done; it can also talk about what the user knows.

3. Write up *use cases*.[6] This helps to refine the features and to dig out new requirements and to expose problems with the features you just created. Use cases are more specific descriptions of how a user accomplishes a task using the program; they describe in more detail how the user interacts with the system. Use cases "...capture the goal of an action, the trigger event that starts a process, and then describe each step of the process including inputs, outputs, errors, and exceptions. Use cases are often written in the form of an actor or user performing an action followed by the expected system response and alternative outcomes."[7] Each scenario or user story might create several use cases.

4. *Break the problem down* into subproblems or subsystems or modules or whatever you want to call them as long as they're smaller, self-contained modules, typically related to functionality.

5. *Map* your features, subsystems, and use cases to domain objects; create abstractions.

6. *Identify* the program's objects, methods, and algorithms.

7. *Implement* this iteration.

8. *Test* the iteration.

9. If you've not finished the feature list and you still have time and/or money left, go back to step 4 and do another iteration, otherwise...

10. Do final *acceptance testing* and release.

---

[6] N.B. In some of the literature on requirements gathering, the definitions of scenario and use case used here are reversed. That is, the use case is a general description of accomplishing a goal and the scenario is the list of explicit steps used to accomplish the task. We prefer the definitions given here. A lively discussion of the differences between user stories and use cases can be found at `https://wiki.c2.com/?UserStoryAndUseCaseComparison`.

[7] Schaeffer, Nadine. "User Stories, Scenarios, and Use Cases," retrieved from `https://cloudforestdesign.com/2011/04/25/introduction-user-stories-user-personas-use-cases-whats-the-difference/` on July 10, 2017.

Note that this process leaves out a lot of details, such as the length of an iteration. How many features end up in an iteration? How and when do we add new features to the feature list? How exactly do we identify objects and operations? How do we abstract objects into classes? Where do we fix bugs that are found in testing? Do we do reviews of code and other project work products? Leaving out some details here is okay; we're mostly concerned with the analysis and design elements of the process. We'll discuss ideas on the rest of the process below; some of the answers are also in Chapter 3 on project management.

Details of the OOA&D Process

How do the process steps above fit into the software development life cycle? Well, we're glad you asked. Recall that the basic development life cycle has four steps:

1. Requirements gathering and analysis

2. Design

3. Implementation and testing

4. Release, maintenance, and evolution

We can easily assign the previous ten steps into these four buckets, as follows:

1. Requirements gathering and analysis:

    1.1. Problem statement

    1.2. Feature list creation

    1.3. Use case generation

2. Design:

    2.1. Break up the problem.

    2.2. Map features and use cases to domain objects.

    2.3. Identify objects, methods, and algorithms.

3. Implementation and testing:

3.1. Implement this iteration.

3.2. Test the iteration.

3.3. If you've not finished with the feature list or are out of time, go back to step 2.1, otherwise go to step 4.

4. Release, maintenance, and evolution:

4.1. Do final acceptance testing and release.

Once again we can ignore the details of each step for now. These details really depend on the process methodology you choose for your development project. The description of the process above uses an iterative methodology and can easily be fitted into an agile process, or a more traditional staged release process.

Note that you'll need to revisit the requirements whenever you get to step 4 because you're likely to have uncovered or generated new requirements during each iteration. Also, whenever your customer sees a new iteration, they'll ask for more stuff (yes, they will; trust us). This means you'll be updating the feature list (and reprioritizing) at the beginning of each new iteration.

Executing the Process

Let's continue by working through an extended example, seeing where the problem statement leads you, and how you can tease out requirements and begin your object oriented analysis.

Step 1: The Problem Statement

Burt, the proud owner of Birds by Burt, has created the ultimate in bird feeders. Burt's Bird Buffet and Bath (B⁴), is an integrated bird feeder and birdbath. It comes in 12 different colors (including camo) and 1, 3, and 5 lb. capacities. It will hold up to one gallon of water in the attached bird bath, it has a built-in hanger so you can hang it from a tree branch or from a pole, and the B⁴ is just flying off the shelves. Alice and Bob are desperate for a B⁴, but they'd like a few changes. Alice is a techno-nerd and a fanatic songbird watcher. She knows that her favorite songbirds only feed during the day, so she wants a custom B^4 that allows the feeding doors to open automatically at sunrise and close automatically at sunset. Burt, ever the accommodating owner, has agreed and the hardware division of Birds by Burt is hard at work designing the B^4++ for Alice. Your job is to write the software to make the hardware work.

Step 2: The Feature List

The first thing you need to do is figure out what the B^4++ will actually *do*. This version seems simple enough. You can almost immediately write down three requirements:

- The feeding doors must all open and close simultaneously.

- The feeding doors should open automatically at sunrise.

- The feeding doors should close automatically at sunset.

So this doesn't seem so bad. The simplified requirements are straightforward and there is no user interaction required. Next you'll consider the use cases so you can see just what the bird feeder is really going to do.

Step 3: Use Cases

A *use case* is a description of what a program does in a particular situation. It's the detailed set of steps that the program executes when a user asks for something. Use cases always have an *actor* (some outside agent that gets the ball rolling) and a *goal* (what the use case is supposed to have done by the end). The use case describes what it takes to get from some initial state to the goal, from the user's perspective.[8] Here's a quick example of a use case for the B^4++:

1. The sensor detects sunlight at a 40% brightness level.

2. The feeding doors open.

3. Birds arrive, eat, drink, and leave.

4. The sensor detects a decrease in sunlight to a 25% brightness level.

5. The feeding doors close.

---

[8] (Cockburn 2000)

Given the simplicity of the B4++, that's about all you can expect out of a use case. In fact, step 3 technically isn't part of the use case because it isn't part of the program, but it's good to have so that you can get a more complete picture of how the B⁴++ is operating. Use cases are very useful in requirements analysis because they give you an idea—in natural language—of what the program needs to do in a particular situation and because they often help you uncover new requirements. Note that in the use case you don't talk about *how* a program does something; you only concentrate on *what* the program has to do to reach the goal. This can also include the inputs, outputs, and errors that occur. It can also include alternative lists of steps for different situations (e.g., if the user makes an error, create two alternative use cases, one for how to treat the error and one for when the user doesn't make the error). Most times there will be several use cases for every program you write. Here you've only got one because this version of the B⁴++ is so simple.

Step 4: Decompose the Problem

So now that you've got your use case you can probably just decompose the problem and identify the objects in the program.

If you look at the use case above and pick out the nouns (including compound nouns), you can identify several objects. Each of these objects has certain characteristics and contributes to reaching the goal of making food available to the birds. While "birds" is a noun in the use case, but they are the actors in this little play so for the purposes of describing the objects you ignore them; they're not really part of the program. On a birdless day, your B⁴++ should continue to operate its business as usual. The other nouns are *sensor, doors,* and *sunlight brightness level*. These are the critical pieces of the B⁴++ because the use case indicates that they are the elements and triggers that accomplish the goal of opening and closing the feeding doors at sunrise and sunset. As any changes in *sunlight brightness level* will be fully handled by the environment and detected by the sensor, you are left with *sensor* and *doors* as the objects to incorporate into your design. Here are the objects for this first version of the B⁴++ and a short description:

BirdFeeder: The top-level object. The bird feeder has one or more feeding doors through which the birds can enter and a sensor to detect changes in light brightness. The BirdFeeder class needs to control the querying of the light sensor and the opening and closing of the feeding doors.

Sensor: An object connected to a hardware light sensor that detects different light levels. You'll need to query it about current light levels.

FeedingDoor: There will be several feeding doors on the bird feeder. They have to open and close when given some trigger.

That's probably about it for classes at this point. Now what do they all do? To describe classes and their components you can use another diagramming feature, a *class diagram*.

Step 5: Class Diagrams

A *class diagram* allows you to describe the attributes and the methods of a class. A set of class diagrams describe all the objects in a program and the relationships between the objects. You draw arrows of different types between class diagrams to describe the relationships. Class diagrams give you a visual description of the object model that you've created for your program. You saw a set of class diagrams for the Fox and Rabbit program in Chapter 7.

Class diagrams have three sections:

- *Name*: The name of the class

- *Attributes*: The data fields (including names and datatypes) available
  to class instances

- *Methods*: The set of methods (including name and visibility) available
  to class instances

You can see an example of a class diagram for your BirdFeeder class in Figure 10-1.

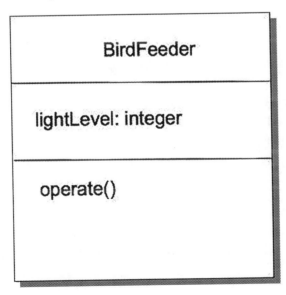

Figure 10-1. *The BirdFeeder class*

The diagram shows that the BirdFeeder class has a single integer attribute, lightLevel, and a single method, operate(). By themselves class diagrams aren't terribly interesting, but when you put several of them together and show the relationships between them, then you can get some interesting information about your program. So what else do you need in the way of class diagrams? In your program, the BirdFeeder class uses the FeedingDoor and Sensor classes, but they don't know (or care) about each other. In fact, while BirdFeeder knows about FeedingDoor and Sensor and uses them, they don't know they are being used. Ah, the beauty of object-oriented programming. This relationship can be expressed in the class diagram of all three classes shown in Figure 10-2.

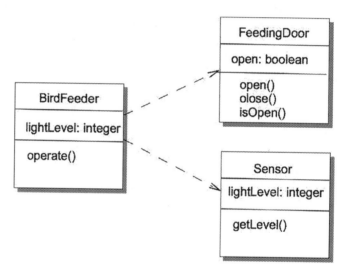

Figure 10-2. *BirdFeeder uses FeedingDoor and Sensor*

In this figure, the dotted line with the open arrow at the end indicates that one class (in your case, BirdFeeder) is *associated* with another class (in your case, either FeedingDoor or Sensor) by *using* it.

Step 6: Code Anyone?

Now that you've got the class diagrams and know the attributes, the methods, and the association between the classes, it's time to flesh out your program with some code.

In the BirdFeeder object, the operate() method needs to check the light levels and open or close the feeding doors depending on the current light level reported by the Sensor object. It does nothing if the current light level is above or below the threshold values.

In the Sensor object, the getLevel() method just reports back the current level from the hardware sensor.

In the FeedingDoor object, the open() method checks to see if the doors are closed. If they are, it opens them and sets a boolean to indicate that they're open. The close() method does the reverse.

Here's the code for each of the classes described.

```java
/**
 * class BirdFeeder
 *
 * @author Agile Programmer
 * @version 1.0
 */

import java.util.ArrayList;
import java.util.Iterator;

public class BirdFeeder {
    /* instance variables */
    private static final int ON_THRESHOLD = 40;
    private static final int OFF_THRESHOLD = 25;
    private int lightLevel;
    private Sensor s1;
    private ArrayList<FeedingDoor> doors = null;

    /*
     * Default Constructor for objects of class BirdFeeder
     */
    public BirdFeeder() {
        doors = new ArrayList<FeedingDoor>();
        /* initialize lightLevel */
        lightLevel = 0;
        s1 = new Sensor();
```

```java
        /* by default we have a feeder with just one door */
        doors.add(new FeedingDoor());

    }

    /*
     * The operate() method operates the birdfeeder.
     * It gets the current lightLevel from the Sensor and
     * checks to see if we should open or close the doors
     */
    public void operate() {
        lightLevel = s1.getLevel();

        if (lightLevel > ON_THRESHOLD) {
            Iterator door_iter = doors.iterator();
            while (door_iter.hasNext()) {
                FeedingDoor a = (FeedingDoor) door_iter.next();
                a.open();
                System.out.println("The door has opened.");
            }
        } else if (lightLevel < OFF_THRESHOLD) {
            Iterator door_iter = doors.iterator();
            while (door_iter.hasNext()) {
                FeedingDoor a = (FeedingDoor) door_iter.next();
                a.close();
                System.out.println("The door has closed.");
            }
        }
    }
}

/**
 * class FeedingDoor
 *
 * @author Agile Programmer
 * @version 1.0
 */
```

```java
public class FeedingDoor {
    /* instance variables */
    private boolean doorOpen;

    /*
     * Default constructor for objects of class FeedingDoors
     */
    public FeedingDoor() {
        /* initialize instance variables */
        doorOpen = false;
    }

    /*
     * open the feeding doors
     * if they are already open, do nothing
     */
    public void open( ) {
        /** if the door is closed, open it */
        if (doorOpen == false) {
            doorOpen = true;
        }
    }

    /*
     * close the doors
     * if they are already closed, do nothing
     */
    public void close( ) {
        /* if the door is open, close it */
        if (doorOpen == true) {
            doorOpen = false;
        }
    }

    /*
     * report whether the doors are open or not
     */
```

```java
    public boolean isOpen() {
        return doorOpen;
    }
}

/**
 * class Sensor
 *
 * @author Agile Programmer
 * @version 1.0
 */
public class Sensor {
    /* instance variables */
    private int lightLevel;

    /*
     * Default constructor for objects of class Sensor
     */
    public Sensor() {
        /** initialize instance variable */
        lightLevel = 0;
    }

    /**
     * getLevel - return a light level
     *
     * @return the value of the light level
     * that is returned by the hardware sensor
     */
    public int getLevel( ) {
        /* till we get a hardware light sensor, we just fake it */
        lightLevel = (int) (Math.random() * 100);
        return lightLevel;
    }
}
```

Finally, you have a BirdFeederTester class that operates the B⁴++.

```java
/**
 * The class that tests the BirdFeeder, Sensor, and
 * FeedingDoor classes.
 *
 * @version 0.1
 */
public class BirdFeederTester {
    private BirdFeeder feeder;

    /*
     * Constructor for objects of class BirdFeederTest
     */
    public BirdFeederTester() {
        this.feeder = new BirdFeeder();
    }

    public static void main(String [] args) {
        BirdFeederTester bfTest = new BirdFeederTester();

        for (int i = 0; i < 10; i++) {
            System.out.println("Testing the bird feeder");
            bfTest.feeder.operate();
            try {
                Thread.currentThread().sleep(2000);
            } catch (InterruptedException e) {
                System.out.println("Sleep interrupted" + e.getMessage());
                System.exit(1);
            }
        }
    }
}
```

When Alice and Bob take delivery of the B⁴++ they are thrilled. The doors automatically open and close, the birds arrive and eat their fill. Birdsong fills the air. What else could they possibly want?

Conclusion

Object-oriented design is a methodology that works for a very wide range of problems. Solutions to many problems in the real world are easily characterized as groups of cooperating objects. This single simple idea promotes simplicity of design, reuse of both designs and code, and the ideas of encapsulation and information hiding that Parnas advocated in his paper on modular decomposition.[9] It's not the right way to solve some problems, including problems like communications protocol implementations, but it opens up a world of new and better solutions for many others and it closes the "intellectual distance" between the real-world description of a problem and the resulting code.

References

Beck, K., and B. Boehm. 2003. "Agility through Discipline: A Debate." *IEEE Computer* 36 (6): 44–46.

Cockburn, Alistair. 2000. *Writing Effective Use Cases*. Boston, MA: Addison-Wesley.

Graham, Paul. 2000. "Why Arc Isn't Especially Object Oriented." Blog. *PaulGraham. Com*. `www.paulgraham.com/noop.html`.

McLaughlin, Brett D., Gary Pollice, and Dave West. 2007. *Head First Object-Oriented Analysis and Design*. Head First Books. Sebastopol, CA: O'Reilly Media, Inc. `www.oreilly.com/products/books-videos.html`.

Parnas, D. 1972. "On the Criteria to Be Used in Decomposing Systems into Modules." *Communications of the ACM* 15 (12): 1053–58.

Wirfs-Brock, Rebecca, and Alan McKean. 2003. *Object Design: Roles Responsibilities, and Collaborations*. Paperback. Boston, MA: Addison-Wesley.

---

[9] Parnas, D. 1972. "On the Criteria to Be Used in Decomposing Systems into Modules." *Communications of the ACM* 15 (12): 1053–58.

CHAPTER 11

Object-Oriented Analysis and Design

When doing analysis you are trying to understand the problem. To my mind this is not just listing requirements in use cases. ... Analysis also involves looking behind the surface requirements to come up with a mental model of what is going on in the problem. ... Some kind of conceptual model is a necessary part of software development, and even the most uncontrolled hacker does it.

—Martin Fowler[1]

Object-oriented design is, in its simplest form, based on a seemingly elementary idea. Computing systems perform certain actions on certain objects; to obtain flexible and reusable systems, it is better to base the structure of software on the objects than on the actions.

Once you have said this, you have not really provided a definition, but rather posed a set of problems: What precisely is an object? How do you find and describe the objects? How should programs manipulate objects? What are the possible relations between objects? How does one explore the commonalities that may exist between various kinds of objects? How do these ideas relate to classical software engineering concerns such as correct-ness, ease of use, efficiency?

---

[1] Martin, Robert, *Single Responsibility Principle*. 2009. `www.butunclebob.com/ArticleS.UncleBob.PrinciplesOfOod` Retrieved on December 10, 2009.

© John F. Dooley and Vera A. Kazakova 2024
J. F. Dooley and V. A. Kazakova, *Software Development, Design, and Coding*,
https://doi.org/10.1007/979-8-8688-0285-0_11

Answers to these issues rely on an impressive array of techniques for efficiently producing reusable, extendible and reliable software: inheritance, both in its linear (single) and multiple forms; dynamic binding and polymorphism; a new view of types and type checking; genericity; information hiding; use of assertions; programming by contract; safe exception handling.

—Bertrand Meyer[2]

When defining object-oriented analysis and design, it's best to keep in mind your objectives. In both the analysis and design process phases you're producing a *work product* that is closer to the code that is your end goal.

In *analysis*, you're refining the feature list you've created and producing a model of what the customer wants. You want to end up with a description of what the program is supposed to do—its *essential features*. This end product takes the form of a *conceptual model* of the problem domain and its solution. The model can be made up of a number of things, including use cases, user stories, scenarios, preliminary class diagrams, user interface storyboards, and possibly some class interface descriptions.

In *design*, you're taking that model produced during analysis and creating the classes that will end up being code. You want to end up with a description of how the program will implement the conceptual model and do what the customer wants. This end product takes the form of an *object model* of the solution. This model is made up of groups of related class diagrams, their associations and descriptions of how they interact with each other. This includes the programming interface for each class. From here you should be able to get to the code pretty quickly.

Analysis

So what is object-oriented analysis? Well, it depends on whom you talk to. For our purposes, we'll define *object-oriented analysis* as a method of *studying the nature of a problem and determining its essential features and their relations to each other.*[3] Your objective is to end up with a conceptual model of the problem solution that you can then

---

[2] Meyer, Bertrand. 2000. *Object-Oriented Software Construction.* 2nd ed. London, England UK: Pearson Education. `https://bertrandmeyer.com/wp-content/upLoads/OOSC2.pdf`.

[3] McLaughlin, Brett D., Gary Pollice, and Dave West. 2007. *Head First Object-Oriented Analysis and Design.* Head First Books. Sebastopol, CA: O'Reilly Media, Inc. `www.oreilly.com/products/books-videos.html`.

use to create an object model—your design. This model doesn't take into account any implementation details or any constraints on the target system. It looks at the domain that the problem is in and tries to create a set of features, objects and relations that describe a solution in that domain. What makes a feature essential? Typically, a feature is essential if it's a feature the customer has said they must have, if it's a non-functional requirement that the program won't run without, or if it's a core program element that other parts of the program depend on.

The conceptual model describes *what* the solution will do and will typically include use cases,[4] user stories,[5] user scenarios, and object sequence diagrams.[6] It can also include a description of the user interface and a preliminary set of class diagrams (but that, of course, is shading over into design).

So how do you create this conceptual model? Just like with all the other methodologies we've talked about, the correct answer is: it depends. It depends on understanding the problem domain, it depends on understanding the feature list you've already come up with, and it depends on understanding how the customer reacts to each of the program iterations they'll see. As you'll see, change is constant.

The key part of object-oriented analysis is the creation of *use cases*. With use cases you create a detailed walkthrough of a scenario from the user's perspective and that walkthrough gives you an understanding of what the program is supposed to do from the outside. A program of any size will normally have several use cases associated with it. In fact, a single use case may have alternative paths through the scenario. When using an agile methodology, you'll normally start with *user stories* that the product owner will create and then a set of *scenarios* that flesh out the user stories. The scenarios are then used to generate use cases. More on this later.

Once you get a few use cases created, how do you get to the class diagrams? There are several methods suggested, but we'll just go over one now and save the rest for later. The first method we'll look at is *textual analysis*, where you take your uses cases and examine the text for clues about classes in your programs. Remember that the object-oriented paradigm is all about objects and the behavior of those objects, so those are the two things to pluck out of your use cases.

---

[4] Cockburn, Alistair. 2000. *Writing Effective Use Cases*. Boston, MA: Addison-Wesley.
[5] Beck, K. 2000. *Extreme Programming Explained: Embrace Change*. Boston, MA: Addison-Wesley.
[6] Sequence diagrams show the sequence of messages passed between objects as your program executes.

In textual analysis, you pluck potential objects out of the text by picking out the *nouns* in your use case. Because nouns are things and objects are (usually) things, the nouns stand a good chance of being objects in your program. In terms of behavior, you look at the *verbs* in the use case. Verbs provide you with action words that describe changes in state or actions that report state. This usually isn't the end, but it gives you your first cut at method names and parameter lists for the methods.

Analysis: An Example

Let's go back to Burt's Bird Buffet and Bath, the B⁴++. When last we left the B⁴++ it automatically opened the feeding doors at sunrise and closed them at sunset. The B⁴++ was a hit and Alice and Bob were thrilled with its performance. Once again the B⁴ models were flying off the shelves.

Then one day Burt gets a call from Alice. It seems she has an issue. While the B⁴++ works just fine, Alice has noticed that she's getting unwanted birds at her bird feeder. Recall that Alice is a songbird fanatic and she's thrilled when cardinals, painted buntings, scarlet tanagers, American goldfinches, and tufted titmice show up at the feeder. But she's not so thrilled when grackles, blue jays, and starlings drive away the songbirds and have their own feast. So Alice wants to be able to close the B⁴++ feeding doors herself when the unwelcome birds show up and open them again when the songbirds come back. And you're just the developer to do it.

The first obvious question you ask Alice is, "How do you want to open and close the feeding doors?" "Well," she says, "how about a remote control? That way I can stay inside the house and just open and close the doors when the birds arrive." And so the game begins again.

Let's assume that you're an agile team and you'll do your updated design using agile techniques. The first thing you'll need is a new user story. Recall that a user story usually takes the form: "As a <role>, I want to <action>, in order to <benefit>." In this case you might say "As Alice, the owner, I want to open and close the bird feeder doors with a remote control, in order to keep the predator birds away from the feeder."

From this user story you can generate a scenario that fleshes out what Alice wants to do. A scenario might look like: "Alice is sitting at her kitchen table having her morning coffee. The B⁴++ doors opened when the sun came out this morning and the feeder has attracted several songbirds. As Alice is watching the songbirds, a couple of blue jays arrive, chase the songbirds off, and begin feasting on the birdseed. Alice reaches for the remote control and presses the button. The bird feeder doors close smoothly and the blue jays fly off. Alice presses the remote control button again and the doors open. After a while the songbirds return and Alice can happily finish her coffee."

Just like last time, you can take this now fleshed-out problem statement and put together a use case. Your previous use case looked like this:

1. The sensor detects sunlight at a 40% brightness level.

2. The feeding doors open.

3. The birds arrive, eat, drink, and leave.

4. The sensor detects a decrease in sunlight to a 25% brightness level.

5. The feeding doors close.

So the first thing you need to decide is whether your new problem is an alternate path in this use case or whether you need an entirely new use case.

Let's try a new use case. Why? Well, using the remote control doesn't really fit into the sensor use case, does it? The remote can be activated at any time and it requires a user interaction, neither of which fits with the sensor. So let's come up with a remote control use case:

1. Alice hears or sees birds at the bird feeder.

2. Alice determines that they are *not* songbirds.

3. Alice presses the remote control button.

4. The feeding doors close.

5. The birds give up and fly away.

6. Alice presses the remote control button.

7. The feeding doors open again.

Does this cover all the situations? Are there any you've missed? There are two things to think of.

First, in step #1 you have "Alice hears or sees birds." The question is should the "or" matter? In this case, the answer is no because Alice is the one deciding and she's the actor in this use case. You can't control the actor; you can only respond to something the actor wants to do and make available options for the actor to exercise. In your case, your program will need to wait for the signal from the remote control and then do the right thing. (Not to get ahead of yourself, but your program is an event-driven system that has to wait (a.k.a. listen) for an event before it does something.)

Secondly, what are the steps in the use case that will help you identify new objects? This is where your textual analysis comes in. In your previous version of this application, you've already got BirdFeeder, Sensor, and FeedingDoor objects. These are identified in the use case easily. So what is new now? The only new object here is the remote control. So what does the remote control do? How many buttons does it have? What does the program do when a remote control button is pressed?

In your example, the remote control seems relatively simple. Opening and closing the feeding doors is a toggle operation: the doors open if they are closed, and close if they are open. Those are the only options, so the remote really just needs a single button to implement the toggle function.

So at the end of your analysis of this new version of the program, you've got a new use case and a new class for the B^4++ program (see Figure 11-1).

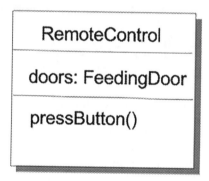

Figure 11-1. *The new RemoteControl class*

This exercise provides a couple of guidelines you can use for analysis.

- First, make *simple classes that work together* by sending and responding to messages. In your example, the simple classes FeedingDoor and Sensor encapsulate knowledge about the current state of the BirdFeeder and allow you to control the bird feeder with simple messages. This simplicity allows you to later easily add a new way of controlling the bird feeder with the RemoteControl class.

- Second, we say that *classes should have one responsibility.* Not only are the FeedingDoor and Sensor simple and easy to control, but they each only do one thing. This makes them easier to change later and easier to reuse.

Design

Now what about design? Assuming you've got a conceptual model from your analysis in the form of a few use cases and possibly a few class diagrams, your more detailed design should follow from this. In object-oriented design, the next steps are to solidify the class designs: decide on the methods your classes will contain, determine the relationships between the classes, and figure out how each of the methods will do what it's supposed to do.

In your current example, you've decided on four classes: BirdFeeder, FeedingDoor, Sensor, and RemoteControl. The first three classes you already developed, so the question here is whether you need to change any of these classes in order to integrate the RemoteControl class into the program. Figure 11-2 shows what you've got right now.

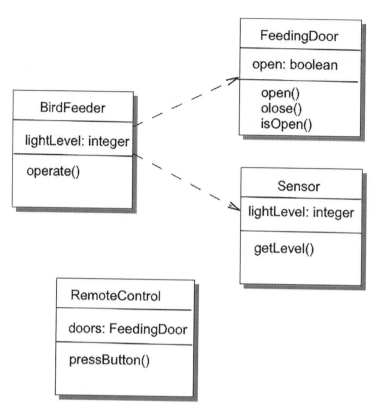

Figure 11-2. *How to integrate the RemoteControl class*

Thinking about it, it seems that nothing in FeedingDoor or Sensor should have to change. Why?

Well, it's because the BirdFeeder class uses these two classes, which in turn don't need to use anything from any other class; they are pretty self-sufficient. If you recall, it's the operate() method in the BirdFeeder class that does all the hard work. It has to check the light level from the Sensor and if appropriate, send a signal to the doors to open or close. So, it seems that maybe the RemoteControl class will work the same way. The question for your design is: does the BirdFeeder class also use the RemoteControl class, or does the RemoteControl class stand alone and just wait for an "event" to happen?

Let's take a look at the code for the operate() method again:

```
public void operate() {
    lightLevel = s1.getLevel();

    if (lightLevel > ON_THRESHOLD) {
        Iterator door_iter = doors.iterator();
        while (door_iter.hasNext()) {
            FeedingDoor a = (FeedingDoor) door_iter.next();
            a.open();
        }
    } else if (lightLevel < OFF_THRESHOLD) {
        Iterator door_iter = doors.iterator();
        while (door_iter.hasNext()) {
            FeedingDoor a = (FeedingDoor) door_iter.next();
            a.close();
        }
    }
}
```

In this method, you check the light level from the Sensor object and if it's above a certain level (the sun has risen), you ask the doors to open. It's the doors themselves that check to see if they are already open or not. Regardless, when the open() method returns, each door is open. The same thing happens with the close() method. Regardless of how they start out, when each invocation of close() returns, its door is closed. This is precisely the behavior you want from the RemoteControl object, except that instead of a light threshold, it responds to a button press. So the pseudo-code for pressButton() will look like:

```
pressButton()
    while (there are still doors left to process) do
        if (the door is open) then
            door.close()
        else
            door.open()
        end-if
    end-while
end-method.
```

And from here you can now write the actual code.

Change in the Right Direction

A key element of the last two sections is that object-oriented analysis and design are *all about change*. Analysis is about understanding behavior and *anticipation of change*, while design is about implementing the model and *managing change*. In a typical process methodology, analysis and design are iterative. As you begin to create a new program, you uncover new requirements; as the user begins to use your prototypes, they come up with new ideas, things that don't work for them or don't spark joy, and new features they hadn't mentioned previously. All of these things require you to go back and rethink what you already know about the problem and what you have designed. In order to avoid what's known as "analysis paralysis," you need to manage this never-ending flow of new ideas and requirements.

Recognizing Change

One way to deal with change is to look for what might change in your design. Let's look at the B⁴++ again. Right now, the B⁴++ will open and close the bird feeder's doors at sunrise and sunset in response to the light levels returned by the sensor. It will also open and close the feeding doors in response to a button push from the remote control. What might change here?

Well, the hardware might change. If the sensor physically changes, that might affect how the Sensor class should work. Getting new hardware can result in the appearance of new use cases or changes to existing use cases, just like the remote control addition we made above. And just like the remote control example, new hardware can result in the appearance of new use cases or changes to existing use cases. These changes can consequently ripple down through your class hierarchy.

The requirements might change and, very likely, new requirements might crop up. A requirement change can lead to alternate paths through use cases, leading to design changes. Design change can happen because requirements change.

By thinking about what things can change in your program and design, you can begin to anticipate change. *Anticipating change* will lead you to be more careful about encapsulation, inheritance, dependencies of one class on another, and so on. Careful is good, but don't let the infeasibility of anticipating everything block you from making progress. You are satisficing here.[7]

---

[7] https://en.wikipedia.org/wiki/Satisficing

Songbirds Forever

While we're talking about change, let's look at B⁴++ again. It's several weeks now since Alice and Bob received delivery of their new and improved B⁴++ with remote control. Alice loves it. She can watch the birds outside the kitchen window and when the grackles swoop in, she just hits the remote control button and the doors shut. The grackles leave disappointed, she hits the button again, and the doors open. The new version works like a charm and does everything they had asked for.

There's just one little thing....

Alice has discovered that sometimes she has to run errands, or go to the bathroom, or watch her favorite nature show on The Discovery Channel. When she does this, she can't close the door with the remote and the grackles can come and feed to their hearts' content, chasing away all the songbirds. So Alice would like yet another teensy change to the B⁴++; hardly worth mentioning, really. She wants the B⁴++ to detect the pesky birds and close the doors automagically. How do you make this happen?

A New Requirement

So the new requirement is that "The B⁴++ must be able to detect the unwanted birds and close the doors automatically." Is this a complete requirement? It doesn't seem so because it begs the obvious question of when do the doors open again? So it seems you have at least a couple of things to decide.

1. How does the bird feeder detect bird types?

2. How do you distinguish between the unwanted birds and the songbirds?

3. When does the bird feeder open the doors again after they've been closed?

Luckily for you, your sensor supplier, SensorsRUs, has just come out with a programmable audio sensor that will let you identify birdsong. So if you integrate their hardware into the B⁴++, that takes care of item #1 above. It also turns out that the pesky birds have way different songs from the songbirds you want to attract, so that the audio sensor can be programmed via firmware to distinguish between the different bird species, so that takes care of issue #2. So what about issue #3, getting the closed doors open again?

It seems as if there are two ways you can get the B⁴++ to open the doors again: timer or sensor. You can have a timer that keeps the doors shut for a specific amount of time and then opens them again. This has the advantage of simplicity of both design and implementation. Simple in the sense that the timer program just implements a countdown timer with no information about the *context* in which it operates. It could easily open the door while there are still a bunch of unwanted birds around. Another way you could implement the bird identifier is to have it only open the door when it hears one of the songbirds. As songbirds leave when there are non-songbirds birds around, then the only time you'd hear songbirds singing is if there are no pesky non-songbirds around, in which case it's safe to reopen the feeding doors.

Let's make a use case. Because opening and closing the feeding doors with the song identifier is a lot like using the remote control, let's start with the RemoteControl use case as the *main path* and then create the alternate new use case directly from it as the *alternate path* in the use case. Table 11-1 shows the main and alternate paths side by side. One or the other path should be taken at any given time.

Table 11-1. *The Song Identifier Use Case and Its Alternate*

Main Path	Alternate Path
1. Alice hears or sees birds at the bird feeder.	1.1 The songbird identifier hears birdsong.
2. Alice determines that they are *not* songbirds.	2.1 The songbird identifier recognizes the song as from an unwanted bird.
3. Alice presses the remote control button.	3.1 The songbird identifier sends a message to the feeding doors to close.
4. The feeding doors close.	
5. The birds give up and fly away.	5.1 The songbird identifier hears birdsong.
	5.2 The songbird identifier recognizes the song as from a songbird.
6. Alice presses the remote control button.	6.1 The songbird identifier sends a message to the feeding doors to open.
7. The feeding doors open again.	

These two paths aren't exactly the same. For instance, in the main path, Alice sees the birds give up and fly away before she presses the remote control button to reopen the doors. In the alternate path, the bird song identifier must wait until it hears birdsong before it can open the feeding doors again. So you could easily make these two different use cases rather than two alternative paths for a simple use case. It is up to *you*. Use cases are there to illustrate different scenarios in the use of the program, so you can represent them in any way you want. If you want to break this use case up into two different ones, feel free. Just be consistent. You're still managing change.

Separating Analysis and Design

As we've said before, it is difficult to separate analysis and design. The temptation for every programmer, particularly beginning programmers, is to start writing code *now*. That temptation leads to thinking about and doing analysis, design, and coding all at once. This is usually a *bad idea* unless your program is only about 10 lines long. It's nearly always better to abstract out requirements and architectural ideas from your low-level design and coding. Chapters 5 and 6 talked about this separation more.

Separating object-oriented analysis and design is a particularly difficult task. In analysis we are trying to understand the problem and the problem domain from an object-oriented point of view. That means we start thinking about objects and their interactions with each other *very* early in the process. Even our scenarios and use cases are littered with loaded object words. Analysis and design are nearly inseparable: when you are "doing analysis" you can't help but "think about design" as well. So what should you do when you actually want to start thinking about design?

Your design must produce, at minimum, the classes in your system, their public interfaces, and their relationships to other classes, especially base or super classes. If your design methodology produces more than that, ask yourself if all the pieces produced by that design have value over the lifetime of the program. If they do not, maintaining them will cost you. Members of development teams tend not to maintain anything that does not contribute to their productivity; this is a fact of life that many design methods don't account for.

All software design problems can be simplified by introducing an extra level of conceptual indirection. This idea is the basis of abstraction, the primary feature of object-oriented programming. The idea is to identify common features in two or more classes and abstract those features out into a higher level, more general class that the lower level classes then inherit from.

When designing, make your classes as atomic as possible; that is, give each class a single, clear purpose. This is the *Single Responsibility Principle*[8] that we'll talk more about in the chapter on design principles. If your classes or your system design grows too complicated, break complex classes into simpler ones. The most obvious indicator of this is sheer size: if a class is big, chances are it's doing too much and should be broken up.

You also need to look for and separate things that change from things that stay the same. That is, search for the elements in a program that you might want to change without forcing a redesign, then encapsulate those elements in classes.

All of these guidelines are key to managing the changes in your design. In the end, you want a clean, understandable design that is easy to maintain.

Shaping the Design

Your goal is to invent and arrange objects in a pleasing fashion. Your application will be divided into neighborhoods where clusters of objects work toward a common goal. Your design will be shaped by the number and quality of abstractions and by how well they complement one another. Composition, form, and focus are everything.

—Rebecca Wirfs-Brock and Alan McKean[9]

Identifying objects (or object classes) is a difficult part of object-oriented design. There is no "magic formula" for object identification. It relies on the skill, experience and domain knowledge of system designers (that would be you). Object identification is an iterative process; you are not likely to get it right the first time.

You begin finding objects by looking for real-world analogues in your requirements. That gets you started, but it's only the first step. Other objects hide in the abstraction layers of your domain. Where do you find these hidden objects? You can look to your own knowledge of the application domain. You can also look for operations that crop up in your requirements and in your architectural concepts of the system. You can even look to your own past experience designing or using other systems.

---

[8] (Martin 2009)

[9] Wirfs-Brock, Rebecca, and Alan McKean. 2003. *Object Design: Roles Responsibilities, and Collaborations.* Paperback. Boston, MA: Addison-Wesley.

Here are some steps to finding candidate objects in your system:

1. *Write a set of use cases* describing how the application will work for a number of different scenarios. Remember that each use case must have a goal. Alternate paths through a use case may indicate new requirements that require a new use case.

2. *Identify the actors* in each use case, the operations they need to perform, and the other things they need to use in performing their actions.

3. *Name and describe each candidate object.* Base the identification on tangible things in the application domain (like nouns). Use a behavioral approach and identify objects based on what participates in what behavior (use verbs).

4. *Objects can manifest themselves* in a number of ways. They can be

   - External entities that produce or consume information

   - Things that are part of the information domain (reports, displays, etc.)

   - Occurrences or events that occur within the system

   - Internal producers (objects that make something)

   - Internal consumers (objects that consume what producers make)

   - Places (remote systems, databases, and so on)

   - Structures (windows, frames)

   - People or characteristics of people (Person, Student, Teacher, etc.)

   - Things that are owned or used by other objects (bank accounts or automobile parts)

   - Things that are lists of other objects (parts lists, any kind of collection, etc.)

5. *Organize the candidate objects into groups.* Each group represents a cluster of objects that work together to solve a common problem in your application. Each object will have several characteristics:

- *Required information*: The object has information that must be remembered so the system can function.

- *Needed services*: The object must provide services relating to the system goals.

- *Common attributes*: The attributes defined for the object must be common to all instances of the object.

- *Common operations*: The operations defined for the object must be common to all instances of the object.

6. Look at the groups you've created and *see if they represent good abstractions for objects* and that work in the application. Good abstractions will help make your application easier to rework when you inevitably need to change some feature or relationship in the application.

Abstraction

Let's change tack here and talk about a different example. Alice and Bob have just moved to a new city and they need to transfer their old Second City Bank and Trust bank accounts to First Galactic Bank. Alice and Bob are middle class and have several bank accounts they need to transfer: a checking account, a passbook savings account, and an investment account.

Nobody actually opens a generic "bank account." Instead they open different types of accounts and each type has different characteristics. You can write checks from a checking account, but you can't write checks from a savings account. You can earn interest on a savings account, but you normally don't earn interest on a checking account; instead, you pay a monthly service fee. Still, all different types of bank accounts have some things in common: all of them use your personal information (name, social security number, address, city, state, ZIP code) and all of them allow you to deposit money and withdraw money.

When putting together a program that handles bank accounts, you may notice that there will be common attributes and behaviors among several classes. Since you know that checking accounts, savings accounts, and investment accounts are all different, let's first create three different classes that contain all the information they would each need and see what you end up with (see Figure 11-3).

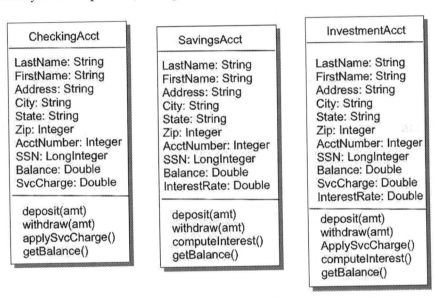

Figure 11-3. *Bank accounts with a lot in common*

Notice that all three classes have a lot in common. One of the things we always try to do, no matter what design or coding techniques we're using, is to avoid duplication of design and code. Not only is this redundant and wasteful, but you will inevitably forget to update one or more of the duplicates when making a change. Avoiding duplication is what abstraction is all about! If you abstract out all the common elements of these three classes, you can create a new (super) class called BankAccount that incorporates all of them. The CheckingAcct, SavingsAcct, and InvestmentAcct classes can then inherit it all from BankAccount, which will greatly simplify the children classes and clean up your design and your code.

So here's BankAccount, in Figure 11-4.

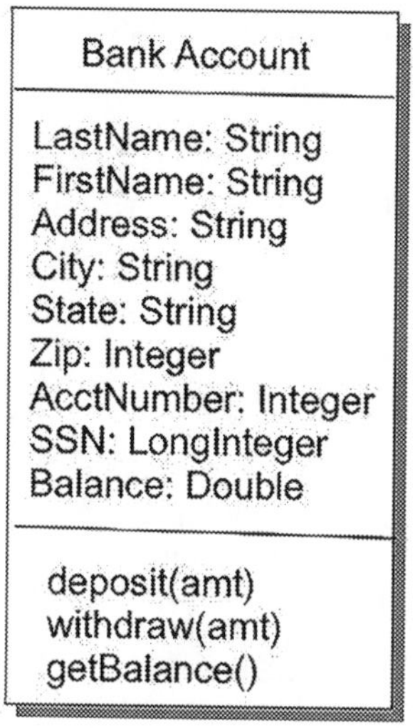

Bank Account

LastName: String
FirstName: String
Address: String
City: String
State: String
Zip: Integer
AcctNumber: Integer
SSN: LongInteger
Balance: Double

deposit(amt)
withdraw(amt)
getBalance()

Figure 11-4. *A cleaner BankAccount class*

But wait! Is the `BankAccount` class one that you would want to instantiate? Each of your original classes was much more specific than this new `BankAccount` class, so there isn't enough information in the `BankAccount` class for you to use it for standalone objects. This means you'll always be inheriting from it but never instantiating it. It's a perfect *abstract class.* (Note that in the diagram below class diagrams of abstract classes put the class name in *italics.*) See Figure 11-5.

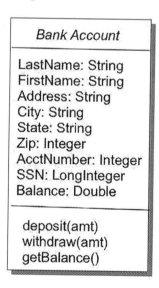

Bank Account

LastName: String
FirstName: String
Address: String
City: String
State: String
Zip: Integer
AcctNumber: Integer
SSN: LongInteger
Balance: Double

deposit(amt)
withdraw(amt)
getBalance()

Figure 11-5. *The BankAccount as an abstract class*

Abstract classes are templates for actual *concrete classes*. They encapsulate shared behavior and define the protocol for all subclasses. The abstract class defines behavior and sets a common state, and then concrete subclasses inherit and implement that behavior. You can't instantiate an abstract class; a new concrete class must be created that extends the abstract class. As a guideline, whenever you find common behavior in two or more places, you should look to abstract that behavior into a class and then reuse that behavior in the common concrete classes.

Figure 11-6 shows what you end up with after abstracting out all the personal data and common behavior into the BankAccount abstract class. Note that class diagrams of abstract classes put the class name in *italics*. Notice also the new arrow types: the open arrow ends indicate *inheritance*. So, the CheckingAcct class inherits attributes and methods from the BankAccount abstract class. This is also called *generalization* because the super class generalizes the subclasses. That's why the arrows point up to the super class.

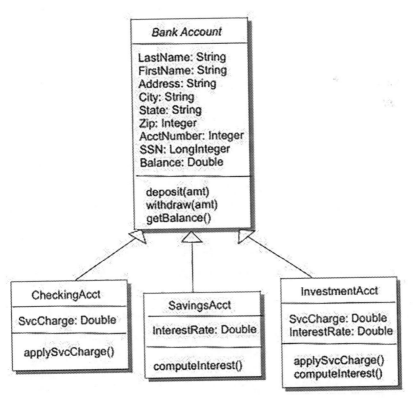

Figure 11-6. *The concrete account classes inherit from the abstract BankAccount class*

Conclusion

In object-oriented analysis and design it's best to keep in mind your objectives.

In analysis, you're refining the feature list you've created and producing a model of what the customer wants. You want to end up with a description of what the program is supposed to do—its essential features. This creates a conceptual model of the problem domain and its solution. The model is made up of a number of things, including user stories, scenarios, use cases, preliminary class diagrams, user interface storyboards, and possibly some class interface descriptions.

In design, you're taking that conceptual model and creating the classes that will end up being code. You want to end up with a description of how the program will implement the conceptual model and do what the customer wants. This is an object model of the solution. This model is made up of groups of related class diagrams, their associations, and the descriptions of how they interact with each other, including the programming interface for each class. This design is an abstraction of the class details and code you'll create later. From here you should be able to get to code pretty quickly.

References

Beck, K. 2000. *Extreme Programming Explained: Embrace Change.* Boston, MA: Addison-Wesley.

Cockburn, Alistair. 2000. *Writing Effective Use Cases.* Boston, MA: Addison-Wesley.

McLaughlin, Brett D., Gary Pollice, and Dave West. 2007. *Head First Object-Oriented Analysis and Design.* Head First Books. Sebastopol, CA: O'Reilly Media, Inc. www.oreilly.com/products/books-videos.html.

Meyer, Bertrand. 2000. *Object-Oriented Software Construction.* 2nd ed. London, England UK: Pearson Education. https://bertrandmeyer.com/wp-content/upLoads/OOSC2.pdf.

Martin, Robert, *Single Responsibility Principle.* 2009. www.butunclebob.com/ArticleS.UncleBob.PrinciplesOfOod retrieved on December 10, 2009.

Wirfs-Brock, Rebecca, and Alan McKean. 2003. *Object Design: Roles Responsibilities, and Collaborations.* Paperback. Boston, MA: Addison-Wesley.

CHAPTER 12

Object-Oriented Design Principles

Devotion to the facts will always give the pleasures of recognition; adherence to the rules of design, the pleasures of order and certainty.

—Kenneth Clark

How can I qualify my faith in the inviolability of the design principles? Their virtue is demonstrated. They work.

—Edgar Whitney

Now that we've spent some time looking at object-oriented analysis and design, let's recapitulate some of what you've already seen and talk about some *common design characteristics.*

First, designs have a purpose. They describe how something will work in a context, using the requirements (lists of features, user stories, and use cases) to define the context.

Second, designs must have enough information in them so that someone can implement them. You need enough details in the design so that someone can come after you and implement the program correctly.

Next, there are different styles of design, just like there are different types of house architectures. The type of design you want depends on what it is you're being required to build. It depends on the context; if you're an architect, you'll design a different kind of house at the seashore than you will in the mountains.

© John F. Dooley and Vera A. Kazakova 2024
J. F. Dooley and V. A. Kazakova, *Software Development, Design, and Coding,*
https://doi.org/10.1007/979-8-8688-0285-0_12

Finally, designs can be expressed at different levels of detail. When building a house, the framing carpenter needs one level of detail, the electrician and plumber another, and the finish carpenter yet another.

There are a number of rules of thumb about object-oriented design that have evolved over the last few decades. These *design principles* act as guidelines for you, the designer, to abide by so that your design ends up being a good one, easy to implement, easy to maintain, and one that does just what your customer wants. We've looked at several of them already in previous chapters, and here we've pulled out nine fundamental design principles of object-oriented design that are likely to be the most useful to you as you become that designer extraordinaire. We'll list and explain them here and then give examples in the rest of the chapter.

List of Fundamental Object-Oriented Design Principles

Here are the nine fundamental principles:

1. *Encapsulate* things in your design that are *likely to change*.

2. *Code to an interface* rather than to an implementation.

3. The *Open-Closed Principle* (OCP): Classes should be open for extension and closed for modification.

4. The *Don't Repeat Yourself Principle* (DRY): Avoid duplicate code. Whenever you find common behavior in two or more places, look to abstract that behavior into a class and then reuse that behavior in the common concrete classes. Satisfy one requirement in one place in your code.

5. The *Single Responsibility Principle* (SRP): Every object in your system should have a single responsibility, and all the object's services should be focused on carrying out that responsibility. Another way of saying this is that a cohesive class does one thing well and doesn't try to do anything else, which also means that each class should have only one reason to change. This says *higher cohesion is better*.

6. The *Liskov Substitution Principle* (LSP): Subtypes must be substitutable for their base types. (In other words, *inheritance* should be well designed and well behaved.)

7. The *Dependency Inversion Principle* (DIP): Don't depend on concrete classes; depend on abstractions.

8. The *Interface Segregation Principle* (ISP): Clients shouldn't have to depend on interfaces they don't use.

9. The *Principle of Least Knowledge* (PLK) (also known as the *Law of Demeter*): Talk only to your immediate friends. This also relates to the idea of *loose coupling*. Objects that interact should be loosely coupled with well-defined interfaces.

As you have probably noticed, there's some overlap here and one or more of the design principles may depend on others. That's okay. It's the fundamentals that count. Let's go through these one at a time.

Encapsulate Things in Your Design That Are Likely to Change

This first principle means to protect your classes from unnecessary change by separating the features and methods of a class that remain relatively constant throughout the program from those that will change. By separating the two types of features, you isolate the parts that will likely change into a separate class (or classes) that you can depend on changing, and we increase our flexibility and ease of change. You also leave the stable parts of your design alone so that you just need to implement them once and test them once. This protects the stable parts of the design from any unnecessary changes.

Let's create a very simple class Violinist. Figure 12-1 is a class diagram for the Violinist class.

Figure 12-1. *A Violinist*

Consider that the setUpMusic() and tuneInstrument() methods are likely pretty stable. But what about the play() method? It turns out that there are several different types of playing styles for violins: classical, bluegrass, and Celtic, just to name three. That means that the play() method will vary depending on the playing style. Since you have a behavior that will likely change, maybe you should abstract that behavior out and encapsulate it in another class? If you do so, you get something like Figure 12-2.

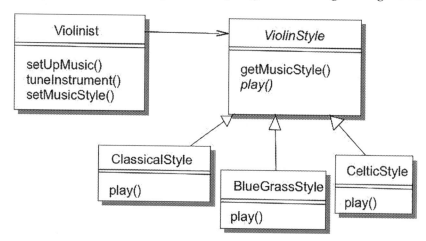

Figure 12-2. *Violinist and playing styles*

You've abstracted out and encapsulated the play() method—which will vary—in a separate class so that you can isolate any changes you want to make to the playing style from the other stable behaviors in Violinist. Notice that you're using association between the Violinist class and the ViolinStyle abstract class, allowing the Violinist to use the concrete style classes that inherit and override the abstract method play() from the abstract ViolinStyle class.

Code to an Interface Rather Than to an Implementation

This principle means to design your code around structures that are less likely to change. Like many of the principles in this chapter, this has to do with inheritance and how you use it in your program. Say you have a program that will model different types of geometric shapes in two dimensions. You'll have a class Point that will represent a single point in 2D space, and you'll have an interface named Shape that will abstract out the things that all shapes have in common—areas and perimeters. (Circles and ellipses call perimeter, circumference instead, but you will use perimeter here.) So here's what you've got (see Figure 12-3).

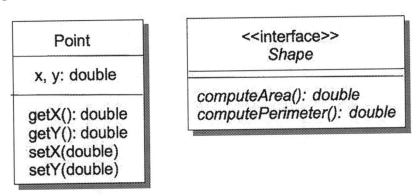

Figure 12-3. *A simple Point class and the common Shape Interface*

If you want to create concrete classes of some different shapes, you *implement* the Shape interface. This means that the concrete classes must implement each of the abstract methods in the Shape interface. See Figure 12-4.

Rectangle	Circle	Triangle
width: double height: double	center: Point radius: double	v1, v2, v3: Point
computeArea(): double computePerimeter(): double	computeArea(): double computePerimeter(): double	computeArea(): double computePerimeter(): double

Figure 12-4. *Rectangle, Circle, and Triangle all implement Shape*

So now you've got a number of classes that represent different geometric shapes. How do you use them? Say you're writing an application that will manipulate a geometric shape. You can do this in two different ways. First, you can write a separate application for each geometric shape. See Figure 12-5.

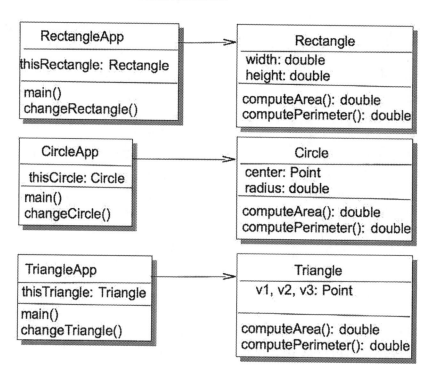

Figure 12-5. *Using the geometric objects*

What's wrong with these apps? Well, you've got three different applications doing the same thing. If you want to add another shape, say a rhombus, you'd have to write two new classes, the Rhombus class (which implements the Shape interface) and a new RhombusApp class. Yuk! This is inefficient. You've coded to the different implementations of the geometric shape rather than coding to the interface itself.

So how do you fix this? The thing to realize is that the interface is the top of a class hierarchy of all the classes that implement the interface. As such, it's a class type and you can use it to help implement *polymorphism* (the idea that a single thing can have many forms) in your program. In this case, since you have some number of geometric shapes that implement the Shape interface, you can create an array of Shapes that you can fill up with different types of shapes and then iterate through. In Java, you'll use the *List* collection type to hold your shapes:

```java
import java.util.*;

/**
 * ShapeTest - test the Shape interface implementations.
 *
 * @author Programmer 1
 * @version 1.0
 */
public class ShapeTest {

    public static void main(String [] args) {
        List<Shape> figures = new ArrayList<Shape>();

        figures.add(new Rectangle(10, 20));
        figures.add(new Circle(10));
        Point p1 = new Point(0.0, 0.0);
        Point p2 = new Point(5.0, 1.0);
        Point p3 = new Point(2.0, 8.0);
        figures.add(new Triangle(p1, p2, p3));

        Iterator<Shape> iter = figures.iterator();

        while (iter.hasNext()) {
            Shape nxt =  iter.next();
            System.out.printf("area = %8.4f perimeter = %8.4f\n",
                nxt.computeArea(), nxt.computePerimeter());
        }
    }
}
```

So, when you code to the interface, your program becomes easier to extend and modify, working with all the interface's subclasses seamlessly.

As an aside, the principles above let you know that you should be constantly reviewing your design. Pride kills good design; don't be afraid to revisit your design decisions. Your design is iterative. Changing your design will also force your code to change, because of the need to *refactor*.

The Open-Closed Principle (OCP)

The Open-Closed principle says that classes should be open for extension and closed for modification.[1]

What this means is to find the behavior in a class that does not vary and abstract that behavior up into a super/base class. That encapsulates and locks the base code away from modification while allowing all subclasses (those classes that extend the base class) to inherit the base behavior and extend it in different ways. The bottom line here is that in your well-designed code, you add new features not by modifying existing code (it's closed for modification), but by adding new code (it's open for extension).

The BankAccount class that you wrote in the previous chapter is a classic example of the Open-Closed Principle at work. In that example, you abstracted all the personal information required by all implementations into the abstract BankAccount class (along with any methods to access and modify the data), closed it from modification, and then extended that class into the different types of bank accounts. This allows you to easily add new types of bank accounts just by extending the BankAccount class again. You avoid duplication of code and you preserve the integrity of the BankAccount properties. See Figure 12-6.

---

[1] Larman, Craig. 2001. "Protected Variation: The Importance of Being Closed." *IEEE Software* 18 (3): 89–91. http://codecourse.sourceforge.net/materials/The-Importance-of-Being-Closed.pdf.

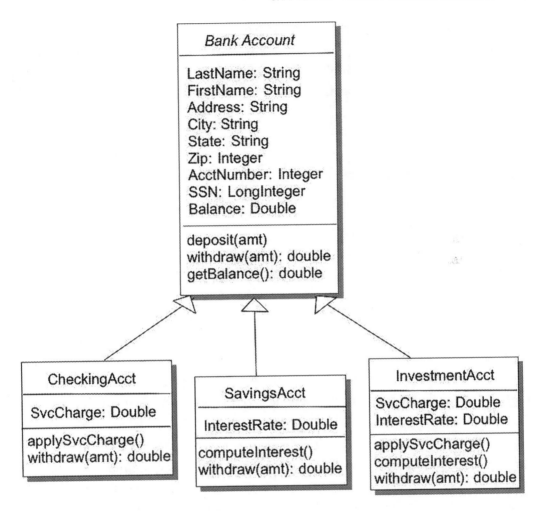

Figure 12-6. *The classic BankAccount example for OCP*

For instance, in the abstract BankAccount class you define the withdraw()
method that allows a customer to withdraw funds from an account. But the way in
which withdrawals occur can differ in each of the extended account classes. While
the withdraw() method is closed for modification in the BankAccount class, it can be
overridden in the subclasses to implement the specific rules for that type of account
and thus alter the behavior of the method to suit is account subtype. It's closed for
modification but open for extension.

The Open-Closed Principle doesn't have to be limited to inheritance. If you have several private methods in a class, those methods are closed for modification, but if you then create one or more public methods that use the private methods, you've opened up the possibility of extending those private methods by adding functionality in the public methods.

The Don't Repeat Yourself Principle (DRY)

This principle says to avoid duplicate code by abstracting out things that are common and placing those things in a single location.[2]

DRY is the motherhood-and-apple-pie design principle: it's been handed down ever since developers started thinking about better ways to write programs. You can revisit Chapters 8 and 9 for a discussion of this. With DRY you have each piece of information and each behavior in a single place in the design. Ideally you have one requirement in one place. This means that you should create your design so that there is one logical place where a requirement is implemented. Then, if you have to change the requirement, you have only one place to make the change. You also remove duplicate code and replace it with method calls. If you are duplicating code, you are duplicating behavior.

DRY applicability extends beyond the code. It's always a good idea to comb you feature list and requirements for duplications. Rewriting requirements to avoid duplicating features in the code will make your code much easier to maintain.

Consider the final version of the B⁴++ bird feeder discussed in the last chapter. The last thing you worked on was adding a song identifier to the feeder so that the feeding doors would open and close automatically. Let's look at the two use cases you ended up with (see Table 12-1).

---

[2] Hunt, Andrew, and David Thomas. 2000. *The Pragmatic Programmer: From Journeyman to Master*. Boston: Addison-Wesley.

Table 12-1. *The Song Identifier Use Case and Its Alternate*

Main Path	Alternate Path
1. Alice hears or sees birds at the bird feeder.	1.1 The songbird identifier hears birdsong.
2. Alice determines that they are *not* songbirds.	2.1 The songbird identifier recognizes the song as from an unwanted bird.
3. Alice presses the remote control button.	3.1 The songbird identifier sends a message to the feeding doors to close.
4. The feeding doors close.	
5. The birds give up and fly away.	5.1 The songbird identifier hears birdsong.
	5.2 The songbird identifier recognizes the song as from a songbird.
6. Alice presses the remote control button.	6.1 The songbird identifier sends a message to the feeding doors to open.
7. The feeding doors open again.	

Notice that you're opening and closing the feeding doors in two different places, via the remote control and via the song identifier. But if you think about it, regardless of where you request the doors to open/close, they always open/close in the same way. So this is a classic opportunity to abstract out the open and close door behaviors and put them in a single place, say a `FeedingDoor` class. DRY at work!

The Single Responsibility Principle (SRP)

This principle says that a class should have one, and only one, reason to change.[3]

Here's an example of the overlap between these design principles that was mentioned above: SRP, the first principle about encapsulation, and DRY all say similar, but slightly different things. Encapsulation is about abstracting behavior and putting things in your design that are likely to change in the same place. DRY is about avoiding

---

[3] McLaughlin, Brett D., Gary Pollice, and Dave West. 2007. *Head First Object-Oriented Analysis and Design*. Head First Books. Sebastopol, CA: O'Reilly Media, Inc. www.oreilly.com/products/books-videos.html.

duplicating code by putting identical behaviors in the same place. SRP is about designing your classes so that each does just one thing.

Every object should have a single responsibility and all the object's services are targeted towards carrying out that responsibility. *Each class should have only one reason to change.* Put simply, this means to beware of having your class try to do too many things.

As an example, say you're writing the embedded code for a mobile phone. After months (really) of discussions with the marketing folks, your first cut at a MobilePhone class looks like Figure 12-7.

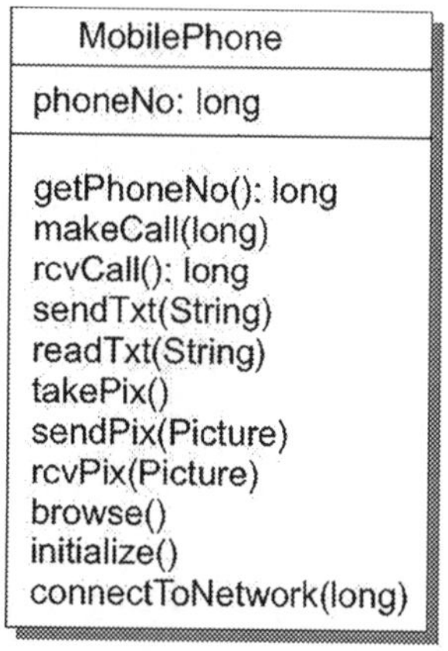

```
┌─────────────────────────────┐
│ MobilePhone                 │
├─────────────────────────────┤
│ phoneNo: long               │
├─────────────────────────────┤
│ getPhoneNo(): long          │
│ makeCall(long)              │
│ rcvCall(): long             │
│ sendTxt(String)             │
│ readTxt(String)             │
│ takePix()                   │
│ sendPix(Picture)            │
│ rcvPix(Picture)             │
│ browse()                    │
│ initialize()                │
│ connectToNetwork(long)      │
└─────────────────────────────┘
```

Figure 12-7. A very busy MobilePhone class

This class seems to incorporate a lot of what you would want a mobile phone to do but it violates the SRP in several ways. The class doesn't have a *single responsibility*; it has many. Instead of trying to do a single thing, it is trying to do way too many things: make and receive phone calls; create, send, and receive text messages; create, send and receive pictures; and browse the Internet. But you don't want a single class to be impacted by all these completely different requirements. You don't want to modify the MobilePhone class every time the picture format is changed or every time you want to add a new picture-editing feature, or every time the browser changes. Rather, you want to separate these functions out into different classes so that they can change independently of each other. So how do you recognize the things that should move out of this class, and how do you recognize the things that should stay? Have a look at Figure 12-8.

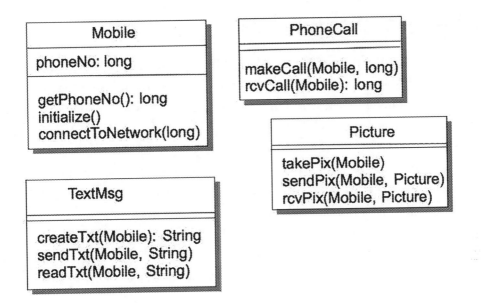

Figure 12-8. *Mobile phone classes each with a single responsibility*

In this example, you ask the question "What does the mobile phone do (to itself)?" as opposed to "What services are offered by the mobile phone?" By asking questions like this, you can start to separate out the responsibilities of the objects in the design. In this case, you can see that the phone itself can get its own phone number, initialize itself, and connect itself to the mobile phone network. The services offered, on the other hand, are really independent of the actual mobile phone and so can be separated out into PhoneCall, TextMsg, and Picture classes. So you divide up the initial one class into four separate classes, each with a single responsibility. This way you can change any of the four classes without affecting the others. You then add a Controller class that runs the phone itself and interfaces with the existing services, which also allows you to add new services/classes in the future. You've simplified the design (although you've got more classes) and made it easier to extend and modify. Is that a great principle or what?

The Liskov Substitution Principle (LSP)

The Liskov Substitution Principle, named after Turing Award winner Dr. Barbara Liskov of MIT, tells us that all subclasses must be substitutable for their base class.[4] This principle requires that inheritance[5] should be well designed and well behaved. Any object instantiated as a subclass should be able to use all the base class functionality seamlessly.

One of the best and canonical examples of violating the Liskov Substitution Principle is the Rectangle/Square example. The example itself is all over the Internet; Robert Martin gives a great variation on this example in his book *Agile Software Development, Principles, Patterns, and Practices*,[6] and we'll follow his version of the example. Here it is in Java.

Say you have a class called Rectangle that represents the geometric shape of a rectangle:

```
/**
 * class Rectangle
 */
public class Rectangle {
    private double width;
    private double height;

    /**
     * Constructor for objects of class Rectangle
     */
```

---

[4] Thorben. 2018. https://stackify.com/solid-design-liskov-substitution-principle/. Retrieved on October 19, 2023.

[5] A Reminder: A superclass is an implemented class that other classes can inherit from, while an interface is a set of method abstractions and must be implemented by other classes. You use a superclass when you want to define a set of methods or properties that can be inherited by other classes. These can include concrete methods that are already implemented in the superclass and abstract methods that must be implemented by subclasses of the superclass. You use an interface when you want to define a set of methods that must be implemented. When your class implements an interface that is a commitment to implement the methods in the interface. In Java, while a class can implement multiple interfaces, only single inheritance is allowed, in a subclass you can only "extend" one class so a subclass can only inherit from a single superclass.

[6] Martin, Robert C. 2003. *Agile Software Development, Principles, Patterns, and Practices*. Upper Saddle River, NJ: Prentice Hall.

```java
    public Rectangle(double width, double height) {
        this.width = width;
        this.height = height;
    }

    public void setWidth(double width) {
        this.width = width;
    }

    public void setHeight(double height) {
        this.height = height;
    }

    public double getHeight() {
        return this.height;
    }

    public double getWidth() {
        return this.width;
    }
}
```

And, of course, one of your users wants to have the ability to manipulate squares as well as rectangles. You already know that squares are just a special case of rectangles. In other words, a square *IS-A* rectangle. Therefore, this problem seems to require using inheritance. So you create a Square class that inherits from Rectangle:

```java
/**
 * class Square
 */
public class Square extends Rectangle {
    /**
     * Constructor for objects of class Square
     */
    public Square(double side) {
        super(side, side);
    }
```

```
    public void setSide(double side) {
        super.setWidth(side);
        super.setHeight(side);
    }

    public double getSide() {
        return super.getWidth();
    }
}
```

Notice that because the width and height of a Square are the same, you couldn't run the risk of changing them individually, so setSide() uses setWidth() and setHeight() to set both for the sides of a Square. No big deal, right?

Well, if you have a function like

```
void myFunc(Rectangle r, double newWidth) {
    r.setWidth(newWidth);
}
```

and you pass myFunc() a Rectangle object, it works just fine, changing the width of the rectangle. But what if you pass myFunc() a Square object? Well, it turns out that in Java the same thing happens as before, but that's *wrong*. It violates the integrity of the Square object by just changing its width without changing its height as well. So you've violated the LSP here and the Square cannot substitute for a Rectangle without changing the behavior of the Square. The LSP says that the subclass (Square) should be able to substitute for the superclass (Rectangle), but it doesn't in this case.

To get around this, you can override the Rectangle class's setWidth() and setHeight() methods in Square like this:

```
public void setWidth(double w) {
    super.setWidth(w);
    super.setHeight(w);
}

public void setHeight(double h) {
    super.setWidth(h);
    super.setHeight(h);
}
```

These will both work and you'll get the right answers and preserve the invariants of the Square object, but if you have to override a bunch of methods you've inherited, then what's the point of using inheritance to begin with? That's what the LSP is all about: getting the *behavior* of derived classes right and thus getting inheritance right. If you think of the base class as being a contract that you adhere to (remember the Open-Closed Principle?), then the LSP is saying that you must adhere to the contract even for derived classes. Oh, by the way, this works in Java because Java public methods are all *virtual methods* and are thus able to be overridden. If you had defined setWidth() and setHeight() in Rectangle with a final keyword or if they had been private, then you couldn't have overridden them. In fact, private versions of those methods would not have been inherited to begin with.

In this example, while a square is mathematically a specialized type of rectangle and one where the invariants related to rectangles still hold, that mathematical definition just doesn't work in Java. In this case, you don't want to have Square be a subclass of Rectangle; inheritance doesn't work for you in this case because you think about rectangles having two different kinds of sides (length and width) and squares having only one kind of side. So if a Square class inherits from a Rectangle class, the image of what a square is versus what a rectangle is gets in the way of the code. Neither of these two classes can meaningfully extend each other. (If you wanted to group both Square and Rectangle under a shared parent class umbrella, you could instead add a Parallelogram class that encapsulates two pairs of parallel and equal length sides.)

Method overriding in derived classes is the biggest cause of LSP violations.[7] Indications that you're violating LSP include the following:

- A subclass doesn't keep all the external observable behavior of its superclass.

- A subclass modifies, rather than extends, the external observable behavior of its superclass.

- A subclass throws exceptions in an effort to hide certain behavior defined in its superclass.

- A subclass that overrides a virtual method defined in its superclass using an empty implementation in order to hide certain behavior defined in its superclass.

---

[7] (Thorben 2018)

Alternatives to Inheritance: Delegation, Composition, and Aggregation

Sometimes inheritance isn't the right way to share the behavior and attributes of other classes. Luckily, you've got options. The three most common are *delegation*, *composition*, and *aggregation*.

Delegation: It's what every manager should do: give away parts of the work for someone else to handle. Delegation says to give responsibility for handling the behavior to another class. This creates an association between the classes, meaning that the classes are related to each other, usually through an attribute or a set of related methods. Delegation has a great side benefit: it shields your objects from any implementation changes in other objects in your program; you're not using inheritance, so encapsulation protects you.[8] Let's see how delegation works with an example.

When last we left Alice and Bob and their B[4]++, Alice was tired of using the remote to open and close the feeding doors to keep away the non-songbirds. So they'd requested yet another new feature: an automatic song identifier. With the song identifier the B[4]++ itself would recognize songbird songs and open the doors, but keep them closed for all other birds. We can think of this in a couple of ways.

The BirdFeeder class, because of the Single Responsibility Principle, shouldn't do the identification of bird songs but it should know what songs are allowed. You need a new class, SongIdentifier, that will do the actual song identification. You also need a Song object that contains a birdsong. Figure 12-9 shows what you've got so far.

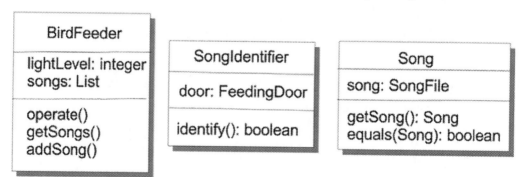

Figure 12-9. *A first cut at the song identifier feature*

---

[8] (Mclaughlin 2007)

The BirdFeeder knows about birdsong and keeps a list of the allowed songs for the feeder. The SongIdentifier has the single job of identifying a given song. There are two ways that this can happen. The first is that the SongIdentifier class can do the work itself in the identify() method. That would mean that SongIdentifier requires an equals() method in order to do the comparison between two songs (any one allowed song from the list of known allowed songs and the song that the new B⁴++ hardware just detected and sent to you). The second way of identifying songs is for the Song class to do it itself, using its own equals() method. Which should you choose?

Well, if you do all the identification in the SongIdentifier class, any time anything changes in a Song, you'll have to change both the Song class *and* the SongIdentifier class. This doesn't sound optimal. But if you delegate the song comparison work to the Song class, then the SongIdentifier's identify() method could just take a Song as an input parameter and call that method, isolating any song changes to just the Song class. Figure 12-10 shows the revised class diagrams.

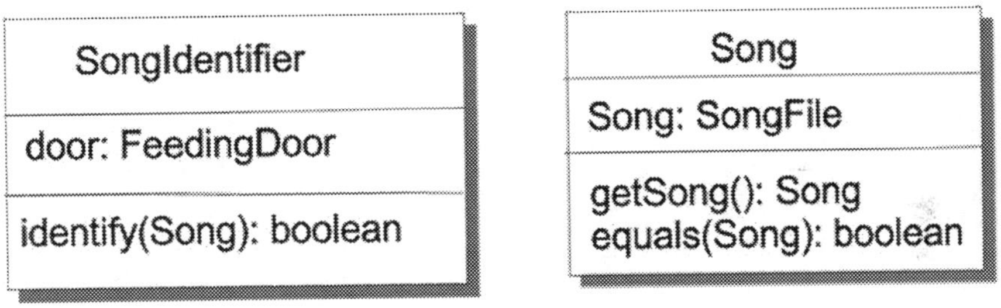

Figure 12-10. Simplifying SongIdentifier and Song

And the corresponding code might look like the following:

```
public class SongIdentifier {
    private BirdFeeder feeder;
    private FeedingDoor door;

    public SongIdentifier(BirdFeeder feeder) {
        this.door = feeder.getDoor();
    }

    public void identify(Song song) {
        List<Song> songs = feeder.getSongs();
        Iterator<Song> song_iter = songs.iterator();
```

```
        while (song_iter.hasNext()) {
            Song nxtSong = song_iter.next();
            if (nxtSong.equals(song)) {
                door.open();
                return;
            }
        }
        door.close();
    }
}

public class Song {
    private File song;

    public Song(File song) {
        this.song = song;
    }

    public File getSong() {
        return this.song;
    }

    public boolean equals(Object newSong) {
        if (newSong instanceof Song) {
            Song newSong2 = (Song) newSong;
            if (this.song.equals(newSong2.song)) {
                return true;
            }
        }
        return false;
    }
}
```

In this implementation, if you change anything with regards to a song, then the only changes you make will be in the Song class, while SongIdentifier is insulated from those changes. The *behavior* of the Song class doesn't change, although how it *implements* that behavior might. SongIdentifier doesn't care how the behavior is implemented, as long as it is always the same behavior. BirdFeeder has delegated the work of handling birdsong to the SongIdentifier class and SongIdentifier has delegated the work of comparing songs to the Song class, all without using inheritance.

Delegation allows you to give away the responsibility for a behavior to another class and not have to worry about changing the behavior in your class. You can count on the behavior in the delegated class not changing. But sometimes you will want to use an entire set of behaviors simultaneously, and delegation doesn't work for that. Instead, you use *composition* to assemble behaviors from other classes.

Say that you're putting together a space-based role playing game (RPG), *Space Rangers*. One of the things you'll model in your game is the spaceships themselves. Spaceships will have lots of different characteristics. For example, there are different types of ships: shuttles, traders, fighters, freighters, capital ships, and so on. Each ship will also have different characteristics: weapons, shields, cargo capacity, number of crew, and so on.

If you want to create a generic Ship class, it will be hard to gather all these things together in a single Ship superclass so you can create subclasses for things like Shuttle, Fighter, Freighter, and the like. These are all quite different, but do all these ships have anything in common? Should you use inheritance here?

You can say that all the ships in *Space Rangers* have just two things in common: each has a ship type and a set of properties that relate to that ship type. This gets you to your first class diagram, shown in Figure 12-11.

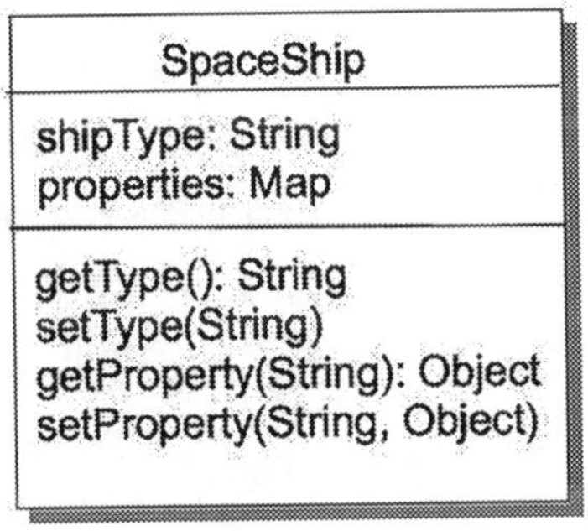

```
            SpaceShip
  ─────────────────────────────
  shipType: String
  properties: Map
  ─────────────────────────────
  getType(): String
  setType(String)
  getProperty(String): Object
  setProperty(String, Object)
```

Figure 12-11. What do all spaceships have in common?

This allows you to store the spaceship type and a map of the various properties for an instance of a ship. It means you can then develop the properties independently from the ships and then different ships can share similar properties. For example, all ships can have weapons, but they can have different ones with different characteristics. This leads you to develop a Weapon interface that you can then use to implement particular classes.

You get to use these weapons in your SpaceShip by using *composition*. Remember that composition allows you to use an entire family of behaviors that you can guaranteed won't change. See Figure 12-12.

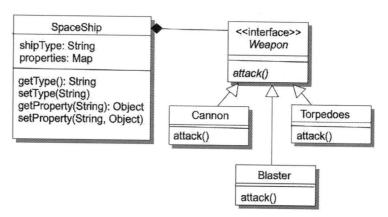

Figure 12-12. *Using composition to allow the SpaceShip to use Weapons*

Recall that the open triangle in the UML diagram means inheritance (or in the case of an interface, it means implements). The closed diamond in UML means composition. So in this design you can add several weapons to your properties Map, where each weapon will have all the capabilities defined by the Weapon interface but each will implement these capabilities in its own way. Through *composition*, you get to use these weapons in your spaceship: capabilities of all the individual weapons on the ship become part of the capabilities of the ship. Different ships will behave differently due to being composed to different weapons and other elements in their properties map.

Note that in composition, the component objects (Weapons) become part of a larger object (SpaceShip) and when the larger object goes away (you get blown up), so do the components. The object that is composed of other behaviors owns those behaviors. When that object is destroyed, so are all of its component parts and their behaviors. The behaviors in a composition don't exist outside of the composition itself. When your spaceship is blown up, so are all your weapons.

Of course, sometimes you want to put together a set of objects and behaviors in such a way that when one of them is removed, the others continue in existence. *Aggregation* is when one class is used as a part of another class but can still exist outside of that other class. Consider, for example, a library: while we often aggregate many books in a library, each book can also exist on its own. If the composing object can sensibly exist on its own (i.e. outside of the composed object), use aggregation; otherwise use composition.

The key to this distinction is to show an instance where it makes sense for a component to exist outside a composition, necessitating that it should have a separate existence.

In *Space Rangers,* you can have Pilot objects in addition to SpaceShip objects. A Pilot can also carry weapons. Different ones, of course; Pilots probably don't carry Cannon objects with them! Say a Pilot is carrying a HandBlaster, so in object-oriented language they are using the behaviors of the HandBlaster. If a mad SpaceCow accidentally crushes the Pilot, is the weapon destroyed along with the Pilot? Probably not, hence the need for a mechanism where the HandBlaster can be used by a Pilot but has an existence outside of the Pilot class. Ta, da! Aggregation!

So you've seen three different mechanisms that allow objects to use the behaviors of other objects, none of which require inheritance. As it's said in *Object-Oriented Analysis and Design,* "If you favor delegation, composition, and aggregation over inheritance your software will usually be more flexible and easier to maintain, extend and reuse."[9]

The Dependency Inversion Principle (DIP)

Robert C. Martin introduced the Dependency Inversion Principle in his C++ Report and later in his classic book *Agile Software Development,*[10] where he defined DIP as

   a. High-level modules should not depend on low-level modules. Both should depend on abstraction.

   b. Abstractions should not depend on details. Details should depend on abstractions.

The simple version of this is, don't depend on concrete classes—depend on abstractions. Martin's contention is that object-oriented design is the inverse of traditional structured design. In structured design, as you saw in Chapter 9, one either works from the top down, pushing details and design decisions as low in the hierarchy of software layers as possible, or one works from the bottom up, designing low-level details first and later putting together a set of low-level functions into a single higher-level abstraction. In both of these cases, the higher-level software depends on decisions that are made at the lower levels, including interface and behavioral decisions.

---

[9] (McLaughlin 2007)

[10] (Martin 2003)

Martin contends that for object-oriented design this is backward. The Dependency Inversion Principle implies that higher-level (more abstract) design levels should create an interface that lower (more concrete) levels should code to. This will mean that as long as the lower level (concrete) classes *code to the interface* of the upper level abstraction, that the upper level classes are safe. As Martin puts it, "The modules that contain the high-level business rules should take precedence over, and be independent of, the modules that contain the implementation details. High-level modules simply should not depend on low-level modules in any way."[11]

Here's a simple example. Traditionally, in structured design you write many programs with the general format of the following:

1. Get input data from somewhere.

2. Process the data.

3. Write output data to somewhere else.

In this example, the Processor uses the Collector to get data, it then packages the data and uses the Writer to write the data to, say, a database. If we draw this out, we get something that looks like Figure 12-13.

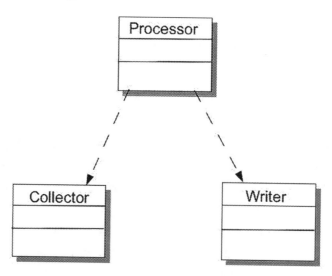

Figure 12-13. *A traditional input-process-output model*

---

[11] (Martin 2003)

One problem with this implementation is that the Processor must create and use the Writer, whose interface and parameter types the Processor must know in order to write correctly. This means that the Processor must be written to a concrete implementation of a Writer and so must be rewritten if we want to change what kind of Writer we want. Say the first implementation writes to a File; if we then want to write to a printer or a database, we need to change Processor every time. This is not very reusable. The Dependency Inversion Principle says that the Processor should be coded to an interface (an abstract Writer) and then the interface is implemented in separate concrete classes for each type of Writer destination. The resulting design looks like Figure 12-14.

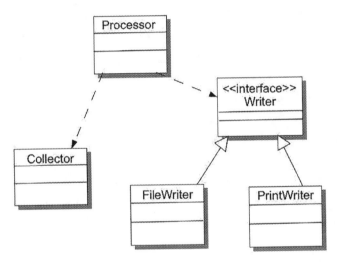

Figure 12-14. *Using an interface to allow different writer implementations*

In this way, different writers can be added and as long as they adhere to the interface, Processor never needs to change. Note that we can do the same thing with the Collector. Note also that the DIP is closely related to Principle #2: Code to an Interface.

The Interface Segregation Principle (ISP)

This principle tells us that clients shouldn't have to depend on interfaces they don't use. In particular, they shouldn't have to depend on *methods* they don't use.[12]

---

[12] (Martin 2003)

We've talked a lot about interfaces in this chapter—coding to interfaces, using interfaces to abstract out common details, and so on. We use interfaces to make our code more flexible and maintainable. So overall, interfaces are a great thing, when used judiciously.

One of the greatest temptations with respect to interfaces is to make them bigger. Expanding an interface can allow it to be implemented by more classes. However, when you start adding new methods to your interface because one of the subclasses that implement the interface needs it, while others do not, you make your interfaces less cohesive, and begin to violate the Interface Segregation Principle. By "generalizing" an interface too much, you are moving away from that single lightning bolt of a set of methods that are all closely related to each other to a jumble of methods which are only tangentially related. Remember *cohesion is good*: your applications should be cohesive and the classes and interfaces they depend on should also be cohesive.

So what's the answer here? How do we keep our interfaces cohesive and still make them useful for a range of classes? The answer is to make more interfaces. The Interface Segregation Principle implies that instead of adding new methods that are only appropriate to one or a few implementation classes, that you *make a new interface*. For any interface that has gotten out of hand, you can divide the bloated interface into two or more smaller, *more cohesive* interfaces. That way, new classes can just implement the interfaces that contain only directly relevant functionality.

The Principle of Least Knowledge (PLK)

The PLK is also known as the *Law of Demeter*. It says, talk only to your immediate friends.[13]

The complement to strong cohesion in an application is *loose coupling*. That's what the Principle of Least Knowledge (PLK) is all about: stating that classes should collaborate *indirectly* with as few other classes as possible.[14]

Let's consider an example derived from one found in Hunt and Thomas.[15]

---

[13] (Martin 2003); `https://en.wikipedia.org/wiki/Law_of_Demeter`. Retrieved September 13, 2023.

[14] Lieberherr, K., I. Holland, and A. Riel. 1988. "Object-Oriented Programming: An Objective Sense of Style." In *Proceedings of OOPSLA '88*, 323–34. San Diego, CA: Association for Computing Machinery.

[15] (Hunt 2000)

You've got a computer system in your car (we all do these days). Say you're writing an application that graphs temperature data in the car. There are a number of sensors that provide temperature data and that are part of a family of sensors in the car's engine. Your program should select a sensor and gather and plot its temperature data. Part of your program might look like the following:

```
public void plotTemperature(Sensor theSensor) {
    double temp = theSensor.getSensorData().getOilData().getTemp();
    ...
}
```

This will likely work, at first... But now you've coupled your temperature plotting method to the Sensor, SensorData, and OilSensor classes. Which means that a change to *any one of them* could affect your plotTemperature() method and cause you to have to refactor your code. Not good.

This is what the PLK urges you to avoid. Instead of linking your method to a hierarchy and having to traverse the hierarchy to get the service you're looking for, just ask for the data directly:

```
public void plotTemperature(double theData) {
    ...
}
...
plotTemperature(aSensor.getTemp());
```

Yes, you had to add a method to the Sensor class to get the temperature but that's a small price to pay for cleaning up the mess (and the possible errors) above. Now your class is collaborating directly with just *one* class and letting that class take care of the others. Your Sensor class will do the same thing with SensorData and so on.

This leads us to a corollary to the PLK—*keep dependencies to a minimum*. This is the crux of loose coupling. By interacting with only a few other classes, you make your class more flexible and less likely to contain errors.

Class Design Guidelines

Finally, we present a list of 23 class design guidelines taken from Davis[16] and McConnell.[17] These guidelines are somewhat more specific than the general design guidelines that we have described above, but they are handy to have around:

1. Present a *consistent level of abstraction* in the class interface.

2. Be sure you understand what abstraction the class is implementing.

3. Move unrelated information to a different class (ISP).

4. Beware of erosion of the class's interface when you are making changes (ISP).

5. Don't add public members that are inconsistent with the interface abstraction.

6. Minimize accessibility of classes and members (OCP).

7. Don't expose member data in public.

8. Avoid putting private implementation details into the class's interface.

9. Avoid putting methods into the public interface.

10. Watch for coupling that's too tight (PLK).

11. Try to implement "has a" relations through containment within a class (SRP).

12. Implement "is a" relations through inheritance (LSP).

13. Only inherit if the derived class is a more specific version of the base class.

14. Be sure to inherit only what you want to inherit (LSP).

---

[16] Davis, Alan M. 1995. *201 Principles of Software Development*. New York, NY: McGraw-Hill, Inc.

[17] McConnell, Steve. 2004. *Code Complete 2: A Practical Handbook of Software Construction*. Redmond, WA: Microsoft Press.

15. Move common interfaces, data, and operations as high in the inheritance hierarchy as possible (DRY).

16. Be suspicious of classes of which there is only one instance.

17. Be suspicious of base classes that only have a single derived class.

18. Avoid deep inheritance trees (LSP).

19. Keep the number of methods in a class as small as possible.

20. Minimize indirect method calls to other classes (PLK).

21. Initialize all member data in all constructors, if possible.

22. Eliminate data-only classes. Classes are supposed to include data and the operations defined on the data, so having data-only classes violates this idea by separating data from operators.

23. Eliminate operation-only classes. Similarly to the principle above, classes that only have operations must get their data from somewhere. This will complicate the method interfaces and require new implementations for different data types.

Conclusion

In this chapter, you explored a number of principles for object-oriented design that have evolved over the last few decades. These design principles act as guidelines for you to follow so that your design ends up being a good one, meaning that it's easy to implement, easy to maintain, and one that does just what your customer wants. Importantly, these design principles give guidance while you're pondering your way from features to design. They offer ways to examine and implement the crucial object-oriented principles of inheritance, encapsulation, polymorphism, and abstraction. They also reinforce basic design principles like cohesion and coupling.

References

Davis, Alan M. 1995. *201 Principles of Software Development*. New York, NY: McGraw-Hill, Inc.

Hunt, Andrew, and David Thomas. 2000. *The Pragmatic Programmer: From Journeyman to Master*. Boston: Addison-Wesley.

Larman, Craig. 2001. "Protected Variation: The Importance of Being Closed." *IEEE Software* 18 (3): 89–91. http://codecourse.sourceforge.net/materials/The-Importance-of-Being-Closed.pdf.

Lieberherr, K., I. Holland, and A. Riel. 1988. "Object-Oriented Programming: An Objective Sense of Style." In *Proceedings of OOPSLA '88*, 323–34. San Diego, CA: Association for Computing Machinery.

Martin, Robert C. 2003. *Agile Software Development: Principles, Patterns, and Practices*. Upper Saddle River, NJ: Prentice Hall.

McConnell, Steve. 2004. *Code Complete 2: A Practical Handbook of Software Construction*. Redmond, WA: Microsoft Press.

McLaughlin, Brett D., Gary Pollice, and Dave West. 2007. *Head First Object-Oriented Analysis and Design*. Head First Books. Sebastopol, CA: O'Reilly Media, Inc. www.oreilly.com/products/books-videos.html.

Thorben. 2018. https://stackify.com/solid-design-liskov-substitution-principle/. Retrieved on October 19, 2023.

CHAPTER 13

Design Patterns

Each pattern describes a problem which occurs over and over again in our environment, and then describes the core of the solution to that problem, in such a way that you can use this solution a million times over, without ever doing it the same way twice.

—Christopher Alexander[1]

Do you reinvent the wheel each time you write code? Do you have to relearn how to iterate through an array every time you write a program? Do you have to reinvent how to fix a dangling else in every if statement you write? Do you need to relearn insertion sort or binary search every time you want to use them? Of course not!

Over the time you've spent writing programs, you've learned a *set of idioms* to employ when writing code. For example, if you need to iterate through and print all the elements of an array, in Java you're likely to do the following:

```java
for (int i = 0; i < myArray.length; i++) {
    System.out.printf(" %d ", myArray[i]);
}
```

or

```java
for (int nextElement: myArray) {
    System.out.printf(" %d ", nextElement);
}
```

---

[1] Alexander, C., Sara Ishikawa, and Murray Silverstein. 1977. *A Pattern Language: Towns, Buildings, Construction.* Oxford, England: Oxford University Press. x.

© John F. Dooley and Vera A. Kazakova 2024
J. F. Dooley and V. A. Kazakova, *Software Development, Design, and Coding*,
https://doi.org/10.1007/979-8-8688-0285-0_13

Without much deliberation, the code just flows out of your fingertips as you type. These *code patterns* are sets of rules and templates for code that you accumulate as you gain more experience writing programs.

Design patterns are the same thing, but for your design.[2] If you take the time to learn a core group of design patterns, it will make your code more uniform and readable and improve its overall quality over time. It will also likely reduce the amount of time you spend designing your coding projects. The famous architect Christopher Alexander, in his book *A Pattern Language*, defined patterns for design in architecture.[3] The same ideas carry over into software design. If you read Alexander's quote at the top of this chapter, you can see the following three key elements in his definition of a design pattern:

- *Recurring*: The problem that evokes the design pattern must be a common one.

- *Core solution*: The pattern provides a template for the solution; pulling out the essence of the solution.

- *Reuse*: The pattern must be easily reusable when the same core problem appears again, even if the context or domain changes.

In fact, you've already seen at least one design pattern so far in this book: the *Model-View-Controller* pattern (MVC) that we discussed in Chapter 7 is one of the earliest published examples of a software design pattern.[4] The MVC design pattern is used with programs that use graphical user interfaces. It divides the program into three parts: the *model* that contains the processing rules for the program, the *view* that presents the data and the interface to the user, and the *controller* that mediates communication between the *model* and the *view*. In a typical object-oriented implementation, each of these abstractions becomes a separate object.

---

[2] Freeman, Eric, and Elisabeth Freeman. 2004. *Head First Design Patterns*. Paperback. Sebastopol, CA: O'Reilly Media, Inc.

[3] (Alexander 1977)

[4] Krasner, G. E., and St. T. Pope. 1988. "A Cookbook for Using the Model-View-Controller User Interface Paradigm in Smalltalk-80." *Journal of Object-Oriented Programming* 1 (3): 26–49.

The *Gang of Four* (Erich Gamma, Richard Helm, Ralph Johnson, and John Vlissides), in their seminal book on design patterns, *Design Patterns: Elements of Reusable Object-Oriented Software*,[5] define a design pattern as something that "names, abstracts, and identifies the key aspects of a common design structure that makes it useful for creating a reusable object-oriented design." In other words, a design pattern is a *named abstraction* from a *concrete example* that represents a *recurring solution* to a *particular, but common, problem*—recurring, core solution, reuse.

But why do we need design patterns in the first place? Why can't we just get along with the object-oriented design principles we studied in Chapter 12 and with our old friends—abstraction, inheritance, polymorphism, and encapsulation?[6]

Well, it turns out that design is hard, that's why. Design for reuse is even harder. Design is also much more of an art than a science or an engineering discipline. Experienced software designers rarely start from first principles; they look for similarities in the current problem to problems they've solved in the past. And they bring to the design table the set of design idioms that they've learned over time. Design patterns provide a *shared vocabulary* that makes this expert knowledge available to everyone.

Design Patterns and the Gang of Four

In their book, the Gang of Four describe design patterns as having four essential features:

- *The Pattern Name* as *"... a handle we can use to describe a design problem, its solution, and consequences in a word or two. Naming a pattern immediately increases our design vocabulary."*

- *The Problem* describes when to use the pattern. *"It explains the problem and its context."*

- *The Solution "... describes the elements that make up the design, their relationships, responsibilities, and collaborations...the pattern provides an abstract description of a design problem and how a general arrangement of elements solves it."*

---

[5] Gamma, Erich, Richard Helm, Ralph Johnson, and John Vlissides. 1995. *Design Patterns: Elements of Reusable Object-Oriented Software*. Addison-Wesley Professional Computing Series. Boston: Addison-Wesley.

[6] Lieberherr, K., I. Holland, and A. Riel. 1988. "Object-Oriented Programming: An Objective Sense of Style." In *Proceedings of OOPSLA '88*, 323–34. San Diego, CA: Association for Computing Machinery.

- *The Consequences,* the results and trade-offs of applying the pattern to a problem. These include time and space trade-offs, but also flexibility, extensibility, and portability, among others.[7]

Design patterns are classified using two criteria: *scope* and *purpose. Scope* deals with the relationships between classes and objects. Static relationships between classes are fixed at compile-time, whereas dynamic relationships are between objects and can change at runtime. *Purpose* deals with what the pattern does with respect to classes and objects. Patterns can deal with object creation, composition of classes or objects, or the ways in which objects interact and distribute responsibilities in the program.

The Gang of Four describe 23 different design patterns in their book, dividing them into three different classes of patterns: *creational, structural,* and *behavioral.*

- *Creational design patterns* deal with when and how objects are created. These patterns typically create objects for you, relieving you of the need to instantiate those objects directly.

- *Structural design patterns* describe how objects are combined into larger groups.

- *Behavioral design patterns* generally talk about how responsibilities are distributed and how communication happens between objects.

The list is not meant to be complete, and over the years since the publication of the Gang of Four's *Design Patterns* book, many more patterns have been added to this original list by developers everywhere. A recent Google search for the phrase "software design patterns" yielded more than 1.8485 million hits, with 90 thousand from the past 24 hours, so it is definitely an active subject of discussion.

The Classic Design Patterns

The 23 (classic) design patterns described by the Gang of Four are listed below. (In the remainder of this chapter we'll go over the design patterns in italics because they are among the most commonly used.)

---

[7] (Gamma, et. al. 1995, 3)

Creational Patterns

1. Abstract Factory

2. Builder

3. *Factory Method*

4. Prototype

5. *Singleton*

Structural Patterns

1. *Adapter*

2. Bridge

3. Composite

4. Decorator

5. *Façade*

6. Flyweight

7. Proxy

Behavioral Patterns

1. Chain of Responsibility

2. Command

3. Interpreter

4. *Iterator*

5. Mediator

6. Memento

7. *Observer*

8. State

9. *Strategy*

10. Template Method

11. Visitor

Patterns We Can Use

The patterns in this section are a representative sample of the classic design patterns and are those that you'll find the most useful right away.

Creational Patterns

Creational patterns all have to do with creating objects. If we think about class definitions as templates for producing objects, then these patterns are all about how to create those templates. The two patterns we'll look at next, Singleton and Factory Method show two different ways of thinking about creating objects.

Creational 1: The Singleton Pattern

Singleton[8] is almost certainly the easiest of the design patterns to understand and to code. The idea is simple: you are writing a program and you have a need for one—*and only one*—instance of a class (and you need to enforce that "and only one" requirement). Examples of programs that use a Singleton pattern are things like print spoolers, window managers, device drivers, and the like.

So what are the implications of the "one, and only one" requirement? First, it means your program can only say new `Singleton()` once, right? But what's to stop other objects in your program (or objects in the program that you didn't write) from issuing another new `Singleton()`? The answer is—nothing! As long as your class can be instantiated once, it can be instantiated again and again.

So what you need to do is to create a class that can be instantiated, once and only once and which *doesn't use* new to do the instantiation. You heard us right: you need a class that can be instantiated without using new. Time to get sneaky!

Here's what you'll do. The method that gets called when an object is instantiated is the constructor. In Java, you can say new `Singleton()` because the `Singleton()`

---

[8] (Gamma, et. al. 1995, 127)

constructor is public—it's visible from outside the class definition. If you want to keep the constructor so you can make instances of Singleton objects, but you don't want anyone to be able to use new to do that, you must make the constructor private. "But wait!" you might think, "If the constructor is private then I can't instantiate the object at all!" However, there is a way around this problem: if the constructor is private, then it can only be accessed from inside the class definition, so it's still entirely possible to instantiate the object from within the class definition itself!

But this then recurses to the problem of how do you get to the constructor from *outside* the class definition? Well, in Java is there a way to access a method inside a class without having to have an instantiation of the class? (Think how you can call Math.abs() without instantiating the Math class.)

Aha! Static class methods! A public static method will be visible outside of the class definition without having the object actually instantiated. So, if you create a class with a private constructor and then use a static method that can conditionally call the private constructor, you can control how many instances of the class you create. Here's the code:

```java
public class Singleton {
    // this is the reference to the instance that will hang around
    private static Singleton uniqueInstance;

    // the private constructor - can't be accessed from outside
    private Singleton() {
        // do stuff here to initialize the instance
    }

    // here's the static method we'll use to create the instance
    public static Singleton getInstance() {
        if (uniqueInstance == null) {
            uniqueInstance = new Singleton();
        }
        // if uniqueInstance is not null, then it already exists
        return uniqueInstance;
    }

    // Other methods - after all Singleton is a real class
}
```

In order to use the `Singleton` class you'd do something like

```
public class SingletonTest {
    public static void main(String [] args) {
        Singleton mySingle;
        mySingle = Singleton.getInstance();
        // and we do other stuff here
    }
}
```

When you instantiate the `Singleton` instance by calling the `getInstance()` method, it will test to see if you've done this before. If not, it creates the instance using the private constructor in the `Singleton` class. If the instance already exists (the `uniqueInstance` variable is not `null`) then you just return the reference to the object.

This version of the Singleton Pattern isn't without its problems. For one thing, it can fail if you are writing a multi-threaded Java program, as the solution above is not "thread safe." It's possible that in between the test for the existing of a `Singleton` instance and the actual creation of an instance that your program could be swapped out while another thread executes. When it swaps back in, it could erroneously create another instance of the `Singleton`. There are relatively easy solutions to this.

The simplest way to make your Singleton Pattern thread-safe is to make the `getInstance()` method a synchronized method. That way it will execute to completion and not be swapped out.

Here's a version of the `getInstance()` method that is thread safe:

```
public synchronized static Singleton getInstance() {
    if (uniqueInstance == null) {
        uniqueInstance = new Singleton();
    }
    return uniqueInstance;
}
```

Notice that the only difference is the inclusion of the synchronized keyword in the method signature. We'll give an example of how to use the Singleton Pattern below.

Creational 2: The Factory Method Pattern

The Factory Method Pattern allows you to define an interface for creating a family of objects, and it allows subclasses to decide which members of the family to instantiate. It defers instantiation down into the subclasses.

Say you've got a small company that is expanding across multiple cities in several states. You have a program to model your operations and compute the sales tax on each sale. Every state and city has a different sales tax rate, so you need to keep track of the locations and only use the correct rate in any specific location. As you add new stores in new locations, you don't want to have to rewrite your code in order to compute the sales tax in each new location. That's where the Factory Method Pattern comes in.

The Factory Method Pattern[9] creates objects for you. You just define an interface (or an abstract class) for creating an object but let the classes implementing that interface (or the subclasses extending that class) decide which class to instantiate. In other words, subclasses are responsible for creating the instance of the class. You use the Factory Method Pattern when you need to create several types of objects that are usually related to each other—they usually have the same abstract parent class so they are in the same class hierarchy—but all are different.

In the Factory Method Pattern, you create an object without exposing the creation logic to the client and refer to the newly created object using a common interface. The Factory Method Pattern allows the subclasses to choose the type of objects to create and they do that at runtime. You ask the factory to create an object of type X and it creates one; you ask it to create an object of type Y and it creates one. This forces the creation of concrete classes to be relegated to subclasses of an interface that knows how to create concrete classes and keeps your other classes closed for modification. All without changing X or Y or the store.

The Factory Method Pattern promotes loose coupling by eliminating the need to bind application-specific classes into the client code. That means the client code interacts solely with the resultant interface or abstract class so that it will work with any classes that implement that interface or that extends that abstract class.

When do you use the Factory Pattern?

- When you don't know ahead of time what class object you will need.

- When all of the potential classes are in the same subclass hierarchy.

---

[9] (Gamma, et. al. 1995, 107)

- To centralize class selection code.

- When you don't want the user to have to know every subclass.

- To encapsulate object creation.

In this example, you can create sales tax calculation objects using a SalesTaxFactory class to generate the objects that will compute sales tax for different locations. You'll have several classes:

SalesTax: An interface that defines your sales tax objects

BostonTax: A concrete class that inherits from Tax

ChicagoTax: A concrete class that inherits from Tax

StLouisTax: A concrete class that inherits from Tax

SalesTaxFactory: Your concrete implementation that makes different Tax objects

SalesTaxDriver: A driver class that lets you sell items and compute sales tax

The Factory Method Pattern depends on defining an interface for the objects you need and then allowing subclasses that implement that interface to actually implement the objects. You can either use a Java interface or an abstract class to define your SalesTax interface. Let's use an abstract class. Your SalesTax abstract class will look like the following:

```
abstract class SalesTax {
    protected double rate;
    abstract void getRate();

    public void calculateTax(double amount) {
        System.out.printf("$%6.2f\n", amount * (1.0 + rate));
    }

}
```

Your SalesTax subclasses end up as concrete classes that override one or more of the methods from the SalesTax abstract class:

```
public class BostonTax extends SalesTax {
    public void getRate() {
        rate = 0.0875;
    }
}
```

```java
public class ChicagoTax extends SalesTax {
    public void getRate() {
        rate = 0.075;
    }
}

public class StLouisTax extends SalesTax {
    public void getRate() {
        rate = 0.05;
    }
}
```

And finally, your concrete SalesTaxFactory, which will actually make a concrete SalesTax object, looks like this:

```java
public class SalesTaxFactory  {
    /**
     * use the makeTaxObject() method to get object of type SalesTax
     */
    public SalesTax makeTaxObject(String location) {
        if(location == null) {
            return null;
        } else if(location.equalsIgnoreCase("boston")) {
            return new BostonTax();
        } else if(location.equalsIgnoreCase("chicago")) {
            return new ChicagoTax();
        } else if(location.equalsIgnoreCase("stlouis")) {
            return new StLouisTax();
        }

        return null;
    }
}
```

In order to test your factory, you create a driver. This is the client code that uses the Factory to create the correct types of objects.

```
/**
 *  Test the Factory Method pattern.
 *  We use the SalesTaxFactory to get the object of concrete classes
 */
import java.io.*;
import java.util.Scanner;

public class SalesTaxDriver {

    public static void main(String args[])throws IOException {
        Scanner stdin = new Scanner(System.in);

        SalesTaxFactory salesTaxFactory = new SalesTaxFactory();
        //get an object of type SalesTax and call its getTax()method.

        System.out.print("Enter the location (boston/chicago/stlouis): ");
        String location = stdin.nextLine();

        System.out.print("Enter the dollar amount: ");
        double amount = stdin.nextDouble();

        SalesTax cityTax = salesTaxFactory.makeTaxObject(location);

        System.out.printf("Bill amount for %s of  $%6.2f is: ", location,
        amount);
        cityTax.getRate();
        cityTax.calculateTax(amount);
    }
}
```

Figure 13-1 is what the design of the entire program looks like.

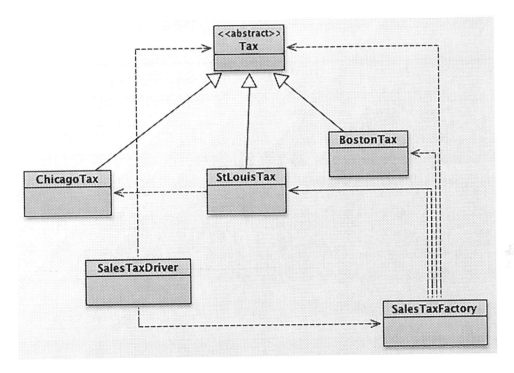

Figure 13-1. *SalesTaxFactory example*

Here are some specifics to notice about how the Factory Method Pattern works in this case:

- The factory method makeTaxObject() encapsulates the creation of the SalesTax object. Your driver just tells the factory which location to use.

- The SalesTax interface provides the interface for the subclasses to create the actual objects.

- The SalesTaxFactory concrete class actually creates the objects by implementing the makeTaxObject() method.

- This leaves the SalesTax classes alone and makes it easier for the SalesTaxDriver to create new objects.

- The SalesTaxDriver class only deals with SalesTax objects. It doesn't have to know anything about particular sales tax rates. The concrete SalesTax objects implement the methods from the SalesTax abstract class and the SalesTaxDriver just uses them regardless of which type of SalesTax object you've created.

- It also means that you can change the implementation of a particular type of SalesTax object without changing either the interface or the SalesTaxDriver.

There is another variation of the Factory Method Pattern. Consider that in your example you only ever need a single factory. In that case, you could use the Singleton Pattern to generate the factory. This would change your SalesTaxFactory and SalesTaxDriver classes. They would end up as follows:

```
public class SingletonTaxFactory  {
    /**
     * We'll just create one SalesTaxFactory using the Singleton pattern
     * To do that we need to make the constructor private and create a
     * variable to hold the reference to the SalesTaxFactory object.
     */
    // this is the instance that will hang around
    private static SingletonTaxFactory uniqueInstance;

    // the private constructor - can't be accessed from outside
    private SingletonTaxFactory() {
        // do stuff here to initialize the instance
    }

    // here's the static method we'll use to create the instance
    public static SingletonTaxFactory getInstance() {
        if (uniqueInstance == null) {
            uniqueInstance = new SingletonTaxFactory();
        }
        return uniqueInstance;
    }
}
```

```
/**
 * use getTax method to get object of type Tax
 */
public SalesTax getTax(String location) {
    if(location == null) {
        return null;
    }
    if(location.equalsIgnoreCase("boston")) {
        return new BostonTax();
    } else if(location.equalsIgnoreCase("chicago")) {
        return new ChicagoTax();
    } else if(location.equalsIgnoreCase("stlouis"))  {
        return new StLouisTax();
    }
    return null;
    }
}
```

The client code becomes the following:

```
import java.io.*;
import java.util.Scanner;

public class SingletonTaxDriver {
    public static void main(String args[])throws IOException {
        Scanner stdin = new Scanner(System.in);

        /* get the single SalesTaxFactory that we need */
        SingletonTaxFactory salesTaxFactory = SingletonTaxFactory.
        getInstance();

        System.out.print("Enter the location (boston/chicago/stlouis): ");
        String location = stdin.nextLine();

        System.out.print("Enter the dollar amount: ");
        double amount = stdin.nextDouble();

        SalesTax cityTax = salesTaxFactory.getTax(location);
```

```
        System.out.printf("Bill amount for %s of  $%6.2f is: ", location,
        amount);
        cityTax.getRate();
        cityTax.calculateTax(amount);
    }
}
```

Structural Patterns

Structural patterns help you put objects together so you can use them more easily.
They are about grouping objects together and providing ways for objects to coordinate
to get work done more easily. Recall that composition, aggregation, delegation, and
inheritance are all about structure and coordination. The first Structural pattern we'll
look at here, the Adapter, is all about getting classes to work together.

Structural 1: The Adapter Pattern

So here's the problem: you've got a class Foo (the client) that wants to access another
class or library or package, Bar (the target). The problem is that Foo is expecting a
particular interface and that interface is different from the public interface that Bar
presents to the world. What are you to do?

You could rewrite Foo to change the interface it expects to conform to the interface
that Bar is presenting. But if Foo is complex, or if it's being used by other classes, that may
not be a viable possibility. Alternatively, you could rewrite Bar to present the interface
that Foo is expecting. But what if Bar is a commercial package and you don't have the
source code?

That's where the Adapter Design Pattern comes in.[10] You use the Adapter Pattern to
create an intermediate class that wraps the target Bar interface inside a set of methods
presenting the interface that client Foo is looking for. The Adapter Pattern will interface
with client Foo on one side and with target Bar on the other, so the interface to Bar
doesn't have to change, and Foo users gets the interface they expect. Everyone is happy!
Due to this wrapping functionality, the Adapter Pattern is also called the Wrapper
pattern.[11] See Figure 13-2.

---

[10] (Gamma, et. al. 1995, 139)

[11] (Gamma, et. al. 1995, 139)

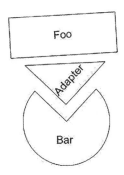

Figure 13-2. *The Adapter lets Foo use Bar*

There are two ways to implement adapters: 1) *class adapters* inherit from the target class and 2) *object adapters* use delegation to create the adapter. Note the difference: a *class adapter* is a subclass of an existing client class and implements the target's interface; an *object adapter* is a subclass of a target class and delegate to an existing class. Figure 13-3 is the graphic for a generic class adapter.

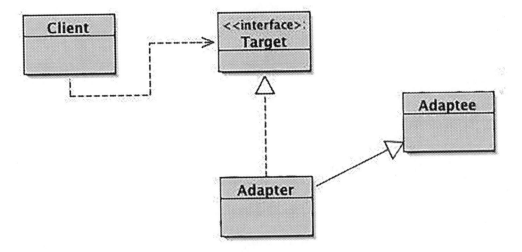

Figure 13-3. *A class adapter example*

Note that the Adapter class inherits from the Adaptee class and implements the same Target interface that the Client class uses. Here's the code for this example:

```
public class Client {

    public static void main(String [] args) {
        Target myTarget = new Adapter();

        System.out.println(myTarget.sampleMethod(12));
    }
}

public interface Target {
    int sampleMethod(int y);
}

public class Adapter extends Adaptee implements Target {
    public int sampleMethod(int y) {
        return myMethod(y);
    }
}

public class Adaptee {

    public Adaptee() {

    }

    public int myMethod(int y) {
        return y * y;
    }
}
```

The object adapter, on the other hand still implements the Target interface, but uses composition with the Adaptee class in order to accomplish the wrapping; it will look like this:

```
public class Adapter implements Target {
    Adaptee myAdaptee = new Adaptee();

    public int sampleMethod(int y) {
        return myAdaptee.myMethod(y);
    }
}
```

In both cases, the Client doesn't have to change! That's the beauty of Adapter. You can change which Adaptee you're using, by changing the Adapter and not the Client.

Structural 2: The Façade Pattern

As a second example of structural patterns, let's try to simplify interfaces. Say you have a set of classes that constitute a subsystem. They could be individual classes that make up a more complex system or part of a large class library. Let's also say that each of those classes in the subsystem has a different interface. Finally, let's say that you want to write a client program that uses some or all of those classes. This would normally mean that to write the client program you'd need to learn all the interfaces of all the relevant classes in the subsystem in order to communicate with the subsystem and get your work done. A visual example is shown in Figure 13-4.

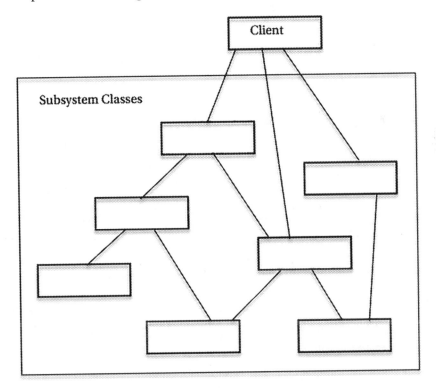

Figure 13-4. *A client using several interfaces*

Clearly, this will make your client program complicated and very hard to maintain. This problem can be addressed using the Façade Pattern[12] Façade provides a single, simple, unified interface that makes it easier for your client to interact with the subsystem classes. When you use Façade, you learn a single interface and use it to interact with all the subsystem classes. A sample visual example of this is shown in Figure 13-5.

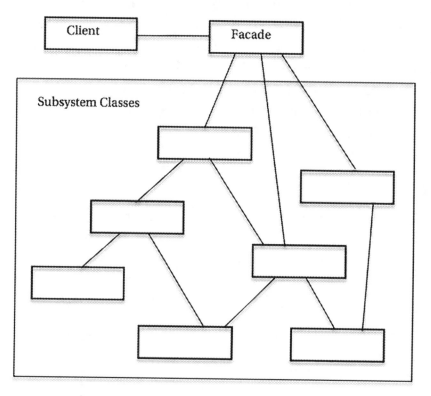

Figure 13-5. *A client using a Façade interface*

In addition to providing a single interface to use, the Façade Pattern also hides any interface changes or additions from the client. It's a classic example of the *Principle of Least Knowledge* from Chapter 12.

---

[12] (Gamma, et. al. 1995, 185)

The Façade Pattern may look similar to the Adapter Pattern above, but they serve different purposes. The Adapter Pattern wraps a target interface and allows a client to use the interface it expects. The Façade simplifies one or more interfaces and presents that simplified interface for the client to use.

For an example of the Façade Pattern, consider creating an online store and putting together a simple program to compute the total amount a customer would have to pay for an item they want to order. In this program, you would need to look up the item, compute the payment, compute the sales tax, compute the delivery charge, total all that up, and send it to the user. That will leave you with classes for SalesTax, Delivery, Payment, and Inventory. If you want to simplify the interface using Façade, you can create a new class, Order, that will hide the multiple interfaces and produce a simpler interface for a Client program to use. In UML, this would look like Figure 13-6.

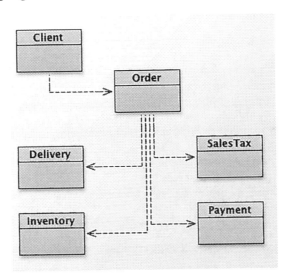

Figure 13-6. *Façade example*

The code for this simple example might look as follows:

```
/**
 * Facade Design Pattern Example
 */

/** Check the Inventory for the item */
```

```java
public class Inventory {
    public String checkInventory(String itemID) {
        /* code in here to check the database */
        return "Inventory checked";
    }
}

/** compute the payment for an item */
public class Payment {
    public String computePayment(String itemID, String currency) {
        return "Payment computed successfully";
    }
}

/** compute the sales tax for an item */
public class SalesTax {
    public String computeTax(String itemID, double rate) {
        return "Tax computed";
    }
}

/** compute the delivery charge for an item */
public class Delivery {
    public String computeDelivery(String itemID, String location) {
        return "Delivery amount computed";
    }
}

/**
 * Here's the Facade
 */
public class Order {
    private Payment pymt = new Payment();
    private Inventory inventory = new Inventory();
    private SalesTax salestax = new SalesTax();
    private Delivery deliver = new Delivery();
```

```java
/**
 * This is the new interface for buying an item
 * it incorporates all the different steps into a single
 * method call
 */
public void placeOrder(String itemID, String currency, String location,
double rate) {
    String step1 = inventory.checkInventory(itemID);
    String step2 = pymt.computePayment(itemID, currency);
    String step3 = salestax.computeTax(itemID, rate);
    String step4 = deliver.computeDelivery(itemID, location);

    System.out.printf("%s\n", step1);
    System.out.printf("%s\n", step2);
    System.out.printf("%s\n", step3);
    System.out.printf("%s\n", step4);
}

    /** add more methods here for performing other actions */
}

/**
 * Here's the client code.
 * Note how the Facade makes ordering something simple
 * by using it's interface
 */
public class Client {
    public static void main(String args[]){
        Order order = new Order();

        order.placeOrder("OR123456", "USD", "Chicago", 0.075);
        System.out.println("Order processing completed");
    }
}
```

Behavioral Patterns

While creational patterns are all about how to create new objects, and structural patterns are all about getting objects to communicate and cooperate, behavioral patterns are all about getting objects to do things. They examine how responsibilities are distributed in the design and how communication happens between objects. The three patterns we'll look at here all describe how to assign behavioral responsibilities to classes: the *Iterator* Pattern lets us traverse a collection of objects, the *Observer* Pattern lets us manage push and pull state changes, and the *Strategy* Pattern lets us select different behaviors behind a single interface.

Behavioral 1: The Iterator Pattern

If you have a *collection of elements*, you can organize them in many different ways. They can be arrays, linked lists, queues, hash tables, sets, and so on. Each of these collections will have its own unique set of operations, but there's usually one operation that you want to perform on all of them: *traverse the entire collection from beginning to end, one element at a time*, without needing *to know the internal structure of the collection.* You may also want to be able to traverse the collection backwards and you may want to have several traversals going on at the same time. The Iterator pattern[13] creates an object that allows you to traverse a collection one element at a time.

Because of the requirement that you shouldn't need to know about the internal structure of the collection, an Iterator object doesn't care about sorting order; it just returns each object as it's stored in the collection, one at a time, from first to last. The simplest iterator needs just two methods:

- `hasNext()`: Which returns a true if there is an element to be retrieved (i.e. we've not reached the end of the collection yet; and false if there are no elements left)

- `getNextElement()`: Which returns the next element in the collection

In the Iterator Pattern, you have an `Iterator` interface that is implemented to make a concrete `Iterator` object that is used by a concrete `Collections` object. A client class then creates the `Collection` object and gets the `Iterator` from there. Figure 13-7 is the UML version of this from Gamma et. al.

---

[13] (Gamma, et. al. 1995, 257)

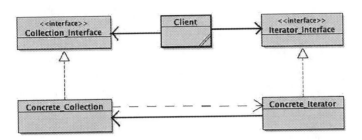

Figure 13-7. *An example of using the Iterator pattern*[14]

You can see that the client class uses the `Collection` and the `Iterator` interfaces, and the `Concrete_Iterator` is part of and uses the `Concrete_Collection`. Note that the `Collection_Interface` will contain an abstract method to create an iterator for the Collection. This method is implemented in the `Concrete_Collection` class and when the client calls the method, a `Concrete_Iterator` is created and passed to the client to use.

Starting in version 1.2, Java contained the Java Collections Framework (JCF) that included a number of new classes and interfaces to allow you to create collections of objects, including an Iterator interface. All of these new types contained iterators. Java even included (just for collections of type List) an expanded `Iterator` called a `ListIterator` which allows going backwards through the list.

Below is an example of typical Iterator code in Java, using both the `Iterator` and the `ListIterator` implementations:

```
/**
 * Iterate through elements Java ArrayList using an Iterator
 * We then use ListIterator to go backwards through the same
 * ArrayList
 */

import java.util.ArrayList;
import java.util.Iterator;
import java.util.ListIterator;

public class ArrayListIterator {
    public static void main(String[] args) {
        //create an ArrayList object
```

---

[14] (Gamma, et. al. 1995, 259)

```
ArrayList<Integer> arrayList = new ArrayList<Integer>();
//Add elements to Arraylist
arrayList.add(1);
arrayList.add(3);
arrayList.add(5);
arrayList.add(7);
arrayList.add(11);
arrayList.add(13);
arrayList.add(17);

//get an Iterator object for ArrayList
Iterator iter = arrayList.iterator();

System.out.println("Iterating through ArrayList elements");
while(iter.hasNext()) {
    System.out.println(iter.next());
}

// Now create a ListIterator for the ArrayList
ListIterator list_iter = arrayList.listIterator(arrayList.size());

System.out.println("Iterating through ArrayList backwards");
while(list_iter.hasPrevious()) {
    System.out.println(list_iter.previous());
}
    }
}
```

Note that when you create the ListIterator object, you pass it the number of elements in the ArrayList. This sets the cursor that the ListIterator object uses to point past the last element in the ArrayList, so it can look backwards using the hasPrevious() method. In both the Iterator and ListIterator implementations in Java, the *cursor* always points between two elements so that the hasNext() and hasPrevious() method calls make sense; for example, when you say iter.hasNext(), you're asking the iterator if there is a next element in the collection. Figure 13-8 is the abstraction of what the cursors look like.

Figure 13-8. *Cursors in the Iterator abstraction*

Finally, some iterators will allow you to insert and delete elements in the collection while the iterator is running. These are called *robust iterators*. The Java `ListIterator` interface (not the `Iterator`) allows both insertion (via the `add()` method) and deletion (via the `remove()` method) in an iterator with restrictions. The `add()` method only adds to the position immediately before the one that would be the next element retrieved by a `next()` or immediately after the next element that would be returned by a `previous()` method call. The `remove()` method can only be called between successive `next()` or `previous()` method calls, cannot be called twice in a row, and never immediately after an `add()` method call.[15]

Behavioral 2: The Observer Pattern

A colleague of ours loves NPR's *Talk of the Nation: Science Friday*, or *SciFri*, radio show (`http://sciencefriday.com`), but they hardly get to listen to it when it is broadcast, because it's on from 2:00–4:00 PM EST on Fridays so they can't listen to it then. They do subscribe to the SciFri podcast and so every Saturday morning when they get a new podcast episode they can listen to it on their iPhone while they mow the lawn. If they ever get tired of *SciFri*, they can just unsubscribe and they won't get any new podcasts. That, dear reader, is the *Observer Pattern*.

According to the Gang of Four, the *Observer Pattern* "...defines a one-to-many dependency between objects so that when one object changes state, all of its dependents are notified and updated automatically."[16] In this SciFri example, NPR is the "publisher" of the SciFri podcast, and all of us who "subscribe" (or register) to the podcast are the observers. You wait for the SciFri state to change (a new podcast gets created) and then the publisher updates you automatically. How the updates happen will differ between two different types of Observer: push and pull. In a *push Observer*, the Publisher (also known as the Subject in object-oriented parlance) changes state and then *pushes* the new state out to all the Observers. In a *pull Observer*, the Subject changes state but

---

[15] `https://docs.oracle.com/en/java/javase/21/docs/api/java.base/java/util/ListIterator.html`

[16] (Gamma, et. al. 1995, 293)

doesn't provide a full update until the Observers ask for it; they *pull* the update from the Subject. In a variation of the *pull* model, the Subject may provide a minimal update to all the Observers notifying them that the state has changed, but the Observers still need to ask for the details of the new state.

With the Observer Pattern, you need a Subject interface so that the Subject, the Observer, and the Client can all tell the state interface they're using. You also need an Observer interface that just tells you how to update an Observer. The publisher will then implement the Subject interface and the different "listeners" will implement the Observer interface. Figure 13-9 depicts these relationships.

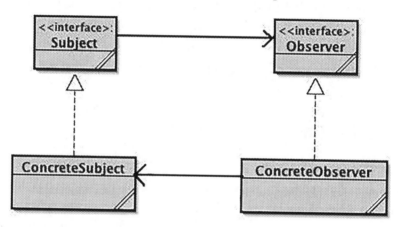

Figure 13-9. *The canonical Observer Pattern[17]*

The client class is missing but it will use both the ConcreteSubject and ConcreteObserver classes. Below is a simple implementation of a *push model* version of all of these. Remember, it's a *push model* because the ConcreteSubject object notifies all the *Observers* whether they request it or not.

First, create the Subject interface that tells you how to register, remove, and notify the Observers:

```
public interface Subject {
    public void addObserver(Observer obs);
    public void removeObserver(Observer obs);
    public void notifyAllObservers();
}
```

---

[17] (Gamma, et. al. 1995, 294)

Next, write the implementation of the Subject interface. This class is the real publisher, so it also needs the attributes that form the state of the Subject. In this simple version, you use an ArrayList to hold all the Observers.

```java
import java.util.ArrayList;

public class ConcreteSubject implements Subject {
    private ArrayList<Observer> observerList;
    // these two variables are our state
    private int subj_id;
    private String msg;

    public ConcreteSubject() {
        observerList = new ArrayList<Observer>();
        this.subj_id = 0;
        this.msg = "Hello";
    }

    public void addObserver(Observer obs) {
        observerList.add(obs);
    }

    public void removeObserver(Observer obs) {
        observerList.remove(obs);
    }

    public void notifyAllObservers() {
        for (Observer obs: observerList) {
            obs.update(this.subj_id, this.msg);
        }
    }

    public void setState(int foo, String bar) {
        this.subj_id = subj_id;
        this.msg = msg;
        notifyAllObservers();
    }
}
```

Next, you write the Observer interface that tells you how to update your Observers:

```
public interface Observer {
    public void update(int obs_id, String msg);
}
```

And then you write the implementation of the Observer interface:

```
public class ConcreteObserver implements Observer {
    private int obs_id;
    private String msg;
    Subject subj;

    /**
     * Constructor for objects of class ConcreteObserver
     */
    public ConcreteObserver(Subject subj) {
        this.subj = subj;
        subj.addObserver(this);
    }

    public void update(int obs_id, String msg) {
        this.obs_id = obs_id;
        this.msg = msg;
        show();
    }

    private void show() {
        System.out.printf("Id = %d Msg = %s\n", this.obs_id, this.msg);
    }
}
```

Finally, you write the driver program that creates the publisher and each of the observers and puts them all together:

```
public class ObserverDriver {
    public static void main(String [] args) {
        ConcreteSubject subj = new ConcreteSubject();
```

```
        ConcreteObserver obj = new ConcreteObserver(subj);

        subj.setState(12, "Monday");
        subj.setState(17, "Tuesday");
    }
}
```

And the output of executing the driver (which all comes from the show() method in the ConcreteObserver object) will look like:

```
Id = 12 Msg = Monday
Id = 17 Msg = Tuesday
```

In many ways, the Observer Pattern works like the Java events interface. In Java, you create a class that registers as a "listener" (the Observer) for a particular event type. You also create a method that is the actual observer and which will respond when the event occurs. When an event of that type occurs, the Java events object (the Subject) notifies your observer by making a call to the method you wrote, passing the data from the event to the observer method; Java events use the *push model* of the Observer Pattern.

For example, if you create a Button object in a Java program, you use the addActionListener() method of the Button object to register to observe ActionEvents. When an ActionEvent occurs all the ActionListeners are notified by having a method named actionPerformed() called. This means that your Button object must implement the actionPerformed() method to handle the event.

Behavioral 3: The Strategy Pattern

Sometimes you have an application where you have several ways of doing a single operation or you have several different behaviors, each with a different interface. One approach is to use a switch statement:

```
switch (selectBehavior) {
    case Behavior1:
        Algorithm1.act(foo);
        break;
```

```
    case Behavior2:
        Algorithm2.act(foo, bar);
        break;
    case Behavior3:
        Algorithm3.act(1, 2, 3);
        break;
}
```

The problem is that the set of behaviors is hard-coded, so expanding the set to add another behavior would require updating this code (and potentially all the other code that has to select different behaviors throughout your program). This is not good.

The Strategy Design Pattern gets you around this. It says that if you have several behaviors (algorithms) you need to select from dynamically, you should make sure that they all adhere to the same interface—a Strategy interface—and then that they are selected dynamically via a driver, called the Context, that is told which to call by the client software. The Strategy Pattern embodies two of the fundamental object-oriented design principles—*encapsulate the idea that varies* and *code to an interface, not an implementation.*[18] This is illustrated in Figure 13-10.

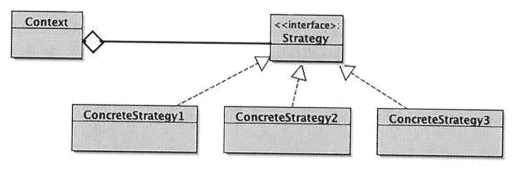

Figure 13-10. *A typical Strategy Pattern layout*[19]

Some examples of when you might use the Strategy Pattern are the following:

- Capturing video using different compression algorithms

- Computing taxes for different types of entities (people, corporations, non-profits)

---

[18] (Gamma, et. al. 1995, 315)

[19] (Gamma, et. al. 1995, 316)

- Plotting data in different formats (line graphs, pie charts, bar graphs)

- Compressing audio files using different formats

In each of these examples you can think of having the application program telling a driver (the Context) which of the strategies to use and then asking the Context to perform the operation.

For a more detailed example, let's say you are a newly minted CPA and you're trying to write your own software to compute your customers' tax bills. (Why a CPA would write their own tax program, we have no idea; work with us on this.) Initially, you've divided your customers into individuals who only file personal income taxes, corporations who file corporate income taxes, and not-for-profit organizations who file hardly any taxes at all. Now, all of these groups have to compute taxes, so the behavior of a class to compute taxes should be the same for all; but they'll compute taxes in different ways. What you need is a Strategy Pattern setup that will use the same interface—to encapsulate what varies in your application and to code the concrete classes to an interface—and allow your client class to select which type of tax customer to use. Figure 13-11 is a diagram of what your program will look like.

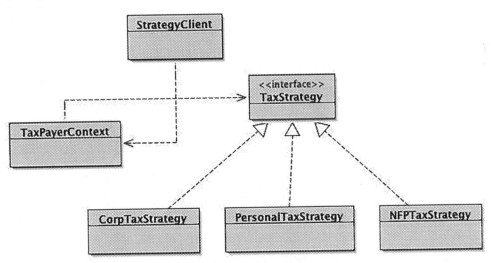

Figure 13-11. *Using the Strategy pattern to select a Tax behavior*

You create a TaxStrategy interface that all the concrete TaxStrategy classes will implement:

```
public interface TaxStrategy {
    public double computeTax(double income);
}
```

Since the only thing that varies here is how the tax is computed, your TaxStrategy interface just includes the computeTax() method.

Then you create each of the concrete TaxStrategy classes, each of which implement the tax computation for that particular type of customer:

```
public class PersonalTaxStrategy implements TaxStrategy {
    private final double RATE = 0.25;

    public double computeTax(double income) {
        if (income <= 25000.0) {
            return income * (0.75 * RATE);
        } else {
            return income * RATE;
        }
    }
}

public class CorpTaxStrategy implements TaxStrategy {
    private final double RATE = 0.45;

    public double computeTax(double income) {
        return income * RATE ;
    }
}

public class NFPTaxStrategy implements TaxStrategy {
    private final double RATE = 0.0;

    public double computeTax(double income) {
        return income * RATE;
    }
}
```

Next, you create the Context class that does the heavy lifting of creating strategy objects requested by the client program and executing the correct ones.

```
public class TaxPayerContext {
    private TaxStrategy strategy;
    private double income;

    /** constructor for Context */
    public TaxPayerContext(TaxStrategy strategy, double income) {
        this.strategy = strategy;
        this.income = income;
    }
    public double getIncome() {
        return income;
    }
    public void setIncome(double income) {
        this.income = income;
    }
    public TaxStrategy getStrategy() {
        return strategy;
    }
    public void setStrategy(TaxStrategy strategy) {
        this.strategy = strategy;
    }
    public double computeTax() {
        return strategy.computeTax(income);
    }
}
```

Note that here you write a separate version of the computeTax() method (you're not overriding the method because you're not extending any of the concrete classes; the Strategy Pattern uses composition, not inheritance). This version calls the computeTax() method of the strategy that the client has selected.

Finally, you implement the client that controls who gets instantiated and when:

```
public class StrategyClient {
    public static void main(String [] args) {
        double income;
        TaxPayerContext tp;

        income = 35000.00;
        tp = new TaxPayerContext(new PersonalTaxStrategy(), income);
        System.out.println("Tax is " + tp.computeTax());

        tp.setStrategy(new CorpTaxStrategy());
        System.out.println("Tax is " + tp.computeTax());
    }
}
```

The client class selects which algorithm to use and then gets the context object to execute it. This way you've encapsulated the tax computation in separate classes. You can easily add new customer types just by adding new concrete TaxStrategy classes and making the change in the client to use that new concrete type. Piece of cake!

Conclusion

Design patterns are a reusable, commonly occurring core solution to a design problem. They are not a finished design, but rather templates you can use to solve similar problems in many different domains. Design patterns offer *proven solutions* for solving common problems, thus streamlining your design process while helping reduce defects in your design.

Be careful, though. Like all design techniques, design patterns are heuristics and so there will be cases where they just don't fit. Trying to squeeze a problem into an unsuitable pattern is asking for trouble.

The goal of design patterns is to define a common vocabulary for design. They may not get us all the way there but design patterns, plus the design principles described in Chapter 10, get us a long way down that road.

References

Alexander, C., Sara Ishikawa, and Murray Silverstein. 1977. *A Pattern Language: Towns, Buildings, Construction.* Oxford, England: Oxford University Press.

Freeman, Eric, and Elisabeth Freeman. 2004. *Head First Design Patterns.* Paperback. Sebastopol, CA: O'Reilly Media, Inc.

Gamma, Erich, Richard Helm, Ralph Johnson, and John Vlissides. 1995. *Design Patterns: Elements of Reusable Object-Oriented Software.* Addison-Wesley Professional Computing Series. Boston: Addison-Wesley.

Krasner, G. E., and St. T. Pope. 1988. "A Cookbook for Using the Model-View-Controller User Interface Paradigm in Smalltalk-80." *Journal of Object-Oriented Programming* 1 (3): 26–49.

Lieberherr, K., I. Holland, and A. Riel. 1988. "Object-Oriented Programming: An Objective Sense of Style." In *Proceedings of OOPSLA '88*, 323–34. San Diego, CA: Association for Computing Machinery.

CHAPTER 14

Parallel Programming

Concurrency is a property of the algorithm. Parallelism is a property of the machine.

—Douglas Eadline

Since the advent of microprocessors, *Moore's Law* has said that the number of transistors on an integrated circuit would double about every eighteen months to two years, while the size of the circuit would stay about the same or get smaller, and the price of that integrated circuit would stay about the same or get cheaper. This meant that we'd have more powerful processors for about the same amount of money on a regular basis. This prediction worked really well until the beginning of the 2000s, when some things changed. First, Moore's Law implies that to get twice as many transistors on a similarly sized chip, the size of the transistors would shrink and the distance between the transistors would also shrink. Clearly, physics being what it is, this couldn't continue indefinitely and by the early 2000s we were beginning to see some problems with making the transistors a lot smaller. The second problem is heat. If you pack twice as many transistors on a chip and expect to run the chip at the same or a higher clock speed, you'll need more electricity going through the circuit. More electricity means more heat. This is known as the "power wall."

Circa 2001, it was becoming clear that the current generation of microprocessors couldn't be pushed much past about 3 or 4 billion cycles per second (3-4GHz); if we wanted to go faster, we needed a different idea. Enter the multi-core microprocessor. The basic idea here is to put two or more CPUs on a single, slightly larger integrated circuit, run them on the same (slower) clock, and have the processors share some cache memory and use a shared main memory. This allows the processors to use less electricity, generate less heat, and be able to run two or more programs simultaneously to make up for the slower clock speed. All the major chip manufacturers got on board

313

© John F. Dooley and Vera A. Kazakova 2024
J. F. Dooley and V. A. Kazakova, *Software Development, Design, and Coding*,
https://doi.org/10.1007/979-8-8688-0285-0_14

with this idea. IBM was first, introducing the POWER4 PowerPC dual-core processor in late 2001, followed by AMD with its Athlon dual-core processor in 2005, and then Intel with its Core Duo in 2006. Since then, nearly all new processors and processor architectures have been multi-core, while programmers and language developers have been working hard to create new software that would take advantage of the new parallel architectures.

In this chapter, we'll first take a brief look at how parallel computers are organized. Then, we'll describe some of the difficulties with writing programs that can take advantage of a parallel computer architecture. Next, we'll talk about how to write parallel programs and how to take a serial program and convert it into a parallel program. Finally, we'll look at writing parallel programs using different computer languages and libraries.

Concurrency vs. Parallelism

Traditionally, software has been written for *serial* or *sequential* computation. A problem solution is broken into a discrete series of instructions that are executed sequentially one after another on a single processor. These (single-core) computers only allow one instruction to execute at any moment in time. A classic example is a loop to sum all the elements of a list: we iterate over all the elements in the list and add each of them to the sum, one at a time, like so:

```
int sum = 0;
for (int i = 0; i < n; i++) {
    sum += list[i];
}
Sytem.out.print(sum);
```

This will normally be executed serially, with results of

sum = 0

sum = sum + list[0]

sum = sum + list[1]

sum = sum + list[2]

...

This is clearly an O(n) operation, requiring n additions and taking about T(n) time proportional to n. We can improve on this by recognizing that we add pairs of numbers together in any order and then add partial sums to get the total. The code might change as follows:

```
sum = 0;
for (int i = 0; i < n-1; i+=2) {
    sum += (list[i] + list[i+1]);
}
System.out.print(sum);
```

Note that because of commutativity of addition, the order in which we execute the two additions inside the loop doesn't matter. While this version goes through the loop half the number of times, it will still require the same overall number of additions and the same amount of time. So with just one processor we don't really gain anything. But this new approach serves as the genesis of an idea: if we had n/2 processors instead of just 1, we could do many of the computations *simultaneously*, using the same number of operations, O(n), but reducing the time T(n) required from proportional to n to proportional to log n (by assuming a binary tree hierarchy of processors), a substantial drop in time, particularly as n gets large. This brings us to the difference between concurrency and parallelism.

Concurrency is the recognition that we can divide up a computation (an algorithm) into separate pieces, where the *order of execution* of the pieces does not matter. Concurrency is a property of an algorithm you use to solve a problem. Note that a concurrent program run on a single processor will still execute serially.

Parallelism is the mechanism used to execute a program on a particular machine (or machine architecture) to improve performance. Parallelism allows a concurrent program to execute on multiple processors simultaneously, potentially improving overall performance of the program.

The left side of Figure 14-1 illustrates a concurrent program broken up into two threads of execution being run on a single processor (the vertical center line of the image), while the right side of the image illustrates running that same program on two processors to execute a program that's divided up into two threads of execution.

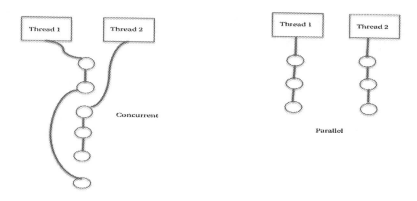

Figure 14-1. *Concurrency vs. parallelism*

Here is an alternative explanation of the difference between concurrency and parallelism, which appeared on the website Stack Overflow[1]:

Assume that your local chess club organizes a demonstration tournament where 10 local players, all with approximately the same skill level, will be pitted against a chess Grandmaster. So the club organizers have to arrange 10 chess games and want to make them time efficient so everyone can go out and celebrate. There are several ways to organize the match.

Serial: The boards are all lined up in a room and the chess master sits down at the first table to play. The game is played to completion and the chess master then moves to the next table to play the next game. If each game lasts 10 minutes, then that's a total of 100 minutes. If it takes the chess master about 6 seconds to move from one table to the next after each game, then that's about another minute (well, it's 54 seconds, but we'll fudge it a bit) for a total of 101 minutes. Not bad.

Concurrent: The boards and players are all lined up the same way, but for this version the chess master only plays one turn at each table. The chess master sits down at the first table to play, makes the first move in 6 seconds, and then immediately moves to the next player to make the next first move. It still takes the chess master 6 seconds to move between tables. This continues until after one minute (6*10 seconds) the chess master is back at the first table for the second move. If we assume that each game still takes 10 total minutes, the same as the serial games took, then we need to know how many rounds through all the tables the chess master will have to make. If each of the local

---

[1]https://stackoverflow.com/questions/1050222/concurrency-vs-parallelism-what-is-the-difference. Retrieved July 24, 2017. If you don't know Stack Overflow, you should go there right now.

players takes about 50 seconds for their move, then we have each complete move taking 50 + 6 = 56 seconds (the 50 seconds for the player move, plus the 6 seconds for the chess master move). Each game takes 10 minutes or 600 seconds, so we have 600 seconds/56 seconds per complete move = about 11 rounds for the chess master to complete all 10 games. The total number of seconds is the sum of all the local player and chess master moves plus the sum of all the times for the chess master to move between boards. This will give us a total of 11*56 + 11*6*10 = 616+660 seconds = 1,276 seconds = 21.27 minutes to complete the match. Much better.

Parallel: Let's say the chess club wants to add a bit more competition to the event and hires a second chess master. With two chess masters, the club organizers can have each master play just 5 games. If they use the serial method from above, then each chess master will sit down, play a complete game and then move to the next table. But this time, since two games are being played simultaneously, the tournament is finished in half the time, 101/2 = 50.5 minutes. Better, but not as good as the concurrent approach.

Concurrent AND parallel: Let's now have our two chess masters play their 5 games at the same time. Each chess master makes a move in 6 seconds and moves to the next table, also in 6 seconds. If the games still take 10 minutes each, and if each player still takes 50 seconds for each move, then we still end up with 11 rounds, but the total time to move between games only takes 30 seconds now (because there are only 5 games going on for each chess master). That gives us 11*56 + 11*30 = 616 + 330 = 946 seconds = 15.77 minutes for the entire match. This is the fastest time from the four different ways of playing the match, so creating a concurrent program and running it on a parallel machine is better than the alternatives.

Remember, concurrency is a property of the algorithm, while parallelism is a property of the machine.[2]

Parallel Architectures: Flynn's Taxonomy

Computer scientists have recognized that parallelism can be used to improve performance and to scale large problems for more than 50 years. In this section, we'll look at some different forms of parallel machines that will allow us to improve the performance of concurrent programs.

---

[2] A great talk on the differences between concurrency and parallelism by Rob Pike (a software engineer who has contributed to Unix, the Go language, the Plan 9 OS, and many other software projects. He was also one of the developers of the Bell Labs Blit terminal, one of the first bit-oriented graphical computer terminals.) is at https://vimeo.com/49718712.

In 1966, Michael Flynn proposed a taxonomy for different types of computer architectures.[3] This taxonomy persists to this day with a couple of extensions we will also mention below.

The taxonomy originally contained four model architectures:

SISD – single instruction stream, single data stream: This is the classic von Neumann computer architecture for uniprocessor computers. A single program runs on the machine at a time, handling a single stream of data.

MISD – multiple instruction stream, single data stream: This architecture assumes that a number of different programs will all execute on the same data stream, producing possibly different results. The programs all run in lock step. Machines that use this architecture are very rare. One possible application is a machine that tries to break a cryptogram, using several different algorithms all running on different processing units.

SIMD – single instruction stream, multiple data stream: This is one of the most common architectures. In it a single program is run on different processors, each using a different data stream. These data streams can be a partitioned set of data where each subset must have the same computation run on it. For example, weather models can use this architecture to predict hurricane paths. One characteristic of the SIMD model is that all the machines in the system are running the same program in lock step. Because all the machines are running the same program at the same time, SIMD machines are not suitable to improve the performance of concurrent programs.

MIMD – multiple instruction stream, multiple data stream: The most general architecture where multiple programs run simultaneously on different machines, each using a different data stream. These programs are not required to run in lock step,

---

[3] Flynn, Michael. 1972. "Some Computer Organizations and Their Effectiveness." *IEEE Transactions on Computers* C-21 (9): 948–60. https://doi.org/10.1109/TC.1972.5009071.

so they can execute concurrent programs and improve their performance. In the early 21st century, this is the most common model for supercomputers. Your multi-core laptop or desktop system is also an MIMD machine.

There are two other variations on these models that evolved in early 2000s or so.

SIMT – single instruction stream, multi-threading: This execution model uses SIMD as its base but allows each instruction stream to execute multiple threads at a time. This model was proposed in the mid-2000s and is generally used in multi-core graphics processors. It is very useful for applications where there is a lot of redundancy in the data stream, for example, processing graphical or video data.

SPMD – single program, multiple data stream: This is a common parallel programming execution model today. It allows each processor to execute a program independently, and so not in step with other processors, all on different (possibly partitioned) data streams. Because the programs run independently, they can take advantage of concurrent sections of the program in order to improve performance. Despite its name, SPMD is a sub-category of the MIMD model above.

Parallel Programming
Some Parallel Programming Definitions

A *thread*, also called *a thread of execution*, is a unit of parallelism. A thread is a piece of code that contains everything it needs to execute a sequence of instructions, a private list of instructions, a call or system stack, a program counter, and a small amount of thread-specific data (usually on its call stack). A thread shares access to memory with other threads. This allows multiple threads to cooperate and communicate via shared variables.

A *process* is a thread that also has its own private address space. Instead of using shared memory, processes communicate with each other using messages so they share an interface for sending and receiving messages. A process is dynamic, while programs are static. In other words, a process is a program in execution. Processes have more state associated with them than do threads, so it costs more to create and destroy processes. It also means that processes are intended to stay around longer.

Latency is the amount of time it takes to complete a given unit of work, whether that is a process, a thread, or a smaller unit of the program. Latency can be a problem in program execution. If one part of a program or process takes much longer to execute than others, then nothing else can get done while we are waiting on that one part. A way around this has been used in operating systems since the early 1970s: context switching. Say you are executing a program and the program attempts to open a file on a hard disk. Disk operations are orders of magnitude slower than other memory operations, and having to wait on the disk operation to complete will slow down your program considerably, while also preventing any other program from executing. In cases like this, the operating system swaps out your program and allows other programs to execute until the disk operation completes. (The system must be able to let the disk perform operations independently for this to work.) It can then switch your program back into memory to continue executing. This context switching does not make the latency any shorter, but it hides the latency from the rest of the system and allows other programs to make progress towards completion. This improves the overall performance of the machine, if not the individual programs. This technique is like the *concurrent* technique in the chess example above.

Throughput is the amount of work that can be computed in a unit of time. Our objective is to use parallelism to increase throughput. For example, a pipelined processor can exhibits a form of parallelism. The pipeline may be made up of different stages, for example, (1) fetch instruction, (2) decode instruction, (3) fetch data, (4) execute instruction, and (5) write data. Here we can have five different instructions all being executed simultaneously as each of them is in a different stage at any given time. This architecture improves the throughput of the machine by allowing it to retire more instructions per unit time than a processor that only has a single instruction active at a time.

Speedup is the execution time of the sequential version of a program divided by the execution time of a parallel version of the same program. *Speedup* = T_s/T_p. (See also *Amdahl's Law* below.) Related to speedup, efficiency is a measure that shows how efficiently each processor is being used. *Efficiency* = *Speedup/P*, where P is the number of processors in the parallel machine.

Performance and Scalability

The two main goals of parallel programming are *improved performance* and *scalability* to a large number of processors. In this section, we'll look at these two goals briefly. For a more detailed look, see Lin & Snyder.[4]

Scalability is the idea that as the amount of input data grows, we want our program to be able to use more processors to efficiently accommodate this input growth. As the amount of data increases, we could spawn more copies of our program and set them loose to act on the data. But there are a number of issues that complicate scalability. Are we using a shared memory or a distributed memory? Does each processor have its own copy of the data? Are we running in lock step or independently and does this matter for this program? What is the topology of the network system that connects the processors and how does that affect communication latency (the time it takes to pass data from one processing element to another when it needs it)? Well-written parallel programs must explore and compensate for all these issues.

Obstacles to Performance Improvement via Parallelism

One might think that *improving performance* by using more processors would also be easy. One would be wrong. Ideally, if a program takes time T to execute to completion on a single processor, we would like it to take T/P time on a machine with P processors. It turns out this is hardly ever the case. There are a variety of potential roadblocks to improving scalability and performance in your parallel programs. Here are a few.

Overhead: When converting a serial program into a parallel one, you may need to add code to *manage* the parallel portions, such as control sections that the program will use to fork off the concurrent pieces of your program. All this code is considered overhead and will impact your performance. There is overhead in creating and destroying your threads of execution; this code is usually in a library or in the operating system and is invisible to you, but nonetheless will slow down your parallel program. *Communication* between threads and other processes is another source of overhead. If you have one thread that must wait on another thread for an event or a computation to complete, that's *synchronization* overhead.

---

[4] Lin, Calvin, and Lawrence Snyder. 2009. *Principles of Parallel Programming*. Hardcover. Boston, MA: Addison-Wesley.

Non-parallelizable code: You must be able to divide your program into P different concurrent sections to take advantage of all P processors. However, even a highly parallelizable serial program is bound to contain code that is inherently serial and thus cannot be parallelized. Loop overhead, input/output, and network communications are all examples of code that normally can't be parallelized. This will impede your efforts to make concurrent sections of your program and it will limit the benefits you can get from parallelizing the program. Non-parallelizable code leads us to the next obstacle.

Amdahl's Law:[5] Even for well-designed parallel programs, scaling your program for larger values of P can create overhead that may drown out any advantage you gain from having more processors. In 1967, Gene Amdahl wrote a paper that tried to express the theoretical speedup of a parallel program over a serial version of the same program. This expression is now known as Amdahl's Law. If the fraction of time for the parallel part of your program to execute on a single processor is P, and the fraction of time for the inherently serial fraction of your program is 1-P, then Amdahl's Law says that the speedup you'll get from using N processors is

$$S(N) = 1 / ((1-P) + P/N)$$

Note that $S(1) = 1$. It is also true that as N goes to infinity, that $S(N) = 1 / (1-P)$. This gives us a limit on the amount of parallelism we can expect for individual programs. It means there is likely an upper bound on the number of processors that we will be able to use to improve the performance of any given program. There are arguments about this conclusion.

Contention: In any computer system, the processors are only one resource that your program will use. There are also various I/O devices, various levels of storage, the connectivity network, and so on. If one of these resources is scarce, or if your program is overly dependent on a single resource, then there may be contention for that resource among your parallel code parts. This will cause some of them to have to wait, slowing down your overall performance.

---

[5] Amdahl, Eugene. 1967. "Validity of the Single Processor Approach to Achieving Large Scale Computing Capabilities." In *AFIPS '67 (Spring): Proceedings of the April 18-20, 1967, Spring Joint Computer Conference*, 483–85. Association for Computing Machinery.

Idle time: Ideally, we'd like all the available processors to be working all the time, but this may not be the case. There may be instances like load imbalances (your concurrent program puts more work on certain parts than others) and delays waiting for memory operations or other resources, which will cause some processors to have to wait. This idling and waiting will hurt your performance gains.

How to Write a Parallel Program

In order to write a parallel program, we will often start with a serial version of the program, or with serial algorithms that implement the solution to a problem we'd like to parallelize. To convert a serial solution into a parallel one, we need to identify the portions of the solution that are inherently serial and those that may be parallelized. We also need a series of abstractions that we can use to think about parallel problems. Finally, we need a set of language features to allow us to talk about the parallel program.

Parallel Programming Models

We can divide parallel computations into several different types:

- Data parallel
- Task parallel
- Shared memory
- Threaded
- Message passing (a.k.a. distributed memory)
- Single program multiple data (SPMD)

In a problem that exhibits *data parallel computations*, we can apply parallelism by performing the same set of computations to different parts of the data all in parallel and hence on different processors. Because we're running the same code on all the processors, but on different data, this type of computation is *scalable*: we can maintain efficiency by just adding more processors as the size of the data increases. One of the most popular current programming languages that work with the data parallel model is Chapel.[6]

---

[6] See http://chapel.cray.com/.

On the other hand, if we can divide a program into a set of independent tasks, each contributing to the overall solution, then we have *task parallel computation*. Because there are a finite number of tasks in any given problem solution, and because there are bound to be some number of dependencies in the computation (some tasks need to execute before others), task parallel types of computations are usually not scalable beyond the number of tasks.

In the *shared memory* model, all the tasks, whether serial or parallel, share the same address space. They read and write to this shared address space asynchronously. This typically requires the use of locks[7] or semaphores[8] to control access to the memory and prevent contention and deadlocks. This is one of the simplest models and is an example of the PRAM (Parallel Random Access Machine) model, which implements a shared memory abstract machine.

In the *threads* model, a single process starts up and acquires a set of resources. It then spawns some number of threads that will execute in parallel. All the threads have some local data (usually on their call stack) but all of them also share the memory and resources of the parent process. This means that the Threads model is a form of Shared Memory model. POSIX Threads, Java Threads, OpenMP, and CUDA threads are all examples of this model.

The *message passing* (distributed memory) model has all the processes on different processors with their own set of memory resources. The processes communicate not by sharing memory but by passing messages over the interconnection network. These messages usually take the form of library subroutine calls. The messages can include control and data messages. All the processes must be programmed to cooperate with the other processes. Messages are usually sent synchronously (e.g. for every send() function call there must be a receive() function call). The standard for this model is the *Message Passing Interface* (MPI) Standard created by the MPI Forum.[9]

---

[7] "In computer science, a lock or mutex (from mutual exclusion) is a synchronization primitive that prevents state from being modified or accessed by multiple threads of execution at once." Retrieved from https://en.wikipedia.org/wiki/Lock_(computer_science).

[8] "In computer science, a semaphore is a variable or abstract data type used to control access to a common resource by multiple threads and avoid critical section problems in a concurrent system such as a multitasking operating system. Semaphores are a type of synchronization primitive. " Retrieved from https://en.wikipedia.org/wiki/Semaphore_(programming).

[9] See https://computing.llnl.gov/tutorials/mpi/

The *single program multiple data* (SPMD) model is a meta-model that can be built on top of any of the models mentioned above. In this model, all the spawned tasks are identical and execute simultaneously, but on different slices of the data stream. Because they act on different parts of the data, each task may, in fact, execute different instructions as they move forward.

Designing Parallel Programs

The first issue with designing parallel program is to decide who is going to do it. Originally it was up you to identify all the parallel parts of a problem solution or an existing serial program, design the program using one of the models above, and then write the program by hand. This process is difficult and prone to many errors. However, over the last few decades, a number of tools have been developed to at least partially automate the parallelization of programs. These tools are generally built into modern compilers.

Modern compilers can parallelize serial programs in two different ways: (1) a fully automatic option where the compiler does all the work or (2) a programmer directed option where the programmer identifies areas of possible parallelization using compiler directives, pragmas, or command-line options. Fully automatic compilers are good at recognizing low-level parallelization opportunities, for example in loops, but they typically do not do large-scale parallelization well. Programmer directed parallelization is more effective because the programmer is explicitly suggesting areas of the program ripe for parallelizing. As a result, modern developers will typically create parallel programs through a combination of manual examination/coding and automated tools. We'll spend the next few sections examining this hybrid approach to parallel programming.

Parallel Design Techniques

As you begin to design a parallel program, there are many aspects to consider. There are entire online courses and books devoted just to that, so we will not provide a full tutorial here. Instead, here is a short list of considerations to get you started:

- First, you must *understand the problem and the solution in terms of concurrency* given an algorithm to solve a problem, you must understand how to create a concurrent solution. If you've already got a serial program that solves your problem, you must understand it before you start thinking of concurrency.

- Once you understand the problem, you should consider whether it can be parallelized at all. Some problems are *inherently sequential*, meaning that they are not amenable to parallelization.

- The biggest thing to look for when you are thinking about parallelism is *data dependency*. If you have a solution where the partial solutions always depend on previous partial solutions, this severely limits your ability to find concurrency and hence to parallelize the algorithm. Computing the Fibonacci sequence (0, 1, 1, 2, 3, 5, 8, 13, 21, 34, ...) is an example of a problem whose solution benefits very little from parallelization. The standard definition of the sequence is that $F(n)$ = $F(n-1)$ + $F(n-2)$, so at every step, the next partial solution in the sequence is dependent on the values of the two previous partial solutions which *must* be computed first. This offers little opportunity in the way of parallelization.

- If you are looking at a serial program, one thing to do is to find the program's *hotspots*—portions of the code where the program spends most of its time. If you can find hotspots in the serial program, and if they can be parallelized, then this is one way to quickly improve the program's performance. Loops and recursive calls are prime places to look for hotspots.

- You should also identify parts of the program that will act as *choke points* or *bottlenecks*—areas where the existing program is considerably slower than other parts. The classic example here are any parts of the program doing input or output (I/O), particularly disk I/O. These parts can't normally be parallelized but you can improve them by taking advantage of things like large, fast, shared memory. For example, instead of reading a single block at a time, you read several blocks at once into main or cache memory, where they can be subsequently accessed much faster.

- *Task decomposition* is another technique that is useful as you are looking at ways to parallelize a program. Just as we looked for opportunities to decompose larger problems into smaller ones in the section on structured decomposition in Chapter 9, you can look for opportunities to break a large amount of work into several smaller tasks that could be executed independently. For example, a climate model is often made up of several smaller independent models: an atmospheric model, an ocean model, a hydrology model, and a land surface model. Each of these smaller pieces of a large problem can be separated out for independent computation, with a fifth piece that brings the partial results together.

- When designing a parallel program you should also always think about *communication* between the different, independent parts of the program. If you have an embarrassingly parallel program (we'll talk more about this in the next chapter), then there will be very little communication between processing units, so communication is not much of an issue. For example, if you have a graphics application that is inverting all the color elements in each pixel, the program is making changes to individual pixels that are independent of the pixels surrounding it. On the other hand, in a hurricane model, computations of things like wind speed and direction and barometric pressure in one small geographic area will affect the same computations in adjacent areas, so communication overhead and synchronization must be taken into account.

- The *memory model* used in the target parallel computer is also an issue that must be considered when writing a parallel program. A shared memory model typically makes reading and writing to and from memory easier but also brings in problems with contention for reads and writes. A distributed memory model typically requires that the program synchronize the memories from time to time, which can hinder performance.

327

- Finally, you should always consider *synchronization* and *coordination*. In some applications, the order in which tasks or threads execute must be coordinated to ensure that any data dependencies are met. This can take the form of language or library features that, for example, allow you to stop execution of a thread until all the other threads catch up. Alternatively, you may also write code to require synchronizing execution, to force memory writes to take place in the correct order.

Programming Languages and APIs (with Examples)

In the next few sections, we'll look at two modern programming languages (as well as libraries and APIs) with parallel programming features: Java and OpenMP. We will not attempt to cover all the features in each language, leaving that to the references at the end of the chapter. We will just try to give a feel for how parallel programming is approached in each language.

Parallel Language Features

Nearly all parallel programming languages, APIs, and libraries include certain features that facilitate the turning your serial solutions into scalable parallel solutions. To get you started, here is a partial list of parallel language features:

Threads: Most parallel languages include the concept of a thread of execution. These languages will typically provide a set of features to allow you to create and destroy threads, to manage them, to cause them to wait, and to join back up to the main program thread. These languages may also allow the threads to share data.

Synchronization: All parallel languages include features that allow you to synchronize the work of different processors and to combine answers from partial solutions. This is particularly important in fine-grained programs running on shared memory machines (like multi-core processors). A common type of synchronization technique is the *barrier*. A *barrier* is a piece of code that will force all threads to stop execution until all other threads have reached the same point in their computation. For example, in OpenMP the loop construct creates a barrier that doesn't let any thread proceed past the loop until all threads have completed executing the loop.

Mutual exclusion and locking: In concurrent programming, two or more threads of execution often must share resources. When this happens, care must be taken to avoid *race conditions.* For example, if one thread changes a shared variable value while another thread is attempting to either read or write that same value, then a race condition occurs. *Mutual exclusion* solves this problem by requiring that each thread include a *critical section* of code where the thread has sole control of the resource, so no other thread can access that resource (i.e., the other thread is forbidden from being in its own critical section at the same time). This exclusion is usually accomplished by using a separate variable (called a *mutex*), which a thread will set to acquire control of the resource and to lock out all other threads until the resource is released. The original idea for mutual exclusion comes from Dijkstra.[10] All parallel programming languages contain features to implement mutual exclusion. As an example of how a mutex works, consider the following class in an object-oriented language:

```
class Mutex {
    public void lock() { // definition in here }
    public void unlock() { // definition in here }
    private boolean locked;
}
```

Mutex objects can be used to demarcate when a thread enters and exits its critical section:

```
Mutex m = new Mutex(); // create a single instance of the Mutex class
...
m.lock();
// critical section
...
m.unlock();
```

Any other threads that call the lock() method will have to wait until the first thread unlocks the mutex. In this way, changes to shared variables are kept inside the critical section and remain synchronized.

---

[10] Dijkstra, Edsger W. 1965. "Solution of a Problem in Concurrent Programming Control." *Communications of the ACM* 8 (9): 569. doi: https://doi.org/10.1145/365559.365617.

Access to shared memory: Most parallel programming languages assume that you are using some variation on the shared memory model and so contain features that allow threads to access shared memory variables and to control access to them (see mutual exclusion above).

Reduction: When your program spawns several threads that are each going to compute part of a solution to a problem, you must have a way to gather the partial solutions together and *reduce* them into a single solution for the entire problem. Many parallel languages provide a feature that lets you tell the program how to do the reduction. You'll see how this works below when we talk about OpenMP.

Parallel Language Features: Java Threads

Java has several libraries that are used for creating parallel programs. The most basic library available is the Thread class in the `java.lang` package. The Thread class provides the basic functionality to create and manage threads of execution. You can also make new Threads by creating a class that implements the Runnable interface or by using the utilities provided in the `java.util.concurrent` package. When a Java program executes, there is always at least one thread of execution running, the main thread.

Here's probably the simplest example of creating and using a new Thread in Java:

```java
/**
 * just about the simplest example of starting and running a Java Thread
 * This new thread will just print "MyThread is running" and exit.
 */
public class MakeAThread {

    /** make an inner class that will be the new thread */
    public static class MyThread extends Thread {
        /** the Thread must have a run method */
        @Override
        public void run(){
            System.out.println("MyThread is running");
        }
    }

    public static void main(String [] args) {
        MyThread myThread = new MyThread();
```

```
    /** always start a new thread using the start() method */
    myThread.start();
  }
}
```

In this program, you create an inner class that is a subclass of the Thread class and whose instances do the work of the new Thread. In your main() method, you create the new Thread and start it. You don't really have a Thread until the start() method is called, at which point you have two threads executing. The start() method automatically called the new thread's run() method and when it exits, the Thread object also exits. You can also create new threads of execution by implementing the Runnable interface and then creating new Thread objects. Here's the same example, but this time using the Runnable interface:

```
/**
 * a second way to
 * make a simple example of starting and running a Java Thread
 */
public class MakeARunnableThread {

    /** make an inner class that will be the new thread */
    public static class MyRunnable implements Runnable {
        /** the Runnable must have a run method */
        @Override
        public void run(){
            System.out.println("MyRunnableThread is running");
        }
    }

    public static void main(String [] args) {
    /* we create a new thread and pass it the Runnable object to execute */
        Thread myThread = new Thread(new MyRunnable());

        /** always start a new thread using the start() method */
        myThread.start();
    }
}
```

Note that in this example you still have to create a new Thread instance, but you can pass the Thread constructor an instance of the new Runnable object. Everything else is the same as above.

When you use Java Threads, each new thread is given a *priority* and the Java Virtual Machine (JVM) contains a thread scheduler that is charged with ordering the thread executions. The scheduler will vary executions based on how many processors are available and the priority of each thread. There are several ways that you can control the scheduling of your threads.

The first is to use the Thread.sleep() method to force a thread to go to sleep. The thread will be blocked and another thread will be selected to execute. When the sleeping thread wakes up, it will be put in a queue to execute. Another way you can change the scheduling of a thread is by changing its priority. All threads are created with an integer value that is the priority of the thread; the values ranging from 1 through 10, with higher numbers indicating higher priority. The Thread methods getPriority() and setPriority() allow you to manipulate a threads priority and hence when it is scheduled to run.

The Threads interface in Java gives you very low-level control over the creation and management of threads. This actually makes programming threads in Java more difficult than it might be otherwise. If you write a program that creates several threads, then the scheduling of these threads and the management of shared variables adds significantly to the overhead of the program. It also can lead to possible runtime errors in the form of *race conditions* and *lost updates*.

In a race condition, two or more threads share a variable and they all want to read and write the variable. The order in which each thread executes and the fact that a thread can be forced to suspend execution either by a sleep() or by the operating system because it has exhausted its current quantum of allowed time can cause the shared variable to have the wrong value when the next thread reads it.

Let's consider an example. Say that Fred and Gladys both share a bank account. Let's also say that the algorithm for withdrawing money from the bank account is as follows:

1. You check the account balance to make sure there's enough money in the account.

2. You withdraw the money you want from the account.

Note that, while each of these two operations are atomic (they can't be interrupted once started), the algorithm could be interrupted between steps 1 and 2. And now let's throw in another step and allow Fred or Gladys to take a nap at some time while they are thinking about withdrawing money. This can lead to the following situation:

1. Fred wants to withdraw $100 from the bank account.

2. He checks the account balance and it is $150.

3. Fred takes a nap.

4. Gladys checks the account balance and it is $150.

5. Gladys withdraws $100.

6. Fred wakes up and tries to withdraw $100.

7. Oops. The account is now overdrawn.

That is a race condition. Here's some source code that can illustrate this problem: you create two threads and have each user withdraw $10 from the account, 10 times in a row.

```java
/*
 * example of a race condition
 * with Java Threads
 *    Here we are going to create two threads and have
 *    each of them withdraw $10 from the account
 *    10 times in a row.
 */
public class FredAndGladys implements Runnable  {
    private BankAccount account = new BankAccount();

    /** The run() method does the actual work of the thread */
    public void run()  {
        for (int x = 0; x < 10; x++) {
            makeWithdrawal(10);
            if (account.getBalance() < 0) {
                System.out.println("Overdrawn!");
            }
        }
    }

    /**
     *   The method that makes each withdrawal.
     *   It checks to see if the balance is OK
     *   goes to sleep for 500msec and then
     *   attempts to withdraw the money.
```

```
        */
    private void makeWithdrawal(int amount)  {
        /** so we know which thread this is */
        String name = Thread.currentThread().getName();
        if (account.getBalance() >= amount) {
            System.out.println(name + " is about to withdraw " + amount);
            try {
                System.out.println(name + " is going to sleep");
                Thread.sleep(500);
            } catch (InterruptedException ex) {
                ex.printStackTrace();
            }

            System.out.println(name + " woke up");
            account.withdraw(amount);
            System.out.printf("%s completes the withdrawal\n", name);
            System.out.printf("New balance is $%d\n", account.
            getBalance());
        } else {
            System.out.println("Sorry, not enough for "
                        + Thread.currentThread().getName());
        }
    }
}

/**
 *  inner class to represent a simple bank account
 */
class BankAccount {
    private int balance = 100;

    public int getBalance () {
        return balance;
    }

    public void withdraw(int amount) {
        balance = balance - amount;
```

```
    }
}
/**
 * the driver to run the experiment
 */
class FGMain {
    public static void main(String[] args) {
        FredAndGladys theJob = new FredAndGladys();

        Thread one = new Thread(theJob);
        Thread two = new Thread(theJob);

        one.setName("Fred");
        two.setName("Gladys");

        one.start();
        two.start();
    }
}
```

When you compile and execute this program, the first part of what you get is below:

```
Gladys is about to withdraw 10
Gladys is going to sleep
Fred is about to withdraw 10
Fred is going to sleep
Fred woke up
Fred completes the withdrawal
Gladys woke up
Gladys completes the withdrawal
New balance is $80
Gladys is about to withdraw 10
Gladys is going to sleep
New balance is $90
Fred is about to withdraw 10
Fred is going to sleep
Fred woke up
```

335

```
Fred completes the withdrawal
New balance is $70
Fred is about to withdraw 10
Fred is going to sleep
Gladys woke up
Gladys completes the withdrawal
New balance is $60
```

All things being equal, Fred and Gladys can alternate making withdrawals, but there's a race condition. Note that the balance is first reported as $80 and then as $90 because both threads are holding copies of the balance variable in their caches before they write it back to memory. Gladys writes first (after Fred has withdrawn) and you see $80. Then Fred writes and you see $90. Gladys then gets in before Fred again and the amount is correct.

This all happens because it's the JVM (or the operating system) that controls when threads get to use the CPU again. Luckily, Java has a way to fix this. There's a keyword, synchronized, that you can use in a method signature to create a critical section so that only one thread at a time is allowed to execute in that method. Any other thread that attempts to enter the synchronized method is blocked. If you synchronize the makeWithdrawal(int amount) method, you'll have everyone in sync[11]:

```
Fred is about to withdraw 10
Fred is going to sleep
Fred woke up
Fred completes the withdrawal
New balance is $90
Gladys is about to withdraw 10
Gladys is going to sleep
Gladys woke up
Gladys completes the withdrawal
New balance is $80
Fred is about to withdraw 10
Fred is going to sleep
Fred woke up
Fred completes the withdrawal
```

---

[11] https://docs.oracle.com/javase/tutorial/essential/concurrency/syncmeth.html

New balance is $70
Fred is about to withdraw 10
Fred is going to sleep
Fred woke up
Fred completes the withdrawal
New balance is $60

Another way to try avoiding race conditions (available since Java 5) is to use the volatile keyword on the variable balance in the BankAccount class. No cached copies of volatile variables are kept so the values are updated correctly, most of the time. Because the volatile variable is always stored in main memory (and not in the cache) and is always written back to main memory, then multiple threads could be writing to a shared volatile variable and still have the correct value stored in main memory. But, if a thread needs to first read the value of a shared volatile variable and then update that value with a new one, then using a volatile variable is no longer good enough to guarantee that the variable's value remains synchronized. Because there is a gap in time between reading the current value of the variable from main memory and then writing the new value, there is still a race condition where Fred and Gladys might both read the current value of balance and generate (the same) new value and write it. The volatile variable is now out of sync. There is no way to fix this other than being careful about when and how a shared volatile variable is used in your program.

One should also be careful about the use of the synchronized keyword because it adds more overhead and thus impacts performance. And while synchronized methods provide mutual exclusion and thread-safe code, they do not protect against a condition called *deadlock*. Deadlock occurs when two processes or threads are contending for the same resources, the resources can get locked, with both processes refuse to give them up. As an example, the following sequence of events leads to deadlock:

- Thread *a* enters *synchronized* method foo (and gets the key, locking out any other thread).

- Thread *a* goes to sleep.

- Thread *b* enters *synchronized* method bar (and gets the key, locking out any other thread).

- Thread *b* tries to enter foo, can't get the key, and waits.

- Thread *a* wakes up, tries to enter bar, can't get the key, and waits.

- *Neither can proceed until they acquire the other key.*

This is known (from Dijkstra) as a *deadly embrace*. So, how to fix a deadlock? Well, you shouldn't depend on Java to do it because Java can't detect a deadlock. The best methods involve prevention: work carefully to make sure that this situation doesn't happen.

For more on concurrency and parallel programming in Java, see the online Java Tutorials.[12]

Parallel Language Features: The OpenMP[13] API

OpenMP stands for Open Multi-Processing. It is a very popular open source applications programming interface (API) that enables simple creation of parallel programs. There are OpenMP implementations for practically all hardware architectures and bindings for C, C++, and Fortran. OpenMP assumes a shared memory model where threads share variables so there are race condition possibilities like in Java above. OpenMP is not really a programming language; instead, it consists of compiler directives (#pragmas in C & C++), library routines (which gives you an API), and environment variables.

OpenMP uses a *fork-join parallelism* model. In this model, there is one *master thread* charged with dynamically creating N parallel threads (called a *"team of threads"*) for a parallel region of the code. The number of threads created depends on OpenMPs assessment of how much parallelism is needed to execute the parallel region. When all those threads finish, program execution goes back to one master thread again until another parallel region is encountered. Figure 14-2 illustrates what fork-join parallelism looks like.

---

[12] https://docs.oracle.com/javase/tutorial/essential/concurrency/index.html
[13] The name OpenMP is the property of the OpenMP Architecture Review Board. See www.openmp.org/.

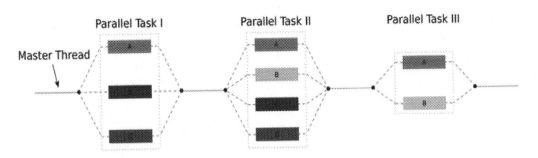

Figure 14-2. *Fork-join parallelism*

The programmer indicates to the compiler where the parallel regions should be using the compiler directive `#pragma omp parallel`. This directive creates an SPMD (single program multiple data) program where each thread executes the same code. The threads are created dynamically as needed. The maximum number of threads can be controlled with the `OMP_NUM_THREADS` environment variable or with the `omp_set_num_threads(N)` OpenMP library function. OpenMP will add parallelism dynamically until the demands of the program are met (or until it reaches the maximum number of threads allowed).

The programmer can determine which thread they currently are using via the `omp_get_thread_num()` library function, which returns the current thread number.

The master thread will create threads with the OpenMP parallel compiler directive. This directive tells the compiler that the next code statement block is to be considered a *parallel region* to be executed by each processor. For example, `#pragma omp parallel num_threads(8)` will instruct OpenMP to create up to seven threads of the parallel region that immediately follows the `#pragma`. Seven threads are created instead of eight because the master thread is also used in the parallel computation. In C or C++ this might look like

```
long list[1000];
#pragma omp parallel num_threads(8)
{
    int threadID = omp_get_thread_num();
    foo(list, threadID);
}
```

Note that because OpenMP uses a shared memory model, we need to guarantee *synchronization* to prevent race conditions. Recall that two common techniques for enforcing synchronization are *barriers* and *mutual exclusion*. OpenMP has a compiler directive to set a barrier, `#pragma omp barrier`. It can also create *critical sections* (and thus enforce mutual exclusion) by using another directive, #pragma omp critical. Only one thread at a time can enter a critical section. OpenMP also allows a very fine-grained form of synchronization by allowing the programmer to create an *atomic* operation. Using the #pragma omp atomic compiler directive, the programmer can apply mutual exclusion to a single statement that must update a memory location. Allowable operations in an atomic region include x op= expression, x++, ++x, x--, and --x.

If the #pragma omp parallel compiler directive creates an SPMD program and forces the program to execute the code in the parallel region, how do we get a loop to divide up the work into the threads (known as *worksharing*) so that we can execute the entire program faster? OpenMP ensures this with another directive, #pragma omp for. This directive has the effect of splitting up the work in the loop among all the threads in the team.

To illustrate how you would use all these OpenMP directives and library functions, let's take a look at a fairly common example in parallel computing. You might remember from calculus that one way to look at the integral is as the area under a curve. In numerical analysis, there is a technique called the *trapezoid rule* that allows you to approximate the definite integral of a function by measuring and summing up the areas of the trapezoids (or rectangles) under the curve drawn by your function. It turns out that the function $f(x) = 1.0 / (1.0 + x^2)$ using values of x from 0.0 to 1.0 approximates $\pi/4$. So, we can write a program that uses the trapezoid rule to compute $\pi/4$ and then just multiply to get a value for π. Figure 14-3 shows us what the function looks like.

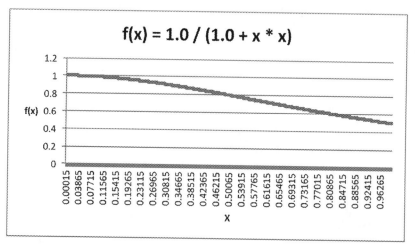

Figure 14-3. Function to compute $\pi/4$

Here is a serial version of this program in C:

```c
/*
 *  Serial program to estimate the area under a curve f(x)
 *  It really computes pi/4 and approximates the trapezoidal rule
 *  using rectangles instead of trapezoids.
 */
#include <stdio.h>
#include <stdlib.h>

/*
 * Here's the function we'll be computing
 */
double f(double x) {
    return 1.0 / (1.0 + x * x);
}

int main (int argc, char **argv) {
    int steps = 1000000000;      /* number of rectangles - 1 billion */
    double width = 0.0;          /* width of each rectangle */
    double x, pi4, sum = 0.0;

    /* get the width of each rectangle */
    width = 1.0 / (double) steps;

    /* loop to compute the area under f(x) */
    for (int i = 0; i <= steps; i++) {
        x = i * width;
        sum = sum + f(x);
    }
    pi4 = width * sum;
    printf("Sum is %8.4f and Area: pi/4 is %8.6f\n", sum, pi4);
    printf("Approximation to pi is %8.6f\n", pi4 * 4.0);
    return 0;
}
```

341

Compiling and executing this program on an eight-core Intel Linux computer running the Fedora operating system, using the GNU C compiler, produces the following results:

```
Sum is 785398164.1474 and Area: pi/4 is 0.785398
Approximation to pi is 3.141593
real 16.19
user 16.11
sys 0.00
```

The real processor time for the execution of 1 billion loop iterations is 16.19 seconds on a lightly loaded machine. Of course, this version of the program is running serially on a single core. To speed it up, we can use OpenMP to parallelize the loop:

```c
/*
 * Parallel program to estimate the area under a curve f(x)
 * it really computes pi/4 and approximates the trapezoidal rule
 * using rectangles instead of trapezoids.
 * Uses OpenMP with the gcc 7.1.0 compiler.
 */
#include <stdio.h>
#include <stdlib.h>
#include <omp.h>

/*
 * Here's the function we'll be computing
 */
double f(double x) {
    return 1.0 / (1.0 + x * x);
}

int main (int argc, char **argv) {
    int steps = 1000000000;     /* number of rectangles - 1 billion */
    double width = 0.0;         /* width of each rectangle */
    double x, pi4, sum = 0.0;

    /* get the width of each rectangle */
    width = 1.0 / (double) steps;
```

```
/*
 * here we define the parallel region to be the for loop
 * We declare x to be private and tell OpenMP
 * to reduce the partial sums as each thread finishes.
 */
#pragma omp parallel for private(x) reduction(+:sum)
/* loop to compute the area under f(x) */
for (int i = 0; i <= steps; i++) {
    x = i * width;
    sum = sum + f(x);
}
pi4 = width * sum;
printf("Sum is %8.4f and Area: pi/4 is %8.6f\n", sum, pi4);
printf("Approximation to pi is %8.6f\n", pi4 * 4.0);
return 0;
}
```

When this version of the program is compiled and run on the same system and using the same compiler (but including the OpenMP library), we get the following results:

```
Sum is 785398164.1475 and Area: pi/4 is 0.785398
Approximation to pi is 3.141593
real 2.24
user 17.06
sys 0.00
```

Note that the sum variable in the program is accumulated in the for loop. How does this work if we do *worksharing* and separate the work in the loop into multiple threads? Accumulating partial values each time we loop is called a *reduction* (converting an expression into a simpler form), achieved here using another OpenMP compiler directive, reduction(<operator> : <list of variables>). This operator causes several things to happen: (1) a local copy of each variable is made and initialized, (2) updates in the thread only happen to the local copy, and (3) at the end of the loop execution, the local copies are reduced into a single value and combined (both using the designated operator) into the original global variable. Operators that can be used for reduction include +, -, *, max, min, &, |, ^, &&, and ||.

In this version, the running time is down to 2.24 seconds, a speedup of 7.2 on a lightly loaded system. This indicates that OpenMP was using all eight cores to do the work and with the for and reduction compiler directives, the compiler was dividing up the work in the for loop efficiently and the answers ended up the same, but in a much shorter time.

Just as in Java, there is much more to the details of OpenMP that we haven't gone into here. This was just a taste of the very cool and interesting things you can do with parallel programming. If you really want to do parallel programming, you are strongly encouraged to go to the references at the end of this chapter and learn more.

Conclusion

Coding is the heart of software development. Code is what you produce. Performance is the key to good code and to programming the solutions to large and interesting problems. With Moore's Law beginning to fade and the power wall a reality, parallel programming is what everyone will be doing in the future.

And finally, a prediction that hasn't quite worked out:

"The way the processor industry is going, is to add more and more cores, but nobody knows how to program those things. I mean, two, yeah; four, not really; eight, forget it."

— Steve Jobs, Apple

References

Amdahl, Eugene. 1967. "Validity of the Single Processor Approach to Achieving Large Scale Computing Capabilities." In *AFIPS '67 (Spring): Proceedings of the April 18-20, 1967, Spring Joint Computer Conference*, 483–85. Association for Computing Machinery. https://doi.org/10.1145/1465482.1465560.

Anonymous. 2007. *Example of fork-join parallelism.* By Wikipedia user A1 - w:en:File:Fork_join.svg, CC BY 3.0, https://commons.wikimedia.org/w/index.php?curid=32004077.

Barney, B. 2017a. *Introduction to Parallel Programming* [government]. `https://computing.llnl.gov/tutorials/parallel_comp/#top`. Retrieved July 31, 2017.

Barney, B. 2017b. *OpenMP* [government]. `https://computing.llnl.gov/tutorials/openMP/`. Retrieved July 31, 2017.

Cherneyshev, A. 2008. *Writing Parallel Programs: a multi-language tutorial introduction* [industrial]. `https://software.intel.com/en-us/articles/writing-parallel-programs-a-multi-language-tutorial-introduction`. Retrieved July 31, 2017.

Dijkstra, E. W. 1965. Solution of a problem in concurrent programming control. *Communications of the ACM, 8*(9), 569. `https://doi.org/10.1145/365559.365617`.

Downey, A. B. 2016. *The Little Book of Semaphores* (2nd ed.). Needham, MA: Green Tea Press. `http://greenteapress.com/semaphores/LittleBookOfSemaphores.pdf`.

Eadline, D.(2009. *Concurrent and Parallel are not the Same* [Online magazine]. `www.linux-mag.com/id/7411/`. Retrieved July 27, 2017.

Flynn, M. 1972. Some Computer Organizations and Their Effectiveness. *IEEE Transactions on Computers, C-21*(9), 948–960. `https://doi.org/10.1109/TC.1972.5009071`.

Hoare, C. A. R. 1978. Communicating Sequential Processes. *CACM, 21*(8), 666–677.

Lin, C., & Snyder, L. 2009. *Principles of Parallel Programming* (Hardcover). Boston, MA: Addison-Wesley.

Mattson, T. G., Sanders, B. A., & Massingill, B. L. 2005. *Patterns for Parallel Programming* (hardcover). Boston, MA: Addison-Wesley.

Parri, J., Shapiro, D., Bolic, M., & Groza, V. 2011. Returning control to the programmer: SIMD intrinsics for virtual machines. *CACM, 54*(4), 38–43. `https://doi.org/10.1145/1924421.1924437`.

Vishkin, U. 2011. Using simple abstraction to reinvent computing for parallelism. *CACM, 54*(1), 75–85. `https://doi.org/10.1145/1866739.1866757`.

CHAPTER 15

Parallel Design Patterns

Software typically outlives hardware, so over the course of a program's life it may be used on a tremendous range of target platforms. The goal is to obtain a design that works well on the original target platform, but at the same time is flexible enough to adapt to different classes of hardware.

—Tim Mattson, et. al.[1]

Design patterns were introduced in the 1990s to "describe simple and elegant solutions to specific problems in object-oriented software design. Design patterns capture solutions that have developed and evolved over time. Hence, they aren't the designs people tend to generate initially. They reflect untold redesign and recoding as developers have struggled for greater reuse and flexibility in their software. Design patterns capture these solutions in a succinct and easily applied form."[2]

A *design pattern* is a representation of a common programming problem along with a tested, efficient solution for that problem. Although design patterns are normally presented in an object oriented programming framework, the idea is completely general and it can be applied to different programming models, including parallel ones.

---

[1] Mattson, T. G., Sanders, B. A., & Massingill, B. L. 2005. *Patterns for Parallel Programming.* Boston, MA: Addison-Wesley.

[2] Gamma, E., Helm, R., Johnson, R., & Vlissides, J. 1995. *Design Patterns: Elements of Reusable Object-Oriented Software.* Boston: Addison-Wesley.

© John F. Dooley and Vera A. Kazakova 2024
J. F. Dooley and V. A. Kazakova, *Software Development, Design, and Coding,*
https://doi.org/10.1007/979-8-8688-0285-0_15

Parallel Design Patterns Overview

Parallel design patterns have the same objectives as the classical sequential design patterns, namely to describe solutions to recurrent problems, but now in the context of parallel software design rather than object-oriented software design.

In this chapter, we'll give an overview of parallel patterns, the computing abstractions typical in parallel programming, and how to think about converting serial programs into parallel programs. We'll also go through several sample parallel design patterns, including those for solving the problems of efficient implementation of recursive, divide and conquer computations, of staged computations, and of computations split into a number of independent tasks. As in Chapter 13, we will not examine all the parallel design patterns, but rather focus on a representative sample, mostly from Mattson et. al.[3]

In the next several sections, we'll introduce a language of parallel patterns, which will allow us to later discuss the different patterns.

Overview: Parallel Design Spaces

One of the most interesting aspects of parallel design patterns is the partitioning of the design of a parallel application into four separate but related design elements called *design spaces* that roughly coincide with the steps in creating a parallel program:

Finding concurrency: This design space is "concerned with structuring the problem to expose exploitable concurrency."[4] The programmer will take a problem or an existing serial program and search out the areas of possible concurrency that can be utilized.

Algorithm structure: In this design phase, the programmer attempts to find and structure the algorithms that can take advantage of the exposed concurrency.

---

[3] (Mattson 2005)

[4] (Mattson 2005, 24)

Supporting structures: Supporting structures is where the programmer begins to map the algorithms to data structures and to more detailed program structures, like loops and recursion.

Implementation mechanisms: Finally, the design is mapped into particular parallel programming frameworks.

Figure 15-1 shows the hierarchy of the design spaces, the general dimensions in which the patterns are organized, and inside those, the parallel meta-patterns associated with each space. The following four sections discuss each of the design spaces in more detail.

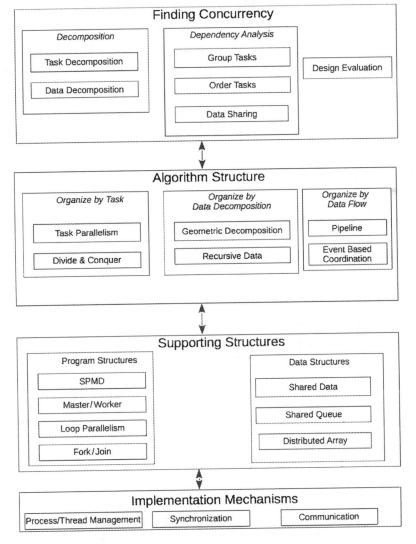

Figure 15-1. *The parallel design spaces and related meta-patterns*

Design Spaces: Finding Concurrency

The meta-patterns in the *Finding Concurrency* design space are used to start designing a parallel application. You will enter this design space after having considered the top-level elements of the problem to be solved. Your objective is to tease out the parts of the algorithm or program that are inherently sequential and those that contain elements of concurrency. This typically has you looking at the parts of the program or algorithm that are the most computationally intensive, as these are the areas where they are most likely to find concurrency. Finding concurrency is divided into three dimensions: Decomposition, Dependency Analysis, and Design Evaluation.

The first two, the *Decomposition* and *Dependency Analysis* dimensions, are related to the ways in which you will implement the parallel application. The *Decomposition* meta-patterns are used to decompose the problem into pieces that can execute concurrently, while the *Dependency Analysis* meta-patterns help group the tasks to be executed and analyze the dependencies among these tasks.

The *Decomposition* dimension includes just two meta-patterns that are used to find and divide the problem into parts that can execute concurrently:

- The *Task Decomposition* pattern views a complex algorithm as a set of instructions that can be grouped into a set of tasks to be executed concurrently.

- The *Data Decomposition* pattern takes the data used by the program and attempts to divide it into chunks which can be used by each of the tasks.

The *Dependency Analysis* dimension includes three different meta-patterns, whose job it is to group the tasks found above and to analyze the dependencies between them:

- The *Group Tasks* pattern is aimed at modeling the more convenient grouping of tasks, such that the management of dependencies is simplified.

- The *Order Tasks* pattern is aimed at figuring out how tasks (or groups of tasks) may be ordered to satisfy the application constraints related to task execution.

- The *Data Sharing* pattern is aimed at modeling the accesses to a shared data structure.

The main forces influencing the design of these meta-patterns are flexibility, efficiency, and simplicity. Flexibility is needed to adapt the program design to different implementation requirements. Efficiency is usually related to scalability: how does the solution scale with the size of the target parallel computer. Finally, simplicity is required for understandability and maintenance.

The third dimension, *Design Evaluation*, is not really a dimension or meta-pattern in the way we've used the words so far. Rather, it is used to "guide the algorithm designer through an analysis of what has been done so far before moving to the patterns in the *Algorithm Structure* design space."[5] Design evaluation is really a process that encourages you to evaluate the design iteratively in order to arrive at the best design possible. In this process, you ask questions that force you to think about the current version of the design. For example, how suitable is the design for the target platform? How many processing elements (PEs) are available, and how many of them and how often will they be used? How are the data structures shared among the PEs? How regular are the tasks and their data dependencies? Are the tasks grouped in the most efficient and scalable way?

The overall output resulting from the analysis of the *Finding Concurrency* design space is a decomposition of the problem into different design elements: i) a task decomposition identifying the tasks that can be executed concurrently, ii) a data decomposition that identifies the data local to each one of the tasks, iii) a way of grouping tasks and ordering these tasks groups in such a way that temporal and data dependencies are satisfied, and iv) an analysis of the dependencies among the tasks.

Design Spaces: Algorithm Structure

The output from the *Finding Concurrency* design space is used in the *Algorithm Structure* design space to refine the design of our concurrent tasks and to create a parallel program structure closer to an actual parallel program, suitable to be run on a parallel target architecture.

There are three major dimensions used in organizing a parallel algorithm's structure: by task, by data decomposition, and by flow of data. Note that, while in the *Finding Concurrency* design space, you will normally go through all the dimensions and their patterns, in the *Algorithm Structure* design space you are required to choose one of these three alternative dimensions and implement one of its parallel design patterns below.

---

[5] (Mattson 2005, 26)

- Organizing the parallel algorithm by *task*. In this dimension, tasks themselves drive your design. That is, you consider the tasks that can be computed in parallel, which tasks in your set are concurrent, and then how the tasks are enumerated, linearly or recursively. The *organize by tasks* meta-pattern group includes two patterns:

    - The *Task Parallelism* pattern governs the efficient execution of collections of tasks and is used for linear decompositions. The common factor here is that "the problem can be decomposed into a collection of tasks that execute concurrently."[6] These tasks can be independent or there can be some dependencies between them. In many cases the tasks are also associated with a loop program structure. The proposed solution to implement the pattern works out three different points: how tasks are defined, the dependencies among tasks, and the scheduling of the tasks for concurrent execution, including assigning tasks to different processors or threads.

    - The *Divide and Conquer* pattern is used for recursive decompositions and implements the well-known divide-and-conquer recursive solution schema where a problem is divided up into a number of smaller, identical, sub-problems, which are then solved, and the solutions are combined together into a single overall solution for the original problem.

- Organizing the parallel algorithm by *data decomposition*, where data is driving the design. Consider the decomposition of data into (possibly disjoint) subsets to be used by each task. Again, this decomposition can be either linear or recursive: if the data can be distributed into discrete data sets and the entire problem can be solved by operating on each of the data sets independently, then choose the linear/geometric meta-pattern; if the data is organized recursively (say as a binary tree), then choose the recursive meta-pattern. The *organize by data* decomposition pattern group includes two meta-patterns:

---

[6] (Mattson 2005, 65)

o The *Geometric Decomposition* pattern represents computations where the algorithm is recognized as a series of computations on some core data structure and where that data structure is inherently linear in nature, like an array or table or matrix. With these types of data structures, the data can be broken up into contiguous subsets and acted on independently by the program. This means that the tasks operating on this data can execute concurrently. See the *Distributed Array* meta-pattern below for an example of how the *Geometric Distribution* pattern would organize its data.

o The *Recursive Data* pattern works with parallel computations created to work with a recursively defined data structure, where the data appears to be acted upon sequentially. These tasks generally use links to move from one data element to another, as in a linked list, a binary tree, or a graph, but the computations involve things like following a path in the tree or partitioning the graph. Solving these problems usually involves restructuring the computations over the linked data structure that exposes more concurrency.

- Organizing the parallel algorithm by *flow of data* when the organizing principle is how the flow of data imposes an ordering on the tasks that make up the algorithm. The *Organize by Flow of Data* pattern group also includes two meta-patterns:

o The *Pipeline* pattern is where the flow of data is traversing a consistent linear chain of stages, each representing a function computed on the input data coming from the previous stage, and whose result is delivered to the next stage. In this pattern, the data flow is assumed to be one way. (This should look and sound just like the idea of a multi-stage CPU architecture, or a pipe-and-filter execution sequence, as seen in Chapter 7.)

o The *Event-Based Coordination* pattern is where a number of semi-independent concurrent activities interact in a dynamic or unpredictable way, and interactions are determined by the flow of data between the concurrent activities. The flow of data implies a set of ordering dependencies between the tasks. In this pattern, the data flow is not assumed to be one way nor linear. There are many examples of problems that fit this pattern, including many discrete event simulation problems. Hence, many of the solutions that use this pattern use events as basic building blocks: there is usually at least one task that generates events and then some number of them that process the events. (Think of a multi-stall car wash where cars arrive at random and are assigned to a stall, or a bank with either a single queue or multiple queues and several tellers to serve customers as they reach the front of the queue. The Bird Feeder example in Chapter 11 is an example of this type of design.)

Design Spaces: Supporting Structures

After having explored different possibilities to find concurrency in *Finding Concurrency* design space and to express parallel algorithms in the *Algorithm Structure* design space, implementation arrives at the *Supporting Structures* design space, which begins to investigate the structures/patterns suitable to support the implementation of the algorithms planned in the preceding design spaces. Two groups of meta-patterns are included in the *Supporting Structures* design space: the *Program Structures* meta-pattern group discusses how to structure the program in order to maximize parallelism and the *Data Structures* meta-pattern group discusses commonly used shared data structures.

The *Program Structures* group includes four meta-patterns:

- The Single Program, Multiple Data (*SPMD*) meta-pattern, where all of the processing elements (PEs) run the same program in parallel, but each PE has its own subset of the data. Unlike in an SIMD architecture, the PEs are not required to stay in lock step and so different parallel tasks may follow different paths through the code. Because each of the PEs runs its own copy of the program, an important feature of the SPMD is that the extra overhead associated with starting and stopping the loops are implemented at the beginning and end of the program, rather than inside the loop itself. Each data set will typically be split, so that a loop in the program runs just a fraction of the total number of iterations. Also, the PEs only communicate infrequently with their neighbors, increasing efficiency.

- The *Manager/Worker* meta-pattern, where a single Manager task will set up a number of concurrent Worker threads or processes, and a single bag of tasks. Each Worker will take a task out of the bag and execute it in parallel; as they finish, Workers will continue to take tasks out of the bag and execute them until the bag is empty, or some other ending condition has occurred. The bag of tasks is typically implemented as a shared queue. The *Manager/Worker* pattern is particularly useful for *embarrassingly parallel* programs (see below), where a large number of worker tasks have no dependencies.

- The *Loop Parallelism* meta-pattern solves the problem of how to execute an algorithm with one or more compute-intensive loops. The pattern describes how to create a parallel program where the distinct iterations of the loop are executed in parallel. The program to compute the value of π using OpenMP[7] in Chapter 14 is an example of the *Loop Parallelism* pattern at work.

- The *Fork/Join* meta-pattern (see the example in Chapter 14) is an example of the concurrent execution of different portions of the overall computation that proceed unrelated, until the (possibly coordinated) collective termination. Typically, a single thread or process will fork off some number of sub-processes that will all execute in parallel. The originating process will typically wait until the child processes all join before resuming its own execution. Each time the original thread forks off subprocesses, there may be a different number of them. This meta-pattern, like many of the patterns you've seen so far, assumes a shared memory model where all the tasks are sharing values and creating results that are available to the Manager at the end. The *Fork/Join* pattern is the standard programming model in OpenMP.

These meta-patterns are well known in the parallel computing community. The *SPMD* pattern is the computational model used by MPI and one of the most popular patterns used to structure parallel computations along with the *Manager/Worker*. *Loop Parallelism* has been exploited in vector architectures, and it is currently one of the

---

[7] See Barney, Blaise 2017a, 2017b, and 2017c in the References for an excellent introduction to parallel programming and the OpenMP library.

main sources of parallelism in both OpenMP and GPUs. Last but not least, the *Fork/Join* pattern perfectly models the pthread_create/pthread_join model of POSIX threads[8] and is also used as the basis for OpenMP.

The *Data Structures* group includes three meta-patterns:

- The *Shared Data* meta-pattern implements the features related to the management of data shared among a number of different concurrent activities. Correct and efficient management of the shared data is usually the most time and effort consuming activity in the entire parallel program development/design process. This pattern requires simplicity of execution, a careful abstraction of how the data will be manipulated, an awareness that explicitly managing the shared data will incur some parallel overhead, and it must guarantee the correctness of any computation regardless of the order of the tasks (reading and writing, in particular).[9] This requires the consideration of locking, memory synchronization, and task scheduling. An example of the use of this meta-pattern is managing shared data in the *Task Parallelism* meta-pattern, where tasks are first duplicated and then partial answers reduced.

- The *Shared Queue* meta-pattern creates queue data types implemented to allow concurrent access to the queues. Shared queues are used to support the interaction of concurrent activities in different contexts, from threads to processes, and concurrent activities running on CPU co-processors. A good example of where this meta-pattern is used is in the *Manager/Worker* meta-pattern to create the concurrent queue that dispenses tasks for the Worker processes.

- The *Distributed Array* meta-pattern models all the aspects related to the management of arrays partitioned and distributed among different concurrent activities. Distributed arrays are often used to implement data structures that are logically shared among concurrent activities, but may be partitioned in such a way that one

---

[8] Barney, Blaise. 2017b. POSIX Threads Programming [government]. Retrieved August 7, 2017, from https://computing.llnl.gov/tutorials/pthreads/.
[9] (Mattson 2005, 174)

of the concurrent activities owns and manages a single portion of the distributed array. "The challenge is to organize the arrays so that the elements needed by each UE are nearby at the right time in the computation. In other words, the arrays must be distributed about the computer so that the array distribution matches the flow of the computation."[10] This meta-pattern is particularly useful for programs using the *Geometric Decomposition* meta-pattern to help with the algorithm construction and to organize the program structure when using the *SPMD* meta-pattern.

Mattson et. al. classify the different meta-patterns in this design with respect to their suitability to support the implementation of the different patterns in the *Algorithm Structure* design space. As an example, *Task Parallelism* is well supported by the four meta-patterns in the *Program Structures* group, whereas the *Recursive Data* pattern is only (partially) supported by the *SPMD* and *Manager/Worker* pattern.

Design Spaces: Implementation Mechanisms

The fourth and final design space related to implementation of parallel applications is the *Implementation Mechanisms* design space, which includes meta-patterns representing the basic mechanisms to support the typical parallel computing abstractions: concurrent activities, synchronization, and communication. The three meta-patterns corresponding to these abstractions above are the following:

- The *UE (Units of Execution) Management* meta-pattern deals with managing the units of execution (processes and threads used to execute the parallel application), handling all aspects related to the concurrent activities in a parallel application, including their creation, destruction, and management. Although in Mattson et. al. only threads and processes are taken into account, the UE Management meta-pattern may be adapted to handle the concurrent activities placed on CPU co-processors (e.g., the GPU kernels).

---

[10] (Mattson 2005, 199)

- The *Synchronization* meta-pattern handles all aspects related to ordering of events/computations in the UE, including synchronization of concurrent activities and memory. This pattern covers aspects such as lock/fence mechanisms, higher level mutual exclusion constructs (e.g., monitors), and collective synchronizations (e.g., barriers).

- The *Communication* meta-pattern manages all the aspects related to communications between the different UEs implementing the parallel application, including data exchange among concurrent activities. This pattern covers different kinds of point-to-point message passing (e.g., send, receive, synchronous and asynchronous) and multi-point or collective communications (e.g., broadcast, scatter, gather, reduce) where multiple UEs are involved in a single communication event.

A List of Parallel Patterns

In this section we examine in more detail some of the meta-patterns discussed above. We also include some other common parallel patterns and match these patterns with the meta-patterns above.[11]

Pattern 1: Embarrassingly Parallel

Not really a pattern, but rather a class of problems where the division of the work into independent tasks is so obvious and simple, that the problem is known as *embarrassingly parallel* or *pleasingly parallel.*

Examples of embarrassingly parallel problems include using the trapezoid rule to compute π (Chapter 14) where we could compute the areas of any number of trapezoids in parallel, any problem solution that uses a loop to accumulate values using

---

[11] McCool, M., Robison, A. D., & Reinders, J. 2012. *Structured Parallel Programming: Patterns for Efficient Computation.* Waltham, MA: Morgan Kaufmann Publishers.

multiplication or addition, password cracking, rendering of computer graphics images, computing the points for the Mandelbrot set, facial recognition systems, and many computer simulations, like climate models.

Other examples can depend on the type and size of the input data. For example, if you have several million (say M) TIFF files that you want to convert to GIF files, using P processing elements (PE), you can distribute M/P TIFF files to each PE and do the conversions there (see the Map pattern below). Or if you have an entire catalog of text documents and you want to compute word frequencies across the entire catalog, you can again divide the documents across all the processing elements you have, do the counts on each subset, and then combine all the subsets (see the MapReduce pattern below). It turns out that there are many these types of pleasingly parallel problems where you have a large number of independently distributed computations across a large set of data that fit this split-compute-combine pattern. You'll see more examples of this in combination with other parallel patterns in the sections below.

Pattern 2: Manager/Worker

In this pattern, a single Manager task will set up a number of concurrent Worker threads or processes, alongside a single bag of tasks. Each Worker will take a task out of the bag and execute it in parallel; as they finish, Workers will continue to take tasks out of the bag and execute them until the bag is empty, or some other ending condition has occurred. The bag of tasks is typically implemented as a shared queue. The *Manager/Worker* pattern is particularly useful for *embarrassingly parallel* programs (see Figure 15-2), where a large number of worker tasks have no dependencies.

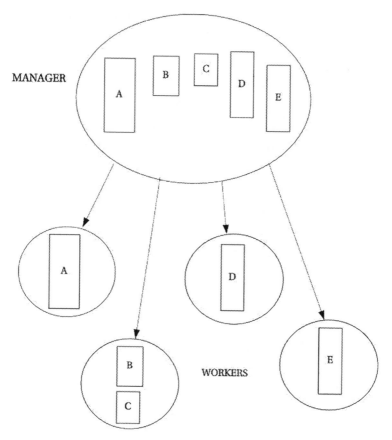

Figure 15-2. *Manager/Worker pattern implementing an embarrassingly parallel problem*

Pattern 3: Map and Reduce

Like *Manager/Worker*, the *Map and Reduce* patterns are very well suited for pleasingly parallel problems. The *Map and Reduce* patterns can be used separately and they often are.

The *Map pattern* is likely the simplest pattern you'll run into. Map applies part of the program, let's call it a function, to every element of the data in parallel. The functions must have no side effects, be identical, and independent. Because of this independence, Map can take advantage of as many units of execution as are available.

Used with the *Map pattern*, the *Reduce pattern* combines all the elements of the collection of partial solutions pairwise and creates a summary value as the overall solution. While commutativity is not required for the combination of the partial solutions, most applications of Reduce assume both commutativity and associativity. Figure 15-3 shows an example of how combining Map and Reduce works.

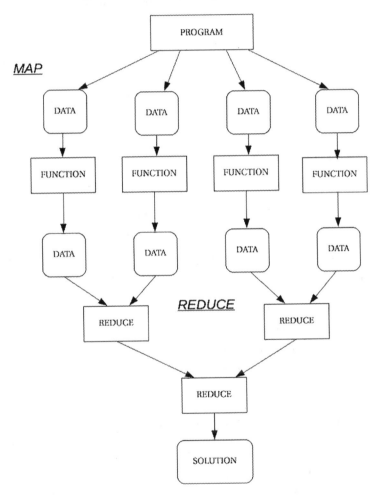

Figure 15-3. *Illustration of an implementation of Map, followed by Reduce*

In OpenMP, the `#pragma omp parallel for` compiler directive will initiate a Map operation for a for-loop that is in a program that is pleasingly parallel. Adding a *reduction(+: <var-list>)* to the compiler directive will add the Reduce component. For the trapezoid rule program in Chapter 14 the main for loop looked like

```
#pragma omp parallel for private(x) reduction(+:sum)
    /* loop to compute the area under f(x) */
    for (int i = 0; i <= steps; i++) {
        x = i * width;
        sum = sum + f(x);
    }
```

Pattern 4: MapReduce

A variation of using the *Map and Reduce* patterns that combines the two to accomplish a common task is the *MapReduce* pattern that was first published in 2004.[12] The *MapReduce* pattern is intended solve problems where the main goal is to input, process, and generate large data sets and where the implementation is scalable across many processors. The implementation of *MapReduce* performs three essential functions:

- *Mapping*, in which the program divides up a large data set (or a large set of files) into N discrete and independent subsets, each of which will be processed on a single processor. The output is typically a map data structure of some kind containing lists of not necessarily unique (key, value) pairs.

- *Shuffle*, in which the program extracts similar (key, value) pairs and assigns them to a new processor where the Reduce operation will happen.

- *Reduce*, where the elements in an input dataset are combined into a single result that is output. The list of the results from each processor constitutes the generated output dataset.

---

[12] Dean, J., & Ghemawat, S. 2004. MapReduce: Simplified Data Processing on Large Clusters. In *Proceedings of the 6th Conference on Symposium on Operating Systems Design & Implementation*. Berkeley, CA, USA: USENIX Association. 137-149.

As an example of a use of MapReduce to solve a large problem, let's say that we have a large catalog of text documents. Our objective is to create a single list of [word, frequency] pairs that tells us all the unique words in all the documents and how many times each of those words occur. A solution to this type of problem would be useful in problems in cryptography or in the statistical analysis of texts, say for author attribution studies. Figure 15-4 shows us how such a system might look.

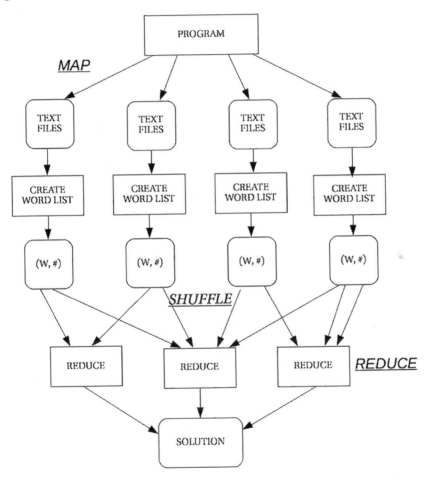

Figure 15-4. *A use of MapReduce to find word frequencies across a large set of text files*

In this solution, we start with a catalog of text files, which we divide into subsets, and assign each subset to an instance of the program on a processor. The program then creates a list of words and their frequencies for each of the words across all the documents in its subset. The shuffle operation then takes each unique word in each of the words lists and assigns it to a reduce process. So, for example, all the ("cat", value) pairs from all the word lists end up as inputs to the same reduce process. Each reduce process then accumulates all the values of all the unique words to create the overall solution.

Pseudo-code for the map and reduce portions of this program might look as follows:[13]

```
map(DocumentID docID_key, String input_value) {
    /* docID_key is the name of the document */
    /* input_value is the contents of the document */
    Create a Map called myMap;
    for each word in input_value do {
        if (myMap.contains(word)) then
            myMap.put(word, myMap.get(word) + 1);
        else
            myMap.put(word, 1);
    }
    return myMap;
}
/* The shuffle operation goes here */
```

The input to the shuffle is the set of all the myMap map output files that contain (word, frequency) pairs for all the words in the text file subsets. The output of the shuffle function is an intermediate key (the word) and the list of all the word frequency counts for that word across all the files in the catalog. Each of these goes to a reduce function and this operation continues until all the myMap output files are exhausted. The shuffle operation can take a long time (longer than the map or reduce) because it will end up doing a lot of I/O between processing elements as it moves data from the map output files to the reduce inputs.

```
reduce(String intermediate_key, Iterator value_list) {
    /* intermediate_key is a word from the documents */
    /* value_list is the list of counts of that word */
    int result = 0;
```

---

[13] (Dean and Gehmawat 2009, 138)

```
    for each value in value_list do {
        result += value;
    }
    return result;
}
```

At the end, we have a final output map that contains entries for each unique word and its total frequency in all the files in the catalog. So, we see that the *MapReduce* pattern is a useful set of operations that allow a parallel program to implement a solution to the split-compute-combine problem.

MapReduce is so common, and the solution is so popular, that a standard framework called Hadoop has been created that has *MapReduce* as its fundamental basis of operation. Hadoop is now part of the Apache project. "Apache Hadoop is a framework for running applications on large clusters built of commodity hardware. The Hadoop framework transparently provides applications both reliability and data motion. Hadoop implements a computational paradigm named MapReduce where the application is divided into many small fragments of work, each of which may be executed or re-executed on any node in the cluster. In addition, it provides a distributed file system, the Hadoop Distributed Files System (HDFS), which stores data on the compute nodes, providing very high aggregate bandwidth across the cluster. Both MapReduce and the Hadoop Distributed File System are designed so that node failures are automatically handled by the framework."[14]

Pattern 5: Divide and Conquer

Among the many problems with recursive solutions, many are amenable to a *Divide and Conquer* strategy. In this strategy, the data is typically large and contiguous, and the problem has the characteristic that smaller versions of the problem are solved independently and the larger solution depends on the smaller solutions. This characteristic of these problems makes them easily amenable to parallelization: the original large problem can be broken down into smaller sub-problems (along with a discretized subset of the data) and each sub-problem can be in turn solved independently and the partial solutions subsequently combined back into a solution for the larger problem. Figure 15-5 shows how divide and conquer works.

---

[14] https://cwiki.apache.org/confluence/display/HADOOP/Home

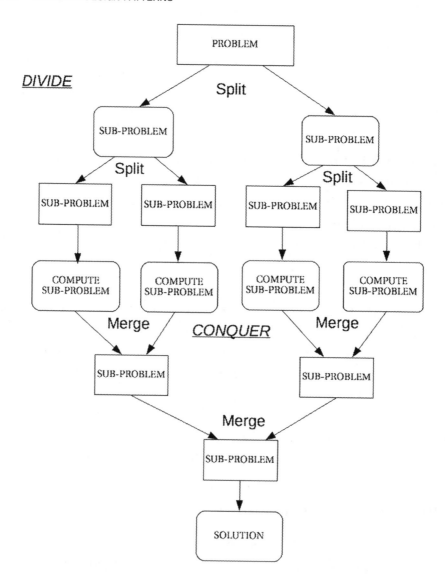

Figure 15-5. *An illustration of the Divide and Conquer strategy*

Note in the example in Figure 15-5 that in a program that uses the *Divide and Conquer* strategy, the amount of concurrency will vary over the course of the execution of the program. At the beginning and end of the program there is little in the way of concurrency, but as the program divides the data into more levels, the amount of concurrency grows, at some point reaching a maximum after which as the merging operations occur the amount of concurrency shrinks. Also, at some level in the recursion, the amount of work involved in coming up with a solution is less than the parallel overhead, and the program should drop out into a sequential algorithm or a base case. There is also the possibility that the division of data will not be regular (a good example here is where the pivot element in Quicksort doesn't divide the current list in half), which also may require more work.

The *Divide and Conquer* strategy is useful for an entire class of recursive problems, including all the O(n log n) sorting algorithms, the Fast Fourier Transform, and problems in linear algebra. This general strategy is typically implemented using either a *Fork/Join* pattern (where a Manager thread or instance will spawn some number of child threads, then wait for their completion and combine the partial answers into a final answer) or a *Manager/Worker* pattern. You'll examine the *Fork/Join* parallel pattern next.

Pattern 6: Fork/Join

In some problems, the number of parallel threads will vary as the program executes, making it more difficult to use simple control structures to invoke the parallelism. One way around this is to fork off a different number of threads at different times during the program execution and then wait for them to finish before proceeding. Typically, a single thread or process will fork off some number of sub-processes that will all execute in parallel. The originating process will typically wait until the child processes all complete and join before resuming its own execution. Each time the original thread forks off sub-processes, there may be a different number of them. This pattern also has the possibility of having *nested parallel execution regions* that can complicate the performance of the program.

Pseudo-code for this strategy retains the recursive nature of sequential divide and conquer algorithms; it looks something like the following:

```
ResultType solve(Problem problem) {
    if (problem.size is small enough)
        return solveSequentially(problem);
    else {
        ResultType left, right;
        Divide problem into K subproblems;
        Fork the K subproblems;
        join; // wait for all the subproblems to finish
        return combine(left, right);
    }
}
```

This code also illustrates a problem with this type of pattern. The `combine()` function looks to be inherently serial and will be executed every time `solve()` is executed. This might slow down the parallel implementation of the problem. To illustrate this, let's examine a version of the mergesort algorithm; the pseudo-code for the parallel version looks as follows:

```
mergesort(list, start, end) {
    if (start < end) then
        mid = floor(start + (end - start)) / 2)
    fork mergesort(list, start, mid)
    mergesort(list, mid+1, end)
    join
    merge(list, start, mid, end)
}
```

We implement this program in C and using the OpenMP parallel package. In C, in the `main()` function we first tell OpenMP to allow nested parallel regions, which is necessary because of the recursion in mergesort. Then, in the `mergeSort()` function we create a parallel region around the two recursive calls to `mergeSort()`. We tell OpenMP to limit the number of threads created in this region to 2, so that each recursive call will get exactly one thread, creating the overall appropriate number of threads of execution.

```
/*
 * parallel version of mergesort in C using openMP
 */
#include <stdio.h>
#include <stdlib.h>
#include <omp.h>

/* Here's the merge; it's sequential and the normal one you'd write */
void merge(int* array, int start, int end) {
    int middle = (start + end) / 2;
    int temp_index = 0;

    /* create a temporary array */
    int* temp = malloc(sizeof(int) * (end - start + 1));

    /* merge in sorted data from the 2 halves */
```

```
int left = start;
int right = middle + 1;

/* while both halves have data */
while((left <= middle) && (right <= end)) {
    /* if the left half value is less than right */
    if (array[left] < array[right]) {
        /* take from left */
        temp[temp_index] = array[left];
        temp_index++;
        left++;
    }
    else {
        /* take from right */
        temp[temp_index] = array[right];
        temp_index++;
        right++;
    }
}

/* add the remaining elements from the left half */
while(left <= middle) {
    temp[temp_index] = array[left];
    temp_index++;
    left++;
}

/* add the remaining elements from the right half */
while(right <= end) {
    temp[temp_index] = array[right];
    temp_index++;
    right++;
}

/* move from temp array to the original array */
int i;
for(i = start; i <= end; i++) {
```

```c
        array[i] = temp[i - start];
    }

    /* free the temporary array */
    free(temp);
}

/* the parallel version of mergesort */
void mergeSort(int* array, int start, int end) {

    if(start < end) {
        int middle = (start + end) / 2;

        /* sort both halves in parallel;
         * we limit the number of threads to 2
         */
        #pragma omp parallel sections num_threads(2)
        {
            /* require that only one thread execute this task */
            #pragma omp section
            {
                mergeSort(array, start, middle);
            }
            #pragma omp section
            {
                mergeSort(array, middle + 1, end);
            }
        }

        /* merge the two halves */
        merge(array, start, end);
    }
}

int main(int argc, char **argv ) {
    int i;
```

```
if (argc < 2) {
    printf("Usage: %s <arraySize>\n", argv[0]);
    exit(1);
}

int SIZE = atoi(argv[1]);
int* nums = malloc(sizeof(int) * SIZE);

/* enable recursive parallel blocks */
omp_set_nested(1);

/* put in random numbers */
for(i = 0; i < SIZE; i++) {
    nums[i] = rand( ) % 1000;
}

/* sort them */
mergeSort(nums, 0, SIZE - 1);

    return 0;
}
```

Notice that we use the OpenMP sections directive in this program. This directive guarantees that each section inside the parallel pragma will be executed once by a thread from the team. Different sections are allowed to be executed by different threads. There is also an implicit barrier at the end of the parallel block so that the merge() function won't be called until the two mergeSort() threads are completed. So, with the *Fork/Join* pattern, we can separate the partitioned array, do the independent mergeSort()s, and then merge when each pair is complete. With this setup, each call to mergeSort(), except for the last ones, will divide the current sub-list in half, then create two new threads of execution which will execute to completion and, when both finish, the merge() function will execute and the thread will end. The array being sorted will be shared among all the threads. The number of threads active will increase until we get to a maximum (after $\log_2$ n steps), at which time the threads will begin to end, and the joins will happen. Note that there is overhead incurred every time a new thread is created and destroyed, so this needs to be taken into account when you consider using OpenMP.

The sequential version of this program executes everything in a single thread, but uses the system stack to keep track of the recursive calls to mergeSort(). Every time mergeSort() is called, a new activation record[15] is created on the system stack, and when each mergeSort() call ends, that activation record is removed. In this way, the system stack grows and shrinks during execution. Again, the array is shared by all the active instances of the mergeSort() function. The temporary array created in the merge() function is local to that function and disappears when merge() exits. The major overhead in the sequential version is the creation and destruction of the activation records on the system stack. As above, you need to consider this overhead when implementing the sequential version of the program.

While this parallel version works and we are able to take advantage of the multiple cores in our test system, it turns out Amdahl's Law[16] will be our undoing here. The merge() function as written is inherently sequential and thus slows down the entire program, so our potential speedup is very small. The parallel version of the mergesort program ends up being slower than the sequential version on a two-core, shared memory system running Linux. With larger sizes of the array, we also have to be careful of how many threads we will create simultaneously (that is why we limited the number of threads in the parallel pragma); most operating systems have limits on the number of simultaneously active threads or processes that a single user can create.

How might we fix this problem with the parallel version? There are two changes that might be made. First, in the mergeSort() function, the test for the base case, if (start < end), can be changed to be a threshold test instead. We can keep track of either the number of recursive calls or the length of the current sub-list and if it drops below a certain threshold, we stop recursing and switch to a different sorting algorithm, say insertion sort, which approaches linear time complexity for small arrays. This fix doesn't change the sequential nature of the merge() function though. We can make the program faster by creating a parallel merge function. The merge function is already a O(n) algorithm, so we don't want to make it any slower. It is also not an obvious candidate for parallelization. The goal should be a parallel algorithm that is O(n) or faster (possibly by reducing the coefficient size in the complexity estimate). A *Divide and*

---

[15] https://en.wikipedia.org/wiki/Call_stack#ACTIVATION-RECORD
[16] See Chapter 14 for a statement of Amdahl's Law.

Conquer algorithm might be what we are looking for. The development of this algorithm is somewhat beyond the scope of this book, but there is a nice parallel merge algorithm in the current edition of the famous CLRS *Introduction to Algorithms* book, which we commend to the interested reader.[17]

Conclusion

As you have likely noticed by now, parallel design patterns can be very similar to each other. This is because they typically follow the process of creating a parallel algorithm/program from a corresponding serial algorithm/program. The process is (1) identify concurrency, (2) split the program into the concurrent pieces, (3) split the data if the updated algorithm calls for it, (4) execute the concurrent pieces in parallel, and (5) put all the answers back together to make a final answer. That said, parallel design patterns provide us with a useful set of abstractions for thinking about parallel programming.

References

Barney, Blaise. 2017a. *Introduction to Parallel Programming* [government]. `https://computing.llnl.gov/tutorials/parallel_comp/#top`. Retrieved July 31, 2017.

    Barney, Blaise. 2017b. POSIX Threads Programming [government]. `https://computing.llnl.gov/tutorials/pthreads/`. Retrieved August 7, 2017.

    Barney, Blaise. 2017c. *OpenMP* [government]. `https://computing.llnl.gov/tutorials/openMP/`. Retrieved July 31, 2017.

    Cormen, Thomas H., Charles E. Leiserson, Ronald L. Rivest, and Clifford Stein. 2022. *Introduction to Algorithms, 4th Edition*. Cambridge, MA: The MIT Press. `https://mitpress.mit.edu/9780262046305/introduction-to-algorithms/`.

    Dean, J., & Ghemawat, S. 2004. MapReduce: Simplified Data Processing on Large Clusters. In *Proceedings of the 6th Conference on Symposium on Operating Systems Design & Implementation*. Berkeley, CA, USA: USENIX Association. 137-149.

    Gamma, E., Helm, R., Johnson, R., & Vlissides, J. 1995. *Design Patterns: Elements of Reusable Object-Oriented Software*. Boston: Addison-Wesley.

---

[17] Cormen, Thomas H., Charles E. Leiserson, Ronald L. Rivest, and Clifford Stein. 2022. *Introduction to Algorithms, 4th Edition*. Cambridge, MA: The MIT Press. `https://mitpress.mit.edu/9780262046305/introduction-to-algorithms/`. 797 – 804.

Mattson, T. G., Sanders, B. A., & Massingill, B. L. 2005. *Patterns for Parallel Programming*. Boston, MA: Addison-Wesley.

McCool, M., Robison, A. D., & Reinders, J. 2012. *Structured Parallel Programming: Patterns for Efficient Computation*. Waltham, MA: Morgan Kaufmann Publishers.

PART III

Coding Practices

CHAPTER 16

Code Construction

Mostly, when you see programmers, they aren't doing anything. One of the attractive things about programmers is that you cannot tell whether or not they are working simply by looking at them. Very often they're sitting there seemingly drinking coffee and gossiping, or just staring into space. What the programmer is trying to do is get a handle on all the individual and unrelated ideas that are scampering around in his head.

—Charles M. Strauss[1]

Great software, likewise, requires a fanatical devotion to beauty. If you look inside good software, you find that parts no one is ever supposed to see are beautiful too. I'm not claiming I write great software, but I know that when it comes to code I behave in a way that would make me eligible for prescription drugs if I approached everyday life the same way. It drives me crazy to see code that's badly indented, or that uses ugly variable names.

—Paul Graham[2]

We are finally getting to the real heart of software development: writing the code. The purpose of this chapter is to provide some tips for writing *better* code, because we can all write better code. Our assumption throughout this discussion is that you already *do* know how to write code in at least one programming language. This chapter presents examples in a couple of languages, each chosen to best illustrate the points being made.

---

[1] https://softwarequotes.com/author/charles-m--strauss

[2] Graham, Paul. 2004. *Hackers and Painters: Big Ideas from the Computer Age.* Sebastopol, CA: O'Reilly Media, Inc. oreilly.com.

© John F. Dooley and Vera A. Kazakova 2024
J. F. Dooley and V. A. Kazakova, *Software Development, Design, and Coding,*
https://doi.org/10.1007/979-8-8688-0285-0_16

For plan-driven process developers (see Chapter 2), coding is the tail that wags the development-process dog. Once you finish the detailed requirements, architecture, and detailed design, the code should just flow out of the final design, right? Well, in 20 years of industry software development experience, we never saw this happen. Coding is hard; translating even a good, detailed design into code takes a lot of thought, experience, and knowledge, even for small programs. Depending on the programming language you are using and the target system, programming can be a very time-consuming and difficult task. On the other hand, for very large projects that employ dozens or even hundreds of developers, having a very detailed design is critical to success, so don't write off the plan-driven process just yet.

For the agile development process, coding is it.[3] The Agile Manifesto (`https://agilemanifesto.org`) says it at the very beginning: "Working software over comprehensive documentation." Agile developers favor creating code early and often; they believe in delivering software to their customers frequently and using feedback from the customers to make the product better. They welcome changes in requirements and see them as an opportunity to refactor the code, make the product more usable for their customer, and easier to maintain for the developers. This doesn't mean that coding gets any easier when using an agile process; it means that your focus is different. Rather than focus on requirements and design and getting them nailed down as early as possible, in agile processes you focus on delivering working code to your customer as quickly and as often as possible. You change the code often, and the entire team owns all the code and so has permission to change anything if it's appropriate.

Your code has three audiences:

- The machine that's the target of the compiled version of the code, what will actually get executed

- The people, including yourself, who will *read* it in order to understand it and modify it

- The user who will use the program that you create to accomplish some goal

---

[3] Martin, Robert C. 2003. *Agile Software Development, Principles, Patterns, and Practices.* Upper Saddle River, NJ: Prentice Hall.

To those ends, your code needs to fulfill the requirements, implement the design, and also be readable and easy to understand. We'll be focusing on the readability and understandability parts of these ends first and then look at some issues related to performance and process.

This chapter is not exhaustive and will not give you all the hints, tips, and techniques for writing great code; there are entire books for that, some of which are mentioned below and in the references at the end of this chapter. Two of the best books on coding around are Steve McConnell's *Code Complete 2: A Practical Handbook of Software Construction*[4] and Hunt and Thomas' *The Pragmatic Programmer*.[5]

Steve McConnell's *Code Complete 2: A Practical Handbook of Software Construction* is a massive, 960-page tome that takes you through what makes good code. McConnell discusses everything from variable names, to function organization, to code layout, to defensive programming, to controlling loops. It is in McConnell's book where the "software construction" metaphor comes from, which suggests that building a software application is similar to constructing a building. Small buildings (Fido's doghouse, for example) are easier to build, require less planning, and are easier to change (refactor) if something goes wrong. Larger buildings (your house) require more detail, more planning, and more coordination largely because it's more than a one-person job. Really big buildings (skyscrapers) require many detailed levels of both design and planning, close coordination, and many processes to handle change and errors. Although the building construction model isn't perfect (it doesn't handle incremental development well and McConnell also talks about an accretion model, where one layer of software is added to an existing layer much like a pearl is created in an oyster), the metaphor gives you a clear view of the idea that software gets much more complicated and difficult to build the larger it gets.

The second classic book is Hunt and Thomas' *The Pragmatic Programmer*, organized as 46 short sections containing 70 tips that provide a clear vision of how you should act as a programmer. It provides practical advice on a range of topics from source code control, to testing, to assertions, to the DRY (Don't Repeat Yourself) principle, some of which we'll cover later in this chapter. Hunt and Thomas themselves do the best job of describing what the book and what pragmatic programming is all about:

---

[4] McConnell, Steve. 2004. *Code Complete 2: A Practical Handbook of Software Construction.* Redmond, WA: Microsoft Press.

[5] Hunt, Andrew, and David Thomas. 2000. *The Pragmatic Programmer: From Journeyman to Master.* Boston, MA: Addison-Wesley.

"Programming is a craft. At its simplest, it comes down to getting a computer to do what you want it to do (or what your user wants it to do). As a programmer, you are part listener, part advisor, part interpreter, and part dictator. You try to capture elusive requirements and find a way of expressing them so that a mere machine can do them justice. You try to document your work so that others can understand it, and you try to engineer your work so that others can build on it. What's more, you try to do all this against the relentless ticking of the project clock. You work small miracles every day. It's a difficult job."

A coding example

In *Code Complete 2*, Steve McConnell gives an example of bad code[6] that is worth examining so we can begin to see what the issues of readability, usability, and understandability are about. We've converted it here from its original version in C++ to Java:

```java
void HandleStuff(CORP_DATA inputRec, int crntQtr, EMP_DATA empRec, Double estimRevenue,
    double ytdRevenue, int screenx, int screeny, Color newColor, Color
    prevColor, StatusType
    status, int expenseType) {
int i;
for ( i = 0; i < 100; i++ )
    {
    inputRec.revenue[i] = 0;
    inputRec.expense[i] = corpExpense[crntQtr][i];
    }
UpdateCorpDatabase( empRec );
estimRevenue = ytdRevenue * 4.0 / (double) crntQtr;
newColor = prevColor;
status = SUCCESS;
if ( expenseType == 1 ) {
    for ( i = 0; i < 12; i++ )
```

---

[6] (McConnell 2004, 162)

```
        profit[i] = revenue[i] - expense.type1[i];
    }
else if ( expenseType == 2 ) {
        profit[i] = revenue[i] - expense.type2[i];
    }
else if ( expenseType == 3 )
        profit[i] = revenue[i] - expense.type3[i];
        }
```

So what's wrong with this code? Well, what isn't? Let's make a list:

- Because this is Java, the HandleStuff method should have a *visibility modifier*. No, it's not required, but you should always put one in. You are not writing for the compiler here; you are writing for the human who will read the code. Visibility modifiers make things explicit for the human reader.

- The method name is terrible. HandleStuff doesn't tell you anything about what the method does.

- The method does too many things. It seems to compute something called profit based on an expenseType. But it also seems to change a color and indicate a success. Method behavior should be confined to handling just one thing.

- Where are the comments? There is no indication of what the parameters are or what the method is supposed to do. All methods should tell you at least that.

- The layout is just awful. It's not consistent, the indentation is wrong, the curly braces are sometimes part of the statement and sometimes they're separators. And are you sure that that last right curly brace really ends the method?

- The method doesn't protect itself from bad data. If the crntQtr variable is zero, then the division in line 8 will return a divide-by-zero exception.

- The method uses hard-coded *magic numbers* including 100, 4.0, 12, 2, and 3. Where do they come from? What do they mean? Magic numbers are bad.

- The method has way too many input parameters. If we knew what the method was supposed to do, maybe we could change this.

- There are also at least two input parameters, screenx and screeny, that aren't used at all. This is an indication of poor design: this method's interface may be used for more than one purpose and so it is "bloated," meaning it has to accommodate all possible uses.

- The variables corpExpense and profit are not declared inside the method so they are either instance variables or class variables. This can be dangerous: because instance and class variables are visible inside every method in the class, we can also change their values inside any method, generating a side effect. Side effects are bad.

- Finally, the method doesn't consistently adhere to the Java naming conventions.

So this example is terrible code for a bunch of different reasons. In the rest of the chapter, we'll take a look at the general coding rules that are violated here and give suggestions for how to make your code more readable, more maintainable, and less error prone.

Size and Focus

First things first: your classes, functions, and methods should all *do just one thing*. This is the fundamental idea behind *encapsulation*. Having your methods do just one thing isolates errors and makes them easier to find. It encourages reuse because small, single feature methods are easier to use in different classes. Single feature (and single layer of abstraction) classes are also easier to reuse.

The phrase "single feature" implies small. Your methods/functions should be small; 20 lines of executable code is a good upper bound for a function. Under no circumstances should you write 300-line functions. We know; we've both done it. It's not pretty. Back in Chapter 9 we talked about *stepwise refinement* and *modular decomposition*. Taking an initial function definition and refactoring it so that it does just a single small thing will decompose your function into two or more smaller, easier to understand and easier to maintain functions. And as you'll see in Chapter 18, smaller functions are easier to test because they require fewer unit tests (they have fewer paths to get through the code). *Small is good, smaller is better.*

Formatting, Layout, and Style

Formatting, layout, and style are all related to how your code looks on the page, which, as you saw above, is also related to its correctness. McConnell's *Fundamental Theorem of Formatting* says, "good visual layout shows the logical structure of a program,"[7] making it more readable and helping reduce the number of errors. So the objectives of good layout and formatting should be

- to accurately represent the logical structure of your program

- to be consistent, so there are few exceptions to whatever style of layout you've chosen

- to improve readability for humans

- to be open to modifications (because things always change)

General Layout Issues and Techniques[8]

Most layout issues have to do with laying out blocks of code. There are different types of block layout, some of which are built into languages and some you get to choose on your own. The three most prevalent kinds of block layouts are built-in block boundaries, begin-end block boundaries, and emulating built-in blocks.

Some languages have *built-in block boundaries* for every control structure in the language. In this case, you have no choice; because the block boundary element is a language feature, you must use it. Languages that have built-in block boundaries include

---

[7] (McConnell 2004, 732)

[8] There are a number of tools available that will help with coding and testing issues. Some links to popular tools are www.owasp.org/index.php/Source_Code_Analysis_Tools, https://en.wikipedia.org/wiki/List_of_tools_for_static_code_analysis, www.jetbrains.com/resharper/, www.softwaretestinghelp.com/tools/top-40-static-code-analysis-tools/

Ada, PL/1, Lisp, Scheme, and Visual Basic. As an example, an if-then statement in Visual Basic looks like the following:

```
if income > 25000 then
    statement1
    statement2
else
    statement3
    ...
end if
```

You can't write a control structure in Visual Basic without using the ending block element, so blocks are easier to find and distinguish.

But most languages don't have built-in block boundary lexical elements, using *begin-end block boundaries* instead: each block is a sequence of zero or more statements (where a statement has a particular definition) that are delimited by *begin* and *end* lexical elements. The most typical begin and end elements are the keywords begin and end or left and right curly braces { and }. For example:

Pascal:

```
if income > 25000 then
    begin
        statement1;
        statement2
    end
else
    statement3;
```

C/C++/Java:

```
if (income > 25000) {
    statement1;
    statement2;
} else
    statement3;
```

Note in both examples that a single statement is considered a block and does not require the block delimiter elements. Note also in Pascal that the semicolon is the statement *separator* symbol so it's required between statements, but because else and end are not the end of a statement, you don't use a semicolon right before else or end. (Confused? Most people are.) In C, C++, and Java, the semicolon is the statement *terminator* symbol, and must be at the end of every statement. This is easier to remember and write: you pretty much put a semicolon at the end of every line except after curly braces. Consistency is good.

Finally, when you format a block, you can try to emulate the built-in block boundary in languages that don't have it, by requiring that every block use the block delimiter lexical elements. Let's see an example:

C/C++/Java:

```
if (income > 25000) {
    statement1;
    statement2;
} else {
    statement3;
}
```

In this example, you want to pretend that the left and right curly braces are part of the control structure syntax, so you use them to delimit the block, no matter how large it is (although single line blocks do not require curly braces here). To emphasize that the block delimiter is part of the control structure, you put it on the same line as the beginning of the control statement. You can then line up the closing block boundary element with the beginning of the control structure. This isn't a perfect emulation of the built-in block element language feature, but it comes pretty close and has the advantage that you're less likely to run into problems with erroneous indentation like the following:

C/C++/Java:

```
if (income > 25000)
    statement1;
    statement2;
    statement3;
```

In this example, the erroneous indentation for `statement2` and `statement3` can lead the reader to believe that they are part of the `if` statement. The compiler is under no such illusions; this code will execute statement1 only if the conditional expression is true. But it will always execute statement2 and statement3.

Overall, emulating a block-boundaries style works very well, is readable, and clearly illustrates the logical structure of your program. It's also a great idea to put block boundaries around every block, including just single statement blocks, to eliminate the possibility of the erroneous indentation seen above. So if you say

```
if (income > 25000) {
    statement1;
}
```

it's then clear that in

```
if (income > 25000) {
    statement1;
}
    statement2;
    statement3;
```

that `statement2` and `statement3` are not part of the block, regardless of their indentation (which is wrong here on purpose). It also means that you can now safely add extra statements to the block without worrying about whether they are in the block or not, because new statements will be inside the curly braces and thus, inside the block.

```
if (income > 25000) {
    statement1;
    statement2;
    statement3;
    statement4;
    statement5;
}
```

White Space

White space is your friend. You wouldn't write a book without any spaces between words, or line breaks between paragraphs, or without chapter divisions, would you? Then why would you write code with no white space? White space allows you to logically separate parts of the program and to line up block separators and other lexical elements. It also lets your eyes rest between parts of the program. Resting your eyes is a good thing. The following are some suggestions on the use of white space:

- Use blank lines to separate groups of statements (just like paragraphs).

- Within a block, align all the statements to the same tab stop (the default tab width is normally four spaces).

- Use indentation to show the logical structure of each control structure and block.

- Use spaces around operators.

- Use spaces around array references and function/method arguments as well.

- Do not use double indentation with begin-end block boundaries.

Block and Statement Style Guidelines

As mentioned, the "emulating block boundaries" style works well for most block-structured languages. Other guidelines include the following:

- *Use more parentheses than you think you'll need.* Especially use parentheses around all arithmetic expressions, mostly to make sure you haven't screwed up the precedence rules.

  ```
  fx = ((a + b) * (c + d)) / e;
  ```

- *Format single statement blocks consistently.* Using the "emulating block-boundaries" technique:

  ```
  if (average > MIN_AVG) {
      avg = MIN_AVG;
  }
  ```

- *For complicated conditional expressions, put separate conditions on separate lines,* aligning them whenever possible for some added readability.

```
if (('0' <= inChar && inChar <= '9') ||
    ('a' <= inChar && inChar <= 'z') ||
    ('A' <= inChar && inChar <= 'Z')) {
    mytext.addString(inChar);
    mytext.length++;
}
```

- *Wrap individual statements at column 70 or so.* This is a holdover from the days of 80-column punch cards, but it's also a great way to make your code more readable. Having very long lines of code forces your readers to scroll horizontally, or it makes them forget what the heck was at the beginning of the line! You may need to print your code and wrapped lines look very messy; you may want to see two chunks of code side by side on a screen; you may want to work on half-screen and use the other half for Stack Overflow; and so on. With shorter lines you have lots of options.

- *Be very sparse in your use of goto, no matter what Don Knuth says.*[9] Some languages, like Java, don't even have goto statements. Most don't need them (assembly languages excepted). Take the spirit of Knuth's paper and only use gotos where they make real sense and make your program more readable and understandable.

- *Use only one statement per line.* (Do not write code as if you were entering the annual International Obfuscated C Code Contest![10]) This is legal, but just doesn't look good, and it's easy to slide right over that statement in the middle:

```
g.setColor(Color.blue); g.fillOval(100, 100, 200, 200);
mytext.addString(inChar);mytext.length++;System.out.println();
```

---

[9] Knuth, D. 1974. "Structured Programming with Goto Statements." *ACM Computing Surveys* 6 (4): 261–301.

[10] https://www.ioccc.org

This looks much, much better:

```
g.setColor(Color.blue);
g.fillOval(100, 100, 200, 200);

mytext.addString(inChar);
mytext.length++;
System.out.println();
```

Declaration Style Guidelines

Just like in writing executable code, your variable declarations need to be neat and readable.

- *Declare variables close to where they are used.* Most procedural and object-oriented programming languages have a *declaration before use* rule, requiring that you declare a variable before you can use it in any expression. In the olden days, say in Pascal, you had to declare variables at the top of your program (or subprogram) and you couldn't declare variables inside blocks. This had the disadvantage that you might declare a variable many lines of code before you'd actually use it. (Though recall that your classes and functions/ methods shouldn't be very long.) Python is one exception to the declaration before use rule. Because Python is usually interpreted (instead of compiled), the interpreter will guess the variable type the first time it is seen, making declaration before use less useful.

  These days most languages allow you to declare variables in any block in your program. The scope of that variable is the block in which it is declared and all the blocks inside that block (children blocks, grandchildren blocks, etc.). It's a good idea to declare those variables in the closest block in which they are used. That way you can see the declaration and the use the variables *right there.*

- *Use only one declaration per line,* or at least one logical variable type per line. For instance, while we think that

  ```
  int max,min,top,left,right,average,bottom,mode;
  ```

is a bit crowded, we'd rewrite this as

```
int max, min;
int top, bottom;
int left, right;
int average, mode;
```

While it's not one per line, the variables that are logically related are grouped together. This makes more sense to us.

- *Order declarations sensibly.* Group your declarations by types and usage (see the previous example).

- *Use white space to separate your declarations.* Once again, white space is your friend. The key idea here is to make your declarations more visible, keeping them near the code where they are used and making their purpose easier to understand.

- *Don't nest header files—ever!* (This is for you C and C++ programmers.) Header files are designed so that you only need to define constants, declare global variables, and declare function prototypes once, and you can then reuse the header file in some (possibly large) number of source code files. Nesting header files hides some of those declarations inside the nested headers. This is bad—because visibility is good. It allows you to erroneously include a header file more than once, which can lead to redefinitions of variables and macros, causing errors.

  The only header files you might nest in your own header files are system headers like `stdio.h` or `stdlib.h` and we don't even like that.

- *Don't put source code in your header files—ever!* (Again, this is for you C and C++ programmers.) Headers are for declarations, not for source code. Libraries are for source code. Putting a function in a header file means that the function will be redefined every place you include the header. This can easily lead to multiple definitions— which the compiler may not catch until the link phase. The only source that should be in your headers are macro definitions in `#define` preprocessor statements, and even those should be used carefully.

Commenting Style Guidelines

Just like white space, comments are your friend. Every programming book in existence tells you to put comments in your code—and none of them (including this one) tell you exactly where to put comments and what your comments must look like. That's because how to write good, informative comments falls in the "it depends" category of advice. A good, informative comment depends on the *context* in which you are writing it, so general advice is pretty limited. Still, here are a few main pointers:

- *Comment first.* Coding following a plan is easiest, so you are not both reasoning out the big problem and also narrowing down the current line's syntax. Keep your thinking at the same level as often as possible, from big picture to details. Use comments as pseudocode for your solution, then write your code in between the lines of comments. In the end, you'll have both the code and the explanations. This also helps you not forget any bits of your solution while down in the coding trenches (e.g., closing your file input stream, deallocating some memory, etc.).

- *Briefly explain reasoning and bigger plans.* Comments are all about quality and not quantity. Another programmer (or you the next morning) will generally be able to understand what your code is doing, but the why tends to be more obscure. So don't explain syntax, or basic language structures, but do explain the utility of your code. If you are doing something that may not be immediately needed here but is needed by something else later, leave a comment explaining that, so it doesn't accidentally get removed later as unnecessary. If you are about to write several lines of code solving a complex problem, it's often a good idea to write an overall planning comment for what the next segment does.

- *Keep comments short and to the point.* Comments must be focused and brief. You don't need full sentences, nor articles.

- *Align comment indentation with its corresponding statement.* This is important for readability, because then the comment and the relevant code line up.

```
/* make sure we have the right number of arguments */
if (argc < 2) {
    fprintf(stderr, "Usage: %s <filename>\n", argv[0]);
    exit(1);
}
```

This has a huge negative impact on readability. Either make the comment shorter or make this a block comment above the statement instead.

- *Don't let comments wrap. Use block comments instead.* This usually occurs if you tack a long, involved comment onto the end of a line of source code, as in

```
if (argc < 2) { // make sure we have the right number of arguments
from the command line
```

- *Set off block comments with blank lines*, if you start the comment right after the start marker /* and stick the end of comment marker */ at the end of a line, follows:

```
/* make sure we have the right number of arguments
from the command line */

if (argc < 2) {
    fprintf(stderr, "Usage: %s <filename>\n", argv[0]);
    exit(1);
}
```

We don't really recommend this style though. Instead, if you line up the start /* and end */ markers on lines by themselves, then you don't need additional blank lines, as these are already mostly blank and create enough separation.

```
/*
 * make sure we have the right number of arguments
 * from the command line
 */
if (argc < 2) {
    fprintf(stderr, "Usage: %s <filename>\n", argv[0]);
    exit(1);
}
```

- *All functions/methods should have a header block comment* so that your reader knows what the method is supposed to do. The need for a detailed header comment is somewhat mitigated if you use good identifier names for the method name and the input parameters. Still, at a minimum, you should tell the user what the method is going to do and what the return values are, if any. In C++ you can say

```
#include <string>
/*
 * getSubString() - get a substring from the input string.
 *  The substring starts at index start
 *  and goes up to but doesn't include index stop.
 *  returns the resulting substring.
 */
string getSubString(string str, int start, int stop) { }
```

In Java, use JavaDoc comments for all your methods. JavaDoc is built into the Java environment and all Java SDKs come with the program to generate JavaDoc web pages, so you might as well use it! JavaDoc can provide a nice overview of what your class is up to at very little cost. Just make sure and keep those comments up to date!

```
/**
 * getSubString() - get a substring from the input string.
 *      The substring starts at index start
 *      and goes up to but doesn't include index stop.
 * @param str the input string
```

```
 *   @param start the integer starting index
 *   @param stop the integer stopping index
 *   @return the resulting substring.
 */
public String getSubString(String str, int start, int stop) { }
```

- *"Self-documenting code" is an ideal,* the Holy Grail of those lazy programmers who don't want to take the time to explain their code to readers. Self-documenting code is the Platonic ideal of coding that assumes that everyone who reads your code can also read your mind. If you have an algorithm that is at all complicated, or input that is at all obscure, you need to explain it. Don't depend on the reader to understand every subtlety of your code. Explain it. Just do it. All that said, some programming languages and tool sets allow you to embed documenting tags in comments in your code. JavaDocs is the canonical example here. That type of feature is semi-self-documenting.

The main advice about writing comments is—do it. Oh, and since you'll change your code—do it again. That's the second hardest thing about comments—keeping them up to date. When you finish your unit testing of a particular function, write a final set of comments for that function by updating the ones that are already there. That way, you'll come pretty close to having an up-to-date set of comments in the released code.

Identifier Naming Conventions

As Rob Pike puts it so well in his terrific white paper on programming style, "Length is not a virtue in a name; clarity of expression *is*."[11] Following a Goldilocks approach, you need identifier names that are not so long that they are unwieldy and annoying, not so short that they are uninformative or confusing, but just right. As with comments, this means different things to different people and in different contexts. Common sense and readability should rule.

---

[11] Pike, Rob. 1989. *Notes on Programming in C,* `www.literateprogramming.com/pikestyle.pdf`.

- *All identifiers should be descriptive.* You might understand what your code does and how it does it today, but eventually you could forget you were even the one who wrote it. It might not even make sense to you the very next day. It often also needs to make sense to others, as we are often not the sole developers over the entire lifetime of the software. Descriptive identifiers make it much, much easier to read your code and figure out what you were trying to do at 3:00 AM. A variable called *interestRate* is much easier to understand than *ir*. Sure, *ir* is shorter and faster to type, but believe us, you'll forget what it stood for about 10 minutes after you ship that program. Reasonably descriptive identifiers can save you a lot of time and effort while coding, debugging, and maintaining software.

- *OverlyLongVariableNamesAreHardToRead (and type).* On the other hand, don't make your identifiers too long. For one thing they are hard to read, for another they don't really add anything to the context of your program, they use up too much space on the page, and finally, they are time-consuming to type out.

- *Andtheyareevenharderwhenyoudontincludeworddivisions.* Well that was painful... If you need multiword identifiers, improve readability by always using camel case: capitalize the first letter of each new word in your multiword identifiers, starting from the second word. For example, maxPhysAddr is easier to read than maxphysaddr. As a bonus, text-to-voice software will be able to read those identifiers correctly, so #pleaseUseItWithAllYourSocialMediaHashtagsAlso.

- *Single-letter variable names are cryptic, but sometimes useful.* Using single letter variable names for things like mortgage payments, window names, or graphics objects is not a good example of readability. M, w, and g don't mean anything even in the context of your code. mortPmnt, gfxWindow, and gfxObj have more meaning. The big exception here is variables intended as index values—loop control variables and array index variables. Here, i, j, k, l, m, etc. are easily understandable, although we wouldn't argue with you about using index or indx instead.

```
for (int i = 0; i < myArray.length; i++) {
    myArray[i] = 0;
}
```

looks much cleaner and is just as understandable as

```
for (int arrayIndex = 0; arrayIndex < myArray.length;
arrayIndex++) {
    myArray[arrayIndex] = 0;
}
```

Still, we recommend you dig a bit deeper and aim for more meaningful letters when dealing with nested loops, multi-dimensional arrays, and such. For example, we often see i used for rows and j used for columns, but using r and c is just so much clearer! This way you way less likely to make mistake when performing, for example, an image rotation.

- *Adhere to the programming language naming conventions when they exist.*

  Somewhere, sometime, you'll run into a document called Style Guide or something like that. If you work in a group with more than one developer, style guidelines are a good idea. They give all your code a common look and feel and they make it easier for one developer to make changes to code written by somebody else. Nearly every software development organization of any size has one. Sometimes you're allowed to violate the guidelines, but most commonly, during a code review, you'll get dinged for not following the guidelines and be required to rewrite your code.

  A common set of guidelines in a style guide is about naming conventions, which specify what your identifier names should look like for different types of identifiers.

Java has a common set of naming conventions:

For classes and interfaces: The identifier names should be nouns, using both upper and lowercase alphanumerics, with the first character of the name in upper case.

```
public class Automobile {}
public interface Shape {}
```

For methods: The identifier names should be verbs, using both upper and lowercase alphanumerics, with the first character of the name in lower case.

```
private double computeAverage(int [] list)
```

For variables: The identifier names can use both upper and lowercase alphanumerics, with the first character of the name in lower case. Variable names may contain but should not start with $ or _ (underscore).

```
double average;
String firstSentence;
```

For all identifiers (except constants): Camel case should be used, so that internal words are capitalized.

```
long myLongArray;
```

For constants: All letters should be uppercase and composing words should be separated by underscores.

```
static final int MAX_WIDTH = 80;
```

Refactoring

An important part of code construction is keeping the design in mind as you code and especially keeping the design as simple as possible. Design simplicity is particularly important when you are fixing a bug or adding something new to existing code. You should think about whether the code you're working on is as simple as it can be, or whether it is getting outdated, crusty, and complicated. If so, consider *refactoring*, meaning changing the code to update, simplify, and clean it up.

Martin Fowler defines refactoring as "a change made to the internal structure of the software to make it easier to understand and cheaper to modify without changing its observable behavior."[12] Refactoring is key to all agile methodologies, which strongly encourage it every time you change code.

---

[12] Fowler, Martin, and Kent Beck. 1999. *Refactoring: Improving the Design of Existing Code*. Paperback. Boston, MA: Addison-Wesley.

When to Refactor

There are a number of times, reasons, and techniques for refactoring code. In *Code Complete 2*, Steve McConnell gives a number of them.[13] Martin Fowler gives a longer list at his website.[14] Let's look at some reasons for refactoring code:

- *If you have duplicate code*, remember the DRY (Don't Repeat Yourself) principle; create a new method that encapsulates the code and then call it as many times as needed.

- *If a function or method is too long*, it's probably doing too many things. A function or method should only ever do one thing, allowing it to stay short. Typically, a method should not be more than one screen height long; that's somewhere between 24 and 50 lines long.

- *If a class has poor (not tight enough) cohesion*, it's likely doing more than one thing (has more than a single responsibility); you should break it up into two or more classes.

- *If a class interface does not project a consistent level of abstraction.* Over time, as you've made changes to a class, its interface may become complicated and difficult to understand. This is the time to simplify the interface by moving methods to other classes or combining methods.

- *A formal parameter list has too many input parameters*, meaning that the method is just being used to transfer data to another method or it is doing too many things. In either case, the parameter list should be simplified.

- *If changes to code require parallel changes to multiple classes or modules*, then you need to think about rearranging data and/or methods to simplify the structure.

---

[13] https://refactoring.com/catalog/index.html
[14] (Fowler and Beck 1999)

- *If related pieces of data that are used together are in different places* (e.g., two or more pieces of data are always used to compute a third, but the input data is in two different places), then they should be moved together to the same class.

- *If a method uses more features of some other class than of its own class,* maybe it should be moved to the other class.

- *If a chain of method calls is used to pass data via parameters* (input parameters to a method that are not used but just passed onto other methods), you should take a look at your flow of control to see if changes need to be made.

- *If a middleman class doesn't do anything itself* (i.e., a class whose main work is just to call methods in another class), then maybe you can eliminate the middleman and call the methods directly.

- *If instance variables are public,* you are breaking one of the fundamental ideas behind object-oriented programming: *information hiding.* All instance variables in an object should be private, accessed via public getter and setter methods.[15]

- *If a subclass uses only a few of its superclass's inherited methods,* you may want to rethink your current hierarchy. As McConnell puts it, "typically this indicates that that subclass has been created because a parent class happened to contain the routines it needed, not because the subclass is logically a descendant of the superclass. Consider achieving better encapsulation by switching the subclass's relationship to its superclass from an is-a relationship to a has-a relationship; convert the superclass to member data of the former subclass, and expose only the routines in the former subclass that are really needed."[16]

---

[15] Lieberherr, K., I. Holland, and A. Riel. 1988. "Object-Oriented Programming: An Objective Sense of Style." In *Proceedings of OOPSLA '88*, 323–34. San Diego, CA: Association for Computing Machinery.
[16] (McConnell 2004, 567-68)

- *If comments are used to document overly convoluted code.* As the saying goes, "Don't document bad code—rewrite it."[17] Additionally, always reconsider your comments when you refactor code.

- *If the code uses global variables.* Avoid using global variables (or at least use them very carefully). If you find global variables in code you are refactoring, consider them carefully and see if you can eliminate them by passing data to methods via parameters. Global variables are dangerous because they can lead to side effects where two or more objects attempt to change the value of the global variable, possibly causing a race condition.

- *If a method uses setup or takedown code with another method call,* reconsider your class's interface. Say you are going to add an item to an inventory of CarParts and your code looks like

```
AddInventory transaction = new AddInventory();
transaction.setPartID(partID);
transaction.setPartName(partName);
transaction.setPartCost(partCost);
transaction.setDate(transactionDate);
```

And then you do the actual add:

```
processAdd(transaction);
```

You might consider whether the method call that requires this type of setup is using the right level of abstraction. In order to eliminate the setup code and make the code simpler, you might change the formal parameter list for the processAdd() method to something like the following:

```
processAdd(partID, partName, partCost, transactionDate);
```

---

[17] Kernighan, Brian W., and P. J. Plauger. 1978. *The Elements of Programming Style, 2nd Edition.* New York, NY: McGraw Hill, Inc.

Types of Refactoring

Let's review some of the types of changes you can make to improve your code:

- *Replace a magic number with a named constant.* Magic numbers are bad for a couple of reasons. First, if you use some magic number more than once, and if you need to change it, then you have to change the number in every line of code you've used it. Second, if someone comes along after you, they may not know what the number means. Named constants allow you to change the value of the number in only one place, and they give a hint as to what the number means.

- *Rename a variable with a name that is more informative.* Always try to keep things brief but meaningful (with the exceptional of occasional basic loop iterators such as i, j, k. et.)

- *Replace variables with expressions.* Examine cases where you may be creating unnecessary intermediate variables that are only used to arrive at the overall answer. Check if you can skip creating these variables, instead using their formula or expression directly in expression for the overall answer.

- *Replace expressions with methods.* If you have an expression that might be duplicated in two or more parts of the code, replace that expression with a single method and just call the method. Again: DRY.

- *Convert a variable that's used for different things into several variables each used for one thing.* Reusing a single variable for two or more different purposes is confusing. Replace all the duplicates with new variables with appropriate names to make the code more understandable.

- *Create a local variable instead of overusing an input parameter.* Repurposing an input parameter in a method is also confusing. Create a dedicated local variable instead; it's just one more entry on the system stack.

- *Create a class instead of using a data primitive.* If you create a variable using a data primitive type (say using *double* to create a variable called money) and if that variable may need extra behaviors, then replace the primitive type with a class declaration.

- *Convert a set of named constants (type codes) into a class or an enumeration.* Earlier we said that using magic numbers was bad and you should use named constants instead. However, if you have a set of named constants that are related to each other, you should consider putting them in a separate class or in an enumeration type instead. It will make your code more maintainable and more readable.

- *Decompose a boolean expression into variables.* If you have a complex boolean expression, you might consider separating the clauses into intermediate variables and then combining the results at the end.

- *Move a complex boolean expression into a method that returns a boolean.* If your boolean expression is complex and likely to be repeated elsewhere in the program, put it into a method that evaluates the expression and returns a boolean result.

- *Use break or return instead of a boolean loop control variable.* Many times you'll see a while loop that looks something like

```
boolean done = false;
while (!done) {
    // do stuff here
    if (some-expression)
        done = true;
}
```

  This creates a bit of unnecessary work and the suggestion here is to replace the done = true; with a return or a break statement.

- *Return from a method as soon as you know the answer.* This also means don't use a boolean or other variable to tell yourself you've found the return value from a method. As soon as you know the answer, just return it.

- *Move the code from simple routines to where it is used.* If you have a method that contains code that is only used in one place, just put the code inline where it is used instead of having it in a method.

- *Separate queries from calculations.* Normally, a query operation will just return a value. If you have a method that does both calculation and returns a value for a query (say something like getAverage() or getTotal()), consider separating it into two methods, one to do the calculation and one to do the query. This allows you to adhere to the "methods should just do one thing" principle.

- *Combine methods that are similar.* You may have two different methods that differ only by a constant used in a calculation. Consider consolidating those methods and making the constant an input parameter instead.

- *Move specialized code into its own class or subclass.* If you have code that is only used by a subset of the instances of a superclass, then move that code into its own class or subclass.

- *Move similar code from classes into a superclass.* On the other hand, if you have code in several classes that is similar, then create a new superclass and move the code up into it.

- *Divide a class with multiple responsibilities into multiple classes,* adhering to the Single Responsibility Principle.

- *Delete a class.* If you have a class that ends up not doing much (e.g., it only has a single method, or it only contains data members), then consider moving that work into another class.

- *Encapsulate public instance variables.* If you have an instance variable declared as public, convert it to private and create a getter method to access it, obeying the information hiding principle.

- *Only use* get() *and* set() *methods when necessary.* By default, all instance variables should be private and accessed via public setter and getter methods. Only create get() methods for instance variables that need to be used outside the object and only create set() methods when need to be able to change the value of an instance variable. For example, if you have an instance variable for a part number, you probably don't need a set() method, because part numbers don't usually change.

- *Hide public methods.* Only expose methods if they need to be in the class's interface. Just like with instance variables, all methods should be private unless there's a good reason to make them public.

- *Combine similar superclasses and subclasses* that are nearly identical by consolidating them into a single class.

Defensive Programming

By defensive programming we mean that your code should protect itself from bad data. The bad data can come from user input via the command line, a graphical text box or form, or a file. Bad data can also come from other routines in your program via input parameters, like in the first example above.

How do you protect your program from bad data? Validate! As tedious as it sounds, you should always check the validity of data that you receive from outside your routine. This means you should do the following:

- Check the number and type of command line arguments.

- Check file operations.

  o Did the file open?

  o Did the read operation return anything?

  o Did the write operation write anything?

  o Did you reach EOF yet?

- Check that all values in function/method parameter lists are of the correct type and size.

- Always initialize variables and do not depend on the system to do the initialization for you.

- Check for null pointers (references in Java), incorrect types, zeros in denominators, and out of range values.

As an example, here's a C program that takes in a list of house prices from a file and computes the average house price from the list. The input file is provided to the program from the command line.

```c
/*
 * Program to compute the average selling price of a set of homes.
 * Input comes from a file that is passed via the command line.
 * Output is the Total and Average sale prices for
 * all the homes and the number of prices in the file.
 *
 * jfdooley
 */
#include <stdlib.h>
#include <stdio.h>

int main(int argc, char **argv){
    FILE *fp;
    double totalPrice, avgPrice;
    double price;
    int numPrices;

    /* check that the user entered the correct number of args */
    if (argc < 2) {
        fprintf(stderr,"Usage: %s <filename>\n", argv[0]);
        exit(1);
    }

    /* try to open the input file */
    fp = fopen(argv[1], "r");
    if (fp == NULL) {
        fprintf(stderr, "File Not Found: %s\n", argv[1]);
        exit(1);
    }
    totalPrice = 0.0;
    numPrices = 0;

    /* read the file, total the prices and count the number of houses */
    while (!feof(fp)) {
```

```
        fscanf(fp, "%10lf\n", &price);18
        if (price <= 0.0) {
            fprintf(stderr, "Bad Data %10.5f\n", price);
            exit(1);
        }
        totalPrice += price;
        numPrices++;
    }

    avgPrice = totalPrice / numPrices;
    printf("Number of houses is %d\n", numPrices);
    printf("Total Price of all houses is $%10.2f\n", totalPrice);
    printf("Average Price per house is $%10.2f\n", avgPrice);

    return 0;
}
```

Defensive Programming: Assertions Are Helpful

Defensive programming can be greatly aided by the use of assertions, if your language supports them. Java, C99, C11, C23, and C++ all support assertions. Assertions will test an expression that you give them and if the expression is false, it will throw an error and normally abort the program. You should use error handling code for errors you think might happen (e.g., bad user input) and use assertions for errors that should *never* happen (e.g., off-by-one errors in loops). Assertions are great for testing your program, but because you should remove them before giving programs to customers (you don't want the program to abort on the user, right?), they aren't good to use to validate input data in a production program.

---

[18] Note that in C, the `fscanf()` function returns an integer which is the number of items read. This number can be zero if the `fscanf()` fails. We don't check for it here because we just used `feof()` to check if we had reached the end of the file. If that passes, then there must be data left in the file to read.

Defensive Programming: Exceptions[19]

Part of defensive programming is making sure your program can gracefully recover from common runtime problems, such as incorrect input, so that the program stays running for as long as possible (making your program robust). While *assertions* are used for errors that should never happen, *exceptions* should be used for handling recoverable errors which are to be expected as part of normal operations (e.g. FileNotFound exception).

You should take advantage of built-in *exception handling* in whatever programming language you're using. What your program does and how it handles the exception depends on the language capabilities (we'll talk about exception handling in Java later). The exception handling mechanism will give your program information about what bad thing has just happened. It's then up to you to decide what to do. Normally in an exception handling mechanism your program will have two choices: 1) handle the exception itself or 2) pass it along (a.k.a. throw) to whoever called it and let that code handle it.

Defensive Programming: Error Handling

Just like with validation, you're most likely to encounter errors in input data, whether it's command line input, file handling, or input from a graphical user interface form. Here we're talking about errors that occur at runtime. Compile time and testing errors are covered in the next chapter on debugging and testing. Other types of errors can be data that your program computes incorrectly, errors in other programs that interact with your program, the operating system (for instance, race conditions), and interaction errors where your program is communicating with another and your program is at fault.

The main purpose of error handling is to have your program run correctly for as long as possible. When it gets to a point where your program cannot continue, it needs to report what is wrong as best as it can and then exit gracefully. Exiting is the last resort for error

---

[19] Note that we define exceptions to be recoverable undesirable behaviors that we can predict during runtime. Since we can predict them, we can write code to handle exceptions if they occur. The goal is to try to handle the behavior so that your program can continue to run. Errors, on the other hand, are unexpected behaviors that occur at runtime and which we must handle in order to keep the program executing. In both cases, if the program can't recover from the unexpected behavior, it should fail gracefully and provide the user with a reason for the failure. Handling and reporting of exceptions and errors is sometimes a built-in language feature.

handling. So what should you do? Well, once again we come to the "it depends" answer. What you should do depends on what your program's context is when the error occurs and what its purpose is. You won't handle an error in a video game the same way you handle one in a cardiac pacemaker. In every case, your first goal should be to try to recover.

Recovery means that your program needs to try to either ignore the bad data, fix it, or substitute something else that is valid for the bad data. See McConnell[20] for a further discussion of error handling. Here are a few examples of how to recover from errors:

- You might just *ignore the bad data and keep going*, using the next valid piece of data. Say your program is a piece of embedded software in a digital pressure gauge. You sample the sensor that returns the pressure 60 times a second. If the sensor fails to deliver a pressure reading once, should you shut down the gauge? Probably not; a reasonable thing to do is just skip that reading and set up to read the next piece of data when it arrives. Now if the pressure sensor skips several readings in a row, then something might be wrong with the sensor and you should do something different (like yell for help or shut down the machine the program is monitoring).

- You might *substitute the last valid piece of data* for a missing or wrong piece. Taking the digital pressure gauge again, if the sensor misses a reading, since each time interval is only a sixtieth of a second, it's likely that the missing reading is very close to the previous reading. In that case you can substitute the last valid piece of data for the missing value.

- There may be instances where you don't have any previously recorded valid data. Your application uses an asynchronous event handler, so you don't have any history of data, but your program knows that the data should be in a particular range. Say you've prompted the user for a salary amount and the value that you get back is a negative number. Clearly no one gets paid a salary of negative dollars, so the value is wrong. One way (probably not the best) to handle this error is to *substitute the closest valid value in the range*, in this case a zero. Although it's not ideal, at least your program can continue running with a valid data value in that field.

---

[20] (McConnell 2004, 187-213)

- In C programs, nearly all system calls and most of the standard library functions return a value. You should test these values! Most functions will return values that indicate success (a non-negative integer) or failure (a negative integer, usually -1). Some functions return a value that indicates how successful they were. For example, the `printf()` family of functions returns the number of characters printed, and the `scanf()` family returns the number of input elements read. Most C functions also set a global variable named `errno` that contains an integer value that is the number of the error that occurred. The list of error numbers is in a header file called `errno.h`. A zero in the `errno` variable indicates success. Any other positive integer value is the number of the error that occurred. Because the system tells you (1) an error occurred and (2) what it thinks is the cause of the error, you can do lots of different things to handle it, including just *reporting the error* and bailing out.

For example, if you try to open a file that doesn't exist, the program

```
#include <stdio.h>
#include <stdlib.h>
#include <errno.h>

int main(int argc, char **argv) {
    FILE *fd;
    char *fname = "NotAFile.txt";

    if ((fd = fopen(fname, "r")) == NULL) {
        perror("File not opened");
        exit(1);
    }
    printf("File exists\n");
    return 0;
}
```

will return the error message

```
File not opened: No such file or directory
```

The function `perror()` reads the `errno` variable and, using the string provided plus a standard string corresponding to the error number, writes an error message to the console's standard error output. This program could also prompt the user for a different file name or it could substitute a default file name. Either of these would allow the program to continue rather than exiting on the error.

There are other techniques to use in error handling and recovery. These examples should give you a flavor of what you can do within your program. The important idea to remember here is to attempt recovery if possible, but most of all, ***do not fail silently!***

Defensive Programming: Exceptions in Java

Some programming languages have built-in error reporting systems that will tell you when an error occurs and leave it up to you to handle it one way or another. These errors that would normally cause your program to die a horrible death are called *exceptions*. The code that encounters the error *throws* the exception. Once something is thrown, it's usually a good idea if some part of the program *catches* it. So there are two sides to exceptions that you need to be aware of when you're writing code:

- When you have a piece of code that can encounter an error you *throw* an exception. Systems like Java will throw some exceptions for you. These exceptions are listed in the `Exception` class in the Java API documentation (see `https://docs.oracle.com/en/java/javase/20/docs/api/index.html`). You can also write your own code to throw exceptions. We'll have an example later in the chapter.

- Once an exception is thrown, some other part of the program has to *catch* it. If you don't do anything in your program, this *uncaught exception* will percolate up the call stack to the Java Virtual Machine (the JVM) and be caught there. The JVM will kill your program and provide you with a stack backtrace that should lead you back to the place in your code that originally caused the exception to be thrown and show you how you got there. On the other hand, you can also write code to encapsulate the calls that might generate exceptions

and catch them yourself using Java's `try-catch` mechanism.
Java requires that some exceptions must be caught. You'll see an
example later.

Java has three different types of exceptions: errors, checked exceptions, and runtime
exceptions.

Errors, on the other hand, are exceptions that usually are related to things happening
outside of your program and are things you can't do anything about except fail
gracefully. You might try to catch the error exception and provide some output for the
user, but you will still usually have to exit.

Checked exceptions are those that you should catch and handle yourself using an
exception handler; they are exceptions that you should anticipate and handle as you
design and write your code. For example, if your code asks a user for a file name, you
should anticipate that they will type it wrong and be prepared to catch the resulting
`FileNotFoundException`. Checked exceptions must be caught.

The third type of exception is the *runtime exception*. Runtime exceptions all result
from problems within your program that occur as it runs and almost always indicate
errors in your code. For example, a `NullPointerException` nearly always indicates a
bug in your code and shows up as a runtime exception.[21] Errors and runtime exceptions
are collectively called *unchecked exceptions* (this is because you usually don't try to
catch them, so they're unchecked). In this program, you deliberately cause a runtime
exception:

```
public class TestNull {
    public static void main(String[] args) {
        String str = null;
        int len = str.length();
    }
}
```

---

[21] A null pointer is a reference variable whose contents are zero, which is an illegal memory
address. So a `NullPointerException` indicates that you have created a reference variable but then
failed to initialize it with a legitimate memory address.

This program will compile just fine, but when you run it, you'll get this as output:

```
Exception in thread "main" java.lang.NullPointerException
        at TestNull.main(TestNull.java:4)
```

This is a classic runtime exception. There's no need to catch this exception because the only thing you can do safely is exit. If you do catch it, the program might look like

```java
public class TestNullCatch {
    public static void main(String[] args) {
        String str = null;

        try {
            int len = str.length();
        } catch (NullPointerException e) {
            System.out.println("Error. Found a pointer: " + e.getMessage());
            System.exit(1);
        }
    }
}
```

which gives us the output

```
Error. Found a pointer: null
```

Note that the getMessage() method will return a String containing whatever error message Java deems appropriate—if there is one. Otherwise, it returns a null. This is somewhat less helpful than the default stack trace above.

Let's rewrite the short C program from the previous section in Java and illustrate how to catch a *checked exception*.

```java
import java.io.*;
import java.util.*;

public class FileTest {
    public static void main(String [] args) {
        File fd = new File("NotAFile.txt");
        System.out.println("File exists " + fd.exists());
```

```
    try {
        FileReader fr = new FileReader(fd);
    } catch (FileNotFoundException e) {
        System.out.println(e.getMessage());
    }
  }
}
```

and the output you get when you execute `FileTest` is

```
File exists false
NotAFile.txt (No such file or directory)
```

By the way, if you don't use the `try-catch` block in the above program, it won't compile. You get this compiler error message:

```
FileTestWrong.java:11: unreported exception java.io.FileNotFoundException;
must be caught or declared to be thrown
                FileReader fr = new FileReader(fd);


                ^


1 error
```

Remember, in Java checked exceptions **must** be caught. This type of error doesn't show up for unchecked exceptions. This is far from everything you should know about exceptions and exception handling in Java; start digging through the Java tutorials and the Java API!

Conclusion

Coding is the heart of software development. Code is what you produce. But coding is hard; translating even a good, detailed design into code takes a lot of thought, experience, and knowledge, even for small programs. Depending on the programming language you are using and the target system, programming can be a very time-consuming and difficult task. That's why taking the time to make your code readable and have the code layout match the logical structure of your design is essential to writing code that works and is understandable by humans. Adhering to coding standards and conventions, keeping to a consistent style, and including good, accurate comments will help you immensely during debugging and testing. And it will help you six months from now when you come back and try to figure out what the heck you were thinking here.

And finally,

I am rarely happier than when spending an entire day programming my computer to perform automatically a task that it would otherwise take me a good ten seconds to do by hand.

—Douglas Adams, "Last Chance to See"

References

Fowler, Martin, and Kent Beck. 1999. *Refactoring: Improving the Design of Existing Code.* Paperback. Boston, MA: Addison-Wesley.

Hunt, Andrew, and David Thomas. 2000. *The Pragmatic Programmer: From Journeyman to Master.* Boston, MA: Addison-Wesley.

Kernighan, Brian W., and P. J. Plauger. 1978. *The Elements of Programming Style, 2nd Edition.* New York, NY: McGraw Hill, Inc.

Knuth, Donald. 1974. "Structured Programming with Goto Statements." *ACM Computing Surveys* 6 (4): 261–301.

Lieberherr, K., I. Holland, and A. Riel. 1988. "Object-Oriented Programming: An Objective Sense of Style." In *Proceedings of OOPSLA '88*, 323–34. San Diego, CA: Association for Computing Machinery.

Martin, Robert C. 2003. *Agile Software Development, Principles, Patterns, and Practices.* Upper Saddle River, NJ: Prentice Hall.

McConnell, Steve. 2004. *Code Complete 2: A Practical Handbook of Software Construction.* Redmond, WA: Microsoft Press.

Pike, Rob. 1989. "Notes on Programming in C." Murray Hill, NJ. www.literateprogramming.com/pikestyle.pdf.

CHAPTER 17

Debugging

As soon as we started programming, we found to our surprise that it wasn't as easy to get programs right as we had thought. Debugging had to be discovered. I can remember the exact instant when I realized that a large part of my life from then on was going to be spent in finding mistakes in my own programs.

—Maurice Wilkes, 1949

It is a painful thing to look at your own trouble and know that you yourself and no one else has made it.

—Sophocles

Congratulations! You've finished writing your code so now it's time to get it working. No matter how good of a programmer you are, mistakes will happen: logical mistakes, typos, forgotten edge cases, off-by-one errors, your keyboard failing to register a keystroke, your cat making some edits while you weren't looking... Mistakes are a natural part of the code's lifecycle. After writing code for many years, we have gotten to the point where most of the time our programs under 50 lines don't have any *obvious* errors and often even compile on the first try, behaving approximately as expected. We think that's a pretty solid place to aim for.

Getting your program to work is a process with three parts, the order of which is the subject of some debate: debugging, reviewing/inspecting, and testing.

Debugging is the process of finding the *root cause* of an error and fixing it. This doesn't mean treating the symptoms of an error by coding around it to make it go away; it means finding the real reason for the error and fixing that piece of code so the error is removed. Debugging is normally done once you finish writing the code and before you do a code review or unit testing (but see *test-driven development* later in this chapter). Debugging and unit testing can also be done simultaneously.

415

© John F. Dooley and Vera A. Kazakova 2024
J. F. Dooley and V. A. Kazakova, *Software Development, Design, and Coding*,
https://doi.org/10.1007/979-8-8688-0285-0_17

Reviewing (or inspecting) is the process of reading the code as it sits on the page and *looking for errors*. The errors can include errors in how you've implemented the design, other kinds of logic errors, wrong comments, and so on. Reviewing code is an inherently *static* process because the program isn't running on a computer—you're reading it off a screen or a piece of paper. So while reviewing is great for finding static errors, it can't find dynamic or interaction errors in your code. That's what testing is for. We'll talk more about reviews and inspections in a future chapter.

Testing is the process of *finding errors* in the code, as opposed to fixing them, which is what debugging is all about. Testing occurs, at a minimum, at the following three different levels:

- *Unit testing*, where you test small pieces of your code, notably at the function or method level.

- *Integration testing*, where you put together several modules or classes that relate to each other and test them together. Integration testing is particularly important when you are working on a team, testing that code you have written works with that written by other team members.

- *System testing*, where you test the entire program from the user's perspective. This is also called *black-box testing* because the tester doesn't know how the code was implemented; all they know is what the requirements are, so they're testing to see if the code as written fulfills all the requirements.

We'll focus on debugging in this chapter. Unit testing involves finding the errors in your program, while debugging involves finding the root cause and fixing those errors. Debugging is about finding out why an error occurs in your program. You can look at errors as opportunities to learn more about the program and about how you work and approach problem solving. After all, debugging is a problem-solving activity, just as developing a program is problem solving. Look at debugging as an opportunity to learn about yourself and improve your skill set.

What's an Error, Anyway?

In code, errors can be of three types: syntactic, semantic, and logic.

Syntactic errors are made with respect to the syntax of the programming language being used. Spelling a keyword wrong, failing to declare a variable before you use it, forgetting to put that closing curly brace in a block, forgetting the return type of a function, and forgetting that semicolon at the end of a statement are all typical examples of syntactic errors. Syntactic errors are by far the easiest to find because the compiler finds nearly all of them for you. Compilers are very rigid taskmasters when it comes to enforcing lexical and grammar rules of a language, so if you get through the compilation process with no errors *and no warnings*, then it's very likely your program has no syntax errors left. Notice the "and no warnings" part of the previous sentence. You should *always* compile your code with the strictest syntax checking turned on, and you should *always* eliminate all errors and warnings before you move on to reviews or testing. Eliminating warnings is especially important when you're working on a team because a warning in your code could end up as an error in someone else's code, once you integrate them.

If you are sure you've not done anything wrong syntactically, that's just one less thing to worry about while you're finding all the other errors. The good news is that modern integrated development environments (IDEs; like Eclipse, NetBeans, XCode, or Visual Studio) do this for you automatically once you've set up the compiler options. Once you set the warning and syntax checking levels, every time you make a change, the IDE will automatically recompile your file and let you know about any syntax errors!

Semantic errors, on the other hand, occur when you incorrectly express what you intended in a programming language, usually due to some misunderstanding of the grammar rules of the language. Not putting curly braces around a block, accidentally putting a semicolon after the condition in an *if* or *while* statement in C/C++ or Java, and forgetting to use a break statement at the end of a case statement inside a switch are all classic examples of semantic errors. Semantic errors are harder to find because they are normally syntactically correct pieces of code, so the compiler will successfully compile your code correctly into an object file. It's only when you try to execute your program that semantic errors surface through incorrect behavior. The good news is that they're usually so egregious that they show up pretty much immediately. The bad news is they can be very subtle. For example, in this code segment

```
while (j < MAX_LEN);
{
    // do stuff here
    j++;
}
```

the semicolon at the end of the *while* statement's conditional expression can be hard to see. Your eyes might slide right over it. But its effect is to either put the program into an infinite loop (if the conditional test passes) or to never execute the loop (if the test fails), but then erroneously execute the block that follows, because it is no longer semantically connected to the *while* statement. Any basic testing should catch this.

Logic errors, on the other hand, are by far the most difficult to find and eradicate. Logic errors are mistakes in the logic of your solutions, which can arise from an incorrect design or during translation of the design into code. Logic errors include computing a result incorrectly, off-by-one errors in loops (which can also be a semantic error if your off-by-one error is because you didn't understand array indexing, for example), misunderstanding a network protocol, misunderstanding the problem, forgetting a step, returning the wrong thing from a function, and so on. With a logic error, either your program seems to execute normally but with wrong answers, or it dies suddenly because you've walked off the end of an array, tried to dereference a null pointer, or tried to go off and execute code in the middle of a data area. Logic errors can be devilishly hard to find.

What Not To Do

While there is no single right way to debug,[1] here are a few things you avoid when debugging your code.[2]

Don't guess. Guessing implies that (1) you don't understand the program you're trying to debug and (2) you're not searching for the root cause of the error systematically. Stop, take a deep breath, and start again.

---

[1] Chelf, Ben. 2006. "Avoiding the Most Common Software Development Goofs." 2006. www.embedded.com/avoiding-the-most-common-software-development-goofs/.

[2] McConnell, Steve. 2004. *Code Complete 2: A Practical Handbook of Software Construction.* Redmond, WA: Microsoft Press.

Don't fix the symptom, fix the problem. Often you can "fix" a problem by forcing the error to go away by adding code. For instance, say the error involves an outlier in a range of values or some other edge case. The temptation here is to special-case the outlier by adding code to handle just that case. Reconsider, as you may just be masking a weak spot instead of fixing it. There is almost always some other special case out there waiting to break free and squash your program. Study the program, figure out what the bigger issue is, and find a general solution to prevent future failures.

Don't use the ostrich algorithm. Don't stick your head in the sand and ignore the problem. It may be tempting to think "it's a fluke," "the IDE is malfunctioning," "the rest of the system must be broken," "Ralph's module is obviously sending me bad data," or some other excuse to avoid digging. While things external to your code go awry, the call is most often coming from inside the house. If you just "changed one thing" and the program broke, then guess who probably just injected an error into the program and where it is? Or at the very least it uncovered an existing issue. Mistakes in code, whether from you or others, are to be expected. One of the best discussions of careful coding and how hard it is to write correct programs is the discussion of how to write a binary search routine in Column 5 of Jon Bentley's book *Programming Pearls*.[3] You should read it.

An Approach to Debugging

The best mindset for debugging is to treat misbehaving code as a challenge or an escape-room full of interconnected puzzles. It's a chance to be clever, to solve a cybercrime scene: who did it ('twas probably you...), how, and where? And the best part is that once you solve it, you can also undo it! Debugging is a battle of wits of You vs. You. We promise, this match will have you on the edge of your seat for years to come!

Remember, you're solving a problem here and the best way to do this is to have a systematic way of sneaking up on the problem and whacking it on the head. The other thing to remember about debugging is that, like a murder mystery, you're working backwards from the conclusion.[4] The bad thing has already happened—your program

---

[3] Bentley, Jon. 2000. *Programming Pearls, Second Edition.* Paperback. Boston, MA: Addison-Wesley.

[4] Kernighan, Brian W., and Rob Pike. 1999. *The Practice of Programming.* Paperback. Boston, MA: Addison-Wesley.

failed. Now you need to examine the evidence and work backwards to a solution. Here's the approach, in the order in which you should work:

1. Reproduce the problem reliably.

2. Find the source of the error.

3. Fix the error (just that one).

4. Test the fix (now you've got a regression test for later).

5. Optionally, look for other errors in the vicinity of the one you just fixed.

Debugging Step 1: Reproduce the Problem Reliably

If your error only shows up sporadically, it will be much, much harder to find. The classic example is the "but it works fine on my computer" problem. This is the one sentence you never want to hear. This is why people in tech support retire early. The key first step is reproducing the problem—in different ways, if possible—allowing you to see what's happening and where. Luckily, most errors aren't hiding too hard: either you get the wrong answer in some print statement and work backwards from there, or your program dies a horrible death and the system generates a backtrace for you. (The Java Virtual Machine does this automatically. With other languages, you may need to use a debugger to get the backtrace.)

Remember, errors are not random events. If the error is showing up sporadically, the culprit is usually one of the following (although this list is not exhaustive):

- *An initialization problem*, possibly due to depending on initialization to happen as a side effect of the variable definition and which is not working as you expect.

- *A timing error*, where something is happening earlier or later than you expect.

- *A dangling pointer problem*, where the pointer was expected to point to an object but the object no longer exists.

- *A buffer overflow or walking off the end of an array*, which happen when code traverses beyond the boundaries of some intended space (such as looping beyond the edge of a collection) and stomping on either another piece of code, another variable, or the system stack.

- *A concurrency issue (a race condition)*, when you've not synchronized your code in a multi-threaded application or in an application that uses shared memory and a variable you need is overwritten by someone else before you get to it.

Reproducing the problem is not enough, however. Instead, you need to reduce the problem to the simplest test case that triggers an error, by eliminating all extraneous conditions. One way to do this is to try to reproduce the problem with binary search: using half the data (or even half the code) you had before. Pick one half or the other. If the error still occurs, try it again. If the error doesn't happen, try the other half of the data. If there's still no error, then try with three-quarters of the data. You get the idea. You'll know when you've found the simplest case because with anything smaller the behavior of the program will change: either the error will disappear, or you'll get a slightly different error.

Debugging Step 2: Find the Source of the Error

Once you can reliably reproduce the problem, you can find where the error is occurring. Once again, you need to do this systematically. There are several straightforward techniques you can use:

- *Read the code.* The first thing you should do once you've run your test case is examine the output, make an educated guess where the error might be (look at the last thing that got printed and find that print statement in the program), and then sit back, grab a cup of coffee, and read the code. Understanding what the code is trying to do in the area where the error occurs is key to figuring out both the source of the problem and the fix. Nine times out of ten, if you sit back and read the code for five minutes or so, you'll find the problem.

- *Explain the code to a rubber ducky.* When reading our own code, we often develop code blindness, missing the obvious problem every time we read it, even though we probably would have caught it immediately had it been someone else's code. A solution to this blindness is to explain our code. This can be to ourselves, to a pet, to a plant, to a rubber ducky... you can choose your own adventure sidekick here. Note that we are not expecting any contributions from the sidekick, only passive listening skills. The adventure will usually unfold as follows: "So here I'm doing [A], then [B], then... Oh...", by which point you'll typically finally see the problem.

- *Gather data.* If the problem is still hiding, since you've now got a test case that will reproduce the error, gather data from running the test case. The data can include what kinds of input cause the error, how long it takes to appear, what steps happen leading up to the error, and the state of the program at the time of the error. Once you have this data, you can form an hypothesis on where the error is in the code. For most types of errors, you'll have some output that is correct, followed by incorrect output or by the program crashing.

- *Insert print statements.* Once you narrow down the incorrect output, the simplest thing to do is to start adding print statements near the code interacting with that output, working backwards from the point where you think the error makes itself known. Remember that many times where an error *exhibits* its behavior may be many lines of code after where the error actually *occurs.* Some informative spots for print statements can be the entrance and exit to functions (where you could print "Entering sort routine," "Exiting partition routine," and so on), the top and bottom of loops, at the beginning of the *then* and *else* blocks of *if* statements, in the default case of a switch statement, and so on. Unless something very spooky is going on, you should be able to isolate where the error is occurring pretty quickly.

In some languages, you can encase your print statements inside debugging blocks that you can turn on and off using compile options. In C/C++, you can insert

```
#ifdef DEBUG
printf("Debug statement in sort routine\n");
#endif
```

around debugging statements that you wish to execute optionally. Before compiling the program, you can either add the following to the header or at the top of the code:

```
#define DEBUG
```

or you can compile the code using

```
gcc -DDEBUG foo.c
```

Leaving out the #define or the -DDEBUG will simply skip executing all #ifdef DEBUG ... #endif blocks. Beware, though, because this technique makes your program harder to read due to all the DEBUG blocks scattered around the code. You should remove DEBUG blocks before your program is released. (Unfortunately, Java doesn't have this facility because it doesn't have a preprocessor.)

In Java, you can get the same effect as the #ifdef DEBUG by using a named boolean constant. Here's an example of code:

```java
public class IfDef {
    final static boolean DEBUG = true;

    public static void main(String [] args) {
    System.out.printf("Hello, World \n");

        if (DEBUG) {
            System.out.printf("max(5, 8) is %d\n", Math.max(5, 8));
            System.out.printf("If this prints, the code was included\n");
        }
    }
}
```

In this example, you set the boolean constant DEBUG to true when you want to turn the DEBUG blocks on, and you then turn it to false when you want to turn them off. This isn't perfect because you have to recompile every time you want to turn debugging on and off, but you have to do that with the C/C++ example above as well.

- *Use built-in debugging features* commonly available when coding in an IDE. Such features allow you to set breakpoints, watch variables, step into and out of functions, single step instructions, change code on the fly, examine registers and other memory locations, and so on so that you can learn as much as possible about what is going on in your code—and all without adding print statements you would later need to remove. Pretty much all the IDEs you'll run into, whether open source or proprietary, all have built-in debuggers. This includes Eclipse, XCode, Visual Studio, VSCode, BlueJ, PyCharm, and many others. If you are not using an IDE, you can use a stand-alone debugger like *gdb*. If a quick-and-dirty look through the code and a sprinkling of print statements doesn't get you any closer to finding the error, then use the debugger. See the next section for more on debuggers.

- *Use logging*: Many IDEs and scripting languages (like JavaScript) have built-in logging routines that you can use in place of putting in your own print statements. Typically, you can identify which variables would be helpful to log for debugging. The logging routines will usually create a log file that you can then examine after running the program. If you're doing interactive debugging, you may be able to examine the log file during program execution.

- *Look for patterns* in the code, in particular for errors that you've seen or have caught yourself making before. Patterns are there because developers make the same mistakes over and over again (we're creatures of habit, after all). As you gain more programming experience and get a better understanding of how you write programs, finding the types of mistakes you make will become easier.

The extra semicolon at the end of the while loop header above can be a pattern. Another could be messing up loop boundaries with a classic *off-by-one* error:

```
for (int j = 0; j <= myArray.length; j++) {
    // some code here
}
```

where you step off the end of the array because you're testing for <= rather than <.

A classic in C/C++ is using one = where you meant to use two == for a conditional expression, ending up with an assignment instead. Say you're checking an array of characters for a particular character:

```
for (int j = 0; j < length; j++) {
    if (c = myArray[j]) {
```

```
        pos = j;
        break;
    }
}
```

The single equals sign will cause the *if* statement to stop early every time; pos will always be zero. Java wouldn't let you get away with this because it requires that a conditional expression evaluate to a boolean type; the Java compiler would error out stating that the type of the assignment expression is not a boolean.

```
TstEql.java:10: incompatible types
found    : char
required: boolean
if (c = myArray[j]) {
         ^

1 error
```

This is because in Java (just like in C and C++) an assignment operator returns a result and every result has a type. In this case, the result type is **char** but the if-statement is expecting a **boolean** expression there. The Java compiler checks for this because it's more strongly typed than C and C++, whose compilers don't perform this check.

Forgetting a break statement after a case in a switch is another possible pattern.

```
switch(selectOne) {
    case 'p':  operation = "print";
        break;
    case 'd':  operation = "display";
    default:   operation = "blank";
        break;
}
```

425

The above will reset `operation` to `blank` whenever `selectOne`'s variable is `'d'` because there is no *break* statement after that case, causing fall-through to the following case.

- *Other problems.* We've only scratched the surface of the possible errors you can make and ways to find them in your code. Because there are an infinite number of programs you can write in any given programming language, there are an infinite number of ways to insert errors into them. Memory leaks, typing mistakes, side effects from global variables, failure to close files, not putting a default case in a switch statement, accidentally overriding a method definition, bad return types, hiding a global or instance variable with a local variable... the Skynet is the limit.

Don't be discouraged, though. Most errors you'll make really are simple. Most you'll catch during code reviews and unit tests. The ones that escape into system test or (heaven forbid) released code are the really interesting and subtle ones. Debugging is like solving a puzzle that might require you to spot the differences, solve some math, untangle some logic, and a bunch more fun all in one. Revel in it; we sure do!

Debugging Step 3: Fix the Error (Just That One)!

Once you've found where the error is, you need to come up with a fix for it. Most of the time the fix is obvious and simple because the error is simple. That's the good news. But sometimes, while you can find the error, the fix isn't obvious, or the fix will entail rewriting a large section of code. In such cases, be careful! Take the time necessary to understand the code, and then rewrite it and fix the error correctly. The biggest problem in debugging is haste.

When you are fixing errors, remember two things:

- Fix the actual error; don't fix the symptom.

- Only fix one error at a time.

This second item is particularly important. We've all been in situations where we're fixing an error and we find another one in the same piece of code. The temptation is to fix them both right then and there. Resist! Fix the error you came to fix. Test it and make sure the fix is correct. Integrate the new code back into the source code base. Then you can go back to step 1 and fix the second error.

But why do all this extra work when you can just make the fix right now? By the time you get to this step in the debugging process you already have a test for the first error, you've educated yourself about the code where the error occurs, and you're ready to make that one fix. Don't confuse things by fixing other extraneous issues. You don't have a test for the second error, so you cannot test that fix. Plus, separate integrations, integration testing, shared repository commits, and dedicated commit messages are the cleanest way to keep track of what was done, when, and for what reason. Trust us. It's a little more work but doing the fixes one at a time will save you lots of headaches down the road (such as when some fix ends up needing further fixing).

Debugging Step 4: Test the Fix

Testing the fix seems obvious, doesn't it? But you'd be surprised how many fixes don't get tested. Or if they're tested, it's a simple test with generic sample data and no attempt to see if your fix broke anything else.

First of all, rerun the original test that uncovered the error. Not just the minimal test that you came up with in step 1, but the original test that caused the error to appear. If the error does not occur, that's a good sign you've at least fixed the proximate cause of the error. Now run every other test in your regression suite (see the next chapter for more discussion on regression tests), so you can make sure you've not rebroken something that was already fixed or added a new error into the code. Finally, integrate your code into the source code base repository, check out the new version, and test the entire thing. If all that still works, you're in good shape. Time for a treat, or a nap, or both.

Debugging Step 5: Look for More Errors

Well, if there was one error in a particular function or method, then there might be another, right? One of the truisms of programming is that 80% of the errors occur in 20% of the code, known as the Pareto Principle.[5] It is likely there is another error close to where you've just fixed one. So while you're here, you might as well take a look at the code in the general vicinity of the error you just fixed and see if anything like it happens again. This is another example of looking for patterns.

---

[5] www.getclockwise.com/blog/pareto-principle-software-development

It also won't hurt to take a look at the whole module or class and see if there are other opportunities for change. In the agile world, this is called *refactoring*. This means rewriting the code to make it simpler. Making your code simpler will make it clearer, easier to read, and it will make finding that next error easier. So grab your refreshing beverage of choice and read some code.

Debugger Tools

So far, we have talked about debugging using compilers to remove syntax errors and warnings, print statements you can insert in your code to give you data on what is happening where, and inline debugging statements that you can compile in or out. A more powerful tool you can use to search for the source of an error is a *debugger*: it's a special program that executes instrumented code and allows you to peek inside your program as it's running to examine what's going on. A debugger allows you to stop your running code (breakpoints), examine variable values as the code executes (watchpoints), execute a single instruction at a time, step into and out of functions, and even make changes to the code and the data while the program is running.

While debuggers are very powerful and convenient, you should use them with caution. Debuggers, by their nature, have tunnel vision when it comes to looking at code. They are great at showing you all the code for the current function, but they don't give you a feel for the organization of the program as a whole. They also don't give you a feel for complicated data structures. Additionally, it's hard to debug multithreaded and multiprocess programs using a debugger. Multithreaded programs are particularly problematic, since execution timing is crucial for the different threads, and running a multithreaded program in a debugger changes the timing.

Gdb

For C and C++ developers, the *gdb* command line debugger that comes with nearly all Unix and Linux systems is usually the debugger of choice, as it is the easiest way to get a backtrace. For Java, gdb is also integrated in some interactive development environments like Eclipse (`www.eclipse.org/`) and comes with a graphical user interface in the DDD debugger (`www.gnu.org/software/ddd/`). The NetBeans IDE (`www.netbeans.org`) comes with its own graphical debugger. The Java debuggers in

Eclipse and NetBeans allow you to set breakpoints at individual lines of code, they let you watch variables values change via watchpoints, and they allow you to step through the code one line or one method at a time.

Eclipse

The Eclipse IDE has a built-in debugger that gives you many tools all in one. We'll focus on the Java debugger that's built into Eclipse. The easiest way to get a debugging session started is first to change to the Java perspective in Eclipse, then open your project, open the files that you're interested in so they appear in the editor pane, then go to the upper right of the screen, and open the Debug perspective. Several new panes will open and your screen will look something like Figure 17-1.

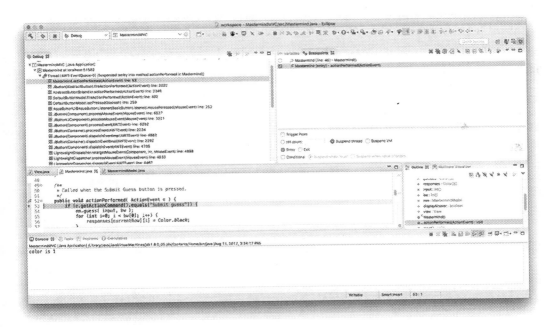

Figure 17-1. *The Debug perspective in Eclipse*

With this new perspective you'll see several panes, including Debug, Variables, Breakpoints, Outline, Mulitcore Visualizer, Console, and the Editor pane. The first thing you should do is to set breakpoints. You can do that in the Editor pane just by double-clicking the line number of a source code file where you want execution to stop. You can now run your program by pressing the bug icon in the upper left of the window. Your program will execute and then stop at the first breakpoint. Look around and examine

429

the current state of your program. The debugger also allows you to set watchpoints on variables, single step-through instructions, skip-over method calls (the method executes, the debugger just doesn't go into the method), change the current value of a variable, and change the code in your program on the fly. The Eclipse website has extensive documentation on the Eclipse debugger.[6]

XCode

Apple's XCode IDE allows you to create applications for Mac OS, iOS, iPadOS, and WatchOS devices. XCode lets you program in several different programming languages including C, C++, Swift, and Objective-C. Just like Eclipse, XCode has a built-in debugger that allows you to set breakpoints, watch variables, step-through code, and make changes on the fly.[7]

XCode's debugger can be enabled to automatically start when you build and execute your program; just insert a breakpoint. You can insert breakpoints by double-clicking the line number to the left of the source line of code where you want to stop execution. Once you've stopped at a breakpoint, XCode also allows you to watch variables and then step through the code execution one line at a time. Figure 17-2 gives you a view of what a stopped program looks like in XCode. Note the left pane of the window that provides options and information about the currently running program. The blue flag in the editing pane indicates the breakpoint where the program is currently stopped (just before it prints "Hello World").

---

[6] http://help.eclipse.org/neon/index.jsp?topic=%2Forg.eclipse.jdt.doc.user%2 Ftasks%2Ftask-running_and_debugging.htm&cp=1_3_6

[7] https://developer.apple.com/library/content/documentation/DeveloperTools/ Conceptual/debugging_with_xcode/chapters/debugging_tools.html#//apple_ref/doc/uid/ TP40015022-CH8-SW4

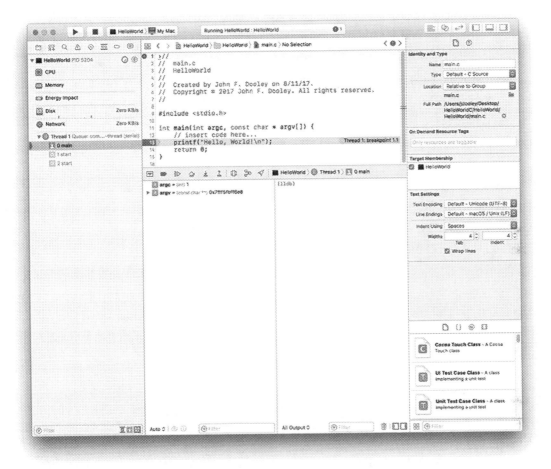

Figure 17-2. *A program stopped in the XCode debugger*

Source Code Control

Earlier is this chapter we mentioned integrating changes into a source code base or repository. Code repositories are used for *source code control*, also known as *software version control*, which is the practice of tracking and managing changes to software.

Whenever you work on a project, whether you are the only developer or you are part of a team, you should keep backups of the work you're doing. A *version control system* (VCS) will not only keep a backup of all the files you create during a project, but it will keep track of all the changes to these files, alongside dates and change authors, so that in addition to saying, "Give me the latest version of PhoneContact.java," you can say, "I want the version of PhoneContact.java from last Thursday with changes made by Dan."

A VCS keeps a *repository* of all the files you've created and added to for your project. The repository can be a flat file or a more sophisticated database, usually organized hierarchically as a file system tree structure. A client program allows you access the repository and retrieve or revert to different versions of one or more of the files stored there. Normally, if you just ask the VCS for a particular file or files, you get the latest version. Whatever version of the file you extract from the repository, it's called the *working copy* in VCS-speak. Extracting the file is called a *check-out*.

If you are working on a project by yourself, then the working copy you check out from the VCS repository is the only one out there and any changes that you make will be reflected in the repository when you check the file back in (yes, that's a *check-in*). The great thing is that if you make a change and it's wrong, you can just check out a previous version that doesn't have the change in it. It's a coding time machine!

When there is more than one developer working on a project, it's quite likely that somebody else on the team may check out and modify the same file that you are working on. If you both attempt to check the file back into the repository, you will end up with a conflict where either one version is lost or the other, or they are carefully manually combined.

Source Code Control: The Collision Problem

Say Alice and Bob both check out PhoneContact.java from the repository and each of them makes changes to it. Bob checks his version of PhoneContact.java back into the repository and goes to lunch. A few minutes later Alice checks in her version of PhoneContact.java. Two problems occur: (1) if Alice hasn't made any changes in the same lines of code that Bob did, her version is still newer than Bob's and it hides Bob's version in the repository. Bob's changes are still there, but they are now in an older version than Alice's; (2) worse, if Alice did make changes to some of the same code that Bob did, then her changes actually overwrite Bob's and PhoneContact.java is a very different file. Bummer. So we don't want either of these situations to occur. How do we avoid this problem? Version control systems use two different strategies to avoid collisions:

- lock-modify-unlock

- copy-modify-merge

Collisions: Using Lock-Modify-Unlock

The first strategy is *lock-modify-unlock*. In this strategy, Bob checks out PhoneContact.java and locks it for edit. This means that Bob now has the only working copy of PhoneContact.java that can be changed. If Alice tries to check out PhoneContact.java, she gets a message that she can only check out a read-only version and can't check it back in until Bob gives up his lock. Bob makes his changes, checks PhoneContact.java back in, and then releases the lock. Alice can now check out and lock an editable version of PhoneContact.java (which now includes Bob's changes) and make her own changes and check the file back in, giving up her lock.

The biggest negative about the lock-modify-unlock strategy is that it has the side effect of *serializing changes* in the repository, meaning changes to the same file cannot happen in parallel, slowing down development. While Bob has the file checked out for editing, Alice can't make her changes and has to wait.

Collisions: Using Copy-Modify-Merge

The second strategy is *copy-modify-merge*. In this strategy, Alice and Bob are both free to check out editable copies of PhoneContact.java. Let's say that Alice makes her changes first and checks her new version of the file back into the repository. When Bob finishes his changes, he tries to check his new version of PhoneContact.java into the repository only to have the VCS tell him his version of the file is "out of date;" Bob can't check in. What happened here?

The VCS stamps each checked out file with a timestamp and a version number. It also keeps track of what is checked out and who checked it out and when. It checks those values when you try to check in. When Bob tried to check in, his VCS realized that the version of the code he was trying to check in was older than the current version in the repository (the new one that Alice had checked in earlier), so it let him know that. So, what is Bob to do? That's where the third part of copy-modify-merge comes in: Bob needs to tell the VCS to merge his changes with the current version of PhoneContact. java and then check in the updated version. This works just fine if Alice and Bob have changed different parts of the file; their changes do not conflict and VCS can just do the merge automatically and check in the new file. On the other hand, if Alice and Bob did make changes to the same lines of code in the file, we end up with a *merge conflict*. In that case, Bob must do a manual merge of the two files. When manual merge is needed, the VCS will normally put both versions of the file on the screen, side by side, highlighting the conflicting lines of code, and then Bob can decide which version he wants, or he can make changes that resolve any inconsistencies. Bob is in control. Bob has to do this because the VCS isn't smart enough to choose between the conflicting changes. Usually, a VCS will provide some help in doing the merge, but ultimately the merge decision must be Bob's. Copy-modify-merge can occasionally make for extra work for whomever checks in second, but it allows both developers to work on the same file simultaneously and it doesn't allow any changes to be lost automatically.

Note, however, that changes can still be lost if Bob is not very careful during the manual merge; he may even want to discuss some conflicting changes with Alice to ensure both sets of modifications are preserved and merged correctly. The merged code should then be fully retested before it is checked into the repository. Another problem with copy-modify-merge is that if your repository allows you to store binary files, you can't merge them. Say you have two versions of the same jpg file. How do you decide which of the bits is correct? In this case, the VCS will require you to use lock-modify-unlock.

A typical working cycle for any version control system will look like the following. Before anything else starts, the developer must create a *local repository* for the project. This can happen automatically using a client program, or the developer can manually create a directory that will house the repository. Some systems allow the developer to do an initial check out and will create the repository for them. Then

1. The developer *checks out* the code they want from the project.

2. The developer edits, compiles, debugs, and tests the code.

3. When ready to upload their changes to the main repository, the developer will *commit* the changes; this will automatically check in the changed files.

4. Usually, the system will attempt to do an *automatic merge* of the changes. If there is a *merge conflict*, the developer will be notified and will be prompted to do a manual merge.

5. Once all merge conflicts are resolved, the changed files are in the main repository and ready to be checked out again by other developers.

Source Code Control Systems

Subversion

Copy-modify-merge is the strategy used by most version control systems these days, including the popular open-source distributed version control system, Subversion (`https://subversion.apache.org`).[8] Subversion (SVN) was first developed in 2000 and is a rewrite and update of an older VCS called the Concurrent Versions System (CVS). CVS itself is a front end to a version control system developed in 1982 called the Revision Control System (RCS). Subversion is much more fully featured and sophisticated than either CVS or RCS. While it is primarily used in software development projects, it can be used as a version control system for any type of file in any type of project. Subversion comes in both command line versions and in GUI versions, like RapidSVN, TortoiseSVN, and SmartSVN. There are also plug-ins for various IDEs, like subclipse[9] for the Eclipse IDE.

Subversion is an example of a *centralized version control* system (also known as client-server), where there is a centralized database of all the source code and users access the database via a local client. This centralized database can be on the local machine, it can be on a remote *svnserve* server machine, or it can be on a remote Apache server. The user can set things up so the local svn client knows where the version control database is located. Checked-out *working copies* of files are a developer's own private copy of the file, stored locally in a tree hierarchy repository. Subversion defaults to the copy-modify-merge version control model but can also be configured to use the lock-modify-unlock model on individual files. For more information and a link to the online copy of the aptly named *Subversion Book*, go to `https://subversion.apache.org`.

Git and GitHub

Git (`www.git-scm.com`), a candidate for most popular open-source *distributed version control system*, uses a model that provides each developer with their own local copies of the source files as well as the entire development history of the project. When a developer makes a change to a file, the changes are synced to the other developers' local

---

[8] Pilato, C., Ben Collins-Sussman, and Brian Fitzpatrick. 2008. *Version Control with Subversion.* 2nd Edition. Sebastopol, CA: O'Reilly Media, Inc. `https://svnbook.red-bean.com/`.

[9] `https://marketplace.eclipse.org/content/subclipse`

repositories via the use of git commands. Git uses a model called an *incomplete merge,* along with a number of plug-in merge tools to coordinate merges across repositories. Git can also connect with and sync remote repositories on different computers across a network (including the Internet). Note that two developers' local repositories may be out of sync at any given time, but the totality of all the developer's repositories is what constitutes the project's source code, making git a distributed version control system. It is up to the developers to keep their repositories in sync (but see GitHub and Bitbucket below). Git's main virtue is speed. It may be the fastest distributed VCS around. Linus Torvalds, who also famously developed the Linux kernel, originally developed Git.

Git is typically run via the command line and by default is only distributed with command line tools (though many GUI versions are readily available). Like other version control systems, git uses the idea of a *main branch* of the code that a developer can *pull* from to get up to date local copies of the code to work on. Developers can also make separate *branches* of the master so that their work doesn't interfere with other developers until they merge. Git makes it trivially easy to create repositories: create a directory, navigate to that directory from a terminal window, and initialize a new repository at that location by typing $ `git init`.

Typical git workflow has the following basic steps[10]:

1. *Pull* from the remote version of the repository to see all changes anyone has made.

2. *Merge* the changes you just pulled into your local repository to update your personal copy.

3. *Branch* off of an existing branch or check out a branch to work directly on it.

4. *Edit* the files as needed.

5. *Compile, debug, and test.*

6. *Add* all or a subset of the changed files to the staging area (an abstract area git uses to indicate which files are candidates for committing back into the source code repository).

---

[10] For a more in-depth primer on git commands, refer to this article by Rik Bose: `https://medium.rbose.dev/yet-another-git-primer-966d14b8ea93`.

7. *Commit* the files from the staging area into the local repository.

8. *Push* to the remote version of the repository because other developers cannot see your local version.

An extension of git called *GitHub* is a web-based version of git that allows the creation and maintenance of remote repositories accessible across the Internet. GitHub provides all the regular services of git, but also features access control, bug tracking, a web hosting service, wikis, and project management services. GitHub has more than 20 million users and hosts more than 50 million repositories. See `https://github.com/`.

You can find all the git commands and tutorials at `https://git-scm.com/doc`.[11] There are also many graphical interfaces to git. The two most popular are the *GitHub Desktop*, which you can find at `https://desktop.github.com/` and *gitKraken* at `www.gitkraken.com/` which works with both *git* and *Mercurial*.

Mercurial

Mercurial is another popular free, *distributed version control system*. Like *git*, it is primarily a command line tool. It uses practically the same repository and workflow models as git, including the ideas of pulling and pushing branches, commits, and merges. Instead of staging, Mercurial has the idea of a *changeset* that is the set of all the files that have been modified since the last commit. It also allows you to view changes between different versions of files, look at the current status of the repository since the last commit, and view a summary of the work that has gone on in the repository. Mercurial is available free online at `www.mercurial-scm.org/` and a free online book and tutorial is available at `https://book.mercurial-scm.org/`.

---

[11] Chacon, Scott, and Ben Straub. 2014. *Pro Git: Everything You Need to Know About Git, 2nd. Ed.* Paperback. New York, NY: Apress. `https://git-scm.com/book/en/v2`.

One Last Thought on Coding and Debugging: Pair Programming

Pair programming[12] is a technique to improve software quality and programmer performance (for more, see Chapter 2). In pair programming, two people share one computer and one keyboard. One person "drives" by controlling the keyboard and writing the code, and the other "navigates" by watching for errors in the code, suggesting changes and test cases. Periodically the driver and the navigator switch places. Pairs can work together for long periods of time on a project, or pairs can change with each programming task. Pair programming is particularly popular in agile development environments; in the *Extreme Programming* model, all developers are required to pair program and no code that has not been written by two people is allowed to be integrated into the project. There have been several studies[13] that show that pair programming decreases the number of errors in code and improves the productivity of programmers. So this is our final debugging technique: pair program!

Conclusion

Just like writing good, efficient code, debugging is a skill that all programmers need to develop. Being a careful coder will mean you'll spend less time debugging, but there will always be debugging. Programmers are all human and we'll always make mistakes. As we get more skilled, we work on harder problems, so the debugging puzzles never end. Having a toolbelt full of debugging skills will help you find the root causes of errors in your code faster and it will help you from injecting more errors. The combination of reviews (Chapter 19), debugging, and unit testing (as you'll see in the next chapter) is the knock-out punch that a developer uses to release defect-free code.

---

[12] Williams, Laurie, and R. Kessler. 2000. "All I Really Need to Know about Pair Programming I Learned in Kindergarten." *CACM* 43 (5): 108–14.

[13] Cockburn, A., and Laurie Williams. 2001. "The Costs and Benefits of Pair Programming." In *Extreme Programming Examined*. Boston, MA: Addison-Wesley Longman.

References

Bentley, Jon. 2000. *Programming Pearls, Second Edition*. Paperback. Boston, MA: Addison-Wesley.

Chacon, Scott, and Ben Straub. 2014. *Pro Git: Everything You Need to Know About Git, 2nd. Ed.* Paperback. New York, NY: Apress. `https://git-scm.com/book/en/v2`.

Chelf, Ben. 2006. "Avoiding the Most Common Software Development Goofs." 2006. `www.embedded.com/avoiding-the-most-common-software-development-goofs/`.

Cockburn, A., and Laurie Williams. 2001. "The Costs and Benefits of Pair Programming." In *Extreme Programming Examined*. Boston, MA: Addison-Wesley Longman.

Kernighan, Brian W., and Rob Pike. 1999. *The Practice of Programming*. Paperback. Boston, MA: Addison-Wesley.

McConnell, Steve. 2004. *Code Complete 2: A Practical Handbook of Software Construction*. Redmond, WA: Microsoft Press.

Pilato, C., Ben Collins-Sussman, and Brian Fitzpatrick. 2008. *Version Control with Subversion*. 2nd Edition. Sebastopol, CA: O'Reilly Media, Inc. `https://svnbook.red-bean.com/`.

Williams, Laurie, and R. Kessler. 2000. "All I Really Need to Know about Pair Programming I Learned in Kindergarten." *CACM* 43 (5): 108–14.

CHAPTER 18

Unit Testing

More than the act of testing, the act of designing tests is one of the best bug preventers known. The thinking that must be done to create a useful test can discover and eliminate bugs before they are coded—indeed, test-design thinking can discover and eliminate bugs at every stage in the creation of software, from conception to specification, to design, coding and the rest.

—Boris Beizer

You can see a lot by just looking.

—Yogi Berra

As was emphasized in the last chapter, nobody is perfect, including software developers. In Chapter 17, we talked about different things to look for when you *know* there are errors in your code. Now we're going to talk about how to determine whether there are errors. Of the three types of errors in your code, the compiler will find the syntax errors and the occasional semantic error. In some language environments, the runtime system will find others (to your users' chagrin). The rest of the errors are found either through testing or through code reviews and inspections. In this chapter, we'll discuss testing: what it is, when to do it, how to do it, what your tests should cover, and the limitations of testing. The next chapter will cover code reviews and inspections.

There are three levels of testing in a typical software development project: unit testing, integration testing, and system testing.

Unit testing is typically done by you, the developer, through testing individual methods and classes. Unit testing typically excludes larger configurations of the program, interfaces, or library interactions—except those that your method might actually be using. Because you are unit testing your own code, you know how all the

© John F. Dooley and Vera A. Kazakova 2024
J. F. Dooley and V. A. Kazakova, *Software Development, Design, and Coding*,
https://doi.org/10.1007/979-8-8688-0285-0_18

methods are written, what the data is supposed to look like, what the method signatures are, and what the return values and types should be. This is known as *white-box testing*, *transparent-box testing*, *clear-box testing*, or *glass-box testing*, all alluding to the direct visibility of the details of the code being tested.

Integration testing is typically done by a separate testing organization and consists of testing the interaction and interfaces of the collection of classes or modules that interact with each other. Testers write their tests with knowledge of the interfaces but not with information about the internal implementation of each module. Because of this, integration testing is sometimes called *gray-box testing*, alluding the fact that testers have only partial, interface-level visibility of the internal structure. Integration testing is done after unit tested code is integrated into the source code base. To find any errors in how the new module interacts with the existing code, a partial or complete version of the product is built and tested. Integration testing is also performed when errors discovered in a module are fixed and the module is reintegrated into the code base.

As a developer, you will do some integration testing yourself: each time you work on a separate code branch, you will integrate your new or updated code into that branch and then test the entire application to make sure you've not broken anything anywhere outside the immediate purview of your unit testing. You will also usually do your own unit and integration testing when you are fixing an error that has been discovered in an already released product. In this case, you'll receive a report from either the customer or from your company's customer support organization that some part of the program is not working correctly. It is then your job to reproduce the error, isolate it, fix it, test it in isolation, integrate the fix, and then test it again in the newly built product to make sure it's actually fixed and you have not introduced a new error. This "bug fixing" role is something that many new developers do when they first start at a company and is an excellent way to get familiar with the company's products, tools, and procedures.

System testing is also typically done by a separate testing organization, testing of the entire software product (the system) on both internal baselines and on the final baseline proposed for release to customers. System testing is like integration testing on steroids. All of the recent changes by all developers are used to build a new version of the product, which is then tested as a whole. The separate testing organization uses the requirements and writes their own tests, usually without knowing anything about the details of how the program is designed or written. This is known as *black-box testing*, because the program is opaque to the tester except for the inputs it takes and the outputs it produces. The job of the testers at this level is to make sure that the program implements all the requirements. Black box testing can also include stress testing, usability testing, and acceptance testing. End users may be involved in this type of testing.

The Problem with Testing

Despite testing to determine whether and when your program doesn't work as expected, there is no guarantee it will lead you to uncover all of the issues in the code. There are a number of reasons why testing isn't perfect.

For one, when testing your own code using your own tests, you can easily miss something. If you didn't think of an edge case while coding, you could just as easily miss a test case that would catch the problem. If you made a mistake when you wrote the code, why should you assume you won't make the same mistake when you read it or try to test it? If you misunderstood the problem in some way, it's unlikely you will catch that misunderstanding right away. This happens for even small programs, but it's particularly true for larger programs. If you have a 50,000-line program, that's a lot to read and understand and you're bound to miss something. Also, static reading of programs won't help you find those dynamic interactions between modules and interfaces. So you need to test more intelligently and combine both static (code reading) and dynamic (testing) techniques to find and fix errors in programs.

Another reason errors escape from one testing phase to another and ultimately to the user is that software, more than any other product that humans manufacture, is very dynamic: even small programs have many pathways through the code and many different types of data errors that can occur. This large number of pathways through a program leads to a *combinatorial explosion* of possibilities. Every time you add an if statement to your program, you double the number of possible paths through the program: you have one path through the code if some conditional expression is true, and a different path if it's false. Every time you add a new input value, you increase system complexity and increase the number of possible errors. As a result, for large programs, you can't possibly test every possible path through the program with every possible input value, as there are an exponential number of code-path and data-value combinations.

So, what to do? If brute force is *intractable*, then you need a better plan. A tangible option is to identify the most probable use cases and test those. You need to identify and test the likely input data values, the boundary conditions for data, and the likely code paths. This, it turns out, will get you most of the errors. Steve McConnell says in *Code*

443

Complete that a combination of good testing and code reviews can uncover more than 95% of errors in a good-sized program.[1] That's a solid goal to shoot for with real-world problems.

Code Creator vs. Code Breaker Mindset

There's actually another problem with testing: you, the developer. Developers and testers have two different, one might say adversarial, roles to play in code construction. Developers are there to take a set of requirements and produce a design that reflects the requirements and write the code that implements the design. Your job as a developer is to *get code to work*. If you implement it according to your solution plan, then it's very natural to assume your code solution will work.

A tester's job, on the other hand, is to take those same requirements, but instead to assume the code does not work and their job is to uncover how it fails. Testers are supposed to do unspeakable, horrible things to your code in an effort to *get the code to break*, to get the errors in it to expose themselves to the light of day before the users or client systems get to it. Breaking stuff is why being a tester can be a very fun job. You, the developer, then get to fix the code.

You can see where this might be an adversarial relationship. You can also see where developers might make pretty bad testers. If your job is to make the code work, you're not focused on breaking it. So your test cases may not be the sneaky, contrived, and even mean test cases that someone whose job it is to break your code may come up with. In short, because they're trying to build something beautiful, *developers make lousy testers*. Developers tend to write tests using typical, clean data. They tend to have an overly optimistic view of how much of their code a test will exercise. They tend to write tests assuming that the code will work; after all, it's their own carefully designed and cleverly implemented brainchild.

This is why most software development organizations have a *separate testing team* for integration and system testing. These testers write their own test code, create their own frameworks, do the testing of all new baselines and the final release code, and report all the errors back to the developers who then must fix them. The one thing testers normally *do not* do is unit testing. Unit testing is the developer's responsibility, so you're

---

[1] McConnell, Steve. 2004. *Code Complete 2: A Practical Handbook of Software Construction*. Redmond, WA: Microsoft Press. 470-471.

not completely off the hook here. You do need to think about testing, learn how to write tests, how to run them, and how to analyze the results. You need to learn to be mean to your code. And you still need to fix the errors.

When to Test?

Before we get around to discussing just how to do unit testing and what things to test, let's talk about *when* to test. There are two major options here: 1) you code then test or 2) you test and then code.

You may find it most natural to first write your code, get it to compile (meaning you've eliminated the syntax errors), and then, *after* you feel the code for a function or a module is finished, you write your tests and do your unit testing. This has the advantage that you've understood the requirements and written the code, which gave you the opportunity to think about test cases while writing the code. This can streamline writing clear test cases. In this strategy, debugging and testing happen concurrently: you find an error, fix it, and then rerun the failed test right away.

An alternative approach is to write your unit tests first, *before* you write any code, and then develop your code until all tests pass. This is known as *test-driven development* (TDD), an approach rooted in agile methodologies (especially out of eXtreme Programming). Clearly if you write your unit tests first, they will all fail, since at most you'll have the stub of a method to call in your test. TDD begins with coding up your benchmark for success. If you've written a bunch of tests, and then write just enough code to make all the unit tests pass, you know exactly when you're done! You can write some new code and test it; if it fails, write some more code; if it passes, stop. This has the advantage of helping you keep your code lean, making it simpler and easier to debug. It also gives you, right up front, a set of tests you can rerun whenever you make a change to your code. If the tests all still pass, then you haven't broken anything by making the changes.

So which way is better? Well, the answer is another of those "it depends" things. Generally, writing your tests first gets you in the testing mindset earlier and gives you definite goals for implementing the code. On the other hand, until you do it a lot and it becomes second nature, writing tests first can be hard because you have to visualize what you're testing. It forces you to come to terms with the requirements and the module or class design early as well. That means that design/coding/testing all pretty much happen at once. This can make the whole code construction process more difficult. Because you are doing design/coding/testing all at the same time, it will also take longer to create that first functional program. However, once you have that first functional piece, your development time can speed up. TDD works well for small- to medium-sized projects (as do agile techniques in general), but it may be more difficult for very large programs. TDD also works quite well when you are *pair programming*. To refresh your memory, in pair programming two developers work on the same task at the same time. They share a single computer with one of them (the *driver*) at the keyboard and writing code, while the second developer (the *navigator*) sits next to the driver and watches for errors, thinks about design issues and testing, and comments. About every half hour or so, the driver and navigator switch places. Later, the driver writes a *test*, while the navigator thinks of more tests to write and thinks ahead of the code. This process tends to make writing the tests easier and then flows naturally into writing the code. Give testing a shot both before and after, and then you can decide which is best for you and your project.

Testing in an Agile Development Environment

While many of the ideas and methods are the same no matter what development process you are using, agile processes have a different viewpoint on testing. Most agile methodologies strongly encourage (and XP requires) the use of TDD so that unit tests are written before the production code is written.

TDD makes a lot of sense on an agile team due to *continuous integration*. In most agile methodologies, every time a developer finishes writing a task or a feature, they are expected to integrate their new code into the code base and test it using an automated test suite. On a team of 10 – 20 developers, this can happen many times a day. One of the rules of *continuous integration* is that if you write a new piece of code that passes the unit tests, but after integration it breaks the product, *you have to fix it right away*. No bug reports, no passing the problem off to a separate bug fixing and integration team; the developer who wrote the code is supposed to fix the problem immediately. This, combined with the fact that most new features or tasks implemented in an agile project are small (remember, tasks are supposed to be 8 hours of effort or less, total) makes integration testing an extension of unit testing. Having the tests ready to go for continuous integration retesting just makes sense.

Another reason for TDD in agile is that many agile approaches recommend (while XP requires) *pair programming*, with two developers taking turns writing code and refining their tests and the code. They test often (say every time they have a new function written) and integrate often, and all of their new tests are added to the automated test suite for the project. It's a win, win, win.

Finally, in an agile project, *the customer is a crucial part of the development team and does system testing.* In many cases, the customer is on site so the system/acceptance tests established by the customer can be run after each integration of code changes.

Consequently, in agile projects, the entire suite of tests (unit tests, integration tests, and system tests) is part of the normal agile development process.

What to Test?

Now that we've talked about different phases of testing and when you should do your unit testing, it's time to discuss just *what* to test. What you're testing falls into two general categories: *code coverage* and *data coverage*.

- *Code coverage* has the goal of executing every line of code in your program at least once with representative data so you can be sure that all the code functions correctly. Sounds easy? Well, remember that combinatorial explosion problem for that 50,000-line program.

- *Data coverage* has the goal of testing representative samples of good and bad data (both input data and data generated by your program), with the objective of making sure the program handles data and particularly data errors correctly.

Of course there is overlap between code coverage and data coverage. For instance, sometimes in order to get a particular part of your program to execute you have to feed it bad data. We'll separate these as best we can and come together when we talk about writing actual tests.

Code Coverage: Test Every Statement

Your objective in code coverage is to test every statement across all the different types of code that compose your program. Let's look at these different code types.

Straight-line code illuminates a single path through your function or method. Normally this will require one test per different data type.

Branch coverage tests everywhere your program can change directions. That means you need to look at control structures here: every `if` and `switch` statement, and every *complex conditional expression* (those that contain AND and OR operators). For every `if` statement, you'll need two tests: one for when the condition is `true` and one for when it's `false`. For every `switch` statement, you'll need a separate test for each `case` clause in the switch, including the `default` clause (all your `switch` statements should have a `default` clause). The logical AND (`&&`) and OR (`||`) operators add complexity to your conditional expressions, so you'll need extra test cases for those. Ideally, you'll need four test cases for each (F-F, F-T, T-F, T-T), but if the language you are using uses *short-cut evaluation* for logical operators (as do C/C++ and Java), then you can reduce the number of test cases.[2] For the OR operator, you'll still need two cases if the first subexpression evaluates to `false`, but you can just use a single test case if the first subexpression evaluates to `true` (as the entire expression will then evaluate to true). For the AND operator, you'll only need a single test if the first subexpression evaluates to `false` (the result will always be false), but you need both tests if the first subexpression evaluates to `true`.

Loop coverage is similar to branch coverage above, as loops contain conditionals. The difference is that in `for`, `while`, or `do-while` loops you have the highest likelihood of introducing an *off-by-one error* and you need to test for that explicitly. First, you'll need a test for a *normal* run through the loop. Then there is the possibility with pretest loops that you never enter the loop body (if the loop conditional expression fails the very first time). Then you'll need to test for an *infinite loop* if the conditional expression never becomes *false*. This is most likely if the loop control variable was not updated in the loop body, or if it was updated incorrectly, or if the loop conditional expression was wrong from the beginning. For loops that read files, you normally need to test for the *end-of-file* marker (EOF). This is another place where errors could occur either because of a premature end-of-file or because (in the case of using standard input) end-of-file is never indicated.

Return values should always be checked, even when they are not the main functional component of the tested code. In many languages, standard library functions and operating system calls all return values. For example, in C, the `fprintf` and `fscanf` families of functions return the number of characters printed to an output stream and the number of input elements assigned from an input stream, respectively. But hardly anyone ever

---

[2] In *short-cut evaluation*, parts of a logical comparison will not be executed, depending on the result of the earlier comparisons. For example, in the conditional expression "if ((a == b) OR (c == d))" if the first comparison a == b evaluates to TRUE, then the second comparison will not be evaluated because the entire expression must evaluate to TRUE. Similarly, in the expression "if ((a == b) AND (c == d))" if the first comparison evaluates to FALSE, then the second comparison will not be evaluated because the entire expression must be FALSE.

checks these return values.[3] You should, as they may reveal the more subtle and sneaky issues with the code! Note that Java is a bit different than C or C++. In Java, many of the similarly offending routines will have return values declared void rather than int as in C or C++. So the above problem occurs much less frequently in Java than in other languages. It's not completely gone however: while the System.out.print() and System.out.println() methods in Java are both declared to return void, the System.out.printf() method returns a PrintStream object that is almost universally ignored. In addition, it's perfectly legal in Java to call a Scanner's next() or nextInt() methods or any of the methods that read data and not save the return value in a variable. Be careful out there.

Data Coverage: Bad Data Is Your Friend?

Remember when we talked about *defensive programming* (in the chapter on code construction), we discussed that the key to defending your program is watching out for, detecting, and handling bad data, so that your program can recover or at least fail gracefully. Well, now is where we see if your defenses hold up. Data coverage should examine two types of data: good data and bad data.

Good data is the typical data your method is supposed to handle, data of the correct type and within the correct ranges. Testing good data is a baseline to verify your program can handle the basics of normal operation normally. Here's the short list of the basic tests to be performed on good data:

- *Test typical data values*: Valid data fields that you might normally expect to get. For example, if your program is computing average grades for a course, the range of values is likely between 0 and 100, inclusive. You might check 35, 50, 67, 75, 88, 93, and so on. If they don't work, it's too soon to test anything else; recheck your solution.

- *Test boundary conditions (or edge cases)*: Data near the edges of the range of your valid data. Off-by-one errors often hide at the edges. For the grading example above, you should test valid grades near both boundaries: 0, 1, 99, and 100. You should also test invalid values close to the range: -1 and 101. If you are assigning letter grades, you

---

[3] Kernighan, Brian W., and Rob Pike. 1999. *The Practice of Programming*. Paperback. Boston, MA: Addison-Wesley.

also need to check the upper and lower boundaries of each letter grade value. So if an F is any grade below a 60, you should check 59, 60, and 61.

- *Test preconditions and postconditions.* Whenever you enter a control structure (a loop or a selection statement) or make a function call, you're making certain assumptions about data values and the state of your computations. These are *preconditions*. When you exit that control structure, you're making assumptions about what those values are now. These are *postconditions*. You should write tests that make sure that your assumptions are correct by testing the preconditions and postconditions. In languages that have *assertions* (including C, C++, and Java), this is a great place to use them.

Bad data is any data that your method is not designed to process, but which it could nevertheless receive through user error, code defects, hardware malfunctions, and such. It is your job to find out how your code behaves given all kinds of bad data and to make a conscious choice about how to address it during development. If you are not investigating interactions with bad data proactively, you are letting unexpected bad things happen to your code out in the real world, as well as letting your code become the unexpected bad thing that happens to others. To responsibly test interactions with bad data, you can start by looking at the following:

- *Illegal data values*: You should test data that is blatantly illegal to make sure that your data validation code is working. We already mentioned testing illegal data near the boundaries of your legal data ranges but do test data blatantly out of the range.

- *No data*: This is where you are expecting data and you get nothing. For instance, when you've prompted a user for input and instead of typing a value and then press the return key, they just press return. Or when you can't open an input file or the file you've just opened is empty. Or when you're expecting command line arguments and you get none. You've got to test all of these cases and more. Get creative!

- *Too little or too much data*: You have to test the cases where you ask for three pieces of data and only get two, or you ask for three pieces and get ten. You have to be careful with the "too much data" case. Many programming languages (C and C++ among them) use a *data input stream* model for data: each time the program needs data, it only reads as much data from the input stream as it needs. If there is more data in the stream, it just sits there waiting for the next read operation. This may not be what you want, particularly if the input is coming from a user typing at a keyboard.

- *Uninitialized variables*. Most language systems will provide default initialization values for any variable that you declare. But you should still test to make sure that these variables are initialized correctly. (Really, you should not depend on the system to initialize your data anyway; you should always initialize it yourself.)

Characteristics of Tests

Robert Martin, in his book *Clean Code*, describes a set of characteristics that all unit tests should have via the acronym F.I.R.S.T.:[4]

> *Fast:* Tests should be fast. If your tests take a long time to run, you're liable to run them less frequently. So make your tests small, simple, and fast.

> *Independent:* Tests should not depend on each other. In particular, one test shouldn't set up data or create objects that another test depends on. For example, the JUnit testing framework for Java has separate setup and teardown methods that make the tests independent. We'll examine JUnit in more detail later on.

> *Repeatable:* You should be able to run your tests any time you want, in any order you want, including after you've added more code to the module.

---

[4] Martin, Robert C. 2009. *Clean Code: A Handbook of Agile Software Craftsmanship*. Paperback. Upper Saddle River, NJ: Prentice-Hall.

Self-validating: The tests should either just pass or fail; in other words, their output should just be Boolean. You shouldn't have to read pages and pages of a log file to see if the test passed or not.

Timely: Your tests should be available when you want to run them. For agile methodologies that use TDD, this means you write the unit tests first, just before you write the code that they will test.

Finally, it is important that just like your functions, your tests should only test one thing; there should be a single concept for each test. This is very important for your debugging work because if each test only tests a single concept in your code, a test failure will point you like a laser at the place in your code where your error is likely to be.

How to Write a Test

Let's now dive into exactly how one writes a unit test. In this section, we will focus on manual testing, but in the next section we'll examine how to make use of a testing framework such as JUnit.

To write a test, imagine that you are writing a part of an application in the form of a user story, as might be done in an agile development environment.[5] In agile methodologies, the developers and the customer conduct an *exploration*: they get together to talk about what the customer wants. The customer writes a series of *stories* that describe features that they want in the program. These stories are taken by the developers, broken up into *implementation tasks*, and estimated. Tasks should be small, no more than 8 hours of effort. Programmers (individually or in pairs) take individual tasks and implement them using TDD. We'll present a story, break it up into tasks, and implement some tests for the tasks to get an idea of the unit testing process.

Writing Tests: The Story

User Story: "Given a flat file of phone contacts, we want to sort the contacts alphabetically, and produce an output table that can be printed."

Really, that's all. Stories in agile projects are typically very short. The suggestion is that they be written on 3x5 index cards or digital post-it notes.

---

[5] Newkirk, James, and Robert C. Martin. 2001. *Extreme Programming in Practice.* Paperback. Boston, MA: Addison-Wesley.

Writing Tests: The Tasks

Now you can break this story up into a set of small tasks. This will look suspiciously like a design exercise. It is.

- Create a class that represents a phone contact.

- Create a phone contact.

- Read a data file and create a list of phone contacts. (This may look like two things, but it's really just one thing: converting a file into a list of phone contacts.)

- Sort the phone contacts alphabetically by last name.

- Create the printable sorted list.

Writing Tests: The Tests

Following TDD, let's work on tests firsts. While you want to test one bit of functionality at a time, some elements cannot be tested separately. In this example above, you need to combine the first two tasks into a single test. Once you've created a phone contact class, you must test its constructors to make sure you can correctly instantiate an object. So, let's create a test.

In your first test, you'll create an instance of your phone contact object and print out the instance variables to prove it was created correctly. You must do a little design work first: you must figure out what the phone contact class will be called and what instance variables it will have.

A reasonable name for the class is PhoneContact, and as long as it's alright with your customer, the instance variables will be firstName, lastName, phoneNumber, and emailAddr. Oh, and they can all be string variables. It's a simple contact list. For this class you can have two constructors: a default constructor that just initializes the contacts to null and a constructor that takes all four values as input arguments and assigns them. That's probably all you need at the moment. Here's what the test may look like:

```
public class TestPhoneContact {
    /**
     * Default constructor for test class TestPhoneContact
     */
```

```java
    public TestPhoneContact() {
    }

    public void testPhoneContactCreation() {
        String fname = "Fred";
        String lname = "Flintstone";
        String phone = "800-555-1212";
        String email = "fred@knox.edu";

        PhoneContact t1 = new PhoneContact();
        System.out.printf("Phone Contact reference is %X\n", t1);
        // reference var address

        PhoneContact t2 = new PhoneContact(fname, lname, phone, email);
        System.out.printf("Contact:\n Name = %s\n Phone = %s\n Email = %s\n",
                        t2.getName(), t2.getPhoneNum(), t2.getEmailAddr());
    }
}
```

Now, this test will fail to begin with because you have not created the PhoneContact class yet. Let's do that now. The PhoneContact class will be simple: just the instance variables, the two constructors, and getter and setter methods for the variables. The resulting code is below:

```java
public class PhoneContact {
    /**
     * instance variables
     */
    private String lastName;
    private String firstName;
    private String phoneNumber;
    private String emailAddr;

    /**
     * Constructors for objects of class PhoneContact
     */
```

```java
public PhoneContact() {
    lastName = "";
    firstName = "";
    phoneNumber = "";
    emailAddr = "";
}

public PhoneContact(String firstName, String lastName,
                    String phoneNumber, String emailAddr) {
    this.lastName = lastName;
    this.firstName = firstName;
    this.phoneNumber = phoneNumber;
    this.emailAddr = emailAddr;
}

/**
 * Getter and Setter methods for each of the instance variables
 */
public String getName() {
    return this.lastName + ", " + this.firstName;
}

public String getLastName() {
    return this.lastName;
}

public String getFirstName() {
    return this.firstName;
}

public String getPhoneNum() {
    return this.phoneNumber;
}

public String getEmailAddr() {
    return this.emailAddr;
}
```

```java
    public void setLastName(String lastName) {
        this.lastName = lastName;
    }

    public void setFirstName(String firstName) {
        this.firstName = firstName;
    }

    public void setPhoneNum(String phoneNumber) {
        this.phoneNumber = phoneNumber;
    }

    public void setEmailAddr(String emailAddr) {
        this.emailAddr = emailAddr;
    }
}
```

The last thing you need is a driver for the test you've just created, essentially somewhere you can call the above code. When you only need a preliminary quick-and-dirty test for a single class, you could test it from a main method within the class, but for more thorough, repeatable, and expandable testing, it's always best to create a separate tester class. For instance, consider that a class's own main method can see non-public class elements directly, while outside of the class the use of public getters and setters would be required. Thus, testing from within a class can obscure access issues.

Here you will create a separate tester class so it's always available for you to call or expand, while cleanly and clearly remaining off the side, not mixed up with the rest of our code. This will complete the *scaffolding* for this test environment.

```java
public class TestDriver {
    public static void main(String [] args) {

        TestPhoneContact t1 = new TestPhoneContact();

        t1.testPhoneContactCreation();
    }
}
```

Now, once you compile and execute the `TestDriver,` the output console will display something like the following:

```
Phone Contact reference is 3D7DC1CB
Phone Contact:
 Name = Flintstone, Fred
 Phone = 800-555-1212
 Email = fred@knox.edu
```

The next task is to read a data file and create a phone contact list. Before you figure out the test or the code, you need to go back to design and decide on some data structures.

Since the story says "flat file of phone contacts" you can just assume you're dealing with a text file where each line contains phone contact information. Say the format mirrors the PhoneContact class and each line contains the following for a single contact: `first_name last_name phone_number email_addr.`

Next, you need a list of phone contacts that you can sort and print out. Because you want to keep the list alphabetically by last name, you can use a `TreeMap` Java Collections type to store all the phone contacts. In that case, you don't even need to sort the list because the `TreeMap` class keeps the list sorted for you. It also looks like you'll need another class to bring the `PhoneContact` objects and the list operations together.

So what does the test look like? Well, in the interest of keeping your tests small and adhering to the "a test does just one thing" maxim, it seems like you could use two tests after all, one to confirm that the file is there and can be opened, and one to confirm that you can create the `PhoneContact` list data structure. For the file opening test, you'll need a new class that represents the phone contact list. You will just stub that class out for now, creating a simple constructor and a stub of the one method that you'll need to test. This way you can write the test (which will fail because you don't have a real method yet). The file opening test looks as follows:

```java
public void testFileOpen() {
    String fileName = "phoneList.txt";

    PhoneContactList pc = new PhoneContactList();
    boolean fileOK = pc.fileOpen(fileName);
```

```
    if (fileOK == false) {
        System.out.println("Open Failed");
        System.exit(1);
    }
}
```

which you add to the testing class you created before. In the TestDriver class above, you just add the following line to the main( ) method:

```
t1.testFileOpen();
```

Once this test fails (as expected), you can then implement the new class and fill in the stubs that we created above. The new PhoneContactList class now looks something like the following:

```java
import java.util.*;
import java.io.*;

public class PhoneContactList {
    private TreeMap<String, PhoneContact> phoneList;
    private Scanner phoneFile;

    /**
     * Constructors for objects of class PhoneContactList
     */
    public PhoneContactList() {
    }

    public PhoneContactList(PhoneContact pc) {
        phoneList = new TreeMap<String, PhoneContact>();
        phoneList.put(pc.getLastName(), pc);
    }

    public boolean fileOpen(String name) {
        try {
            phoneFile = new Scanner(new File(name));
            return true;
```

```
    } catch (FileNotFoundException e) {
        System.out.println(e.getMessage());
        return false;
    }
  }
}
```

This is how your *test-design-develop* process will work. Try creating the rest of the tests listed above and finish implementing the PhoneContactList class code. You've got this.

JUnit: A Testing Framework

In the previous section, you created your own test scaffolding and hooked your tests into it. Many development environments have the facilities to do this for you, alongside a number of helpful components. One of the most popular for Java is the JUnit framework for developing unit tests for Java classes, originally created by Eric Gamma and Kent Beck.[6]

JUnit provides a base class called TestCase that you extend to create a series of tests for the class you are developing. JUnit contains a number of other classes, including an assertion library used for evaluating the results of individual tests and several applications that run the tests you create. A very good FAQ for JUnit is at https://junit. org/junit5/docs/current/user-guide/.

To write a test in JUnit, you must import the framework classes, and then extend the TestCase base class. A very simple test looks like this:

```
import junit.framework.TestCase;
import junit.framework.Assert.*;

public class SimpleTest extends TestCase {

    public SimpleTest(String name) {
        super(name);
    }
```

---

[6] https://junit.org/junit5/

```java
    public void testSimpleTest() {
        LifeUniverse lu = new LifeUniverse();
        int answer = lu.ultimateQuestion();
        assertEquals(42, answer);
    }
}
```

Note that the single-argument constructor is required. The assertEquals(parameter1, parameter2) method is one of the assertion library (junit.framework.Assert) methods which tests to see if the expected answer (the first parameter) is equal to the actual answer (the second parameter). There are many other convenient assert*() methods available.

Because JUnit is packaged in a Java jar file, you either need to add the location of the jar file to your Java CLASSPATH environment variable or add it to the line when you compile the test case from the command line. For example, to compile your simple test case you can use the following:

```
% javac -classpath $JUNIT_HOME/junit.jar SimpleTest.java
```

where $JUNIT_HOME is the directory where you installed the junit.jar file.

Executing a test from the command line is just as easy as compiling. There are two ways to do it. The first is to use one of the JUnit prepackaged runner classes, which takes as its argument the name of the test class:

```
java -cp .:./junit.jar junit.textui.TestRunner SimpleTest
```

which results in

```
.
Time: 0.001

OK (1 test)
```

where there is a dot for every test that is run, the time the entire test suite required, and the results of the tests.

You can also execute the JUnitCore class directly, also passing the name of the test class as an argument to the class:

```
java -cp .:./junit.jar org.junit.runner.JUnitCore SimpleTest
```

which results in

```
JUnit version 4.8.2
.
Time: 0.004

OK (1 test)
```

JUnit is included in many standard integrated development environments (IDEs). BlueJ, NetBeans, and Eclipse all have JUnit plug-ins, making the creation and running of unit test cases nearly effortless.

For example, with the example above and using BlueJ[7], you can create a new Unit Test class and use it to test your PhoneContact and PhoneContactList classes. See Figure 18-1.

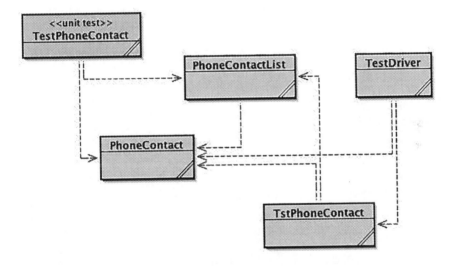

Figure 18-1. *The PhoneContact Test UML diagrams*

Your test class TestPhoneContact now looks as follows:

```
public class TestPhoneContact extends junit.framework.TestCase {
    /**
     * Default constructor for test class TestPhoneContact
     */
    public TestPhoneContact(String name) {
```

---

[7] www.bluej.org/

461

```java
        super(name);
    }

    /**
     * Sets up the test fixture.
     * Called before every test case method.
     */
    protected void setUp() {
    }

    /**
     * Tears down the test fixture.
     * Called after every test case method.
     */
    protected void tearDown() {
    }

    public void testPhoneContactCreation() {
        String fname = "Fred";
        String lname = "Flintstone";
        String phone = "800-555-1212";
        String email = "fred@knox.edu";

        PhoneContact pc = new PhoneContact(fname, lname, phone, email);
        assertEquals(lname, pc.getLastName());
        assertEquals(fname, pc.getFirstName());
        assertEquals(phone, pc.getPhoneNum());
        assertEquals(email, pc.getEmailAddr());
    }

    public void testFileOpen() {
        String fileName = "phoneList.txt";

        PhoneContactList pc = new PhoneContactList();
        boolean fileOK = pc.fileOpen(fileName);
        assertTrue(fileOK);
```

```
        if (fileOK == false) {
            System.out.println("Open Failed, File Not Found");
            System.exit(1);
        }
    }
}
```

To run this set of tests in BlueJ, select Test All from the drop-down menu shown in Figure 18-2.

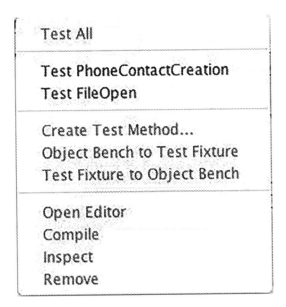

Figure 18-2. *The JUnit Menu - Select Test All to run the tests*

Because you don't have a phoneList.txt file created yet, you get the output shown in Figure 18-3.

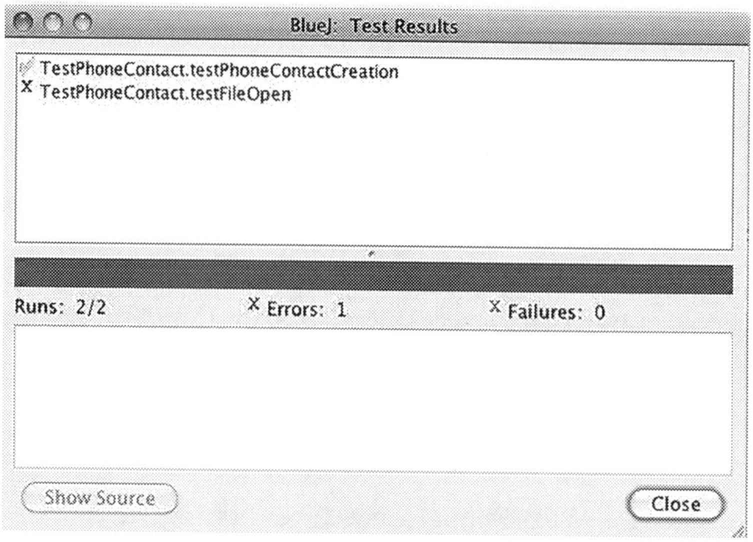

Figure 18-3. *JUnit Testing output*

Here, note that the `testFileOpen()` test has failed.

Every time you make any changes to your program, you can add another test to the `TestPhoneContact` class and rerun all the tests with a single menu selection. The testing framework makes it much easier to create individual tests and whole suites of tests that can be run every time you make a change to the program. This lets you know every time you make a change if you've broken something or not. Very cool.

Testing Is Critical

At the end of the day, unit testing is a critical part of your development process and of your peace of mind. Done carefully and correctly, it can help you remove the vast majority of your errors even before you integrate your code into the larger program. TDD, where you write tests first and then write the code that makes the tests succeed, is an effective way to catch errors in both low-level design and coding, while allowing you to easily and quickly create a regression test suite that you can use for every integration and every baseline of your program.

Conclusion

From your point of view as the developer, unit testing is the most important class of testing your program will undergo. It's the most fundamental type of testing, making sure your code meets the requirements of the design at the lowest level. Even though developers are more concerned with making sure their program works than with breaking it, developing a good unit testing mindset is critical to your development as a mature, effective programmer. Testing frameworks make this job much easier and cleaner, so learning how your local testing framework operates and learning to write good tests are crucial skills you must develop. Better that you find your own bugs than have the customer find them for you.

References

Kernighan, Brian W., and Rob Pike. 1999. *The Practice of Programming*. Paperback. Boston, MA: Addison-Wesley.

Martin, Robert C. 2009. *Clean Code: A Handbook of Agile Software Craftsmanship*. Paperback. Upper Saddle River, NJ: Prentice-Hall.

McConnell, Steve. 2004. *Code Complete 2: A Practical Handbook of Software Construction*. Redmond, WA: Microsoft Press.

Newkirk, James, and Robert C. Martin. 2001. *Extreme Programming in Practice*. Paperback. Boston, MA: Addison-Wesley.

CHAPTER 19

Code Reviews and Inspections

Our objective with Inspections is to reduce the Cost of Quality by finding and removing defects earlier and at a lower cost. While some testing will always be necessary, we can reduce the costs of test by reducing the volume of defects propagated to test.

—Ron Radice (2002)

When you catch bugs early, you also get fewer compound bugs. Compound bugs are two separate bugs that interact: you trip going downstairs, and when you reach for the handrail it comes off in your hand.

—Paul Graham (2001)

Here's a shocker: your main quality objective in software development is to get a working program to your user that meets all their requirements and has no defects. That's right: your code should be perfect, having no errors and meeting all user's requirements when you deliver it. Impossible? Can't be done? Well, *software quality assurance* is all about trying to get as close to perfection as you can—albeit within time and budget.

© John F. Dooley and Vera A. Kazakova 2024
J. F. Dooley and V. A. Kazakova, *Software Development, Design, and Coding*,
https://doi.org/10.1007/979-8-8688-0285-0_19

Software quality is usually discussed from two different perspectives: the user's and the developer's. From the *user's perspective*, quality has a number of characteristics in order to be accepted, including the following:[1]

- *Correctness*: The software has to work, period.

- *Usability*: It has to be easy to learn and easy to use.

- *Reliability*: It has to stay up and be available when you need it.

- *Security*: The software has to protect your data and prevent unauthorized access.

- *Adaptability*: It should be easy to add new features.

From the *developer's perspective*, software quality hinges on a different set of characteristics:

- *Maintainability*: It has to be easy to make changes to the software.

- *Portability*: It has to be easy to move the software to a different platform.

- *Readability*: You and anyone who comes after you needs to be able to read the code. This usually means that the code must have a consistent style and flow.

- *Understandability*: The code design should be understandable by developers other than the original author.

- *Testability*: It should be straightforward to fully test the code. Code that is created in a modular fashion, with short functions that do only one thing, is much easier to understand and test than code that is all just one big main() function.

Software quality assurance (SQA) is a set of activities that ensure software is implemented correctly. SQA has three major components:

- *Testing (or dynamic analysis)*: Finding errors that surface during execution

- *Debugging*: Getting all the obvious errors (found by testing) out of your code

- *Reviews (or static analysis)*: Finding inherent errors in your code as it sits there

---

[1] McConnell, Steve. 2004. *Code Complete 2: A Practical Handbook of Software Construction.* Redmond, WA: Microsoft Press, 463-465.

Many developers—and managers—think that you can test your way to quality. You can't. As you saw in the last chapter, tests are limited. You often can't explore every code path, you can't test every possible data combination, and often your tests themselves are flawed. Tests can only get you so far. As Edsger Dijkstra famously said: "...program testing can be a very effective way to show the presence of bugs, but it is hopelessly inadequate for showing their absence."[2] Testing alone is not a particularly effective way of finding errors in your code. In many cases, the combination of unit testing, integration testing, and system testing will only find about 50% or so of the errors in your program.[3] But, if you add some type of code review (reading the code to find errors) to your testing regimen, you can bring that percentage up to between 93% and 99% of all the errors in your code. Now that's an objective to shoot for, so in this chapter we'll focus on reviewing your code.

Walkthroughs, Reviews, and Inspections

Reviewing your code—reading it and looking for errors on the page—provides another mechanism for making sure that you've implemented the user's requirements and the resulting design correctly. In fact, most development organizations that use a plan-driven methodology will not only review code, but also review all the *work products* produced by the software development organization: the requirements document, the architecture, the design specification, the test plan, the tests themselves, and the user documentation. Organizations that use an agile development methodology don't necessarily have all the documents mentioned above, but they do have requirements, user stories, user documentation, and especially code to review.

There are three major approaches to reviewing code: walkthroughs, code reviews, and inspections. These three work their way up from very informal techniques to very formal methodologies. Code is typically reviewed either right after you've got a clean compile of your code and before you unit test, or right after you finish your unit testing. It's better to do the reviews right after unit testing, because then you've got your changes made, you've got a clean compile, and you've done the first round of testing. This is a great time to have someone else take a look at your code.

---

[2] Dijkstra, E. 1972. "The Humble Programmer." *CACM* 15(10): 859–66.

[3] (McConnell 2004, 472).

Walkthroughs

Walkthroughs (also known as *desk checks* or *code reads*) are the least formal type of review, typically used to confirm small changes to code, say a line or two, that you have just made to fix an error. If you've just added a new method to a class, or you've changed more than about 25 or 30 lines of code, do not do a walkthrough; do a code review instead.

Walkthroughs involve two or at most three people: the author of the code and the reviewer. The author's job in a walkthrough is to explain to the reviewer what the change is supposed to do and to point out where the change was made. The reviewer's job is to understand the change, read the code, and make one of two judgments: either they agree that the change is correct, or they do not. If not, the author has to go back, fix the code again, and then do another walkthrough. If the reviewer thinks the change is correct, then the author can integrate the changed code back into the code base to proceed with integration testing.

If you're pair programming, a code walkthrough happens concurrently as you are implementing a task. The driver is writing the code and the navigator is looking over their shoulder, checking for errors, and thinking ahead; this can be considered as an ongoing walkthrough happening in parallel with coding. In this case, it's acceptable to use a walkthrough for a larger piece of code, although for a complete task or for each user story that is implemented you should do a code review or an inspection, which we will talk about next.

Code Reviews

Code reviews are somewhat more formal than walkthroughs and are what most software developers do. You should always do a code review if you've changed a substantial amount of code, if you've written brand new code, or if you've added more than just a few lines of new code to an existing program. Agile programmers may do code reviews when they finish a user story.

Code reviews are real meetings with three to five attendees, each bringing a different perspective:

- The *moderator* of the code review is usually the *author*. It's the moderator's job to call the meeting, send out the work to be reviewed well before the meeting time, and to run the code review meeting. The moderator may also take notes at the meeting.

- There should be one or more *developers* at the meeting who are working on the same project as the author, contributing the perspective of detailed knowledge of the project.

- There should be a *tester* at the code review, bringing the testing perspective of not only reading the code being reviewed but also thinking about ways the code should be tested.

- Finally, there should be an experienced developer present who is not on the same project as the author. This person is the *disinterested third-party* who represents the quality perspective, providing a more strategic vision about the code and how it fits into the project. Their job at the code review is to understand the code and get the author to explain the changes clearly.

- *No managers are allowed at code reviews.* The presence of a manager changes the dynamics of the meeting and makes the code review less effective. People who might be willing to honestly critique a piece of code among peers will clam up in the presence of a manager; this doesn't help find errors. No managers, please.

The objective of a code review is to find errors in the code, not to fix them. Code reviews are informal enough that some discussion of fixes may occur, but that should be kept to a minimum. Before the code review meeting, all participants should go over the materials sent out by the moderator and prepare a list of errors they find. This step is critical to making the review meeting efficient and successful. Do your homework!

This list should be given to the moderator at the beginning of the meeting. The author (who may also be the moderator) goes through the code changes, explaining them and how they either fix the error they were intended to fix or add the new feature that was required. If an error or a discussion leads the review meeting into code that was not in the scope of the original review, stop! Be very careful about moving off into territory that hasn't been preread. You should treat any code not in the scope of the review as a black box. Schedule another meeting instead. Remember, the focus of the code review is on a single piece of code and finding errors in that piece of code. Don't get distracted.

A computer and view-sharing (projected or screen-shared) are essential at the code review so that everyone can see what's going on all the time. A second computer should be used so that someone (usually the author) can take notes about errors found in the code. A code review should not last more than about two hours, nor review more than about 200–500 lines of code, because everyone's focus and productivity will begin to faulter after that amount of time or reading. If you run out of time, schedule another review.

After the code review, the notes are distributed to all the participants and the author is charged with fixing all the errors that were found during the review. While metrics aren't required for code reviews, the moderator should at least keep track of how many errors were found, how many lines of code were reviewed, and if appropriate, the severity of each of the errors. These metrics are very useful to gauge productivity and should be used in planning the next project.

Code Inspections

Code inspections are the most formal type of review meeting, with the sole purpose of finding defects in any work product the development team produces.[4] Inspections can be used to review planning documents, requirements, designs, and code. Code inspections have specific rules regarding how many lines of code to review at once, how long the review meeting must be, and how much preparation each member of the review team should do, among other things. Inspections are typically used by larger organizations because they take more training, time, and effort than walkthroughs or code reviews. They are also used for mission and safety-critical software, where defects can cause harm to users. In 1979, Michael Fagan invented the most widely known and influential inspection methodology, which became the first formal software inspection process. [5] Most organizations that use inspections use a variation of the original Fagan software code inspection process.[6]

Code inspections have several very important criteria, including the following:

- The focus of the inspection meeting is solely on finding errors; no solutions are permitted.

- Inspections use checklists of common error types to focus the inspectors.

[4] Ackerman, A. and et al. 1989. "Software Inspections: An Effective Verification Process." *IEEE Software* 6 (3): 31–36.

[5] Fagan, Michael. 1979. "Design and Code Inspections to Reduce Errors in Program Development." *IBM Systems Journal* 15 (3): 182–211.

[6] Doolan, P. 1992. "Experience with Fagan's Inspection Method." *Software - Practice & Experience* 22 (2): 173–82.

- Reviewers are required to prepare beforehand; the inspection meeting will be canceled if everyone isn't ready.

- Each participant in the inspection has a distinct role.

- All participants have had inspection training.

- The moderator is not the author and has had special training in addition to the regular inspection training.

- The author is always required to follow up on errors reported in the meeting with the moderator.

- Metrics data is always collected at an inspection meeting.

Inspection Roles

The following are the roles used in code inspections:

- *Moderator*: The moderator gets all the materials from the author, decides who the other participants in the inspection should be, and is responsible for sending out all the inspection materials as well as scheduling and coordinating the meeting. Moderators must be technically competent; they need to understand the inspection materials and keep the meeting on track. The moderator schedules the inspection meeting and sends out the checklist of common errors for the reviewers to peruse. They also follow up with the author on any errors found in the inspection, so they must understand the errors and the corrections. Moderators attend an additional inspection-training course to help them prepare for their role.

- The *author* distributes the inspection materials to the moderator. The author is responsible for all rework that is created as a result of the inspection meeting. During the inspection, the author answers questions about the code from the reviewers but does nothing else. Sometimes, if many of the reviewers are not familiar with the project, an initial overview meeting is necessary; the author chairs it and explains the overall design to the reviewers. Overview meetings are discouraged in code inspections because they can "taint the evidence" by injecting the author's opinions about the code and the design before the inspection meeting.

- The *reader* paraphrases the code. This implies that the reader has a good understanding of the project, its design, and the code in question. The reader does not explain the code; they just paraphrase it. The author should answer any questions about the code. That said, if the author has to explain too much of the code, that is usually considered a defect to be fixed; such code should be refactored to make it simpler.

- The *reviewers* do the heavy lifting in the inspection. A reviewer can be anyone with an interest in the code who is not the author; typically reviewers are other developers from the same project. As in code reviews, it's usually a good idea to have a senior person who is not on the project also be a reviewer. There are usually between two and four reviewers in an inspection meeting. Reviewers must do their prereading of the inspection materials and are expected to come to the meeting with a list of errors that they have found. This list is given to the recorder.

- The *recorder* is one of the reviewers who is charged with taking notes (required at each inspection meeting). The recorder merges the defect lists of the reviewers, classifying and recording errors found during the meeting. After the meeting, the recorder prepares the inspection report and distributes it to the meeting participants. Additionally, if the project is using a defect management system, then it is up to the recorder to enter defect reports for all major defects from the meeting into the system.

- *Managers are not invited to code inspections* (just as with code reviews).

Inspection Defect Types

Defects to be reported can be classified by types and severity. Fagan inspections specify only two types of defects: 1) *minor defects*, such as typographic errors, errors in documentation, small user interface errors, and other miscellany that don't cause the software to fail and 2) *major defects*, which are all the errors that do cause the software to fail. We think that this is a bit extreme, as two levels are usually not sufficient for prioritizing the fixes. Most development organizations will have at least a five-level defect structure:

1. *Fatal:* The program fails, usually resulting in a core dump and/or a backtrace being produced. Fatal errors usually indicate that there is something fundamentally wrong with part of the program.

2. *Severe:* A major piece of functionality fails and there is no workaround for the user. Say that in a first-person shooter game, the software doesn't allow reloading your weapon and doesn't let you switch weapons in the middle of a fight. That's bad.

3. *Serious:* The error is severe, but with a workaround for the user. For example, the software doesn't let you reload your weapon, but if you switch weapons and then switch back, you can reload.

4. *Trivial:* A small error, something like incorrect documentation or a minor user interface problem. For example, a text box is 10 pixels too far from its prompt in a form.

5. *Feature request:* A brand new feature for the program is desired. This isn't an error; it's a request from the user (or marketing) for new functionality in the software. In a game, this could be new weapons, new character types, new maps or surroundings, and so on. This is a request that should be considered for the next software version.

Ideally, of course, no errors ship to a user, but let's be realistic. In most organizations, software is not allowed to ship with known severity 1 and 2 errors still in it. Still, severity 3 errors really make users unhappy, so software should really never ship with any know errors of severity 1 through 3.

Under Fagan classification, the above severity 1 through 3 defects are all classified as major and are required to be fixed. It is usually up to the recorder to correctly classify defects found in the code as major (this classification can be changed later).

Inspection Phases and Procedures

Fagan inspections have seven phases that must be followed for each inspection:[7]

1. Planning

2. The overview meeting

3. Preparation

4. The inspection meeting

5. The inspection report

6. Rework

7. Follow up

Phase 1: Planning

In the planning phase, the moderator organizes and schedules the meeting and picks the participants. The moderator and the author get together to discuss the scope of the inspection materials (for code inspections, typically between 200 and 500 non-commented lines of code will be reviewed). The author then distributes the code to be inspected to the participants.

Phase 2: The Overview Meeting

An overview meeting is a presentation by the author of the project architecture and design and is necessary if several participants are unfamiliar with the project or its design and need to be brought up to speed before they can effectively read the code. Like the inspection meeting itself, overview meetings should last no longer than two hours. If an overview meeting is necessary, the author will call and run the meeting. As mentioned, overview meetings are discouraged, because they tend to taint the evidence.

---

[7] Fagan, M. 1986. "Advances in Software Inspections." *IEEE Transactions on Software Engineering* 12 (7): 744–51.

Phase 3: Preparation

In the preparation phase (required in Fagan inspections), each reviewer reads the work to be inspected. The inspection meeting can be canceled if the reviewers have not done their preparation. Preparation should take no more than 2–3 hours. The amount of work to be inspected should be 200-500 non-comment lines of code, or 30-80 pages of text. Studies have shown that reviewers can typically review about 125–200 lines of code per hour. The amount of time each reviewer spent in preparation is one of the metrics that is gathered at the inspection meeting.

Phase 4: The Inspection Meeting

The moderator is in charge of the inspection meeting, keeping it on track and focused. The inspection meeting should last no more than two hours. If there is any material that has not been inspected at the end of that time, a new meeting is scheduled. At the beginning of the meeting, the reviewers turn in their list of previously discovered errors to the recorder.

During the meeting, the reader paraphrases the code and the reviewers follow along. The author is there only to clarify any details and answer any questions about the code, doing nothing else so as not to taint the process. The recorder writes down all the defects reported, their level, and their classification. Resolving defects is strongly discouraged; participants are encouraged to have a separate meeting to discuss solutions.

Phase 5: Inspection Report

Within a day of the meeting, the recorder distributes the inspection report to all participants. The central part of the report are the defects that were found in the code during the meeting.

The report also includes metrics data, such as

- The number of defects found

- The number of each type of defect by severity and type

- The time spent in preparation (total time in person-hours and time per participant)

- The time spent in the meeting (clock time and total person-hours)

- The number of uncommented lines of code or pages of text reviewed

Phase 6: Rework and Follow Up

The author fixes all the major (severity 1-3) defects found during the meeting. If excessive defects were found, or if extensive refactoring or code changes had to occur, then another inspection is scheduled. While definitions of what is excessive/extensive vary, we have typically used 10% of the code inspected (e.g., changing over 20 lines of code when inspecting 200 lines). If it's less than 10% of the code was reworked, the author and the moderator can do a walkthrough instead. Regardless of how much code is changed, the moderator must check all the changes as part of the *follow up*. As part of the rework, another metric should be reported: the amount of time required by the author to fix each of the defects reported. The easiest way to track this accurately is for developers to use a defect tracking system. This metric, plus the number of defects found during the project, are critical to doing accurate planning and scheduling for the next project.

Reviews in Agile Projects

Let's face it: the sections on walkthroughs, code reviews, and inspections above don't really seem to mesh well with agile and lean methodologies. Instead, these seem like heavyweight processes that fit well in very large projects, but can they benefit XP or Scrum or lean development? The last thing we need during a Scrum sprint is a meeting every time we finish a task and want to integrate the code. Well, it turns out that doing reviews in agile projects is a pretty good idea and can work well with some changes to the process.

Let's remember what the Agile Manifesto says agile developers value:

- individuals and interactions over processes and tools,

- working software over comprehensive documentation,

- customer collaboration over contract negotiation, and

- responding to change over following a plan.[8]

Over the last 40 years or so, there has been quite a bit of research that shows that code reviews produce software with fewer defects, which aligns nicely with the agile

---

[8] https://agilemanifesto.org/

emphasis on working software. What could be more interactive than software developers collaborating about the code and making real-time improvements? Code reviews also fully support agile tenets by promoting the development of working software, collaboration and interaction among teams, continuous attention to technical excellence and the ability to respond to change—all while maintaining a high level of quality. The only question is, how do you do code reviews in an agile project?

Firstly, let's change the name; instead of talking about walkthroughs or code reviews, let's instead talk about *peer code reviews*. This emphasizes the fact that in our agile project, *peers* do the reviewing of code. Remember that a typical agile team has members with a wide variety of skills; there are developers, designers, testers, writers, architects, and, usually, the customer. Also remember that one of the hallmarks of agile teams is that they are *self-organizing*. In this case, what we want is for anyone on the team to be able to be in a peer code review. This spreads around the knowledge of the code, just as with pair programming, and gives everyone on the team more skills and knowledge; remember that *collective code ownership* is also a trait of agile methodologies.

Secondly, we don't really need a meeting to review the code. You'll hold the *peer code review* after the code has been written (or fixed) and after all the unit tests have been run. Whoever is to participate in the peer code review will need to read the code before the code review. In addition, if your project is using pair programming, there have already been two sets of eyes on the code and the design and the requirements. It turns out that, in the context of these practices, the probability of finding more major defects in a dedicated code review meeting is pretty low. According to a research study by Votta,[9] code inspection meetings add only about 4% more defects to the list than those already brought to the meeting by the participants. In other words, the dedicated code review meetings are not likely to add much in the agile development context. Also, remember the ultimate purpose of a peer code review: producing working software. In agile, anything that detracts from producing working software is to be shunned, and meetings take time away from producing working software.

The case for having a peer code review is the research that says that code reviews *do* find new defects in code and one of the reasons for agile processes (described in Kent Beck's *Extreme Programming Explained* book[10]) is that the earlier you find defects, the

---

[9] Votta, Lawrence. 1993. "Does Every Inspection Need a Meeting?" *SIGSOFT Software Engineering Notes* 18(5): 107–14.

[10] Beck, K. 2000. *Extreme Programming Explained: Embrace Change.* Boston, MA: Addison-Wesley.

cheaper they are to fix. The trick is to *peer review code* without slowing down the flow of an iteration/sprint. To achieve this, the team should allocate part of everyone's time to doing peer code reviews when they are doing the task estimations at the beginning of an iteration. Making peer code reviews part of the culture and the work effort will make it easier for developers to fit it into their day.

Performing an Agile Peer Code Review

There are several ways that you can do a peer code review without having a long drawn-out meeting and without requiring lots of heavyweight documentation and reporting. Here are a few suggestions.

Over the shoulder is like the walkthrough you visited at the beginning of this chapter. Whether pair-programming or not, add one more person at the end: go over the code with that person one more time before you integrate the changes. That's all. You can give the new person a heads-up and have them read the code beforehand, or (if their personal working process allows) drag them over to your code and do it immediately.

Email review: You email one or more of your colleagues a link to the code and ask them to read it and provide comments. Assuming your team has built-in code review time into task estimation, this should be something that everyone on the team is on board with. The only downside to an email review is that if the reviewer has any questions about the code, they must reach back out to the author, potentially with much back and forth. In asynchronous communications such as emails, this can cause unnecessary delays and task switching costs, which argues for just having a quick meeting instead.

Summary of Review Methodologies

Table 19-1 summarizes the characteristics of the three review methodologies we've examined. Each has its place and you should know how each of them works. The important thing to remember is that reviews and testing go hand in hand; both should be used to get your high-quality code out the door.

Table 19-1. *Comparison of Review Methodologies*

Properties	Walkthrough	Code Review	Code Inspection
Formal moderator training	No	No	Yes
Distinct participant roles	No	Yes	Yes
Who drives the meeting	Author	Author/moderator	Moderator
Common error checklists	No	Maybe	Yes
Focused review effort	No	Yes	Yes
Formal follow up	No	Maybe	Yes
Detailed defect feedback	Incidental	Yes	Yes
Metric data collected and used	No	Maybe	Yes
Process improvements	No	No	Yes

Defect Tracking Systems

Most software development organizations and many open-source development projects will use an automated *defect tracking system* to keep track of defects found in their software and to record requests for new features in the program. Popular free and open source defect tracking systems include Bugzilla (`www.bugzilla.org`), YouTrack (`www.jetbrains.com/youtrack/`), Jira (`www.atlassian.com/software/jira`), Mantis (`www.mantisbt.org/`), and Trac (`https://trac.edgewall.org/`).

Defect tracking systems keep track of a large amount of information about each defect found and entered. A typical defect tracking system will keep track of at least the following:

- The *number* of the defect (a unique ID for this project assigned by the tracking system itself)

- The current *state* of the defect in the system (Open, Assigned, Resolved, Integrated, Closed)

- The *fix* that was made to correct the error

- The *files* that were changed to make the fix

- Which *baseline* the fix was integrated into

- What *tests* were written and where they are stored (ideally, tests are stored with the fix)

- The *result* of the code review or inspection

Defect tracking systems assume that at any given time a defect report is in some state that reflects where it is in the process of being fixed. Figure 19-1 shows the states of a typical defect tracking system and the flow of a defect report through the system. In brief, all defects start out as New. They are then assigned to a developer for Analysis. The developer decides whether the reported defect is

- A *duplicate* of one already in the system

- *Not a defect* and so should be rejected

- A real *defect* that should be worked on by someone

- A real *defect* whose resolution can be postponed to a later date

Defects that are worked on are eventually fixed and moved to the *Resolved* state. The fix must then be subjected to a code review: if the code review is successful, the defect fix is then *Approved*. From Approved, the fix is scheduled for integration into the next baseline of the product. If the integration tests of that baseline are successful, the defect is *Closed*.

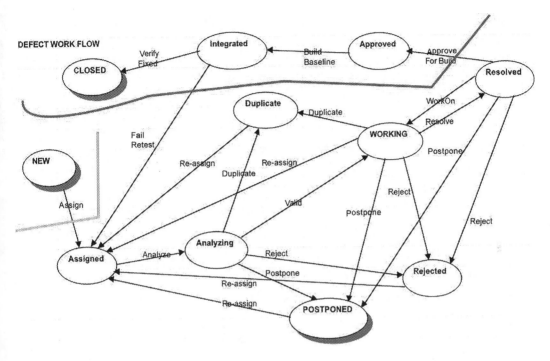

Figure 19-1. *Defect tracking system workflow*

Defect Tracking in Agile Projects

Once again, a lot of what we've said about defect tracking is pretty heavyweight and so you may ask, how does this apply to agile projects?

Well, first of all, you can ask yourself when these defects occur and which defects you want to track. When defects occur can be divided up into before and after an iteration and before and after the product release. Which defects occur can be those that affect the customer and that they care about, and those that the customer doesn't care about. Let's discuss each of these.

Defects that are found before the end of an iteration or sprint are ones you can easily fix. These will normally be found either via unit test failures, during peer code reviews, or by the customer when they are testing an intermediate product build. These defects are typically fixed immediately or, if they uncover some other problem (like in the requirements), they can be made into new tasks that are added to the product or sprint backlog.

Defects that are found after the end of an iteration or sprint, but before the final product release, should probably be made into new tasks that must be added to the backlog for the next iteration. These defects can also lead to refactoring or new tasks that reflect changing requirements.

Defects that are found after product release are all errors that customers find and report. Here, the decision of whether to fix them depends on whether the customer cares about the error or not. If the customer does care, then the error should be tagged and tracked, added to the product backlog and fixed in a subsequent release of the product. If the customer doesn't care, then just ignore it.

This leads us to the problem of who fixes defects found in the product code.

If the defect is found during development (during an iteration or a sprint and before product release), then the development team in consultation with the customer should decide whether the error should be fixed. If yes, then the development team should fix it by making it a task and adding it to the backlog for the next iteration or sprint. If no, then everyone just moves on.

If the defect is found after the product release, then it is likely that the development team has moved on to another project and may even have dispersed into several projects. This calls for the creation of a separate support team whose job it is to evaluate and fix errors in released code. Ideally, people on this support team will rotate in and out from the company's development teams, so that some institutional memory of the project is present on the support team.

Conclusion

A second or third set of eyes on your code is always a good thing. Code that is reviewed by others is improved and brings you closer to the Platonic ideal of defect-free software. Walkthroughs, code reviews, and formal code inspections each have their place in the array of tools used to improve code quality. The more of these tools you have in your toolbox, the better programmer you are. The combination of reviews, debugging, and unit testing will find the vast majority of defects in your code and is the best thing that a developer can do to help release defect-free code.

References

Ackerman, A., et al. 1989. "Software Inspections: An Effective Verification Process." *IEEE Software* 6(3): 31–36.

Beck, K. 2000. *Extreme Programming Explained: Embrace Change*. Boston, MA: Addison-Wesley.

Dijkstra, Edsger W. 1972. "The Humble Programmer." *Communications of the ACM* 15(10): 859–66.

Doolan, P. 1992. "Experience with Fagan's Inspection Method." *Software - Practice & Experience* 22 (2): 173–82.

Fagan, Michael. 1979. "Design and Code Inspections to Reduce Errors in Program Development." *IBM Systems Journal* 15 (3): 182–211.

Fagan, M. 1986. "Advances in Software Inspections." *IEEE Transactions on Software Engineering* 12 (7): 744–51.

Martin, Robert C. 2003. *Agile Software Development, Principles, Patterns, and Practices*. Upper Saddle River, NJ: Prentice Hall.

McConnell, Steve. 2004. *Code Complete 2: A Practical Handbook of Software Construction*. Redmond, WA: Microsoft Press.

Votta, Lawrence. 1993. "Does Every Inspection Need a Meeting?" *SIGSOFT Software Engineering Notes* 18 (5): 107–14.

CHAPTER 20

Wrapping It All Up

All programmers are optimists. Perhaps this modern sorcery especially attracts those who believe in happy endings and fairy godmothers. Perhaps the hundreds of nitty frustrations drive away all but those who habitually focus on the end goal. Perhaps it is merely that computers are young, programmers are younger, and the young are always optimists.

—Frederick Brooks, Jr.[1]

It's the only job I can think of where I get to be both an engineer and an artist. There's an incredible, rigorous, technical element to it, which I like because you have to do very precise thinking. On the other hand, it has a wildly creative side where the boundaries of imagination are the only real limitation.

—Andy Hertzfeld

Reading Alex E. Bell's[2] and Mark Guzdial's[3] "Viewpoint" columns in the August 2008 issue of *Communications of the ACM*, we were struck by the synergy of the two articles. One is a cautionary tale about the tools to use in professional software development, and the other is, at least in part, a cautionary tale about language and syntax use in teaching programming. This got us thinking about all the silver bullets we've tried in both development and education, and why most of them don't matter to real software development. This seems like an appropriate way to wrap up this extended discussion on software development.

---

[1] Brooks, Frederick P. 1995. *The Mythical Man-Month: Essays on Software Engineering, Silver Anniversary Edition.* Boston, MA: Addison-Wesley.

[2] Bell, A. E. 2008. "Software Development Amidst the Whiz of Silver Bullets." *Communications of the ACM* 51 (8): 22–24.

[3] Guzdial, Mark. 2008. "Paving the Way for Computational Thinking." *Communications of the ACM* 51 (8): 25–27.

© John F. Dooley and Vera A. Kazakova 2024
J. F. Dooley and V. A. Kazakova, *Software Development, Design, and Coding,*
https://doi.org/10.1007/979-8-8688-0285-0_20

What Have You Learned?

As we've maintained throughout this book, software development is hard. It takes a lot of dedication and practice to do it and even more to do it well. This, of course, is the attraction. Easy problems are boring, without mystery, without the thrill of the chase, and without the reward of accomplishment. The challenge is to work on something you've never done before, something you might not even know if you can solve. That's what has you coming back to the puzzles of software creation again and again.

Software development is one of the most creative and powerful things a human can do. Out of nothing, one takes a problem, wrestles with it, explores it, pokes at it, rips it apart, puts it back together in a different form, comes up with that bit of problem-solving inspiration, and then converts it all into an artifact that others can use effortlessly. Addressing real-world needs with your software is just the coolest thing.

Writing software is also a humbling experience. It is so hard to get software right and so easy to get it wrong. In writing software, you've learned to embrace failure. Failure is an exciting and frustrating part of the process. Failure teaches you about the problems, but also about yourself: you learn how you approach problems, the types of mistakes you're prone to make, and how to work around them. Failure teaches you perseverance because you are unlikely to get everything right on the first try, so you just have to keep working until the program does.

Small teams build most software, and they build the best software. Small, highly motivated and empowered teams are the most productive. Small teams also tend to use a slimmed down development process. Unless you work for a large company that's desperate to be at SEI Capability Maturity Model Level 5,[4] your processes can be very sparse. Detailed problem descriptions (most recently in the form of user stories), brainstorming design sessions, simple configuration management, peer code reviews, and a separate testing team take care of everything necessary to create almost defect-free code. Process flexibility, effective communication, and common product ownership are the keys to project success.

---

[4] Paulk, Mark C. 1995. *The Capability Maturity Model: Guidelines for Improving the Software Process*. The SEI Series in Software Engineering. Reading, Mass.: Addison-Wesley Pub. Co.

A lot of really good software gets written, tested, and shipped every year; much more than the alleged "failure" numbers would have one believe.[5,6,7] The main drivers of plan-driven development and agile development are the recognition of the constant changes in requirements, and the idea that the end goal is always working software. The best thing about agile development is that it recognizes these facts and builds refactoring into its simple process.

Simple tools are the most effective. Simple tools allow you to get to the core of the puzzle and examine it closely with nothing in your way. They allow you to take it out, hold it in your hands, turn it over, and poke at it quickly and easily. Simple tools also allow you to combine them together to do more complicated things. We refer you to Stephen Jenkins' article on "Old School" programming,[8] where he said it much better than we could.

Coding, debugging, and unit testing are at least as important as design. Experience gives a good programmer a deep sense of design and a wealth of patterns to draw on; experience gives a great programmer a deep, intimate knowledge of the programming language that is their tool. It's this deep, intimate knowledge that produces beautiful code.

The process of debugging a long, complex program is an immensely rewarding endeavor. Isolating a problem, uncovering mistakes, building debugging scaffolding, hypothesizing a solution, reworking a design, finally identifying the error, and then creating a correct fix gives one such a rush of elation and satisfaction that it's at times nearly overwhelming.

What to Do Next?

So now that you've read all about software development and maybe tried some of the examples, what do you do next? How do you continue becoming a better software developer? Well, here are some suggestions.

---

[5] Glass, Ron. L. 2006. "The Standish Report: Does It Really Describe a Software Crisis?" *CACM* 49 (8): 15–16.

[6] DeFranco, J. F., and J. Voas. 2022. "Revisiting Software Metrology." *Computer* 55 (06): 12–14. https://doi.org/10.1109/MC.2022.3146648.

[7] Dolfing, Henrico. 2020. "Project Failure Is Largely Misunderstood." *HenricoDolfing* (blog). November 26, 2020. www.henricodolfing.com/2020/11/project-failure-is-largely-misunderstood.html.

[8] Jenkins, Stephen B. 2006. "Musings of an 'Old-School' Programmer." *CACM* 49 (5): 124–26.

Write code, lots of code. Experience helps a lot. Programming is a craft that requires practice and constant reinforcement. You will inevitably need to learn new things almost every day, and it's very likely that you'll need to learn a whole new set of tools and programming languages every few years. Having written lots of code will make that task easier and more fun. It's like leveling up: takes work but gets you ready for the next big battle against even more interesting problems.

Learn simple tools. Simple tools give you flexibility. They also help you learn the fundamental skills that you can then take to more complicated IDEs. And when those IDEs get replaced (as they will) you can fall back on the simple tools till you learn the new IDE.

Read about problem solving and design. People have been solving problems for thousands of years and designing solutions for just as long. Don't ignore the classics in the computer science literature, like Dijkstra's *Structured Programming* book,[9] Brooks' classic *The Mythical Man-Month,*[10] Bentley's *Programming Pearls,*[11] McConnell's *Rapid Development,*[12] and Beck's *Extreme Programming Explained.*[13] Research and developments in other areas can also communicate common problem solving strategies that can also work for software development. For instance, Polya's *How to Solve It* book was written to solve math problems, but it translates very, very well to software.[14]

Read about programming and read about programmers. There is a plethora of literature on programming. A number of books have been mentioned in the previous chapters, but two that bear repeating are Hunt and Thomas' *The Pragmatic Programmer*[15] and McConnell's *Code Complete 2.*[16] It's also a great idea to read about

---

[9] Dahl, O. J., E. Dijkstra, and C. A. R. Hoare. 1972. *Structured Programming.* London: Academic Press.

[10] (Brooks 1995)

[11] Bentley, Jon. 2000. *Programming Pearls, Second Edition.* Boston, MA: Addison-Wesley.

[12] McConnell, Steve. 1996. *Rapid Development: Taming Wild Software Schedules.* Redmond, WA: Microsoft Press.

[13] Beck, Kent. 2000. *Extreme Programming Explained: Embrace Change.* Boston, MA: Addison-Wesley.

[14] Polya, G. 1957. *How To Solve It: A New Aspect of Mathematical Method, 2nd Edition.* Princeton, NJ: Princeton University Press.

[15] Hunt, Andrew, and David Thomas. 2000. *The Pragmatic Programmer: From Journeyman to Master.* Boston: Addison-Wesley.

[16] McConnell, Steve. 2004. *Code Complete 2: A Practical Handbook of Software Construction.* Redmond, WA: Microsoft Press.

how great programmers think, work, and generally write great code. Two notable books are Lammer's *Programmers At Work*[17] and Oram and Wilson's *Beautiful Code*.[18]

Talk to other programmers. Books and articles are a good way to gather information, but don't discount talking to your peers. A side effect of pair programming is that you get to see how someone else works, how they approach problems, how they code, debug, and write tests. Code review meetings are also a great way to learn how others work. Additionally, code reviews reinforce Gerald Weinberg's idea of *egoless programming*.[19] Once you get over the idea that you "own" the code in a software product (your employer owns it; read some of those documents you had to sign on the first day of work and see Chapter 5 on intellectual property rights), you gain the ability to look at your code and the code of your coworkers more objectively, allowing yourself to learn from its strengths and shortcomings.

Join the ACM and the IEEE-CS: The Association for Computing Machinery (ACM; www.acm.org) and the IEEE Computer Society (IEEE-CS; www.computer.org) are the two main professional organizations for computer scientists. Their journals contain a wealth of information about all things related to computers and computing, their conferences are worth attending, and they have free online books and courses for members. You will not regret joining one or both of them.

Be humble: The following quote from Dijkstra says it all.

> *The competent programmer is fully aware of the strictly limited size of his own skull; therefore he approaches the programming task in full humility...*
>
> —Edsger Dijkstra[20]

Software development is hard. Programs of any size can be extremely hard to understand completely. Besides being one of the most creative things that humans have ever done, computer software is one of the most complex. Be humble. Work hard. Have fun! And lastly, we couldn't resist a quote that had both the words *magic* and *computer* in it...

---

[17] Lammers, Susan. 1986. *Programmers At Work*. Redmond, WA: Microsoft Press.

[18] Oram, Andy, and Greg Wilson, eds. 2007. *Beautiful Code: Leading Programmers Explain How They Think*. Sebastopol, CA: O'Reilly Media, Inc.

[19] Weinberg, Gerald M. 1998. *The Psychology of Computer Programming, Silver Anniversary Edition*. New York: Dorset House.

[20] Dijkstra, Edsger W. 1972. "The Humble Programmer." *Communications of the ACM* 15 (10): 859–66.

The magic of myth and legend has come true in our time. One types the correct incantation on a keyboard, and a display screen comes to life, showing things that never were nor could be. Programming then is fun because it gratifies creative longings built deep within us and delights sensibilities we have in common with all [people]. ... The computer resembles the magic of legend in this respect, too. If one character, one pause, of the incantation is not strictly in proper form, the magic doesn't work. Human beings are not accustomed to being perfect, and few areas of human activity demand it. Adjusting to the requirement for perfection is, I think, the most difficult part of learning to program.

—Frederick Brooks[21]

References

Beck, Kent. 2000. *Extreme Programming Explained: Embrace Change.* Boston, MA: Addison-Wesley.

Bell, A. E. 2008. "Software Development Amidst the Whiz of Silver Bullets." *Communications of the ACM* 51 (8): 22–24.

Bentley, Jon. 2000. *Programming Pearls, Second Edition.* Boston, MA: Addison-Wesley.

Brooks, Frederick P. 1995. *The Mythical Man-Month: Essays on Software Engineering, Silver Anniversary Edition.* Boston, MA: Addison-Wesley.

Dahl, O. J., E. Dijkstra, and C. A. R. Hoare. 1972. *Structured Programming.* London: Academic Press.

DeFranco, J. F., and J. Voas. 2022. "Revisiting Software Metrology." *Computer* 55 (06): 12–14. https://doi.org/10.1109/MC.2022.3146648.

Dijkstra, Edsger W. 1972. "The Humble Programmer." *Communications of the ACM* 15 (10): 859–66.

Dolfing, Henrico. 2020. "Project Failure Is Largely Misunderstood." *HenricoDolfing* (blog). November 26, 2020. www.henricodolfing.com/2020/11/project-failure-is-largely-misunderstood.html.

Glass, Ron. L. 2006. "The Standish Report: Does It Really Describe a Software Crisis?" *CACM* 49 (8): 15–16.

---

[21] (Brooks 1995, 7-8)

Guzdial, Mark. 2008. "Paving the Way for Computational Thinking." *Communications of the ACM* 51 (8): 25–27.

Hunt, Andrew, and David Thomas. 2000. *The Pragmatic Programmer: From Journeyman to Master*. Boston: Addison-Wesley.

Jenkins, Stephen B. 2006. "Musings of an 'Old-School' Programmer." *CACM* 49 (5): 124–26.

Lammers, Susan. 1986. *Programmers At Work*. Redmond, WA: Microsoft Press.

McConnell, Steve. 1996. *Rapid Development: Taming Wild Software Schedules*. Redmond, WA: Microsoft Press.

McConnell, Steve. 2004. *Code Complete 2: A Practical Handbook of Software Construction*. Redmond, WA: Microsoft Press.

Oram, Andy, and Greg Wilson, eds. 2007. *Beautiful Code: Leading Programmers Explain How They Think*. Sebastopol, CA: O'Reilly Media, Inc.

Paulk, Mark C. 1995. *The Capability Maturity Model: Guidelines for Improving the Software Process*. The SEI Series in Software Engineering. Reading, Mass.: Addison-Wesley Pub. Co.

Polya, G. 1957. *How To Solve It: A New Aspect of Mathematical Method, 2nd Edition*. Princeton, NJ: Princeton University Press.

Weinberg, Gerald M. 1998. *The Psychology of Computer Programming, Silver Anniversary Edition*. New York: Dorset House.

Index

A

Abstract classes, 170, 211, 242, 243

Abstraction mechanism, 210

Acceptance tests, 4, 32, 133, 135, 212, 447

Act utilitarianism, 95–96, 98

Adams, Douglas, 414

Aggregation, 211, 262–267, 290

Agile activities, 20

Agile development, 4, 12, 17–18, 30

Agile development methodology, 4, 469

Agile development process, 4, 81, 378

Agile development project, 131

Agile Manifesto, 12, 19, 378, 478

Agile methodologies, 20–21, 126, 129, 131, 167

Agile principles, 19

Agile processes, 5, 17, 19, 20, 30, 124, 378, 479

Agile projects, 4, 51, 52, 129, 131, 446, 447, 478, 479, 483

Agile teams, 51, 228, 446, 479

Agile values, 19–21

Amdahl's Law, 320, 322, 372

Apple's XCode IDE, 430

Apple *vs.* Microsoft, 115

Applications programming interface (API), 338–344, 413

Architectural patterns, 146, 160

    client-server, 156–157

    layered architectural approach, 157–160

    main program–subroutine, 147–148

    MVC (*see* Model view controller (MVC))

    pipe-and-filter, 148–150

Architectural style, 146, 160

assertEquals(), 460

Association for Computing Machinery (ACM), 99, 491

Automation, 57

B

BankAccount class, 210, 241–242

    abstract class, 242

    CheckingAcct class, 243

    concrete class, 243

Bank accounts, 209, 240–241, 333

Beck, Kent, 31, 33, 139, 459, 479

Behavioral design patterns, 278

Behavioral patterns, 279

    classes, 298

    Iterator pattern

        code, 299–300

        Concrete_Collection class, 299

        cursors, 300–301

        interfaces, 299

        Iterator interface, 298

        ListIterator object, 300

        methods, 298, 300–301

        object, 298

        robust iterators, 301

        UML version, 298–299

© John F. Dooley and Vera A. Kazakova 2024
J. F. Dooley and V. A. Kazakova, *Software Development, Design, and Coding*,
https://doi.org/10.1007/979-8-8688-0285-0

Behavioral patterns (*cont.*)
    Observer Pattern, 301
        Button object, 305
        classes, 302
        Java, 305
        Observer interface, 302, 304–305
        pull Observer, 301
        push Observer, 301
        Subject interface, 302–303
    Strategy pattern
        client class, 310
        computeTax() method, 309
        Context class, 306, 309
        customers' tax bills, 307
        layout, 306
        switch statement, 305–306
        tax behavior, 307
        TaxStrategy classes, 308
        TaxStrategy interface, 308
        use, 306
Benefit, 14
Binary-coded decimal (BCD), 119
BirdFeeder class, 216–220, 232, 262–263
BirdFeederTester class, 223
Black-box testing, 416, 442
Blocks and statements, style
    guidelines, 387
Bob's changes, 432, 433
Built-in block boundaries, 383
Business policy, 138

C

C, 338, 385
C++, 380, 385
Change control board (CCB), 53
CheckingAccount class, 210
Chess tournament, 316

Class diagram, 217–218, 227, 247, 263, 265
Classes, 209
    single-feature classes, 382
Classic design patterns, 278, 280
Clients, 6, 17, 66, 89, 105, 156, 269
Client-server architecture, 156–157
Code, 2, 3, 7, 344
Code and fix model, 29–30
Code construction, v, 367, 444, 445, 449
Code coverage
    checking return values, 448
    definition of, 447
    off-by-one error, 448
    testing every program statement, 447
    testing for an end-of-file (EOF)
        marker, 448
Code inspections, 472–473
    author distributes, 473
    moderator, 473
    reader paraphrases, 474
    recorder, 474
    reviewers, 474
    roles, 473
Code of Ethics, principles, 100–102
Code patterns, 276
Code reviews, 470, 484
    computer and view-sharing, 471
    developers, 471
    metrics, 472
    moderator, 470
    objective, 471
    tester, 471
Coding, 344
    Adams, Douglas, 414
    bad code example, critique of, 381
    bad code example, Java code
        listing, 380
    block layouts, types of, 383

blocks and statements, style guidelines, 387

built-in block boundaries, emulating, 385, 387

C, 385

C++, 380, 385

camel case, using, 395

comments, 381

comments, style guidelines, 391

comparing the plan-driven and agile development processes, 378

declaration before use rule, 389

defensive programming, definition of, 404

error recovery, suggestions for, 408–410

exceptions, checked, 411–413

exceptions, in Java, 410

exceptions, runtime, 411

exceptions, throwing and catching, 410

exceptions, uncaught, 410

fat interfaces, 382

getMessage(), 412

good layout and formatting, objectives of, 383

goto statements, 388

handling errors that occur at run time, 407

having your methods do just one thing, 382

Hunt, A., 379

identifier naming conventions, 394

indentation, using, 387

Java, 385

layout of, 381

McConnell, Steve, 380

NullPointerException, 411

parentheses, using, 387

Pascal, 385

Pike, Rob, 394

printf(), 409

protecting a program from bad data, guidelines for, 404

scanf(), 409

software construction metaphor, 379

statement separator symbol, 385

statement terminator symbol, 385

style guidelines, using for a developer team, 396

Thomas, D., 379

variable declarations, style guidelines, 389

visibility modifiers, 381

Visual Basic, 384

white space, suggestions for using, 387

writing good, informative comments, 391

Coding

  adhering to a programming language's naming conventions, 396

  errno global variable, 409

  header files and source code, 390

  header files, nesting, 390

  JavaDoc comments, 393

  magic numbers, 382

  putting separate conditions on separate lines, 388

  taking advantage of built-in exception handling, 407

  wrapping individual statements, 388

Coding standards, 34, 414

Collection of elements, 298

Collective code ownership, 479

Collective ownership, 33, 36

Comments, 381

  keeping comments up to date, 394

  style guidelines, 391

  writing good, informative comments, 391

Communication pattern, 358
Communications protocols, 157, 158, 224
Computer ethics, 89
Computers, 97, 99, 104
Computer worm, 96, 97
Concurrency, 315–317
Concurrent, 316–317
Concurrent Versions System (CVS), 435
Consequentialism, *See* Utilitarianism
Continuous integration, 33, 446
Control coupling, 191
Copy-modify-merge, 433–435
Copyright
    cannot copyright, 114
    conflicts, 115
    definition, 112
    fair use, 116
    law, 112
    rights, 113
    works, 113–114
Copyright Act, 112
Cost, 12, 13
Coupling, 168–170, 191
Creational design patterns, 278
Creational patterns, 279–280, 298
    Factory Method
        client code, 283, 289–290
        design, 286–287
        interface, 283
        objects, 283
        SalesTax abstract class, 284
        SalesTaxDriver class, 288, 289
        SalesTaxFactory class, 284, 288
        SalesTax object, 285
        SalesTax subclasses, 284
        specifics, 287
        subclasses, 283
        testing, 286

        use, 283–284
    Singleton
        getInstance() method, 282
        new Singleton(), 280
        programs, 280
        public static method, 281
        Singleton class, 282
        Singleton() constructor, 281
Crystal, 30, 34–36, 51

D

Data coverage
    definition of, 447
    good data and bad data,
        examining, 449
    illegal data values, testing, 450
    pre-conditions and post-conditions,
        testing, 450
    too little or too much data, testing
        for, 451
    uninitialized variables, testing for, 451
Debug, 418, 423, 429, 491
Debugging, 415, 427–428, 438
    Boolean constant, 423
    debugging statements, 422
    features, 423
    gather data, 422
    IDEs and scripting languages, 424
    patterns, 424
    print statements, 422
    read the code, 421
    rubber ducky, 421
Decomposition patterns, 350, 352, 353
Defect-free software, 484
Defects
    debugging as rewarding, 489
Defect tracking systems, 481–483

Defensive programming, 449
  C program code example, 405
  definition of, 404
  errno global variable, 409
  error recovery, suggestions for, 408–410
  exceptions, checked, 411–413
  exceptions, in Java, 410
  exceptions, runtime, 411
  exceptions, throwing and
    catching, 410
  exceptions, uncaught, 410
  getMessage(), 412
  handling errors that occur at run
    time, 407
  NullPointerException, 411
  protecting a program from bad data,
    guidelines for, 404
  taking advantage of built-in exception
    handling, 407
Delegation, 262–267, 290, 291
Deontological approach, 93–94
Deontologists, 91–92
Deontology, 91
Dependency analysis patterns, 350
Dependency Inversion Principle
    (DIP), 247
  abstractions, 267
  definition, 267
  implementation, 269
  input-process-output model, 268
  levels, 268
  Processor, 269
  programs, 268
  Writer, 269
Derivative work, 121, 122
Design, 245, 277
  characteristics
    cognitive activity, 173–174

    extensibility, 169
    fitness of purpose, 167
    high cohesion, 168
    iterative, 173
    loose coupling, 168
    maintenance, 168
    opportunistic, 174
    portability, 169
    separation of concerns, 167
    simplicity, 167
  and creativity, 171–173
  decomposing, 166
  heuristics, 166–167, 169
    abstraction, 169
    adheres, 171
    design patterns, 171
    diagrams, 171
    identify parts, 170
    information hiding, 170
    loose coupling/interfaces/abstract
     classes, 170
    modular design, 170
    real-world object, 169
  levels, 246
  problems, 166, 173
  styles, 245
Designers, 167, 173
Design evaluation pattern, 351
Designing software, 173
Design patterns, 276–277, 310, 347
  classes, 278
  classic, 278, 280
  classification, 278
  Gang of Four, 277–278
  goal, 310
  key elements, 276
  MVC, 276
  static/dynamic relationships, 278

Design principles, 273
    code to an interface
        geometric objects, 249–250
        implement shape, 249
        List collection, 250–251
        Point class, 248–249
        polymorphism, 250
        RhombusApp class, 250
        Rhombus class, 250
        Shape interface, 248–249
    encapsulate, 247–248
    fundamental principles, 246–247
    guidelines, 272–273
Design techniques, 178, 310
Developers, 3, 13, 50, 126
Development managers, 105, 128
Development teams, 4, 6, 18, 37, 38, 50,
    53, 77, 135, 177, 484
Digital rights management (DRM), 90
Dijkstra, Edsger, 491
Distributed array pattern, 353, 356, 357
Divide and Conquer pattern, 352
Divide and Conquer strategy, 365–367
Don't Repeat Yourself (DRY) principle,
    246, 254–255

E

Eclipse IDE, 429
Egoless programming, 491
Eight queens problem
    alternatives, 182–183
    anti-diagonal, 185
    backtracking, 183
    board configuration, 181, 182
    board positions, 182
    Boolean information, 186–187
    brute force, 181
    column, 181
    data structure, 184
    index, 187
    isSafe() method, 189
    Java method, 188
    Java program, 189, 199–201
    main diagonal, 185
    one-dimensional array, 186–187
    partial solution, 183
    possible choices, 181–182
    possible solution, 180
    pseudo-code, 183–184
    queen position, 185, 187
    q(x) test, 181
    row check, 185
    safety check, 183, 187
    stepwise refinement, 184
    tasks, 187–189
    verification, 184
Embarrassingly parallel pattern, 327,
    355, 358–360
Empathy, 60, 73, 75
Encapsulation, 170, 190–191, 209, 255,
    382, 399
Engineering principles, xxi
Errno global variable, 409
Errors
    error recovery, suggestions for, 408–410
    exceptions, checked, 411–413
    exceptions, in Java, 410
    exceptions, runtime, 411
    exceptions, throwing and
        catching, 410
    exceptions, uncaught, 410
    getMessage(), 412
    handling errors that occur at run
        time, 407
    NullPointerException, 411

taking advantage of built-in exception
   handling, 407
Ethical drivers
   legal driver, 99
   professional driver, 99
      clauses, 100
      code, 100–101
Ethical principles, 102, 106–107
Ethical problems, 106
   analyzing, 103
   computer, 105
   copying software, 104
   identifying/describing, 102
   revealing, 105
   testing, 105
   workspace behavior, 106
Ethical rules, 90, 91, 94–98
Ethical situations, 89, 90, 94, 102, 104, 106
Ethical tensions, 100
Ethical theories, 90
   deontological school, 91
   deontological theory
      deontological argument/
         problems, 93
      deontologists, 92
      ideas, 92
      moral rule, 92–93
   teleological theory, 94
      ethical problem, 97
      harm, 97–98
      principles, 98
      stakeholders, 98
Ethics, 89–90, 94
Event-based coordination pattern, 353
Expert systems, 163
Extreme Programming model, 438
eXtreme programming (XP), 30
   direct communication, 32

ideas, 31
implementation tasks, 452
practices, 32–34
productive technical development, 31
stories in XP projects, 452

F

Fagan classification, 476
Fagan inspections, 475–477
FeedingDoor class, 219–221
Fixing errors, 168, 426
Flynn's Taxonomy, 317–319
Fork/Join pattern, 355
   combine() function, 368
   merge() function, 371–372
   mergeSort() function, 368–372
   originating process, 367
   parallel version, 372
   pseudo-code, 367
   sequential version, 372
Formal code inspections, 484
Functional specification, 124, 126, 142
   Author's name, 128
   disclaimer, 128
   open issues, 130
   overview, 128
   time, 131
   typical usage scenarios, 129

G

Gamma, Eric, 277, 298, 459
gdb command line, 428
Generalization, 171, 209, 243
Generally Accepted Accounting Principles
   (GAAP), 125
Geometric decomposition pattern, 353, 357

getMessage(), 412
getNextElement() methods, 298
Git, 81, 435–437
GitHub, 437
Git workflow, 436
Global-data coupling, 192
Global System for Mobile communication (GSM), 125
Goto statements, 177, 388
Graphical user interface (GUI), 115, 120, 209, 276, 407, 428
Gray-box testing, 442

H

Hadoop Distributed Files System (HDFS), 365
hasNext() method, 298, 300
Header files
    nesting, 390
    source code and, 390
Healthier workplace culture, 62
40-hour week, 34
Hunt, A., 379
Hybrid software development approaches, 44–46

I

Identifiers
    camel case, using, 395
    naming conventions, 394
    using descriptive identifiers, 395
IEEE Computer Society (IEEE-CS), 99
Implementation tasks, 452
Incomplete merge, 436
Indentation, using, 387
Individual work, 121

Information hiding, 170, 190, 192, 209, 399
Inheritance, 210, 211, 226, 243, 262, 267
Inheritance graph, 210
Inspection Defect Types
    fatal, 475
    feature request, 475
    severe, 475
    and severity, 475
    trivial, 475
    workaround, 475
Inspection report, 477
Integration testing, 416
    definition of, 442
    gray-box testing, 442
Intellectual property (IP)
    copyright (see Copyright)
    definition, 110
    law, 111
    ownership, 121–122
    patents (see Patents)
    protections, 111
    public domain, 111
Interface Segregation Principle (ISP), 247, 269–270
International Standards Organization (ISO), 158–159

J

Java, 330, 385
Java Collections Framework (JCF), 299
JavaDoc comments, 393
Java Virtual Machine (JVM), 332, 336, 410, 420
Jenkins, Stephen, 489
Joint work, 110, 121–122
JUnit
    assertEquals(), 460

assertion library methods, list of, 460

Beck, Kent, 459

definition of, 459

executing a test from the command line, 460

Gamma, Eric, 459

JUnitCore class, executing directly, 460

TestCase base class, extending, 459

TestPhoneContact class, code listing, 461

writing a test in, 459

K

Kanban

notions, 42

pull system, 43

swimlanes, 42

tasks, 43–44

WIP, 44

Kanban board, 42, 43

Keyword in Context (KWIC)

create, 193

down decomposition, 194–195

Java program, 197, 202–203, 205–208

modular decomposition, 195

input.txt file, 196

Java classes, 196

Line module, 196

list of modules, 195

output, 196

result, 193

shifting, 194

L

Latency, 320

Layered architectural approach, 157, 159–160

Layered protocols, 158–160

Lean principles

builds quality in, 24

create knowledge, 24

defer commitment, 25

deliver fast, 25

eliminate waste, 22

optimize the whole, 26

respect people, 25

Lean software development, 21–22

Library, 266, 293, 321, 330

Linear problem-solving approach, 164

Liskov Substitution Principle (LSP), 247

inheritance, 258

myFunc(), 260

Rectangle class, 258–261

Square class, 259–261

superclass, 258

violations, 261

virtual methods, 261

Loan terms, 138

Lock-modify-unlock strategy, 433

Logic errors, 416, 418

Loop

additions, 315

iterators, 401

parallelism, 355

sum elements list, 314–315

Loose coupling, 168, 170, 191–192, 247, 270

M

Magic numbers, 382, 401

Manager/Worker pattern, 355, 357, 359–360, 367

Map pattern, 359–361

MapReduce pattern
    functions, 362
    Hadoop, 365
    myMap, 364
    pseudo-code, 364
    text files, 363
    word frequencies, 363
Martin, Robert, 451
McConnell, Steve, 380, 443
Mercurial, 437
Message Passing Interface (MPI), 324, 355
Metaphor, 32
Methods
    doing too many things, 381
    fat interfaces, 382
    having your methods do just one
        thing, 382
    magic numbers, 382
    naming, 381–382
    protecting from bad data, 381
    smaller functions as easier to test, 383
    using and re-using small,
        single-feature methods, 382
    using too many input parameters, 382
Metrics data, 473, 477
Microprocessors, 313
Minimum Viable Product (MVP),
    17, 36, 51, 81
Model-View-Controller (MVC), 150, 276
    architecture, 150
    controller, 151, 155
    flow, 151
    fox and rabbit hunt, 152–154
    model, 151, 154–155
    view, 151, 155
Moderator, 470–473, 476–477
Modular decomposition, 190, 195–196,
    198, 224

Modularity, 190
    characteristics, 190
    encapsulation, 191
    information hiding, 192
    loose coupling, 191–192
Multiple instruction stream, multiple data
        stream (MIMD), 318–319
Multiple instruction stream, single data
        stream (MISD), 318
Mutex, 324, 329

N

Natural languages, 17, 124, 127, 129, 216
Networking, 59, 125
Not-for-profit organization, 165, 307

O

Object identification, 238
Object-oriented analysis and design
        (OOA&D), 190, 209–213, 226,
        237, 267
Object-oriented analysis (OOA), 234, 244
    BirdFeeder class, 219–220
    BirdFeederTester class, 223
    Burt's Bird Buffet and Bath (B⁴++), 228
        agile techniques, 228
        feeding doors, 228
        issue, 228
        remote control, 229–230
        scenario, 228
        steps, 230
        use case, 229
    class diagram, 217–218
    conceptual model, 226–227
    decompose, problem, 216
    definition, 226

essential features, 226–227

feature list, 215

FeedingDoor class, 219–221

guidelines, 230–231

problem statement, 210, 214

process, 211–213

Sensor class, 219, 222

textual analysis, 227–228

use cases, 215, 227

Object-oriented design (OOD), 224, 226, 244

    anticipate change, 234

    BirdFeeder class, 232

    candidate objects, 239–240

    class designs, 231

    classes, 231

    close() method, 233

    identifying objects, 238

    object model, 226

    objects, 211

    and OOA, 237–238

    operate() method, 232, 233

    pressButton(), 233

    process, 211–213

    RemoteControl class, 231–232

    requirements, 234–237

    Sensor class, 234

    songbirds, 235

Object-oriented programming (OOP), 152, 178, 190, 209, 210, 218, 389, 399

Objects, 150, 153, 154, 209, 210, 239

Off-by-one error, 406, 415, 418, 424, 448, 449

On-site customer, 32, 34, 139

Open-Closed principle (OCP)

    BankAccount class, 252–253

    classes, 246, 252

    private/public methods, 254

    withdraw() method, 253

Open Multi-Processing (OpenMP), 338–344, 355, 356, 362

Open Systems Interconnection (OSI), 158–159

Operating systems (OSs), 56, 96, 157–158

Opportunity-driven development approach, 164

Organization, 51

Overview meeting, 473, 476

Ownership, 18, 33, 110, 121–122

P

Pair programming, 23, 33, 53, 70, 136, 438, 446, 480, 491

Palo Alto Research Center (PARC), 115

Parallel, 317

Parallel architectures, 314, 317–319

Parallel computers, 314

Parallel design patterns, 348, 373

Parallel design spaces, 348, 373

    algorithm structure, 348

        data decomposition, 352–353

        dimensions, 351

        flow of data, 353–354

        tasks, 352

    finding concurrency, 348, 350–351

    implementation mechanisms, 349, 357–358

    meta-patterns, 349

    supporting structure, 349

        distributed array, 356

        Fork/Join meta-pattern, 355

        loop parallelism meta-pattern, 355

        manager/worker meta-pattern, 355

        meta-patterns, 354–355, 357

        shared data, 356

Parallel design spaces (*cont.*)
  shared queue, 356
  SPMD, 354
Parallelism, 315–317
Parallel programming
  data parallel model, 323
  latency, 320
  message passing model, 324
  models, 323
  performance, 321
  process, 319
  scalability, 321
  shared memory model, 324
  speedup, 320
  SPMD model, 325
  task parallel model, 324
  thread, 319
  threads model, 324
  throughput, 320
Parallel programming features
  Java threads
    BankAccount class, 337
    creation, 330
    deadlock, 337–338
    interface, 332
    main() method, 331
    makeWithdrawal(int amount)
      method, 336, 337
    objects, 331
    priority, 332
    race condition, 332–336
    start() method, 331
    Thread.sleep() method, 332
  lock() method, 329
  locking, 329
  mutex, 329
  mutual exclusion, 329
  OpenMP, 338

    critical sections, 339
    directives, 340
    fork-join parallelism model,
      338–339
    loop parallelization, 342–343
    omp_get_thread_num() library
      function, 339
    reduction, 343
    results, 342–343
    running time, 344
    serial version, 341
    SPMD, 339
    sum variable, 343
    synchronization, 339
    threads, 339
    trapezoid rule, 340
  reduction, 330
  shared memory, 330
  synchronization, 328
  threads, 328
Parallel programs
  Amdahl's Law, 322
  contention, 322
  designing, 325
  design techniques, 325
    choke points/bottlenecks, 326
    communication, 327
    data dependency, 326
    hotspots, 326
    inherently sequential, 326
    memory model, 327
    problem/solution, 326
    synchronization/coordination, 328
    task decomposition, 327
  idle time, 323
  non-parallelizable code, 322
  overhead, 321
Parentheses, using, 387

Pareto Principle, 427

Pascal, 384, 385, 389

Patents, 117

    can't patient, 118

    definition, 117

    public domain, 117

    software patent, 118–119

    types, 120

Peer code reviews, 479, 480

Performance, 344

Permuted index, 192, 193, 196

Phone contacts example

    creating the tests, 453

    establishing the tasks, 453

    file opening test, code example, 457

    PhoneContact class, code listing, 454

    PhoneContactList class, code

        listing, 458

    TestDriver class, code example, 456

    TestPhoneContact class, default

        constructor, 453

    writing the story, 452

Pike, Rob, 394

Pipeline pattern, 353

Plan-based development, 12, 16

Plan-driven process, vi, 27, 50, 53, 124,

    126, 135, 378

Policies, 98, 138

Preparation phase, 477

Principle of Least Knowledge (PLK),

    247, 270–271

printf(), 409

Print spooler application, 156

Process, 319

Processing elements (PEs), 351, 354,

    359, 364

Product backlog, 37, 38, 41, 53, 57, 124,

    135–137, 139, 484

Product owner, 37, 41, 126, 132, 134, 135

Programmers, 33

Programming, 1, 7

Programming languages, 21, 127, 177, 328,

    329, 338, 410, 417, 451

Project management, 29, 47, 49,

    58, 84, 437

Project management

    tools, 57

Project managers, 59, 66, 105, 128–130

Project planning, 50

    contract, 50

    defect management, 58

    organization, 51

    resource requirements, 54

    risk analysis (*see* Risk analysis)

    schedule, 56–57

    task estimation, 55

        effort, 55

        size, 55

        velocity, 56

    tasks, 49–50

Project schedule, 54, 57

Project status, 57, 81

Public domain, 111, 117

Q

Quality, 13, 23, 44, 61, 133, 468

R

RabbitHunt class, 154

Ralph's module, 419

Recursive data pattern, 353, 357

Reduce pattern, 360–362, 365

Refactoring, 34, 397–398, 401, 428

Remote procedure call (RPC), 96, 97

Requirements, 123
  analysis, 140–141
  design/feature ideas, 130
  domain requirements, 125
  dragging requirements
    non-technical difficulties, 140
    scope, 138–139
    understanding, 139
    volatility, 139–140
  functional requirements, 124, 127
  non-functional requirements, 125
  non-requirements, 125
  user requirements, 124
Requirements digging, 137–138
Return values, checking, 393, 402, 448, 449
Reuse mechanism, 210
Reviewing, 416, 479
Reviewing code, 416, 469
Review Methodologies, 480–481
Risk, 5, 14, 77
Risk analysis
  avoidance, 53
  defect rate, 52
  identifiable risks, 54
  misunderstood requirements, 52
  mitigation, 53
  requirements churn, 52
  schedule slips, 51
  turnover, 53
Role playing game (RPG), 265
Rule utilitarianism, 96, 98

S

Scalability, 321, 351
scanf(), 409
SciFri podcast, 301
Scope, 13, 139, 471

Scrum, 36, 45
  backlogs, 38
  board, 38–39
  ceremonies
    backlog refinement, 41
    daily stand-up, 40
    sprint planning, 39
    sprint retrospective, 40–41
    sprint review, 40
  end of project, 41
  explicitly, 73
  increment, 38
  requirements, 129
  roles, 37
  tasks, 136
  team management/structure, 36
  values, 39
  velocity, 41
Scrum master, 37, 40, 62, 66
Scrum teams, 37–39
Self-documenting code, 394
Semantic errors, 417, 418, 441
Semaphore, 324
Sensor class, 218, 234, 271
Separation of concerns, 152, 167, 190
Serial, 316
Servers, 156
Set of idioms, 275
Shared data pattern, 356
Shared ownership, 70
Shared queue pattern, 356, 359
Simple data coupling, 191
Single instruction stream, multiple data stream (SIMD), 318, 319, 354
Single instruction stream, multi-threading (SIMT), 319
Single instruction stream, single data stream (SISD), 318

Single program multiple data (SPMD),
319, 323, 325, 339, 354
Single Responsibility Principle (SRP),
238, 246
  classes, 257
  Controller class, 257
  encapsulation, 255
  MobilePhone class, 256–257
  object/object's services, 256
Skilled disagreement techniques, 78
Social-emotional learning, 60, 62
Soft-Aware development, vi, 60
  clarity, safety, 71–72
  conflicts, 75
    constructive controversy, 76
    management styles, 76
    opinions, 75
    outcomes, 76
    personal conflicts, 77
    rumble, 77
    skilled disagreement techniques, 78
    task conflicts, 77
    timely proactive resolution, 78
    workplace hierarchy, 78
  developers, 62
  diversity
    equity, 73
    makers, 74
    meetings, 74
    missteps, 75
    neurodivergence, 74
    social interactions, 75
    teammates, 74
  employees/teammates, 61
  individuals, 65
    developers, 66, 68
    drivers, 66
    leaders, 67
    managers, 65
    mutual dedication, 68
    overtime, 68
    product owner, 66
    stakeholder, 67
    teammates, 67
  learning
    developers, 69
    experimentation, 71
    growth, 69
    joint ownership, 70
    mistakes, 69
    safe environment, 69–70
    teamwork, 69
    unsustainable/self-preserving
      behaviors, 70
  power, 61
  team, 61
  teamwork, 62–65
  teamwork artifacts
    challenges/lessons, 83
    meetings, 82
    postmortems, 83
    practices, 79–80
    retrospectives, 82
    status reviews/demos/
      presentations, 81
  workers, 62
Software architect, 146
Software architecture, 145–146, 160
Software design, 145, 167, 237, 348
Software design patterns, 276, 278, 347
Software design problems, 237
Software development, 2, 487
  code, 2
  communication, 4
  debugging as rewarding, 489
  definition, 1

Software development (*cont.*)
   Dijkstra, Edsger, 491
   egoless programming, 491
   embracing failure when writing
      software, 488
   Jenkins, Stephen, 489
   joining the ACM and the IEEE-CS, 491
   key issue that divides plan-driven
      development and agile
      development, 489
   meetings, 5
   models, 26
   pair programming, 491
   principles, 22
   process, 4
   project plan, 5
   projects, 3
   project schedules, 6
   reading about how great programmers
      think, work and code, 490
   reading about problem solving and
      design, 490
   risks, 5
   small teams build the best software, 488
   software project, 3, 7
   suggestions on becoming a better
      software developer, 489
   team members, 4
   teams, 3
   tools/practices, project, 6
   using simple tools, 489
   variables, 12–15
   writing lots of code, 490
   writing software as a creative activity, 488
Software Development Lifecycle (SDLC),
   11, 12, 213–214
Software engineering, 1, 3, 7, 101, 137, 225
Software problems, 161, 162

Software projects, 3, 6, 7, 17, 50, 105, 166
Software quality, 468
   maintainability, 468
   portability, 468
   readability, 468
   testability, 468
   understandable, 468
Software quality assurance (SQA)
   debugging, 468
   debugging as rewarding, 489
   dynamic analysis, 468
   static analysis, 468
Song class, 263–265
SongIdentifier class, 262
   code, 263
   equals() method, 263
   identify() method, 263
   Song class, 264
Song Identifier, 236–237, 355, 362
SongIdentifier class, 263, 265
Source code control, 379, 431–432, 435
Space Rangers, 265
   component objects, 266
   composition, 266
   Pilot objects, 267
   Ship class, 265
   ships, 265
   spaceships, 265
   subclasses, 265
   Weapon interface, 266
Speedup, 320, 322, 344
Start-ups, 110, 121
Statement separator symbol, 385
Statement terminator symbol, 385
Stepwise refinement, 178
   bottom-up, 179
   eight queens problem (*see* Eight
      queens problem)

notation, 178

top-down, 178–179

Structural design patterns, 278

Structural patterns

adapter pattern

Adapter class, 291, 292

adapters, 291

Bar interface, 290–291

Foo class, 290

intermediate class, 290

Target interface, 292

Façade pattern

vs. Adapter Pattern, 295

client, 294

interfaces, client, 293

online store, 295–297

objects, 290

Structured data coupling, 191

Structured design, 24, 177, 198, 267, 268

Structured programming, 177–178, 188

Subversion, 435

Synchronization, 321, 327, 328, 339, 357, 358

Synchronization meta-pattern, 358

Syntactic errors, 417

System testing

black-box testing, 442

definition of, 442

T

Tame problems, 161, 165–166

Task parallelism pattern, 352

Team projects, 59, 110, 121, 122

Teamwork, 59, 62–63, 68, 69, 79, 81, 110

Technical specification, 126

Test-driven development (TDD), 19, 21, 31, 134, 415, 445

definition of, 445

Testing, 416

adversarial roles of developers and testers, 444

Beck, Kent, 459

binary search, 421

black-box testing, 442

characteristics of, 451

code coverage, 447

code traverses, 420

combinatorial explosion problem, 443, 447

combining static (code reading) and dynamic (testing) techniques, 443

dangling pointer problem, 420

data coverage, 447

developers as lousy testers, 444

errors, 420

Gamma, Eric, 459

gray-box testing, 442

how to write a test, 452

implementation tasks, 452

increasing code complexity and increasing the number of possible errors, 443

initialization, 420

integration testing, 416, 442

JUnit, 459

Martin, Robert, 451

McConnell, Steve, 443

mindset, 419

off-by-one error, 448

stories in XP projects, 452

system testing, 442

test-driven development (TDD), 445

testing only a single concept in your code, 452

three levels of, 441

timing error, 420

Testing (*cont.*)
  unit, 416
  unit testing, 441, 444
  what to test, 447
  when to test, 445
  writing unit tests after coding, 445
Thomas, D., 379
Thomas-Kilmann Conflict Mode
      Instrument (TKI), 76
Threads, 319, 328
Throughput, 44, 320
Time, 13
Traceability, 135
Transistors, 313

U

UE (Units of Execution) management
      pattern, 357, 360
Unified Modeling Language (UML), 129, 146
Unit testing, 416
  characteristics of, 451
  definition of, 441
  developer's responsibility for, 444
  how to write a test, 452
  importance of, 465
  writing unit tests after coding, 445
Unix command name, 192
Unix documentation, 192, 193
User stories, 142
  advantages, 129
  characteristics
    estimable, 134
    independent, 133
    negotiable, 133
    small, 134
    testable, 134
    valuable, 134

components
  cards, 132
  confirmation, 132
  conversation, 132
contents, 131
sprint/iteration backlog, 137
tasks, 136–137
  achievable, 136
  measurable, 136
  relevant, 137
  specific, 136
  time-boxed, 137
Utilitarianism
  computer worm, 96
  happiness, 95
  highway construction, 95–96
  local county, 95
  Principle of Utility, 95
  problem of moral luck, 96
  Welchia, 97

V

Variables
  declaration before use rule, 389
  variable declarations, style
      guidelines, 389
Version control system (VCS), 431,
      432, 434
  repository, 432
  stamps, 433
Visibility modifiers, 381
Visual Basic, 384

W

Walkthroughs, 470, 484
Waterfall approach, 164

Waterfall model, 27–28, 162, 164

Welchia, 97, 98

White space, suggestions, 387

Wicked problems, 28, 161

    characteristics, 162–163

    expert systems, 163

    linear problem-solving approach, 164

    opportunity-driven development
        approach, 164

    prototypes, 165

waterfall approach, 164

    web pages, 165

    word processing program, 163

Work in progress (WIP), 42–44

World Wide Web, 156

X, Y, Z

XCode's debugger, 430

X Window System, 157

Printed in the United States
by Baker & Taylor Publisher Services